Lecture Notes in Computer Science 7343

Commenced Publication in 1973
Founding and Former Series Editors:
Gerhard Goos, Juris Hartmanis, and Jan van Leeuwen

Oscar Dieste   Andreas Jedlitschka
Natalia Juristo (Eds.)

Product-Focused Software Process Improvement

13th International Conference, PROFES 2012
Madrid, Spain, June 13-15, 2012
Proceedings

 Springer

Volume Editors

Oscar Dieste
Natalia Juristo
Universidad Politécnica de Madrid
Facultad de Informática
Campus de Montegancedo s/n, 28660 Boadilla del Monte, Madrid, Spain
E-mail: {odieste, natalia}@fi.upm.es

Andreas Jedlitschka
Fraunhofer Institute for Experimental Software Engineering (Fh IESE)
Fraunhofer Platz 1, 67663 Kaiserslautern, Germany
E-mail: andreas.jedlitschka@iese.fraunhofer.de

ISSN 0302-9743   e-ISSN 1611-3349
ISBN 978-3-642-31062-1   e-ISBN 978-3-642-31063-8
DOI 10.1007/978-3-642-31063-8
Springer Heidelberg Dordrecht London New York

Library of Congress Control Number: 2012939226

CR Subject Classification (1998): D.2, K.6, J.1, H.3-4, C.2.4, J.3

LNCS Sublibrary: SL 2 – Programming and Software Engineering

Typesetting: Camera-ready by author, data conversion by Scientific Publishing Services, Chennai, India

Printed on acid-free paper

Springer is part of Springer Science+Business Media (www.springer.com)

Preface

On behalf of the PROFES Organizing Committee, we are proud to present the proceedings of the 13th International Conference on Product-Focused Software Process Improvement (PROFES 2012) held in Madrid, Spain.

Since 1999, PROFES has established itself as one of the recognized international process improvement conferences. The main theme of PROFES is professional software process improvement (SPI) motivated by product, process and service quality needs. PROFES 2012 addressed both quality engineering and management topics including processes, methods, techniques, tools, organizations, and enabling SPI. Both solutions found in practice and relevant research results from academia were presented.

The technical program was selected by a committee of leading experts in software process improvement, software process modeling, and empirical software engineering research. This year, 49 papers from 29 countries were submitted, with each paper receiving at least three reviewers. After thorough evaluation, the Program Committee finally selected 21 technical full papers (43% acceptance rate). The topics addressed in these papers indicate that SPI is still a vibrant research discipline, but is also of high interest for industry; many papers report on case studies or SPI-related experience gained in industry.

The technical program consisted of the tracks Process-Focused Software Process Improvement, Open-Source and Agile and Lean Practices, Product and Process Measurements and Estimation, Distributed and Global Software Development, Quality Assessment, and finally, Empirical Studies.

Since the beginning of the series of PROFES conferences, the purpose has been to bring to light the most recent findings and novel results in the area of process improvement. To fulfill that purpose, in this edition we organized a Special Session on Self-Organizing Systems, chaired by Horst F. Wedde (TU Dortmund). In this session, three high-quality papers about this topic were presented.

We were also proud to have one keynote speaker, Frank Houdek (Daimler AG), who presented the talk "Improving Requirements Engineering Processes. Impressions During One Decade of Improvement at Daimler".

Several events were co-located with PROFES 2012:

- The Second VALOIR workshop (Managing the Client Value Creation Process in Agile Projects), organized by Jeniffer Pérez, Luigi Buglioni and Maya Daneva
- The First INTEAMSE workshop (Managing the Influence of People and Team Factors in Software Engineering), organized by Silvia T. Acuña, Marta Gómez and Kostadin Koroutchev

- The tutorial "Requirements Meet Interaction Design," delivered by Hermann Kaindl
- The tutorial "Business IT Alignment Using the GQM+Strategies® Approach," delivered by Jens Heidrich and Martin Kowalczyk

We are thankful for the opportunity to have served as Program Co-chairs for this conference. The Program Committee members and reviewers provided excellent support in reviewing the papers. We are also grateful to the authors, presenters, and Session Chairs for their time and effort in making PROFES 2012 a success.

In addition, we sincerely thank Natalia Juristo for her work as a General Chair of PROFES 2012. Last, but not least, many thanks to Silvia T. Acuña and Sira Vegas for the local organization of this conference.

April 2012   Oscar Dieste
                                                  Andreas Jedlitschka
                                                     Natalia Juristo

Preface to the Short Papers Track

PROFES 2012 short papers present recent ideas or work based on research, practice or experience. Contributions of this track serve a distinct purpose and are subject to requirements different than those of full technical papers. Short papers may represent research work still under progress with preliminary results, ideas that may not be mature enough to be featured in a full technical paper, or experience with existing approaches or technologies that can be told in a compact form.

This year we received eight short paper submissions. The submissions underwent a rigorous review process by a separate, international Program Committee of 19 members. Each submission received at least four reviews. Based on these reviews and the Program Committee's overall assessments, we selected three submissions to be presented at the conference and to be included in these proceedings.

All of the accepted short papers focus on software process, hence they are best suited for the process-oriented reader. Two papers suggest frameworks for process conformance and one paper studies the effectiveness of effort estimation models. We hope that you will find their insights useful.

We thank the Program Committee for their diligence in reviewing the submissions and help with the selection process.

April 2012

Hakan Erdogmus
Sandro Morasca

Organization

General Chair

Natalia Juristo   Technical University of Madrid, Spain

Program Co-chairs

Oscar Dieste   Technical University of Madrid, Spain
Andreas Jedlitschka   Fraunhofer IESE, Germany

Short Papers and Posters Co-chairs

Hakan Erdogmus   Kalemun, Research, Canada
Sandro Morasca   University of Insubria, Italy

Doctoral Symposium Co-chairs

Stefan Biffl   Technical University of Vienna, Austria
Maya Daneva   University of Twente, The Netherlands

Tutorial and Workshop Chair

Burak Turhan   University of Oulu, Finland

Organizing Co-chairs

Silvia T. Acuña   Autonomous University of Madrid, Spain
Sira Vegas   Technical University of Madrid, Spain

Publicity Co-chairs

Marcela Genero   Castilla-La Mancha University, Spain
Guilherme Travassos   Federal University of Rio de Janeiro, Brazil
Lucas Layman   University of Maryland, USA

Program Committee

Zeiad A. Abdelnabi   Garyounis University - IT College, Libya
Pekka Abrahamsson   Free University of Bolzano, Italy

Silvia Abrahâo	Technical University of Valencia, Spain
Muhammad Ali Babar	ITU of Copenhagen, Denmark
Maria Teresa Baldassarre	University of Bari, Italy
Stefan Biffl	Technical University of Vienna, Austria
Andreas Birk	Software.Process.Management, Germany
Luigi Buglione	ETS/Engineering.IT, Italy
Danilo Caivano	SER&Practices, Italy
Gerardo Canfora	University of Sannio, Italy
Marcus Ciolkowski	QAware GmbH
Reidar Conradi	Norwegian University of Science and Technology, Norway
Beniamino Di Martino	Second University of Naples, Italy
Torgeir Dingsoyr	SINTEF, Norway
Marlon Dumas	University of Tartu, Estonia
Tore Dybâ	SINTEF, Norway
Davide Falessi	University of Rome "Tor Vergata" Italy and Simula Research Labs, Norway
Rudolf Ferenc	University of Szeged, Hungary
Xavier Franch	Technical University of Catalonia, Spain
Marcela Genero	Castilla-La Mancha University, Spain
Paul Grunbacher	Johannes Kepler University Linz, Austria
Jens Heidrich	Fraunhofer IESE, Germany
Yoshiki Higo	Osaka University, Japan
Martin Host	Lund University, Sweden
Frank Houdek	Daimler AG, Germany
Hajimu Iida	NAIST, Japan
Letizia Jaccheri	Norwegian University of Science and Technology, Norway
Michel Jaring	Fluxica, Finland
Janne Järvinen	F-Secure, Finland
Petri Kettunen	University of Helsinki, Finland
Casper Lassenius	Technical University of Helsinki, Finland
Marek Leszak	Alcatel-Lucent, Germany
Lech Madeysky	Wroclaw University of Technology, Poland
Kenichi Matsumoto	Nara Institute of Science and Technology, Japan
Emilia Mendes	Zayed University, United Arab Emirates
Maurizio Morisio	Politecnico di Torino, Italy
Mark Müller	Robert Bosch GmbH, Germany
Jürgen Münch	University of Helsinki, Finland
Haruka Nakao	Japan Manned Space Systems Corporation, Japan
Risto Nevalainen	FiSMA ry, Finland
Mahmood Niazi	Keele University UK/ KFUPM Saudi Arabia
Makoto Nonaka	Toyo University, Tokyo, Japan
Markku Oivo	University of Oulu, Finland

Paolo Panaroni   INTECS, Italy
Oscar Pastor   Technical University of Valencia, Spain
Dietmar Pfahl   Lund University, Sweden
Minna Pikkarainen   VTT, Finland
Teade Punter   Embedded Systems Institute (ESI),
                                    The Netherlands
Austen Rainer   University of Hertfordshire, UK
Daniel Rodriguez   University of Alcalá, Spain
Barbara Russo   Free University of Bolzano-Bozen, Italy
Outi Salo   Nokia, Finland
Klaus Schmid   University of Hildesheim, Germany
Kurt Schneider   Leibniz Universität Hannover, Germany
Michael Stupperich   Daimler AG, Germany
Guilherme Travassos   COPPE/UFRJ, Brazil
Markku Tukiainen   University of Joensuu, Finland
Mark van den Brand   Eindhoven University of Technology,
                                    The Netherlands
Rini van Solingen   Delft University of Technology,
                                    The Netherlands
Sira Vegas   Technical University of Madrid, Spain
Matias Vierimaa   VTT, Finland
Hironori Washizaki   National Institute of Informatics, Japan
Claes Wohlin   Blekinge Institute of Technology, Sweden
Bernhard Wong   University of Technology, Australia

Short Papers Program Committee

Aybuke Aurum   Univesity of New South Wales, Australia
Teresa Baldassarre   Università degli Studi di Bari, Italy
Ayse Bener   Ryerson University, Canada
Nils Brede Moe   SINTEF, Norway
Madeline Diep   Fraunhofer Institute Maryland, USA
Yael Dubinsky   Technion, Israel
Hakan Erdogmus (co-chair)   Kalemun Research, Canada
Juan Garbajosa   Universidad Politecnica de Madrid, Spain
Cigdem Gencel   Blekinge Institute of Technology, Sweden
Luigi Lavazza   Università degli Studi dell'Insubria, Varese,
                                    Italy
Sandro Morasca (co-chair)   Università degli Studi dell'Insubria, Como,
                                    Italy
Ipek Ozkaya   Software Engineering Institute, USA
Gregorio Robles   Universidad Rey Juan Carlos, Spain
Alberto Sillitti   Free University of Bozen-Bolzano, Italy
Daniela Soares Cruzes   NTNU, Norway
Davide Taibi   Università degli Studi dell'Insubria, Como,
                                    Italy

Additional Reviewers

Silvia T. Acuña	Autonomous University of Madrid, Spain
Marcel van Amstel	Eindhoven University of Technology, The Netherlands
Muhammad Aufeef Chauhan	IT University of Copenhagen, Denmark
Frank Elberzhager	Fraunhofer IESE, Germany
Javier González-Huerta	Technical University of Valencia, Spain
Marta López	Xunta de Galicia, Spain
Alexander Serebrenik	Eindhoven University of Technology, The Netherlands

Table of Contents

Open-Source, Agile and Lean Practices

Distributed and Global Software Development

Empirical Studies

Quality Assessment

Special Session on Self-Organizing Systems

Short Papers

Workshops and Tutorials

Improving Requirements Engineering Processes
Impressions during One Decade of Improvement at Daimler

Frank Houdek

Daimler AG
Research and Development
Wilhelm-Runge-Str. 11
D-89081 Ulm, Germany
frank.houdek@daimler.com

Abstract. Requirements play an important role in the automotive business, as most components (like electronic control units) are developed by suppliers basing on specification documents. While a decade ago mainly sketches had been handed over to the supplier, now fully elaborated specification documents are written.

The presentation gives an impression on the several stages of improvement of requirements engineering processes at Mercedes-Benz Passenger Car Development along with some typical improvement patterns and lessons learned.

1 Motivation

Requirements specification documents are a core development artifacts within each car development project. They are use during call-for-tender, act as reference during component development and provide the reference for component testing activities. In a modern Mercedes-Benz car we typically find more than 50 ECUs. Each of them is nowadays specified by a component specification consisting of several hundred pages; additionally, for each component a set of supplementary specification documents (like ISO or internal standards) apply, that again often sum up to several thousand pages of specification volume.

This specification volume was not always that high. A decade ago, we often found sketches rather than real specification documents. Quality problems and the recognition that specifications form a significant lever for supplier's development results initiated first improvement projects addressing the requirements engineering (RE) process.

2 Guided Tour through a Decade of Requirements Engineering Improvement at Daimler

In the early beginning, some individuals and small groups who felt uncomfortable with the situation in requirements engineering, started small projects aiming to improve their situation locally. Here, often tools with their specific capabilities and

O. Dieste, A. Jedlitschka, and N. Juristo (Eds.): PROFES 2012, LNCS 7343, pp. 1–2, 2012.
© Springer-Verlag Berlin Heidelberg 2012

features acted as catalyst. Beside toy examples, first applications in real projects (e.g. the specification document for a single ECU) have been created. An important argument for real world projects was to have an "emergency shutdown" option, i.e. there is fall-back scenario that could be used if the new approach fails.

After that, we saw local initiatives to improve RE practice in larger organizational units covering several dozens to several hundred people. As a consequence, local process improvement groups and support structures had been created. The key success factor in this phase was to have strong support by the head of the organizational unit. As a consequence of this phase, we saw a number of local RE solutions with only few commonalities.

After these local revolutions, we moved towards an evolutionary phase. During that, the number of user constantly increases; additionally, we saw standardization endeavors. Some of them (e.g. standard specification template) were quite successful, others (like a standardized data model for specification documents) ended without significant impact.

In the mid 2000s, we saw so many users (the early majority, according to the innovation adoption curve [1]) that a large-scale rollout of tool-based requirements engineering to all organizational units within research and development had been decided. The initial idea was "just" to disseminate the successful solutions to all users. However, during this rollout we encountered a number of questions that had to be solved, so we saw again methodological improvement along with process rollout.

Now, the vast majority of entire Mercedes-Benz Passenger Car Development uses a common requirements engineering methodology (incl. tool support). Cross-sectional tasks like tool operation, maintenance of specification templates, or tool support have been established.

3   Lessons Learned

Among many others, three main lessons learned are the following ones:

- Rollout and improvement does not happen linear; there are (often small) windows of opportunity that offer that chance to move a significant step ahead.
- Do not feel desperate by the fact that after two steps ahead one step back follows (e.g. due to organizational changes)
- Tools and their capabilities play a dominant role in designing requirements engineering processes.

Reference

[1]   Rogers, E.M.: Diffusion of Innovations. Free Press, Glencoe (1962)

Defect Data Analysis as Input
for Software Process Improvement

Anu Raninen[1,2], Tanja Toroi[1], Hannu Vainio[1], and Jarmo J. Ahonen[1]

[1] University of Eastern Finland, School of Computing,
PL 1627, FI-70211 Kuopio, Finland
{anu.raninen,tanja.toroi,hannu.vainio,jarmo.ahonen}@uef.fi
http://www.uef.fi/cs/
[2] Lero - The Irish Software Engineering Research Centre,
University of Limerick, Ireland

Abstract. In this paper, we present the results of defect data analysis done with three software companies' defect databases. 11879 software defects were classified and analyzed in order to find out what the real world defect distributions are like and what are the most common defect types. The most common defects in every company were functional defects (65.5%), i.e. defects in computation and/or functional logic. The defect types that were most uncommon were defects due to misunderstood or poorly written requirements (0.2%) or documentation (0.4%).The results of the analysis offer practical data to be used to support Software Process Improvement (SPI).

Keywords: Defect database, Testing, Defect Analysis, Software Process Improvement, SPI.

1 Introduction

Software companies usually maintain a defect database where they report the defects detected in their software products in order to manage their testing processes. The defect databases contain a lot of valuable history data that companies can exploit, for example to improve their testing or inspection activities [11]. In addition, product and process problems can be detected through monitoring the distribution of defects by type [5]. Further, defects detected in software projects and their classification provide a basis for product quality evaluation and process improvement [10].

To be able to exploit defect data in improving the operations of a software company the defect data must be unambiguous and the classification of the defects repeatable [10]. To enable this, a number of classification schemes for software defects have been developed. Perhaps to most widely applied classification scheme is IBM's Orthogonal Defect Classification (ODC) [7]. In addition, IEEE provides a Standard Classification for Software Anomalies [1]. Furthermore, Hewlett-Packard have also developed their own "Company-wide Software Metrics" scheme [12].

O. Dieste, A. Jedlitschka, and N. Juristo (Eds.): PROFES 2012, LNCS 7343, pp. 3–16, 2012.
© Springer-Verlag Berlin Heidelberg 2012

Defect data analysis is shown to help companies in process improvement [4,17]. However, in recent studies this approach has not been much discussed. The research presented in this paper aims aim at helping software companies to better exploit their defect data in order to improve their processes. To reach our research goals the first step was to make the three companies' defect data comparable and repeatable. To enable this the defect data was classified using an unambiguous defect distribution scheme.

While researching for a suitable defect distribution scheme we applied the criteria presented in [2]. We wanted to make sure that 1) it is possible to decide the defect type for each defect as unambiguously as possible, and 2) the information necessary for the decision can be collected easily from the materials available.

It was soon perceived that none of the existing defect distribution schemes we found from literature was suitable for our needs without alterations. Hence, we created a defect distribution scheme based on the schemes by Humphrey [13] and Beizer [3]. Humphrey's defect classification alone is very near to our needs. However, we also wanted to find out whether we would be able to identify defects caused by misunderstood requirements. In addition, we had a specific interest in integration problems and component interface errors. Hence, we added "Requirements" and "Integration" defect types, adopted from Beizer [3], to our scheme.

When initiating the defect classification we assumed that the defect distributions would differ notably from company to company as stated in [12]. This was assumed because the three companies differ in number of ways. They have considerable differences in the line of business they provide software to as well as in the processes they use. In addition, they are different in size. However, this assumption was proven false. The defect distributions in each company are remarkably similar. In each case the most common defects were functional defects, i.e. defects in computation and/or functional logic. The defect types that were most uncommon were defects due to misunderstood requirements or documentation. In addition, defects due to version control related issues ("Build, package, environment" defect type) were rare. The results presented in the paper were applied to support the target companies Software Process Improvement (SPI) efforts. The companies were provided with improvement suggestions based on the defect data.

The overall structure of this paper is: Section 2 presents the previous research of the subject. In section 3, the research setting is presented and section 4 describes the results of the research. The results are discussed in section 5 and section 6 provides the conclusion.

2   Previous Research

Previous research has shown that the classification of defects is important when aiming at measurement-based process and product improvement [10]. In addition, the defect classifications can be used to identify product and process problems [5] and to improve the testing or inspection activities [11].

There are numerous defect distribution schemes available in the literature. To name a few, IBM has generated Orthogonal Defect Classification (ODC) [7] and IEEE provides a Standard Classification for Software Anomalies [1]. In addition, Hewlett-Packard also has their own "Company-wide Software Metrics" scheme [12]. Further, Humphrey [13] and Beizer [3] also present possible defect distribution schemes in their work.

Despite the numerous defect distribution schemes published, there are limited examples of their usability and suitability in real-world systems. Such rare real-world examples can be found in e.g. [10] and [3] and [6]. The defect distributions used in these real-world studies and the schemes most important for this research are presented in Table 1. The most common defect types in these studies are marked with an asterisk (*).

Table 1. The defect distribution schemes found in the literature

#	ElEmam	Beizer	RefinedODC	Humphrey
1	Assignment	Data	Algorithm*	Assignment
2	Build/ Package	Features and functionality	Assignment	Build, package
3	Checking	Implementation and coding	Build/Package/ Merge	Checking
4	Data	Integration	Checking	Data
5	Documentation*	Requirements	Documentation	Documentation
6	Environment	Structural bugs*	Function	Environment
7	Function	System, Software architecture	Interface	Function
8	Interface	Test definition and execution	Timing/ Serialization	Interface
9	Memory	Other, unspecified		Syntax
10	Naming Conventions			System
11	Understandability			

* The most common defect type in the study.

3   Research Setting

Our experience working with software companies has shown that especially smaller software companies do not efficiently exploit the defect data they collect. This paper presents the first step in a research project aiming at preventing the most common software defect types through defect data analysis. In addition, we aim at using the defect data in order to improve the processes of the target companies. The research is conducted using the defect data of three software companies.

To be able to reach the goals of the research project the first step was to make the defect data comparable and repeatable. In order to do so, an unambiguous defect distribution scheme was needed. Before the classification, the defect distributions were assumed to be dissimilar because the companies differ remarkably.

The research questions for which the answers are sought in the research presented here are:

1. What are the most common defect types?
2. Is our defect distribution scheme suitable for its purpose?
3. Can defect data analysis provide practical input for SPI?

3.1   The Target Companies

The defect databases of three software companies were classified and analyzed in this research. In this paper, the companies are referred to with acronyms Company A, Company B and Company C.

Company A is a multinational company whose software development unit is located in Finland. The company is a large one (more than 250 employees) with 1340 employees. The software engineering unit employs 24 people. The company produces off-the-shelf software product's for the use of metal industry. The company concentrates on developing and maintaining 3-5 products.

Company B is an SME (Small and Medium sized Enterprise, over 25 but less than 250 employees) with 36 employees. 30 of them are software engineering personnel. Company B's products' main market is telecommunications.

Company C is a small company (less than 25 employees) with 18 employees. Their business is mainly off-the-shelf software products for the use of financial management. The company has six products in their product line.

Despite being product companies [9], as opposed to producing bespoke software, the three companies are dissimilar in many ways. For example, they produce software products for very different business domains. In addition, the companies differ in size. Further, their processes and work methods are quite dissimilar. The characteristics of the companies are compared in Table 2.

3.2   The Data Set

The defect data analyzed in this research consists of 11879 defects in three different databases of three different companies. All three companies use different tools to maintain their defect databases. Company A applies Jira[1], commercial issue and project tracking tool. Company B uses HP Quality center[2] which is an extensive requirement, test and defect management system. Company C does nicely with non-commercial, open-source Mantis[3] bug tracker. The specifics of the defect databases are presented in Table 2.

The defect distribution schemes used in the target companies were very general ones. Despite being general, the defect schemes used were not comparable.

---

[1] http://www.atlassian.com/software/jira/
[2] https://h10078.www1.hp.com/cda/hpms/display/main/
     hpms_content.jsp?zn=bto&cp=1-11-127-24^1131_4000_100__
[3] http://www.mantisbt.org/

Table 2. Characteristics of the companies and their defect databases

Characteristic	Company A	Company B	Company C
Market1	Metal industry	Telecom-munications	Financial management
Market2	I	N	N
Size	Large	SME	SC
Employees	1340 (24)	36 (30)	18 (9)
Business	product	product	product
Location	Multinational	Finland	Finland
Company age	42	12	23
Database	Jira	HP QC	Mantis
No. of defects	555	8321	3003
DB age (y)	3	8	7
Critical defects	63%	41%	31%

Market2: Scope of the company (I: international or N: national)
Employees: Number of employees (employees working in software development and maintenance)
Business: Is the business of the company based on project or product work [9]
Critical defects: Number of defects considered to be serious ones.

None of the companies had paid serious attention to the defect classification used. The classification schemes were established just to help the software engineers know in which order the bugs should be fixed. Company A was using five scale model classifying the defects from blocker, i.e. a defect that prevents the whole software product from working, to a trivial defect. In company B a scale of four, beginning from 0 – Emergency and ending in C – Cosmetic was being used. Company C also applied four classes for their defects, the most serious ones belonging to "Crashes the system" type and the defects giving company the least problems to "Small bug" type. The defects recorded in the databases were reported by both, the companies own testers and the customers in a case when a defect had slipped through the testing operations.

3.3 Defect Distribution Scheme

Despite the fact that there are plenty of defect distribution schemes available, it was not a simple task choosing one for our study. The classifications often are either missing defect types or use restrictive definitions, as stated also in [15].

The defect distribution scheme used in this research is a combination of schemes by Humphrey [13] and Beizer [3]. We ended up enhancing the defect distribution presented by Humphrey with "Requirements" and "Integration" types. "Requirements" was added because we wanted to find out whether we could identify the defects from the designing phases of software development.

In addition, we had a specific interest in integration problems and component interface errors. This was because our target companies were all producing software products, rather than bespoke software, where the interfaces are often especially problematic areas. The applied defect scheme is presented in Table 3.

Table 3. Defect distribution scheme applied

ID	DefectClass	Description	Questions
1	Assignment	Declaration, duplicate names, scope, limits	• Parameter boundaries defined incorrectly? • Output parameters in an incorrect format? • Problem with the punctuation?
2	Build, package, environment	Change management, library, version control	• Bug due to changes in the new version? • Bug due to features of the old version missing from the new one?
3	Checking	Error messages, inadequate checks	• Missing/unclear error message? • Something wrong with the error checking? • Bug due to user inputs not checked?
4	Data	Database structure and content	• Bug due to error in the structure of the database? • Bug due to the availability of the data? • Bug due to difficulties in obtaining the data?
5	Documentation	Comments and messages	• Problem with the output documents? • Problem with the user instructions? • Code comments do no correspond to the implementation?
6	Function	Logic, pointers, loops, recursion, computation, function defects	• Software not functioning as expected?
7	Integration	Integration problems, component interface errors	• Bug due to an interface error? • Bug due to the misfunction between the sofware components? •Bug due to communication problems with other systems?

Table 3. (*Continued*)

8 Requirements	Misunderstood customer requirements	• Software functions incorrectly compared to the requirements? • Bug due to misunderstood requirement? • Requirements not taken into account in implementation?
9 System	Configuration, timing, memory, hardware	• Problem with the functional capacity of the system? • Bug due to system configuration? • Delays in the execution of a function?
10 User Interface	Procedure calls and references, I/O, user formats	• Incorrect output data from the user point of view? • Problem with usability? • Trivial defects in layout (e.g. overlapping windows)?

Questions: Questions explaining the nature of the defects located in each type.

The defect types presented in Table 3 are designed to classify the defects in an unambiguous manner. In addition, the aim is to make the classification repeatable. The scheme includes ten defect types in total. Nine of the types are adopted from Humphrey [13] and two from Beizer [3]. Humphrey's "Environment" type is merged to the "Build and package" type because, in our opinion, these two types are very hard to distinguish from each other.

The nine types derived from Humphrey's classification [13] are "Assignment", "Build and package, (which includes the "Environment" type), "Checking", "Data", "Documentation", "Function", "Interface" (here: "User Interface"), and "System".

"Assignment" type refers to defects in declaration and scope of the variables. These errors indicate a few lines of code, such as the initialization of control blocks or data structure. "Build, package and environment" type contains defects that affect version management and change management. These defects occur due to mistakes in library systems, management of changes, or version control. "Checking" type addresses program logic that has failed to properly validate data and values before they are used, including errors in error messages and inadequate checks. "Data" defects include defects in the structure and content of the database. "Documentation" type includes defects in comments and messages to the user. These defects can affect both, publications and maintenance notes. "Function" type refers to defects in computation and functional logic. "Interface" type in Humphrey includes procedure calls and references, input and output, and user formats. We mean by "User Interface" defects, such as input and output anomalies, that are visible to the user. "System" type defects refer to problems in configuration, timing, memory and hardware.

The two remaining defect types, "Requirement" and "Integration" are adopted from Beizer [3]. "Requirement" type refers to defects due to misunderstood or poorly described and/or documented customer requirements. This type was added to our scheme because the misunderstood/poorly documented requirements often cause costly defects not detected early enough. The earlier a defect is found, the cheaper it is usually to fix [14]. It would be valuable to learn more from these defects and ultimately find out how the prevent them. "Integration" type includes component interface defects and all kinds of integration problems. We wanted to include this type to our scheme because nowadays modularity has been more and more promoted and component cooperation has become very common. However, cooperation is very error-prone and often produces problems in component integration. [16,8]

3.4   Applying the Defect Distribution Scheme

The defect data classification was performed by one researcher based on rules and criteria adopted from Humphrey [13] and Beizer [3]. The questions in Table 3 help to understand how the classification was carried out. To ensure the validity of the classification two additional researchers inspected the results at regular intervals. Lastly, classified data was inspected together with each company's representatives.

The target companies delivered the defect data in Excel data sheets. Due to the data form some fields of the database were missing from the sheets (e.g. notes, comments fields, formatting history). Hence, the researchers also had access to the defect database software of each company. The classification decisions were made based on the defect descriptions. The descriptions were not written in a specified form in any of the databases. Due to this they were often deficient. In problematic cases the defect database software was accessed to gain further information of the defect.

4   Results of the Classification

The defect distributions of all the companies were perhaps even surprisingly similar. The distributions are illustrated in Figure 1 and in Table 4. The most common defect type is "Function". For each company majority of the defects are located there with a total of 7780 defects, 65.5% of the data. The second most common is "User interface" with 1865 defects (15.7%). The rarest defect types are "Requirements" (total of 24 defects, 0.2%) and "Documentation" (47 defects, 0.4%).

The defect distributions are compared in Table 5. From the table it can be seen that "Function", "User Interface", "Assignment" and "Checking" are the

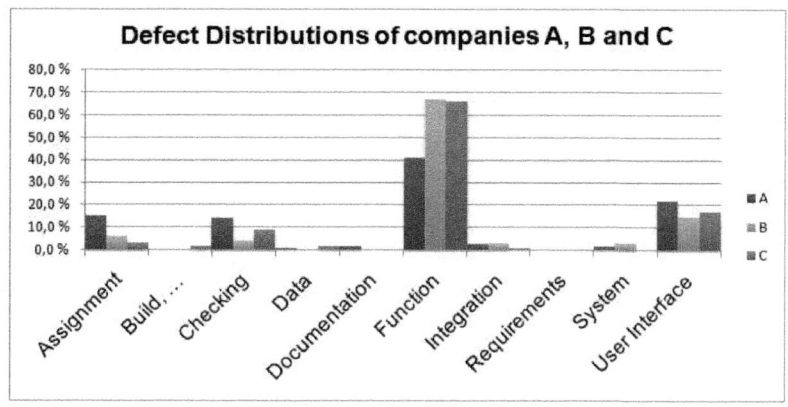

Fig. 1. Defect distributions of companies A, B and C

Table 4. Defect distribution in the three companies' databases

DefectType	A	%	B	%	C	%	Total	%
Assignment	85	15.3 %	514	6.2 %	91	3.0 %	690	5.8 %
Build, packace, environment	1	0.2 %	38	0.5 %	50	1.7 %	89	0.7 %
Checking	80	14.4 %	338	4.1 %	270	9.0 %	688	5.8 %
Database	4	0.7 %	46	0.6 %	55	1.8 %	105	0.9 %
Documentation	11	2.0 %	34	0.4 %	2	0.1 %	47	0.4 %
Function	228	41.1 %	5574	67.0 %	1978	65.9 %	7780	65.5 %
Integration	14	2.5 %	267	3.2 %	29	1.0 %	310	2.6 %
Requirements	0	0.0 %	18	0.2 %	6	0.2 %	24	0.2 %
System	10	1.8 %	260	3.1 %	11	0.4 %	281	2.4 %
User Interface	122	22.0 %	1232	14.8 %	511	17.0 %	1865	15.7 %
Total	555	100 %	8321	100 %	3003	100 %	11879	100 %

A,B,C: Amount of defects in databases of companies A, B and C

four most common defect types in every database. Further, it can be noted that there is only relatively small variation in the positions after these four most common defect types.

4.1 Improvement Suggestions

The results of the defect data analysis were translated to practical improvement suggestions. The improvement suggestions are mainly targeted to the most common and uncommon defect types. Five improvement suggestions provided for all of the companies can be seen below.

Table 5. Comparing the defect distributions

Company A	%	Company B	%	Company C	%
Function	41.4	Function	67.0	Function	65.5
User Interface	22.0	User Interface	14.8	User Interface	17.0
Assignment	15.3	Assignment	6.2	Checking	9.0
Checking	14.4	Checking	4.1	Assignment	3.0
Integration	2.5	Integration	3.2	Data	1.8
Documentation	2.0	System	3.1	Build, . . .	1.7
System	1.8	Data	0.6	Integration	1.0
Data	0.7	Build, . . .	0.5	System	0.4
Build, . . .	0.2	Documentation	0.4	Requirements	0.2
Requirements	0.0	Requirements	0.2	Documentation	0.1

1. The companies were encouraged to create the link between requirements, documentation and the defect databases.
2. The companies were recommended to take a closer look at the functional defects. Closer analysis might reveal problematic areas in the software products in which more test resources should and could be targeted.
3. The companies might benefit from further defining the usage of their bug trackers.
4. The companies should start recording the defects revealed in other software engineering phases than testing.
5. The companies should classify the defects in an informative way.

The defect data analysis and discussions with the target companies indicated that the rarest defect types, "Requirements" and "Documentation", are rare because of the way the defects are reported. The first improvement suggestion was related to the target companies not having defect databases in use during the design phase. Hence, defects related to documentation and requirements are rarely entered in the database.

The second and third improvement suggestions are related to the function defect class. Taking a closer look at functional defects was suggested because there was a majority of them in each company. Closer analysis of the functional defects might reveal problematic areas in the software products in which more test resources should and could be targeted. In addition, it was suggested that the companies might benefit from further defining the usage of their bug trackers. To be able to properly benefit from the defect data, all defects, including the minor ones should be recorded in the defect database. If there is no process defined on how and what to report, it is likely that a part of the defects are fixed without reporting them to the database. In addition, monitoring to ensure the process is followed is needed.

The fourth suggestion was made keeping the defect data analysis viewpoint in mind. To be able to conduct reliable analysis on defect data, all defects, including the minor ones should be recorded in the defect database. In addition, it was recommended that the companies would start recording the defects revealed in other software engineering phases than testing. A rough division to design, code, function test, and system test phases, as presented in [6], could be useful.

Last but not least, the companies were recommended to start applying a meaningful classification of defects in stead of their very general classifications currently in use (see Section 3.2). Applying a classification like the one presented in this paper would enable the companies to better understand the problematic areas of their software products. This would help in test resource allocation and also give the companies the opportunity to benchmark their defect distributions against other companies distributions made public.

5   Discussion

The results of the defect classification are interesting. The defect distributions of each company are quite similar. This was an unexpected result in the light of previous research where it is stated that it is normal for defect distributions to be dissimilar between companies [12]. The companies in our study are different in number of ways as shown in Table 2.

The most common defect type in every company is "Function". The results presented in [3] and [6] show that functional defects have also been common in other studies. One probable reason for this type's conventionality is it's generality. It includes defects related to logic, pointers, loops, recursion, computation and other functional areas. Further, the large amount of defects in this type can be partially explained by the process used in updating the defect databases. When a defect is detected, its cause is rarely known. In later phases, when the defect is currently being fixed or has already been dealt with, the cause is not always updated to the database. In addition, part of the defects manage to pass the testing and are reported by the customer. The customers more easily report a functional defect than, for example, a user interface defect. Core software functionality is usually more acute than inconveniences caused for the users. However, functional defects obviously are very common and need to be researched more carefully to learn how to prevent them, despite the "Function" types' perhaps too general nature.

The least common defect types, "Requirements" and "Documentation", were both often hard to detect from the defect data. "Requirements" defects were problematic because the databases are not linked to the requirements documentation. "Documentation" defects were rare because these defects are usually discovered during the design phase while reviewing the documentation. The target companies do not have defect databases in use during the design phase. Hence, documentation defects are rarely entered in the database. As an improvement suggestion, after the classification efforts, the companies were encouraged to create the link between requirements, documentation and the defect databases.

The defect distribution scheme used was mostly suitable for it's purpose. The classification was relatively easy and the defects are now in a comparable and easily understandable form. However, distinguishing some of the defect types from each other was a little problematic. For example, situations where erroneous input had caused software to behave irregularly. This could be a "Function" defect. However, if software has deficiencies in input checking and it allows the user to enter inputs in an incorrect form this is a defect of the "Checking" type. Another example of the challenging decision making is related to the "Integration" defect type. For example, when there are interface defects related to input checking these defects belong to the "Integration" type. Even though it might first seem that they are part of the "Checking" type. This is due to the fact that if an interface accepts erratic inputs, this is not a "Checking" defect because it only causes problems in integration.

The companies were recommended to take a closer look at the functional defects, the most common defect type of the study. Closer analysis might reveal problematic areas in the software products in which more test resources should and could be targeted. The companies might benefit from further defining the usage of the tools they use to report the defects. To be able to properly benefit from the defect data, all defects, including the minor ones should be recorded in the defect database. In addition, it was recommended that the companies should start recording the defects revealed in other software engineering phases than testing. In addition, the target companies were suggested to start classifying their defects in an informative way, for example, applying a structure similar to the defect scheme applied here. Informative classification would enable the companies to more easily conduct defect data analysis and learn from their defects in a more profound way.

It appears that defect data analysis provides practical input for software process improvement. The results of the analysis were easily translated to improvement suggestions. Process improvement through defect analysis appears to be a promising area as stated in [12]. Further, the companies experienced that comparing their defect data analysis results to other companies' data was a productive exercise. Taking a closer look at the defects helped them understand their products and processes more deeply.

The usage of defect distribution schemes have been criticized as a subjective exercise [10]. In the research presented the potential subjectivity was dealt with regular inspections of the classification by researchers and in the final phase by the company representatives. These inspections helped to gain a mutual understanding of the defect scheme and to increase the validity of the classification.

The results presented can be applied in software companies producing software products in order to benchmark the defect distributions. This exercise probably is not as beneficial in companies producing bespoke software. Defect distributions are useful, for example, for practitioners who want to learn from patterns of real defect data distributions. In addition, we believe that the accumulation of defect distribution patterns is important and should be shared among the research community. Further, these results strengthen the ones presented in previous studies. Functional defects are common [3,6], and we believe that a closer look should be taken into this defect type. In addition, defect classification appears to be beneficial in order to enable process improvement [12].

6 Conclusion

The objective of this study was to present the results of defect data classification in three software companies. In order to analyze the defect data, the data was made comparable by using a common defect distribution scheme. This paper presents the distribution scheme used and the results of the classification.

The results of the classification showed that the defect distributions of each company were quite similar. The most common defect type was "Function" (65.5%) and the most uncommon types were "Requirements" (0.2%) and "Documentation" (0.4%).

The new defect distribution scheme used is considered suitable for it's purpose. However, there were some data types that were sometimes hard to distinguish from each other, i.e. "Function" vs. "Checking". In addition, the defect data was found to be often insufficient or inconsistent which caused problems with the classification.

Further, the defect data analysis helped to identify problematic areas in the processes of the target companies. Based on the analysis it was possible to provide improvement suggestions for the use of software process improvement in the target companies. In addition, the target companies evaluated that they benefited from comparing their defect data to that of the other companies.

Future research will be conducted in analyzing the defect distributions. In addition, a closer look will be paid to the "Function" type's defects to get a clearer image of what the main problems inside this defect type are. Further, additional research will be conducted in order to make the improvement suggestion generation more systematical.

Acknowledgments. This research was funded by the Finnish Funding Agency for Technology and Innovation (Tekes) with grant 70030/10 for METRI (Metrics Based Failure Prevention in Software Engineering) project and supported, in part, by Science Foundation Ireland grant 03/CE2/I303 1 to Lero - the Irish Software Engineering Research Centre (www.lero.ie).

References

1. IEEE standard classification for software anomalies. IEEE Std 1044-2009 (Revision of IEEE Std 1044-1993) pp. C1 –C15 (2010)
2. Basili, V.R., Rombach, H.D.: Tailoring the software process to project goals and environments. In: Proceedings of the 9th International Conference on Software Engineering, ICSE 1987, pp. 345–357. IEEE Computer Society Press, Los Alamitos (1987), http://portal.acm.org/citation.cfm?id=41765.41804
3. Beizer, B.: Software Testing Techniques. International Thomson Computer Press (1990)
4. Bhandari, I., Halliday, M., Tarver, E., Brown, D., Chaar, J., Chillarege, R.: A case study of software process improvement during development. IEEE Transactions on Software Engineering 19(12), 1157–1170 (1993)

5. Bhandari, I., Halliday, M.J., Chaar, J., Chillarege, R., Jones, K., Atkinson, J.S., Lepori-Costello, C., Jasper, P.Y., Tarver, E.D., Lewis, C.C., Yonezawa, M.: In-process improvement through defect data interpretation. IBM Systems Journal 33(1), 182–214 (1994)

6. Bridge, N., Miller, C.: Orthogonal defect classification using defect data to improve software development. Software Quality 3(1), 1–8 (1997)

7. Chillarege, R., Bhandari, I., Chaar, J., Halliday, M., Moebus, D., Ray, B., Wong, M.Y.: Orthogonal defect classification – a concept for in-process measurements. IEEE Transactions on Software Engineering 18(11), 943–956 (1992)

8. Clements, P.: From subroutines to subsystems: Component-based software development. American Programmer 8(11), 31–38 (1995)

9. Cusumano, M.: The business of software: What every manager, programmer, and entrepreneur must know to thrive and survive in good times and bad. Free Press (2004)

10. El Emam, K., Wieczorek, I.: The repeatability of code defect classifications. In: Proceedings of the Ninth International Symposium on Software Reliability Engineering, pp. 322–333 (November 1998)

11. Freimut, B.: Developing and using defect classification schemes. Fraunhofer IESE IESE-Report No 72 (2001)

12. Grady, R.: Practical software metrics for project management and process improvement. Prentice-Hall, Inc., Upper Saddle River (1992)

13. Humphrey, W.: A discipline for software engineering. Addison-Wesley (1995)

14. Kit, E., Finzi, S.: Software testing in the real world: improving the process. ACM Press/Addison-Wesley Publishing Co. (1995)

15. Mantyla, M., Lassenius, C.: What types of defects are really discovered in code reviews? IEEE Transactions on Software Engineering 35(3), 430–448 (2009)

16. Vigder, M., Gentleman, W., Dean, J.: Cots software integration: State of the art (1996), http://nparc.cisti-icist.nrc-cnrc.gc.ca/npsi/ctrl?action=rtdoc&an=8914327&lang=en

17. Vinter, O.: Using defect analysis to initiate the improvement process (1998), http://www.iscn.at/select_newspaper/measurement/bruelkjaer.html

A Test Process Improvement Model for Automated Test Generation

Henri Heiskanen, Mika Maunumaa, and Mika Katara

Tampere University of Technology, Department of Software Systems
{firstname.lastname}@tut.fi

Abstract. Automated test generation is gaining popularity in the software industry, largely due to its labor-saving benefits and its ability to achieve high test coverage. The introduction of this technology into an organization does not, however, always meet with success. One reason for this is often the fact that the testing process and organization are not adjusted accordingly. Thus, in order for an organization to successfully pursue automated test generation, the test process must also be improved to enable this development. In this paper, we introduce an automated test generation add-on for the popular test process improvement model, TPI. We also present a baseline TPI profile for successful introduction of automated test generation.

Keywords: test automation, model-based testing, TPI.

1 Introduction

As the interest of today's software testing industry is to an increasing extent shifting to *automated test generation (ATG)* practices [14], such as *model-based testing*, the expectations of it are often set unreasonably high. In the end, the introduction of a new test automation tool into an organization solves few problems by itself. Instead, in order for the ATG approach to be successful, the test process itself must also be adapted to the needs of ATG. This raises the question on how the test process can be improved to accommodate the ATG approach, and what it requires to sustain the use of the new technology and working methods.

Test Process Improvement (TPI) [10] is a widely known software testing process improvement model that is often applied to determine the present standard of the test process of an organization and identify areas that have room for improvement. TPI has many advantages over other test process improvement models and is therefore used by many organizations, especially in Europe. One of the chief strengths of TPI is the fact that it enables simultaneous progress in many different *Key Areas*, as opposed to being limited to one-dimensional progress. This is reflected in the *maturity matrix* representing the test process maturity of an organization with respect to each Key Area, allowing organizations to focus their improvement efforts on select areas.

O. Dieste, A. Jedlitschka, and N. Juristo (Eds.): PROFES 2012, LNCS 7343, pp. 17–31, 2012.

Even though test automation is one of the Key Areas of TPI, the ATG approach, or the use of formal methods in general, is not addressed in it [17]. This is a major shortcoming as the ATG approach is not only about automation, but it also sets certain requirements for the practices and methods used by an organization and also affects other phases in the software development life cycle besides testing. New roles must also be created and introduced into the organization in the ATG transition. In the end, the overall effect of this change is significant, being not limited to technological aspects.

In this paper, we will present an ATG add-on for TPI [6]. The add-on provides support for the assessment process of organizations that are using, or contemplating using, ATG practices. As the original TPI, the ATG-tailored TPI version also includes a number of Key Areas that each have a number of *maturity levels* and *checkpoints* specifying the steps toward reaching these maturity levels. We also provide a baseline TPI profile for successful introduction of ATG practices. This profile outlines the minimum level of organizational maturity that, based on our earlier work, should be reached before engaging in ATG. In addition, we present the results of an industrial case study that was conducted to establish the validity of our model.

The rest of the paper is organized as follows: Section 2 serves as an introduction to TPI and ATG, Section 3 introduces our ATG add-on for TPI, Section 4 outlines the baseline maturity profile for successful introduction of ATG, Section 5 presents a case study conducted with the ATG-tailored TPI, and Section 6 concludes the paper.

2   Background

In this section we present the background of our work. First we present TPI and its main points, after which we briefly compare TPI with a few other prominent test process improvement models that have gained currency in industry. Finally, the concept of automated test generation is discussed.

2.1   Test Process Improvement

No matter how well testing is performed, there is still always room for improvement. In order to improve, the present situation needs to be determined. TPI is a method for such assessment, providing a frame of reference to identify the strengths and weaknesses of the process and suggesting actions to improve it. TPI is based on a structured test approach called *TMap* [13], which was developed at a Dutch company IQUIP in 1995. Based on the experiences of using TMap, the company and its clients arrived at the conclusion that they needed a method that would support their improvement efforts. The development of TPI began in 1996 and its final version was introduced in 1998. Subsequently, the TPI model has been adapted to various domains to better suit their specific needs, for example embedded systems [9] and the automotive industry [1].

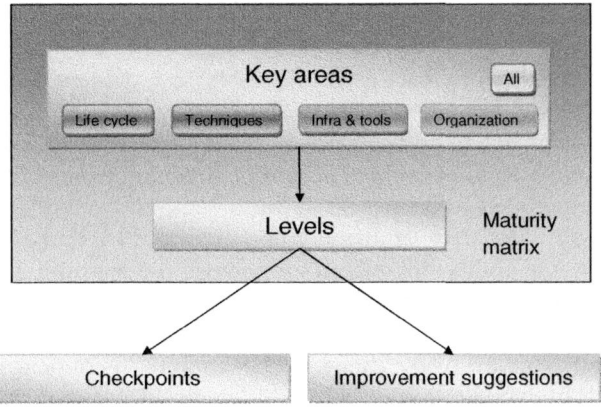

Fig. 1. TPI structure

TPI is based on four cornerstones (Figure 1) that describe various important aspects of the software development process, namely Life cycle, Techniques, Infrastructure and tools, and Organization. In addition, there is a general category for other items. The four cornerstones group together several interrelated Key Areas, which each represent different aspects of software testing. Each Key Area has several maturity levels, on a scale of one to four, and each maturity level in turn contains several checkpoints that specify the required steps to reach that particular level of maturity. TPI also provides practical improvement suggestions for each maturity level.

2.2 Review of Process Improvement Models for Software Testing

Currently the most prominent process improvement models for software testing are TPI, its newly introduced successor *TPI NEXT* [15] and the *Test Maturity Model Integration (TMMi)* [16], which is based on the *Testing Maturity Model (TMM)* [4] developed at Illinois Institute of Technology.

What all these models have in common is that they have a certain number of areas in which one can conduct process improvement. In TPI and TPI Next, these are called Key Areas, while in TMMi they are termed *process areas*. Furthermore, the notion of maturity level figures prominently in all these models. In TPI and TPI Next one can, however, proceed rather freely within different Key Areas and simultaneously be at different maturity levels in different Key Areas. By contrast, in TMMi one can only be at one maturity level at a time, and the process areas of TMMi each belong under a certain maturity level.

Another significant difference between TMMi and the TPI models is the underlying methodological context these models are based on. While TMMi is strongly connected with the *Capability Maturity Model Integration (CMMi)*, TPI and TPI Next in turn are based on testing approaches called TMap and *TMap Next* [3], respectively. TPI also draws a distinction between high-level and low-level testing, whereas TPI Next and TMMi are not concerned with the actual level of testing. Of all these models, TMMi is probably the one that enables the highest degree of development, as it addresses test process optimization issues in areas that are not accommodated in the TPI models.

As for the most salient differences between TPI and its newly introduced successor TPI NEXT, some of the less important Key Areas of the original TPI have not been included in TPI Next in an attempt to remove overlap between some of the Key Areas. In addition, the original TPI had proved somewhat rigid and its applicability to different business models and needs was found inadequate. Hence, TPI Next is more adaptable to different business drivers through highly customizable process improvement patterns. Furthermore, TPI NEXT has only 16 Key Areas and 157 checkpoints, as opposed to the 20 Key Areas and nearly 300 checkpoints of the original TPI. However, TPI NEXT is also less detailed than its predecessor, which can be seen by the reduction in the number of checkpoints. The checkpoints of TPI NEXT are also more abstract than those of the original TPI.

From our point of view, the most important difference between TPI, TPI Next and TMMi is that TPI is more technical by nature and therefore suitable for specific test projects or approaches, whereas TMMi and TPI Next are more managerial and emphasize issues related to stakeholder commitment and process management, for example. Thus, the ATG add-on was build on the original TPI, which we think is better suited for accommodating technological issues, such as ATG, due to its higher level of detail. The original TPI model has also attained a strong foothold in industry.

2.3   Automated Test Generation

Conventional test automation relies on scripts written in different languages and by different people. Sometimes script authors have proper software engineering backgrounds, but often that is not the case. Writing a test script that verifies a set of functionality thoroughly, or at least adequately, can be a tiresome task. Often there are dozens of scripts to test just one feature adequately. A test script must be small and simple to be maintainable, or else it will face the same problems as the code it is intended to test. To circumvent these problems, automated test generation can be used to generate tests automatically, both before and after the completion of the test object.

Generation of test cases always requires some kind of source from which the tests are generated. The source itself can have many forms, for example, requirements, design models, source code of the test object, user documents and/or conventional test scripts – we call these collectively the *ATG basis*, in keeping with the terminology of TMap. The key issue is that the ATG basis is expressed in a form that is computable, i.e., it can be processed on a computer. If the ATG basis is not in computable form, it must be converted to such. The result of such conversion is called the *test model*.

In practice, the test model can be one monolithic model or comprised of several component models, specified with some modeling formalism. The formalism depends on the perspective by which the system is modeled and the model can, in turn, contain information from one or many perspectives, for example, system/design and testing perspectives. An essential requirement for models is that there be a description for both functionality (control flow) and data (input/output values). The functionality is often modeled using some form of state machine, whereas the data can be provided as a simple *data table* [8], although it can also be incorporated into a state machine, for instance in Statecharts.

Depending on the nature of the test object and available tools, tests can be generated prior to test execution (offline) or during test execution (online). Both these approaches have their respective advantages and disadvantages, but in many contexts one way works better than the other [5]. The main difference is that offline generation can produce huge numbers of traditional test cases, which can then be executed and measured using conventional methods and metrics. And since they are reminiscent of traditional test cases, they are easy for testers to relate to and accept. In online testing, on the other hand, test execution can be arbitrarily long and its content can vary between consecutive executions. Accordingly, one execution can contain various traditional test cases. The actual trace (execution path) depends on what opportunities the model provides and what kind of feedback the test object provides in response to test steps. Thus, the online approach is especially suited for robustness testing.

An inherent aspect of ATG is modeling. As already explained, the model is a representation of the information contained in the ATG basis at a certain level of abstraction. It can be explicitly modeled by a *modeler* (explicit model) or implicitly conceived, for example during test execution (implicit model). A case in point of an implicit model is a random monkey test for a GUI, where test automation identifies items on screen and issues write-text and press-button commands randomly [12].

Regardless of how the test model is created, ATG requires new expertise from the organization especially in mapping the product requirements to test purposes that yield both positive and negative tests. Moreover, since requirements change and software is constantly updated, the selected ATG approach needs to be flexible enough to allow easy maintenance.

3   TPI for Automated Test Generation

TPI has 20 Key Areas that cover several aspects of testing. However, the ATG approach has some particularities that need special attention and are not addressed in the original TPI model. The modification process resulted in the creation of four new Key Areas and slight changes in some pre-existing Key Areas in the form of new maturity levels and/or checkpoints. The modifications also prompted the revision of the dependencies between the maturity levels of the Key Areas, as the dependencies caused by the modification process had to be mapped out. Next, we introduce the ATG add-on with a special focus on the new Key Areas and added maturity levels. First, the special process-related requirements of ATG are explained to justify our additions.

3.1   Why Test Process Must Change for ATG

As stated earlier, the ATG approach requires a source from which to generate tests. However, it is not necessarily easy to create this source. For example, in model-based testing the creation of an explicit test model is a time-consuming and exacting process. As such, it must be properly accommodated in the entire software development process. Moreover, the model also dictates what actions are available for testing, so it is crucial that the test model be designed and constructed so as to cover all relevant system functionality. This acts as an inducement to start modeling early on in the overall software development process.

Manual test modeling also has a significant organizational impact, as an entirely new role needs to be created for this purpose. Hence, the role of modeler is a vital addition to the composition of the test team. This role also requires a somewhat different skill set than is required of ordinary testers; a more formal background is often preferred for this task. Still, there is a need for other testers as well to design the actual tests that are based on modeled functionality.

In addition, as modeling is such a critical task in ATG-based testing, it should preferably co-occur with design modeling of the system. Although test models and design models are created from different perspectives, they still have much in common [11]. This, however, is not obligatory for a model-based testing process to be successful.

In industry, the adoption of ATG techniques has met with some difficulty due in part to the difficulty of creating and maintaining the test models, which is liable to deter organizations from adopting the ATG approach. This hardship can, however, be alleviated by earlier experience with ATG practices and proper training of testing personnel.

3.2   Changes to Existing Key Areas

As discussed earlier, the ATG approach involves the creation and use of the test model, which is the main attribute that differentiates ATG-based testing from traditional testing. The modeling process should be conceived as distinct from other testing-related activities due to the fact that the completion of the test model is a prerequisite for running the actual tests. Therefore, modeling should be integrated into the software development life cycle and, preferably, be started early on in a project for maximum gain. As argued earlier, the testing organization and its composition must conform to these special requirements. In practice, this is achieved with the creation of new roles, such as test modeler. All these considerations have been given due attention in the TPI add-on.

On the other hand, modeling can also be conceived as a static testing method, and a thorough one at that – it has been reported that during the modeling phase as much as around 60% of the total number of defects discoverable by ATG-based testing can be uncovered [7,17]. This led to the addition of a new maturity level to the Key Area of Static Test Techniques. Another maturity level

Table 1. Modified checkpoint list for KA03 Moment of Involvement (level B)

B	Checkpoints
1.	The activity "testing" starts simultaneously with or earlier than the phase in which the test basis (often the functional specification) is defined.
2.	**Modeling of functionality has been started (abstract models may be created to aid this process).**

that was added to the TPI model is one for the Key Area of Test Specification Techniques. This is because with some ATG techniques it is possible to derive test specifications from a computational model, which would provide further enhancements in this particular Key Area.

In addition to the new maturity levels, changes were introduced to various existing Key Areas in the form of new checkpoints (see example in Table 1). Most of these new checkpoints specify the necessary adjustments to the test process in terms of ATG and modeling, while some of them act more as additional tips for an established ATG-based test process. The former category covers the aforementioned issues of introducing test modeling into the software development life cycle and retooling the test organization for the purposes of ATG. The latter category, on the other hand, is more concerned with improving an existing ATG-based test process and, to this end, includes checkpoints on, for example, evaluations and defect management. The changes to the original TPI are presented in Figure 2. The new maturity levels are shaded with a darker color and altered original maturity levels with a lighter color.

However, not all of the necessary changes could be made by adding new checkpoints and maturity levels to the existing Key Areas. Some new Key Areas had to be introduced to better accommodate the special needs of ATG.

3.3   New Key Areas

The modeling process and concept of test model were also major reasons that prompted the addition of the new Key Areas (presented in Figure 3). The first new Key Area, *Modeling Approach*, is concerned with the process of modeling, measuring the reusability of models produced and the extent to which test modeling is connected with the use of design models. Reusability is a highly important characteristic of produced test models, particularly when the test models are created explicitly. With a certain level of abstraction and granularity it is possible to gain considerable benefits as far as reusability is concerned (level B).

As argued earlier, another important facet of the test modeling process is its connection with the design phase of the software development life cycle. Being able to derive the test model, at least partially, from existing design models can save plenty of time in the modeling phase, with less need to replicate work already done (level C, see Table 2 for details). The test modeling process would ideally be closely synchronized with design modeling, which would have the dual

Key area / Maturity level		A	B	C	D
Life cycle	1 Test strategy	Strategy for single high-level test	Combined strategy for high-level tests	Combined strategy for high-level tests plus low-level tests or evaluation	Combined strategy for all test and evaluation levels
	2 Life cycle model	Planning, Specification, Execution	Planning, Preparation, Specification, Execution and Completion		
	3 Moment of involvement	Completion of test basis	Start of test basis	Start of requirements definition	Project initiation
Infrastructure and Tools	4 Estimating and planning	Substantiated estimating and planning	Statistically substantiated estimating and planning		
	5 Test specification techniques	Informal techniques	Formal techniques	Computational techniques	
	6 Static test techniques	Inspection of test basis	Check-lists	Modeling of test basis	
	7 Metrics	Project metrics (product)	Project metrics (process)	System metrics	Organization metrics (>1 system)
Techniques	8 Test automation	Use of tools	Managed test automation	Optimal test automation	
	9 Test environment	Managed and controlled test environment	Testing in the most suitable environment	"Environment-on-call"	
	10 Office environment	Adequate and timely office environment			
Organization	11 Commitment and motivation	Assignment of budget and time	Testing integrated in project organization	Test-engineering	
	12 Test functions and training	Test manager, modeler and testers	(Formal) Methodical, Technical and Functional Support, Management	Formal Internal Quality Assurance	
	13 Scope of methodology	Project specific	Organization generic	Organization optimizing, R&D activities	
	14 Communication	Internal communication	Project communication (defects, change control)	Communication in organization about the quality of the test processes	
	15 Reporting	Defects	Progress (status of tests and products), activities (costs and time, milestones), defects with priorities	Risks and recommendations, substantiated with metrics	Recommendations have a Software Process Improvement character
	16 Defect management	Internal defect management	Extensive defect management with flexible reporting facilities	Project defect management	
	17 Testware management	Internal testware management	External management of test basis and test object	Reusable testware	Traceability system requirements to test cases
	18 Test process management	Planning and execution	Planning, execution, monitoring and adjusting	Monitoring and adjusting in organization	
All	19 Evaluation	Evaluation techniques	Evaluation strategy		
	20 Low-level testing	Low-level test life cycle model (planning, specification and execution)	White-box techniques	Low-level test strategy	

Fig. 2. TPI Key Areas with changes

Automated Test Generation	21 Modeling approach	Monolithic test model	Abstract and domain-specific test model	(Re-)Use of design models	Test modeling integrated to design modeling
	22 Use of models	Input generation with context knowledge	Input generation with domain knowledge	Test object output verification	
	23 Test confidence	Critical (path) functionality confidence	Shallow functionality confidence	Thorough functional confidence	Non-functional requirements covered
	24 Technological & methodological knowledge	Project-specific knowledge	Testing personnel has adequate knowledge and training in preferred technologies and practices	Organization is committed to the use of technologies and practices that have been found well suited to existing needs	

Fig. 3. New Key Areas

Table 2. Checkpoints for KA21 Modeling Approach (level C)

C	(Re-)use of design models
1.	The test model can, at least partially, be derived from design models that are of a higher level of abstraction than the test model itself.
2.	Design models used in the design phase, if such exist, are reused in the test modeling phase so as to avoid duplicate effort.

benefit of producing design models with a high level of testability and ensuring the consistency between the models (level D).

The second new Key Area, *Use of Models*, is also closely related to the concept of test model, measuring the degree to which the test model can be leveraged in testing. Some, often implicit, test models might only be capable of simple input generation (as in dumb monkey testing), while other, more advanced and explicitly crafted models can hold extensive knowledge of the system (level B), and possibly even verify the output of the test object (level C). Of course, this distinction might not be meaningful for all systems, but generally the capabilities of the test model affect the extent to which the ATG approach can provide added value to its users.

The third new Key Area, *Test Confidence*, was added to emphasize the area that probably benefits the most from the use of ATG. The attainable level of confidence in the quality of the test object is an important measure of the utility of any ATG technology. The ATG system should at least be capable of covering the most critical functionality of the test basis, but naturally, being able to cover all functional (level B), and possibly even nonfunctional (level D), requirements of the test basis is desirable. In addition, being able to thoroughly cover all functional requirements by testing them in multiple ways (level C) can further increase the attainable level of confidence.

While the other three new Key Areas directly address issues related to modeling, the fourth new Key Area, *Technological and Methodological Knowledge*, is in itself not connected with the ATG approach, or any technical aspect thereof. Still, this Key Area might well be the most important one for the successful and sustainable use of ATG over the long haul. This is because any new technology and working method must be effectively communicated within the organization in order for them to gain currency with the people who may become involved with them at some later time. This applies to any new technology that is introduced into an organization, but is particularly important for ATG since it necessitates significant changes to prevailing testing practices and organizational composition. This Key Area also covers the organizations' experience with the chosen technologies, tools and methods, and the higher the maturity in this Key Area is, the more people in the organization are familiar with the chosen methods.

In economic terms, it is usually costly to develop and maintain an ATG technology and the necessary infrastructure. So in order to recoup the initial investments in the technology, the organization must commit to using it for the long term. In practice, this can be achieved by appropriate training of testing personnel (level B) and, better yet, overall commitment to the new technology at organization level (level C).

4   Baseline Maturity Profile for Introduction of ATG

It is possible that after an ATG technology is introduced into an organization, it can be found unsuited to existing needs and, consequently, be abandoned. This might be due to the organization being immature in terms of Key Areas that are vitally important for the ATG transition, even if the organization were otherwise relatively mature in terms of its testing process. This section presents a baseline maturity profile for organizations envisioning the introduction of ATG into its testing practices. The profile is based on an informed estimate of issues considered key to successful introduction of ATG.

	Key Area	Scale 0	1	2	3	4	5	6	7	8	9	10	11	12	13
		Initial	Controlled					Efficient					Optimizing		
1	Test Strategy		A					B				C		D	
2	Life Cycle Model		A			B									
3	Moment of Involvement			A				B				C		D	
4	Estimating and Planning				A							B			
5	Test Specification Techniques		A		B										
6	Static Test Techniques					A		B							
7	Metrics						A			B			C		D
8	Test Automation				A				B			C			
9	Test Environment			A					B						C
10	Office Environment			A											
11	Commitment and Motivation		A				B						C		
12	Test Functions and Training				A			B			C				
13	Scope of Methodology					A						B			C
14	Communication			A		B							C		
15	Reporting		A			B		C							
16	Defect Management		A				B		C						
17	Testware Management			A			B			C					D
18	Test Process Management		A		B							C			
19	Evaluation						A			B					
20	Low-level Testing				A		B		C						

Fig. 4. Baseline maturity profile

The profile is given in terms of the original, unaltered TPI, not the retooled, ATG-tailored version. In addition, the profile outlines both the minimum and recommended levels of maturity for the introduction of ATG. The profile is described in Figure 4. The minimum maturity level of each Key Area is indicated by a darker color, whereas the recommended maturity level is represented with lighter shading. Note also that some Key Areas have no recommended maturity level to them, and in these cases the minimum maturity level doubles as the recommended maturity level. The gradations on the scale (1-13) are not important, and only serve to illustrate the relative difficulty of reaching a particular maturity level in a given Key Area.

We have identified minimum and recommended maturity levels for most Key Areas of the original TPI, each of which will next be discussed. Note, however, that some TPI Key Areas only require the maturity level A in our baseline profile and have no recommended maturity level either. These Key Areas, being not essential to ATG, have been omitted in the following analysis.

Test Strategy. There should be adequate degree of consideration as to how high-level testing is to be performed. The strategy should consider product risks and the depth and breadth of testing (level A). It would be better if there were a combined test strategy for multiple high-level tests that would complement each other (level B). For example, there should be a strategy on how manual and automated testing interleave so that gaps in test coverage are filled.

Life Cycle Model. Even though Life Cycle Model can be at the lowest maturity level (A), there are some distinct characteristics in ATG that almost require the higher level (B). This is mostly because the B level includes a preparation phase in the life cycle whose one purpose is to evaluate whether the test basis is suitable for the selected testing method. It is not unheard of that automation tools are selected to remedy a testing problem that cannot easily be remedied by automation.

Moment of Involvement. The preparation and planning for testing should be started as early as possible. Even though an early start has some benefits, it is always a tradeoff between valuable information and a waste of time. For example, starting to model the behavior of some part of a system while the particular functionality is still in its infancy can result in a great deal of rework. A good starting point for testing would arguably be when some part of the test basis is complete (level A), but an even better point would be at the beginning of test basis definition (level B).

Estimating and Planning. The ATG domain involves a great amount of planning and preparation before the actual tests can be executed. However, traditional test estimation techniques are not applicable to all ATG approaches due to the fact that some online ATG techniques do not have clear-cut concepts for conventional testing terms such as "test case" etc. Thus, it is necessary to devise appropriate metrics to support the estimation of testing. In addition, the preparation for testing often requires more time with ATG since the test model must also be created. Accordingly, we think that level A should be the minimum, whereas it is recommended to be at level B.

Test Specification Techniques. Test specification techniques are in a very important role in ATG since many ATG techniques require elaborate modeling of system behavior. Thus, well-defined and formal ways to create test specifications (B) are a vital prerequisite for long-lived use of ATG techniques. However, formal in this context does not mean the specification techniques are mathematical techniques, but rather well-defined documentation techniques. In our opinion informal techniques (A) are not adequate because they are not rigorous enough and often produce test specifications that are not as thorough as required.

Static Test Techniques. Static test techniques are important for verifying that the test basis is stable and testable enough. There are also some other benefits, but from the point of view of ATG, the maturity of the test basis is the most important aspect as far as avoiding unnecessary work is concerned. For some ATG approaches, however, this is not a very critical Key Area, if, for example, the test model can be derived by automatic means. Hence, we think it is recommended to be at level A.

Test Automation. This is the most important Key Area for ATG, as it measures the level of test automation. Level A verifies that the organization uses tools for managing budget, progress, defects etc. At level B, there are actual test automation tools in use for test planning and execution. This is the minimum level, but the recommended level is C because it checks whether the use of those tools is actually optimized for the testing task at hand.

Commitment and Motivation. There should be enough vision and support from management for the deployment of ATG into the testing process (level A) in order that it not fail at the first hurdle. In addition, the test team should have enough knowledge and training to deploy ATG into the testing process. Even better results can be achieved if testing constitutes a fixed part of the overall development process (level B).

Test Functions and Training. A substantially large portion of motivation and commitment originates from the fact that one has adequate skills for the task at hand and one's role in the organization is clearly defined. The latter is addressed at level A, while the former is addressed at level B. Since both are equally important for success, we argue that the minimum and recommended maturity level is B.

Scope of Methodology. If an organization has a fixed set of methods in use at organization level (level B) instead of letting individual projects decide what methods to use (level A), the organization has better chances at succesfully applying the chosen methods over the long haul.

Communication. Having internal communication is important for the successful completion of a project (level A), but many ATG practises require that there be a constant feed of information about changes in the test basis and defects discovered in the test object (level B).

5   Case Study

In order to establish the validity of our TPI add-on, an case study was conducted with an organization that practices automated test generation. In this section the main findings of this study are presented in detail.

Execution. The case study was conducted in the form of a *TPI assessment*, which is usually performed to determine the present status of an organization in terms of its testing process. The more thorough the assessment is, the more areas to improve it can identify. As our primary objective was to dry-run our TPI add-on in a real industrial environment, we concentrated on determining the impact of our changes to the original TPI model, not so much on the process improvement side of the assessment. An interesting case question for us was whether the changes we introduced to the TPI model would radically impact the assessment results derived by the original TPI. But, most importantly, we wanted to establish whether our additions would be workable in practice, and whether the requirements for reaching the different maturity levels of the new Key Areas would be reasonable.

A TPI assessment involves asking the interviewees a series of questions to determine the maturity of each TPI Key Area. In practice, the questions are the same as TPI checkpoints, and are all answered either "yes" or "no". All told, there are around 300 checkpoints in the TPI model, which is also the maximum number of assessment questions. All the questions regarding the higher maturity levels do not need to be covered during the assessment if the requirements of these higher maturity levels are not met. Once all the questions have been answered, the matrix representing the test process maturity of the organization being assessed can be constructed. On finishing the assessment, we determined the organization's maturity by both the original TPI and our ATG-tailored TPI. This was done to establish the impact of our additions to the TPI model on the overall maturity of the organization, and to determine whether the organization's maturity agreed with our baseline maturity profile given in Section 4.

The organization for which the assessment was carried out was a medium-sized multiplatform IT company whose mobile software development organization was evaluated. The organization had incorporated the ATG approach into its testing stategy for mobile applications. As an established ATG practitioner, the company was ideally suited as our object of assessment because the new Key Areas on ATG could be thoroughly covered during the assessment.

In addition, the organization has adopted agile working methods, which, as it turned out, had a minor effect on the results of the assessment. This is because TPI is based on a plan-driven software testing and development mindset, and some issues, such as documentation, are not equally important in agile development. Due to a rapid development cycle exploratory testing [2] is heavily used among other testing activities. Two roles were represented in the assessment: a quality manager and a quality engineer. Both had experience in the field of testing mobile applications and test automation solutions in that context.

Assessment Findings. As for the original Key Areas, the result is in agreement with the minumum maturity profile for the ATG approach given in Section 4, and in some Key Areas the minimum levels are even exceeded. In addition, the organization could reach the recommended levels in Key Areas "Test Automation", "Scope of Methodology" and "Commitment and Motivation". These are all exceedingly important areas for ATG, test automation infrastructure being vital to this approach and the sustenance of ATG practices at organization level (Scope of Methodology, level B) at least equally critical. The Key Area of Commitment and Motivation is also important, as it tells that testing has been acknowledged as an essential part of the software development life cycle. Furthermore, the Key Area of Communication was found to exceed the recommended level, which may also have contributed to the fact that the organization has successfully applied ATG for a long time.

As for the new Key Areas added to the TPI model, all of them were found to be sound, without attracting considerable criticism. The new maturity levels added to the Key Areas of Test Specification Techniques and Static Test Techniques also proved workable. Still, some details of the new Key Areas were found to be somewhat ill-defined, needing further elaboration.

The most important observation regarding the new Key Areas was probably the fact that a previously selected or implemented ATG technology can impose some constraints, precluding the possibility of advancing to the next level in the Key Area of Modeling Approach, especially when the technology has been in use for a long time. Accordingly, substantial changes to test tool infrastructure might be necessary when one looks to advance further in this Key Area.

Interestingly enough, in terms of the 20 original Key Areas, our TPI add-on had no effect on the maturity results derived from the TPI assessment, as compared with the results by the original, unmodified TPI. All the original Key Areas reached the very same maturity levels whether it was the original TPI or the ATG-tailored TPI that was applied. Even though many of the original Key Areas were changed to better accommodate ATG, the new checkpoints added to the model did not affect the overall assessment results. This is definitely a major positive with our ATG add-on, as the maturity results derived by it seem to be very compatible with those by the original TPI.

Although this case study only included one single organization, it still demonstrated that the ATG add-on for TPI worked well and we are heading in the right direction with our model. Still, more assessments need to be conducted with the ATG add-on to confirm its utility. We also identified details in our model that need further revision.

6 Conclusion

In this paper we have presented a test process improvement model for automated test generation. This model reflects the particularities that characterize ATG-based testing and provides improvement ideas for organizations operating in this particular area of testing. We have also presented a baseline profile for the application of our model, and more importantly, of the ATG approach itself. This profile outlines both the minimum organizational maturity that should be met before the introduction of ATG into an organization, as well as the recommended organizational maturity for the sustained use of ATG practices.

The industrial case study that was conducted to establish the validity of our model yielded encouraging results. The model was found to be sound and applicable to organizations practicing automated test generation. Still, more assessments with the new model are required in order to conclusively determine its practical value. Minor additions to the model were also made after the case study to further refine it. Future work will involve a closer study of the new TPI NEXT model and other significant test process improvement models from the perspective of automated test generation.

References

1. TPI Automotive. Tech. rep., Sogeti Deutschland GmbH (2004), http://www.tpiautomotive.de/produkte.html, version 1.01 (cited May 2011)
2. Bach, J.: Exploratory testing explained (April 2003), http://www.satisfice.com/articles/et-article.pdf (cited May 2011)
3. Broekman, B., Koomen, T., van der Aalst, L., Vroon, M.: TMap Next for result-driven testing. UTN Publishers (2006)
4. Burnstein, I.: Practical Software Testing. Springer-Verlag New York, Inc. (2003)
5. Hartman, A., Katara, M., Olvovsky, S.: Choosing a Test Modeling Language: A Survey. In: Bin, E., Ziv, A., Ur, S. (eds.) HVC 2006. LNCS, vol. 4383, pp. 204–218. Springer, Heidelberg (2007)
6. Heiskanen, H., Maunumaa, M., Katara, M.: Test process improvement for automated test generation (April 2010), http://practise.cs.tut.fi/files/publications/AMOEBA/reports/Atg-tpi_report.pdf
7. Jääskeläinen, A., Katara, M., Kervinen, A., Maunumaa, M., Pääkkönen, T., Takala, T., Virtanen, H.: Automatic GUI test generation for smart phone applications – an evaluation. In: Proc. of the Software Engineering in Practice track of ICSE 2009, companion volume, pp. 112–122. IEEE CS (2009)
8. Jääskeläinen, A., Kervinen, A., Katara, M.: Creating a test model library for GUI testing of smartphone applications. In: Proc. QSIQ 2008 (short paper), pp. 276–282. IEEE CS (2008)
9. Jung, E.: A test process improvement model for embedded software developments. In: Proc. QSIC 2009, pp. 432–437. IEEE CS (2009)
10. Koomen, T., Pol, M.: Test Process Improvement: A practical step-by-step guide to structured testing. Addison–Wesley (1999)
11. Malik, Q.A., Jääskeläinen, A., Virtanen, H., Katara, M., Abbors, F., Truscan, D., Lilius, J.: Model-based testing using system vs. test models – what is the difference? In: Proc. ECBS 2010 (poster session), pp. 291–299. IEEE CS (2010)
12. Newman, N.: Using monkey test tools. Software Testing and Quality Engineering 2(1), 18–21 (2001)
13. Pol, M., Teunissen, R., van Veenendaal, E.: Software Testing: A guide to the TMap Approach. Addison–Wesley Professional (2001)
14. Rushby, J.: Automated Test Generation and Verified Software. In: Meyer, B., Woodcock, J. (eds.) VSTTE 2005. LNCS, vol. 4171, pp. 161–172. Springer, Heidelberg (2008)
15. Sogeti: TPI Next – Business Driven Test Process Improvement. UTN Publishers (2009)
16. TMMi Foundation homepage, www.tmmifoundation.org/ (cited May 2011)
17. Utting, M., Legeard, B.: Practical Model-Based Testing – A Tools Approach. Morgan Kaufmann (2007)

Software Process Improvement and Certification of a Small Company Using the NTP 291 100 (MoProSoft)

Verónica Ñaupac[1], Robert Arisaca[2], and Abraham Dávila[3]

[1] Facultad de Ingeniería de Sistemas,
Universidad Nacional de San Agustín, Arequipa, Perú
veronica.naupac@gmail.com
[2] Departamento Académico de Ingeniería de Sistemas e Informática,
Universidad Nacional de San Agustín, Arequipa, Perú
rarisaca@unsa.edu.pe
[3] Departamento de Ingeniería, Pontificia Universidad Católica del Perú, Lima, Perú
abraham.davila@pucp.edu.pe

Abstract. Today we recognize the strong influence of the software in our world and the need for it to have the right quality. However, the software industry has remained in a crisis for many years. Faced with this situation, the quality of process models are presented as an interesting opportunity that can help to change it. This article presents the experiences, challenges and lessons learned in the processes improvement and subsequent certification with the NTP 291 100 (based on MoProSoft) of a small software-development company located in the city of Arequipa in Peru.

Keywords: Software Process Improvement, Software Quality, MoProSoft, COMPETISOFT, NTP 291.100.

1 Introduction

The software industry is conformed mainly of small and medium enterprises (SMEs) [1], [2], [3], [4], [5] and in most cases these companies have problems with their software development projects, that is, the way they perform their processes. This situation involves a series of facts such as the high level of disorder, inadequate or lack of technical documentation of the artifacts produced or rework for not meeting customer needs or critical defects [2], [6] [7], [8]. This implies that the product is software of poor quality and the project was carried out with development times above the estimated and costs over budget [9].

The problem with software quality, at least in Peru, is complicated: (i) by the pressure from clients asking for shorter delivery deadlines, (ii) the increasing complexity that computer systems have with integration needs to legacy systems, and (iii) by the high turnover with the development in business, among others. This product complexity makes projects more difficult to structure and manage, so it is necessary to establish clearly the way to work, in other words, the process to be performed to increase the chances of success.

O. Dieste, A. Jedlitschka, and N. Juristo (Eds.): PROFES 2012, LNCS 7343, pp. 32–43, 2012.
© Springer-Verlag Berlin Heidelberg 2012

At the international level, there has been developed models for the improvement and assessment the software processes, most notably CMMI [10], ISO/IEC 12207 in conjunction with ISO/IEC 15504 [11], ISO 9001 [12], and so on. However, it is noted that these models are geared mainly to large enterprises [13], [14], and its adoption by SMEs in the software industry, is difficult and costly [14], [15]. Given this scenario, some Latin American countries in isolation have been some initiatives such as: MoProSoft in Mexico [16], MPS-Br in Brazil [17], or SIMEP-SW in Colombia [18]. In this same line of proposals for SMEs, the project COMPETISOFT was developed (with CYTED funds) to increase the competitiveness of Ibero American software industry [19], [20]. Subsequently COMPETISOFT-Peru Project 2nd and 3rd phase [21], as a sequel to the international efforts to improve productivity through the implementation of the Peruvian Technical Standard MoProSoft 291.100 (in Spanish is NTP 291.100) for SMEs that develop software with less than 25 workers. Finally, ISO published in 2011 the ISO/IEC 29110 Part -5-1-2 Basic Profile (VSE Project) that include only two processes [30] and based on MoProSoft [14].

This article describe the problems, experiences and lessons learned from the implementation of MoProSoft and subsequent certification with the NTP 291,100 in a small enterprise in Arequipa, a city in southern Peru. The article is organized as follows: in section 2, gives a brief description of the NTP 291 100 (MoProSoft) and ISO / IEC 15504; in section 3, presents the description and the improvement project, and the results of the evaluations, the problems identified and lessons learned; in section 4, the effort to get the certification made in the company; and, finally, in section 5, shows the final discussion and future work.

2 Models in the SPI Project

The project COMPETISOFT-Peru 2nd and 3rd phase was developed according to established guidelines: (i) with the MoProSoft (NTP 291 100) for the definition of processes, (ii) process asessment model based on ISO/IEC 15504 for assessing MoProSoft, and (iii) pmCompetisoft to guide the process improvement [19]. Here is a briefly presentation of models used in the Project:

2.1 MoProSoft

MoProSoft is a Software Process Model and it is aimed at SMEs in software development [16]. This model compile a set of best practices from other models such as CMMI, ISO 9001, ISO/IEC 12207, among others, adapting to the needs of SMEs [22]. The MoProSoft was developed for the Mexican software industry government initiative in 2003 [23] and adopted as Mexican National Standard in 2005 [24]. The MoProSoft was introduced to Peru by COMPETISOFT Project in 2007, with the aim of improving competitiveness in the software industry, and in May 2009 was adopted in Peru as a National Technical Standard under number 291.100 [22].

The MoProSoft has been developed considering that it should be easy to learn, easy to apply and that its adoption in the SME will be not expensive, among others requirements [22], resulting in a model with follow features: (i) has a pattern process to document their processes and it can be used as a basis for defining processes in the company, (ii) every process in the model is defined at a level of detail that can be adopted for each business situation and (iii) provides a guide for adoption through the color that identifies the level that corresponds to each processing element [16]. Mo-ProSoft consists of nine processes organized by three categories of processes: (i) "Top Management" category contains the process "Business Management", (ii) Management category which contains the processes "Process Management", "Project Portfolio Management " and "Resources Management" that also comprises 3 sub processes, and (iii) Operation category that contains the processes "Specific Projects Management" and "Software Development and Maintenance" [16].

2.2   EvalProSoft and ISO/IEC 15504

The 3rd phase of CompetiSoft project [21] in Peru established as one result the certification scheme definition based on the NTP 291,100, EvalProSoft [25] and the ISO/IEC 15504-2 [29]. EvalproSoft is an assessment method that applies to development organizations and / or maintenance of software, so particular to those who have used MoProSoft as a reference model for the implementation of their processes [25]. However, EvalProSoft does not meet the ISO/IEC 15504-2 requirements, so it was necessary to develop some extensions to meet them.

The assessment process was conducted according to the ISO/IEC 15504-2 [30] works with: (a) six levels of process capability from 0 to 5; (b) a measurement framework that includes the rating of process attribute based on four level: (i) N, Not achieved, representing between 0 and 15% of the fulfillment of the purpose of the process, (ii) P, Partially achieved, representing between 15 and 50%, (iii) L Largely achieved, representing 50 to 85% and (iv) Fully achieved, which represents between 85 and 100%; (c) nine process attributes, taking one for the first level and two for the each following capability levels and (d) indicators for every attibute used in an assessment process.

2.3   pmCOMPETISOFT

PmCOMPETISOFT is an agile software process improvement model developed as part of COMPETISOFT and used to make improvements in small and medium software companies [26]. This process has an iterative and incremental approach, which aims to meet the principles as: (i) early delivery and continued improvement, (ii) rapid diagnosis and continuous of the processes, (iii) basic measurement process, (iv) effective collaboration between groups, and (v) continuous learning [26].

PmCOMPETISOFT model consists of one or more cycles of improvement, each of which consists of 5 macro activities: (i) installation, (ii) diagnosis, (iii) development, (iv) improvement, and (v) review cycle [27]. Activities that allow the software process improvement in an organization based on business objectives [28].

3   Software Process Improvement in the Company

In order to present the results of the company participating in this project and maintain the confidentiality agreements in place, it was agreed to use the alias "Aqp-Alpha" for any reference to it. The following describes the Company to process improvement and certification process followed.

3.1   Company under Study

Aqp-Alpha is a small company that provides service and consulting in software development and external training in IT tools. The company is mainly focused on developing new computer systems with a continuous incorporation of new technologies, providing solutions to different organizations in Peru. The company has 15 employees including managers, administrative and technical team.

In Aqp-alpha is considered that the software process improvement is important and represent the opportunity to grow and mature as an organization. For this reason, agreed to adopt and implement MoProSoft in all processes of the Company. A special situation in Aqp-Alpha was that the General Manager had knowledge and experience in process improvements using MoProSoft. This situation facilitated the decision to improve processes, allocate time to human resources and material resources to make a success of the improvement effort.

3.2   Software Process Improvement

The improvement project encompassed the macro-activities defined in pmCompetisoft but with some adjustments in its execution according to the coordination of the improvement team. The important aspects of the improvement project are showed in the next section.

Installing the Improvement Cycle. General Manager decided to implement MoProSoft as a part of the 3rd Phase COMPETISOFT Peru, for which they signed an agreement to improve processes between the company and the project COMPETISOFT-Peru. In this agreement established some guidelines given below:

- The nine MoProSoft processes will implement at the capability level 1. The improvement cycle will estimated in 8 month and two iterations. The first iteration will cover the processes of the Top Management category and three of the processes of Management category (Process Management, Project Portfolio Management and Resource Management). The second iteration will cover the remaining MoProSoft processes.
- It will form a team of improvement in the Company, including a Junior Consultant trained in the models and a process quality manager from the company dedicated for 20 hours per week along the Project. The manager will be trained on a continue way on MoProSoft model.

- The kick-off meeting of software process improvement will announced to all company employees through a special meeting.

All the guidelines included in the agreement were met. Particularly, in relation to the socialization, the general manager showed great confidence in the software process improvement and its benefits for the employees and the company.

Diagnostic Assessment. To perform the diagnosis process we used instruments developed by COMPETISOFT-Peru Project, collected and reviewed the documentation from de processes and held a series of interviews with employees. Using the process defined in ISO/IEC 15504, we determined process capabilities profile against MoProSoft. The profile was obtained using a spreadsheet where they had registered all relevant process elements (inputs, outputs and activities) at capability level 1 from MoProSoft. The assessment was conducted for each process attribute using a measurement framework defined by ISO/IEC 15504: (N) Not achieved, (P) Partially achieved, (L) Largely achieved, and (F) Fully achieved. However, to facilitate understanding of the level of compliance was defined a metric of compliance coverage by counting the elements that do meet over the total of possible elements. Figure 1 shows profile process capabilities with baseline adherence rates of each process.

The assessment results shows that some processes reached the qualification N and other the qualification P, which means that all processes are at the capacity level 0.

It may be noted that although the company believes it does things well, they recognized that little formality in its processes has caused problems when they perform their projects. This is shown in the partial or total absence of various practices or documents needed (defined in MoProSoft) such as: strategic plan, process pattern, assessment and improvement process plan, sales plan, project portfolio management plan, record of progress and project activities, knowledge base, project risk management, change management and updating of technical documents, etc.

Proposal and Process Improvement. To develop the Improvement Plan is needed to carry out a series of meetings with the CEO of the company, to develop a list of the most important problems and current business objectives. Considering both lists, we performed the analysis of the impact of implementing each MoProSoft processes to support the scope and achievement of business objectives and to contribute to solve existing problems. The Table 1 presents the problems found and business objectives.

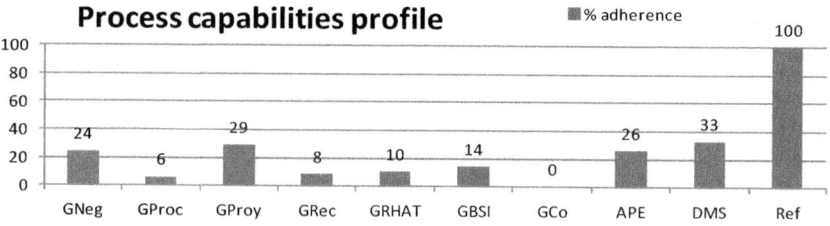

Fig. 1. Processes capabilities profile of Aqp-Alfa (Diagnostic Assessment)

Table 1. Business goals and issues in Aqp-Alfa

Business goals of the company
O1. Maximize your profits through the efficient use of resources.
O2. Having highly trained and certified personnel, to ensure a proper process of developing an IT product or service.
O3. Create strategic alliances with other key organizations.
O4. Using national and / or international standards in the process of software development and IT services, to ensure the delivery of a quality product or service.
O5. Achieving customer loyalty as well as confidence in their services.
O6. Achieving internal staff satisfaction.
Business issues (related to goal affect)
- Business Management erratic for some businesses because of lack of clarity in the direction of the company or absence of a Strategic Plan for Business. O1, O5.
- Business processes are not formally defined. O1, O2.
- Lack of management of a portfolio, which is why there was no proper management of each project. O1, O4, O5.
- There was no proper management of resources, since it is not planned how they were going to find and buy each one of these. O1, O2, O3.
- There was no knowledge of training needs that required human resources. O2, O5.
- Members of the company had never gone through a process of performance evaluation. O2, O4.
- The procurement of goods and / or services are performed taking into account only the costs thereof, and the same evaluation was not performed its suppliers. O1, O3, O4.
- You had a Maintenance Plan, of which only maintenance was done to their property whenever they had a problem. O1, O3, O4.
- Information relevant to the company generally was discarded each time you did maintenance on personal computers of members of the company and in some cases lost due to problems with software like virus and presence of others. Therefore most of them chose to save your data to your email or external memories. O1, O4.
- Absence of a Plan for each Project, which describes issues such as risk management, cost and time estimate, etc. for each of these, which the team carried out the activities that the project leader destined for each week. O1, O3, O4, O5.
- Lacking internal projects deliverables such as requirements specification, analysis and design. O4, O6.
- In some projects there was no user manual nor a manual, because the customer does not demand as project deliverable. O4, O6.

These results together with the initial diagnosis allowed to define what processes will be designed and/or redesigned in the improvement cycle. Also, define two iterations for the improvement project. In Table 2 presents the general activities undertaken during the iterations.

Table 3 shows the processes and other information about iteration where were developed, capability levels in each iteration, times demanded to implement improvements in these processes without considering the time of the pilots and coverage level.

The pilot was conducted over a period of 6 months and a half. During which time, the activities demanded more time and control were the creation of standard templates for documenting each process and the continue training to those process responsible.

Table 2. Activities in both iterations

#	Activity	1	2
A1	Training on the model	x	
A2	Planning of the Iteration	x	x
A3	Formulation of the improvements	x	x
A4	Review of the improvements	x	x
A5	Training on each process	x	x
A6	Pilot of the improvements	x	x
A7	Documentation of the process	x	x
A8	Monitoring of the pilot	x	x
A9	Evaluation of the Iteration	x	x

Table 3. Actions and results in SPI

Abbrev. (In Spanish)	Process	Iteration	Action	Duration (weeks)	Iteration 1			Iteration 2		
					% Adher	Qualif Iter 1	Capab Proc	% Adher	Qualif Iter 2	Capab Proc
G.Neg.	Business Management	1	Design	5	56	L	1	96	F	1
G.Proc.	Process Management	1	Design	7	59	L	1	76	L	1
G.Proy.	Project Management	1	Redesign	5	47	P	0	80	L	1
G.Rec	Management of exceptions	1	Design	3	36	P	0	52	L	1
GRHAT	Human Relations Management and Work Environment	2	Redesign	4	N.A	N.A	N.A	69	L	1
GBSI	Properties, Services and Infrastructure Management	2	Redesign	6	N.A	N.A	N.A	51	L	1
GCO	Knowledge of the Organization	2	Design	4	N.A	N.A	N.A	98	F	1
APE	Software development and maintenance	2	Redesign	3	N.A	N.A	N.A	67	L	1
DMS	Specific Project Management	2	Redesign	3	N.A	N.A	N.A	69	L	1
Evaluation	Final 1st iteration	1	---	1	---	---	---	---	---	---
Evaluation	Final 2nd iteration	2	---	1	---	---	---	---	---	---

When the improvement cycle started, some members of the company were showed unbelievers about whether this improvement process would help them improve their work or it will become a waste of time. As it was developing the pilot, also became clearer about the objectives sought through the implementation of this improvement cycle. Shortly after the end of the improvement process responsible for almost all processes were identified with their functions and roles within the company, only presented the case of Responsible Management Goods, Services and Infrastructure, which did not stop to understand some MoProSoft requirements. For example, what was the purpose of making an assessment providers working with the company? nor the need to the maintenance plan. But, this case was settled satisfactorily using training in MoProSoft model and shows him how his works affect the software projects and impact in the company objectives.

The improve in the Project Management process implied a change in the way of working in the company, since the model aims to work hand in hand between the Portfolio of Projects and Sales Plan. In the case of process management, they customized the process guidance, which defined the activities, products and responsibilities according to the capability level 1 in MoProSoft. Also due to lack of knowledge in risk management has defined a template for monitoring these. The Organizational Knowledge process brought the most radical change in the cycle of process improvement, since it created a Knowledge Base, which had a design that meets the needs of each user (role), as well as usage rules this. By creating such a knowledge base all members of the company were forced to train in the tool that allowed use, forcing them to migrate to a new way to store your information.

During the implementation of Improvement Plan several issues were resolved immediately, because almost all were identified before in the Risk Management Plan and there were tracked every week. The issues detected out of the Risk Management Plan were resolved in the best way possible, trying to reduce their impact in the execution of the plan and do not affect future activities. Table 4 contains the most striking problems encountered and the solutions given for each case.

Assessment and Improvement Cycle Review. In each iteration there was a quick review of the documents worked and the process defined with respect to the pilot and the provisions made based on MoProSoft. The assessment identified some minor deficiencies in some key business documents such as: strategic plan, sales plan, risk matrices and the evaluation plan of processes among others. The grade obtained by each process according to the iteration can be appreciated in Table 3, where the "% of adher" is the coverage calculated by counting process elements compliments against to the total, the column of qualification corresponds to that given using the ISO/IEC 15504-2.

Table 4. Issues and action taken into SPI Project

Issues	Solutions
Lack of experience of the quality manager.	Regular training by the COMPETISOFT Peru team.
Lack of organization improvement group.	Make a plan of weekly activities, further indicating that the products should be developed, as well as responsible for this.
Delays in the Improvement Plan activities.	Modify calendar giving more time to achieve these activities.
Lack of MoProSoft as a role model by all members of the company.	Trainings were held constant for all members of the company, trying to give greater emphasis to the processes which were part of each of them and always stressing the importance of this process of improvement in their daily
Poor understanding of how to develop a sales plan, the responsible person understood how to do market analysis.	Currently the company only detects potential customers and how to reach them, but still lacks a formal Marketing Plan.
Lack of experience in managing portfolios of projects, since there was no concise Project Plan (with information relevant to the charge of this).	Currently responsible for project portfolio AQP-ALFA managed the details of each project separately, but produces a list of projects with useful information for him.
Poor performance of some processes responsible because they did not understand as they should generate some of their processes or products that the new process to work harder.	The group members had to improve continuously support and guide the development of the products of these processes. As well as continually insist on the development of these.
Non-compliance of the design of the Knowledge Base on the part of those responsible.	Meetings were held with each of these to know what their non-conformity so we can modify the design of the base to fit into their daily work.
Non-compliance with the standard nomenclature defined for storing files in the Knowledge Base.	A meeting was held to present the reasons why that standard was applied naming.
Failures in the repository of the knowledge base because the programmers to code updates daily.	It was determined that only be stored in the Knowledge Base stable versions, and developers would use a separate repository for their daily actions.

In the definition of project management process was introduced some mistakes because the new definition confused some activities of two processes: project management and project portfolio management. It also recommended using a simple sales plan including the minimum elements that suggested the model

4   Certification Process

The internal assessment at the end of each iteration was very useful to those responsible because they were more aware of how to operate their processes and make appropriate adjustments. These assessments detected some deficiencies that were quickly adjusted. Upon completion of the improvement project, the Company chose to certify their processes using the Peruvian Technical Standard NTP 291.100 (MoProSoft) that is assessed to ISO / IEC 15504 by the Quality Institute of the Pontificia Universidad Católica del Perú.

After finishing administration activities, the company presented the list of projects to choose the projects to be evaluated. Once selected the projects proceeded to define the schedule of meetings with those responsible for processes and leave all the evidence on hand for meetings with the evaluators.

The evaluation lasted 3 days at the company, reviewing all the evidence presented and conducting interviews with staff provided in the schedule. At the end of the assessment results were presented detailing strengths and weaknesses that were found in every process. In Table 5 presents the ratings for each of the processes. Getting an F level of compliance (fully achieved in 3 of the 9 processes) and L (Largely achieved in the remaining 6 processes), which allowed the certification of the Company at a capability level 1 in NTP 291100 (MoProSoft.

5   Final Discussion y Future Work

The company Aqp-Alpha formally began its process improvement project in August 2010 and ended in March 2011 and then started the certification process, to be evaluated in April 2011 and obtained certification in June 2011. This chronology shows how a small company where all employees and their managers are committed to the work, it achieves the expected results in the projects. It should be noted that both CEO and Junior consulting already had knowledge and experience in MoProSoft which was a contribution to their success.

In the first iteration of the improvement, the processes selected were those managed by a few persons. This idea allowed the company to learn about this type of effort. Also, they achieved satisfactory results because they spent much time analyzing business information to formalize the process and to adapt it to work their way today. In this iteration, it was created formats for the documents required in each of formalized processes and the members of the company were trained in changes and quality concepts and their importance for the company and for their work.

Table 5. Pro-cess capability profile in certification process

Id Process	Process	Qualification
G.Neg.	Business Management	F
G.Proc.	Process Management	F
G.Proy.	Project Management	L
G.Rec	Management of exceptions	L
GRHAT	Human Relations Management and Work Environment	L
GBSI	Properties, Services and Infrastructure Management	L
GCO	Knowledge of the Organization	F
APE	Software development and maintenance	L
DMS	Specific Project Management	L

In the second iteration it was noted that activities in the first iteration established a good reference to deploy the new activities. The format of documents to be generated and also each responsible for each process was which were fully informed of the activities to be performed and the evidence to be generated. The results of the iteration were satisfactory, because it achieved the goals set at the beginning of the improvement cycle. The ratings at the end of the process improvement were considered acceptable and the goal of certification as a real possibility. We developed a work plan to monitor and improve the weaknesses and maintain good practice.

The achievements at the end of the improvement cycle showed that not only raised the level of compliance of processes, but also noted other changes in the company, such as the use of a risk matrix for each project to be developed, the generation of project plans, the use of software to plan and monitor progress of the activities of each project, the use of a repository as a knowledge base and what better security what were the activities that each person must perform in the company according to the role represented in this.

The small company achieved good results in a short time because there was a real commitment and effective general management and professionals involved. Employees in the pilots appreciated the benefits of process improvement as more organized clarity at work, among others. The training was very convenient to facilitate the adoption of improvements.

Acknowledgements. This work is framed within COMPETISOFT Peru Project 3rd Phase 009-FINCyT-PITEI-2010/ACKLIS which tittle was: cMoProSoft *"Definición de una Certificación de Procesos para pymes de tecnología de Información basada en Normas Internacionales ISO/IEC usando un Método de Evaluación Propio y una Herramienta de Soporte"* and, the Engineering Department of Pontificia Universidad Católica del Perú.

References

1. Fayad, M.E., Laitinen, M., Ward, R.P.: Software Engineering in the Small. Communications of the ACM 43(3), 115–118 (2000)
2. APESOFT: Programa de Apoyo a la Competitividad de la Industria del Software, Perú, Diciembre (2008)

3. Laporte, C.Y., April, A., Renault, A.: Applying ISO/IEC Software Engineering Standards in Small Settings: Historical Perspectives and Initial Achievements. In: Proceedings of SPICE 2006 Conference, Luxembourg, May 4-5 (2006)
4. MCT: Pesquisa de Qualidade no setor de Software Brasilero (2009), http://www.mct.gov.br/upd_blob/0214/214567.pdf (last visit December 15, 2011)
5. CETIC: Thailand Initial Implementation of ISO/IEC 29110, http://www.cetic.be/IMG/pdf/Thailand_Initial_Implementation_ISO29110.pdf (last visit December 15, 2011)
6. Pino, F.J., García, F., Piattini, M., Oktaba, H.: COMPETISOFT: Revisión sistemática de mejora de procesos software en pequeñas y medianas empresas de software (2006), http://alarcos.inf-cr.uclm.es/competisoft/publico/downloads/Inf_T%C3%A9cnicos/COMPETISOFT_IT_1.pdf (last visit November 16, 2011)
7. Bertone, R., Pasini, A., Ramón, H., Esponda, S., Pesado, P., Mon, A., Gigante, N., De Maria, E., Estayno, M.: Un Modelo para PyME'S. In: XXV Jornadas IRAM – Universidades, San Juan, Argentina (2006), http://www.uniram.com.ar/jornadas/XXV/TC-19.pdf
8. García Romero, C.: El Modelo de Capacidad de Madurez y su Aplicación en Empresas Mexicanas de Software. Tesis Licenciatura. Ingeniería en Sistemas Computacionales. Departamento de Ingeniería en Sistemas Computacionales, Escuela de Ingeniería, Universidad de las Américas – Puebla, Mayo (2001)
9. Chudnovsky, D., López, A., Melitsko, S.: El sector de software y servicios informáticos (SSI) en la Argentina: Situación actual y perspectivas de desarrollo (2008), http://www2.netvision.com.py/demos/ctip/v2/wp-content/uploads/2008/04/la-industria-de-ssi-en-mercosur_caso-de-argentina.pdf
10. SEI: CMMI for Development, Version 1.3 (2010), http://www.sei.cmu.edu/library/abstracts/reports/10tr033.cfm
11. Pino, F., García, F., Ruiz, F., Piattini, M.: Adaptación de las normas ISO/IEC 12207:2002 y ISO/IEC 15504:2003 para la evaluación de la madurez de procesos software en países en desarrollo. IEEE América Latina 4(2), 17–24 (2006)
12. ISO: ISO 9001, Quality management systems – Requirements, Geneva (2008)
13. Gresse, C., Anacleto, A., Salviano, C.: Helping Small Companies Assess Software Processes. IEEE Software, 91–98 (January-February 2006)
14. Laporte, C., Simon, A., Renault, A.: The application of International Software engineering Standards in Very Small enterprise. SQP 10(3), 4–11 (2008)
15. Richardson, I., Gresse, C.: Why are small software organizations different? IEEE Software 24(1), 18–22 (2007)
16. Oktaba, H., Esquivel, C., et al.: Modelo de Procesos para la Industria del Software. MoProSoft. Versión 1.3. Mayo (2005)
17. Softex: MPS.BR - Mejora de Proceso del Software Brasileño Guía de Implementación – Parte 7: Fundamentos para Implementación del Nivel A del MR-MPS (2011)
18. Ariel, J., Bastarrica, C.: Proyecto SIMEP-SW Trabajo de Investigación: Hacia una Línea de Procesos Ágiles Agile SPsL (2005)
19. CYTED: COMPETISOFT. Mejora de Procesos para Fomentar la Competitividad de la Pequeña y Mediana Industria del Software de Iberoamérica (2006), http://www.cyted.org/cyted_investigacion/detalle_accion.php?un=9c838d2e45b2ad1094d42f4ef36764f6&lang=es

20. Oktaba, H., Felix, G., Mario, P., Francisco, R., Francisco, P., Claudia, A.: Software Process Improvement: The Competisoft Project. IEEE Computer 40(10) (October 2007)
21. COMPETISOFT – PERU 2. Mejora de Procesos para Incrementar la Competitividad de la Pequeña y Mediana Industria del Software de Iberoamérica. Componente – Perú. Proyecto DAI – 2009 – 008 – PUCP, de sitio web (2010),
https://sites.google.com/site/competisoft2peru/
22. Basurto, C.: MOPROSOFT (2011), http://www.acklis.com/moprosoft
23. Reyes, P., Margain, L., Alvarez, F., Munoz, J.: Aplicación de instrumento diagnóstico en proceso "gestión de procesos" con base en MoProSoft. Investigación y Ciencia, enero-abril (43), 30–37 (2009)
24. Oktaba, H.: MoProSoft: A Software Process Model for Small Enterprises. In: Proceedings of the First International Research Workshop for Process Improvement in Small Settings, pp. 93–100 (2006), Special Report CMU/SEI-2006-SR-001
25. Oktaba, H., Alquicira, C., Su, A., Palacios, J., Pérez, C., López, F.: Método de Evaluación de procesos para la industria del software EvalProSoft, Versión 1.1., Marzo, México (2004)
26. Pino, F.J., Hurtado Alegría, J.A., Vidal, J.C., García, F., Piattini, M.: A Process for Driving Process Improvement in VSEs. In: Wang, Q., Garousi, V., Madachy, R., Pfahl, D. (eds.) ICSP 2009. LNCS, vol. 5543, pp. 342–353. Springer, Heidelberg (2009)
27. Pino, F., Vidal, J., Hurtado, J.: Guía del Consultor para la Mejora de Procesos Software (2007),
http://alarcos.inf-cr.uclm.es/competisoft/publico/downloads/
Inf_T%C3%A9cnicos/COMPETISOFT_IT_18%20Marzo%2015%202007%20Gu
ia%20del%20consultor.pdf
28. Pino, F., Vidal, J., García, F., Piattini, M.: Modelo para la Implementación de Mejora de Procesos en Pequeñas Organizaciones Software. In: XII Jornadas de Ingeniería del Software y Bases de Datos (JISBD 2007), Zaragoza, Spain, September 11-14 (2007)
29. ISO: ISO/IEC 15504-2 Information Technology – Process Assessment – Part 2: Performing an assessment, Geneva (2003)
30. ISO: ISO/IEC 29110 Software engineering — Lifecycle profiles for Very Small Entities (VSEs) — Part 5-1-2: Management and engineering guide: Generic profile group: Basic profile (2011)

Derivation of Process-Oriented Logical Architectures: An Elicitation Approach for Cloud Design*

Nuno Ferreira[1], Nuno Santos[2], Ricardo J. Machado[3], and Dragan Gašević[4]

[1] I2S Informática, Sistemas e Serviços S.A., Porto, Portugal
[2] CCG - Centro de Computação Gráfica, Campus de Azurém, Guimarães, Portugal
[3] Centro ALGORITMI, Escola de Engenharia, Universidade do Minho, Guimarães, Portugal
[4] School of Computing and Information Systems, Athabasca University, Canada

Abstract. The benefits of cloud computing approaches are well known but designing logical architectures for that context can be complicated. Prior to designing a logical architecture, a proper requirements elicitation must be executed. When requirements are not properly elicited, and there are insufficient inputs for a product approach to requirements elicitation, a process-level perspective is an alternative way for achieving the intended base requirements for the logical design. Our proposed solution regards the adaptation and extension of the 4SRS (Four-Step-Rule-Set) method to derive logical architectural models, in a process-level perspective. This perspective creates context for the product-level requirements elicitation conducing to cloud design. We present a real industrial case where the method was applied and assessed. The method application results in the creation of a validated architectural model and in the uncovering of hidden requirements for the intended cloud design.

Keywords: Requirements Elicitation, Logical Architectures, Application Architectures, Development Methods for Cloud Applications.

1 Introduction

The design of software architectures for systems to be executed in a cloud computing environment brings many difficulties to system architects. Instead of designing a cloud computing architecture based on user requirements traditionally defined in a product-level perspective, we propose the use of a process-level perspective for the requirements definition and design of the logical model of the system architecture. This is built upon the premise that such an approach contributes to a more accurate definition of product requirements and understanding of the project scope.

The term *process*, in a generic context, is hard to define. In the definition given in [1], a process is a specific ordering of work activities across time and place, with a beginning, an end, and clearly identified inputs and outputs. Software architecture deals with the design and implementation of the high-level structure of the software [2].

---

* This work has been supported by project ISOFIN (QREN 2010/013837).

O. Dieste, A. Jedlitschka, and N. Juristo (Eds.): PROFES 2012, LNCS 7343, pp. 44–58, 2012.

This paper describes the extensions introduced into the 4SRS method to be adopted at the process-level perspective in large-scale projects. The 4SRS method was first defined and detailed in [3, 4]. The described extensions are focused on a process-level perspective to deliver a logical architectural model. This logical architectural model contributes to the context definition of a proper requirements elicitation. This paper additionally illustrates the applicability of the proposed approach in a real industrial case: the ISOFIN project (Interoperability in Financial Software). This project aims to deliver a set of cloud-based functionalities enacting the coordination of independent services relying on private clouds. The resulting ISOFIN platform will allow the semantic and application interoperability between enrolled financial institutions (Banks, Insurance Companies and others). In the presented real industrial case, the process-level 4SRS is used to create the necessary context to elicit the requirements for designing an architecture capable to be implemented in the three typical cloud-layers: Infrastructure-as-a-Service (IaaS), Platform-as-a-Service (PaaS), and Software-as-a-Service (SaaS), as defined in [5]. The transformation of such context into product-level requirements does not belong to the scope of the present work.

This paper is structured as follows: section 2 describes the problem associated to the real industrial case study which is presented in this paper, as well as some related work concerning the core topics and the reason for the new approach; section 3 presents the main differences between the traditional approach of the 4SRS method and the proposed process-level approach; section 4 presents the designed logical architecture as context for elicitation; and in section 5, we present our conclusions and some future work.

2   Problem Overview

This work is based on a premise that the process-level 4SRS method can be used when there is no agreed on or defined context for requirements elicitation. Requirements Elicitation is concerned with where software requirements come from and how they are collected [6] within the Requirements Engineering area. The objective of a requirements elicitation task is to communicate the needs of users and project sponsors to system developers [7]. A proper requirements elicitation task must encompass an understanding of the organizational environment, through their business processes [8].

An accurate requirements elicitation can be assured through the use of requirements elicitation methodologies, methods or techniques. The Work System Method [9] presents a combined static view of the current (or proposed) system and a dynamic view of the system evolution over time. The Soft Systems Methodology (SSM) [10] is a domain-independent analysis methodology designed for tackling problematic situations where there is neither clear problem definition nor solution.

Our approach suggests the derivation of a process-level logical architecture for creating context for cloud design. There are several approaches to support the design of software architectures, in a product-level perspective, like RSEB [11], FAST [12], FORM [13], KobrA [14] and QADA [15]. The product-level perspective of the 4SRS [4] method also promotes functional decomposition of software systems.

Tropos [16] and 4SRS (in [17]) are process-level requirement modeling methods. Tropos uses notions of actor, goal and (actor) dependency as a foundation to model early and late requirements, architectural and detailed design. The 4SRS method is usually applied in a product-level perspective. Our presented approach formalizes the process-level perspective that was firstly used in [17]. Use cases act as input for the 4SRS method and, in the 4SRS process-level perspective, portray the activities (processes) executed by persons or machines in the scope of the system, instead of the characteristics (requirements) of the intended products to be developed. According to [18], and in a business context, a process is executed to achieve a given business goal and where business processes, human resources, raw material, and internal procedures are combined and synchronized towards a common objective. Our processes represent the real-world activities of a software production process, like in [19]. A software process is composed of a set of activities related to the software development life-cycle. Designing a process comprises the development of a process architecture that continually aggregates process elements to support tailoring and enhancements of processes. Implementing a process encompasses the specification of the requirements for process execution.

The requirements for process execution can be represented in a logical architecture. A logical architecture can be considered a view of a system composed of a set of problem-specific abstractions supporting functional requirements [20]. The process architecture represents the fundamental organization of service development, service creation, and service distribution in the relevant enterprise context [21]. A process architecture can also be defined as an arrangement of the activities and their interfaces in a process [22], takes into account some non-functional requirements, such as performance and availability [2], and can be represented with components, connectors, systems/configurations of components and connectors, ports, roles, representations and rep-maps [23], as well as by architectural elements' static and temporal features [24]. The result of the application of the 4SRS method is a logical architecture.

Existing approaches for designing software architecture do not support any specific technique for requirements elicitation; rather, they use the information delivered by an adopted elicitation technique. One problem arises when typical (product-oriented) elicitation techniques cannot properly identify the necessary requirements. With the real industrial case described in this paper we demonstrate that firstly adopting process-level techniques allows for better understanding of the project scope since it allows for the elicitation of the activities that will be supported by the product to be developed.

2.1   The ISOFIN Project

The logical process-level architecture of the ISOFIN solution [25] has embedded design decisions that are initially injected in the processes descriptions. The design decisions concern the deployment of the system in a public cloud environment and its interoperability with several other private clouds as defined in the project objectives.

The resulting logical model of the system architecture, based on the processes that are intended to be executed, shows a software solution able to be deployed in an IaaS layer. That layer will support the execution of a set of services that will allow suppliers to specify the behaviour of the services they intend on supplying, in a PaaS layer. This will allow customers, or third-parties, to use the platform's services, in a SaaS layer and be billed accordingly. This paper only presents a subset of the proposed process-level architecture related to the customer perspective, as seen in Fig. 1. Processes regarding the provider perspective (e.g., infrastructure management) are not considered. We present subsets of two use case models concerning two distinctive functionalities provided by the platform.

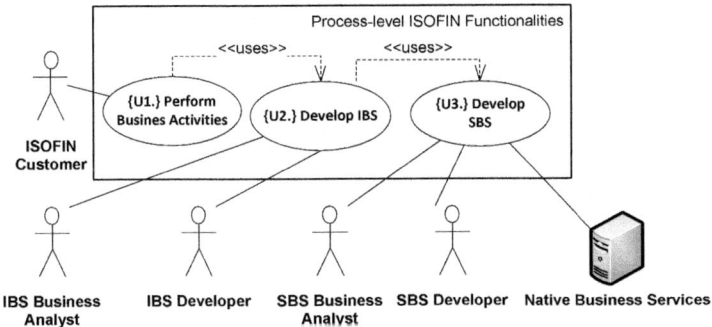

Fig. 1. Use Case Model Regarding the ISOFIN Process-level Perspective Functionalities

The process-level architecture focuses on two sets of functionalities: Interconnected Business Service (IBS) and Supplier Business Service (SBS). IBSs concern a set of functionalities that are exposed from the ISOFIN SaaS Platform to ISOFIN Customers. An IBS interconnects one or more SBSs and/or IBSs exposing functionalities that relate directly to business needs. SBSs are a set of functionalities that are exposed from the ISOFIN Supplier private cloud.

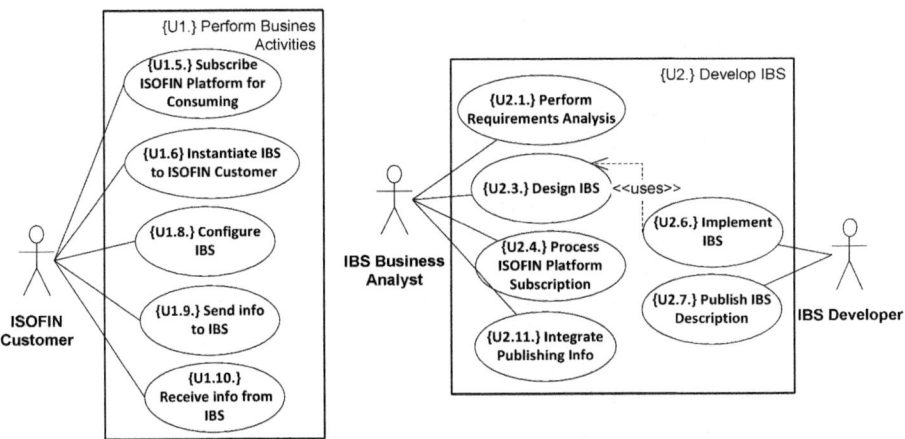

Fig. 2. Refinement of Use Case 1 and Use Case 2 (subset)

In Fig. 2 there is a description of the execution of a set of economically-related business processes within the context of the project. They are executed through the SaaS layer, since the software components and applications are hosted by third-party service providers in the cloud. By accessing the services functionalities (represented by implemented IBSs), ISOFIN Customers fulfills their business needs.

Most of these processes, namely the ones regarding the design and implementation efforts, are executed through the PaaS layer. The defined processes will correspond to some of the services and applications that the ISOFIN Platform will support, when executed in the SaaS layer. The model encompasses the analysis, design and implementation of IBSs, accessed externally, through the SaaS layer, and providing ISOFIN Customers with added business value.

3   Process-Level 4SRS as an Elicitation Method for Cloud Design

The 4SRS method allows for the transformation of user requirements into an architectural model representation. This paper presents an extension of the traditional (product-level perspective) usage of the 4SRS method (presented in [4]) to allow its application in a process-level perspective supporting the creation of context for the product-level requirements elicitation. This application differs from the traditional by defining a set of rules that must be observed when reasoning about the execution of the method steps. Our extension of the method also defines additional micro-steps to the existing ones. Alongside the method presentation there will be included some examples created during the method application to derive a logical architecture that acts as a basis for the requirements elicitation of a cloud SaaS solution, in this case, a subset of the ISOFIN project.

The 4SRS method takes as input a set of use cases describing the requirements for the cloud-specific processes that tackle the initial problem. These use cases are refined trough successive 4SRS iterations, representing the intended cloud concerns of the involved business and technological stakeholders. Neither KobrA, RSEB, nor Tropos make use of techniques for refining use cases like the 4SRS method does. Application of the 4SRS method requires the creation of "architectural elements" (AEs). The nature of AEs varies according to the type of system under study and also with the context where it is applied. In the specific context of logical architectures, the term architectural element refers to the pieces from which the final logical architecture can be built. We deliberately use this term to distinguish those artifacts from the components, objects or modules used in other well established contexts, like in the UML structure diagrams.

The execution of the 4SRS transformation steps can be supported in tabular representations as it can be seen in [4]. Moreover, the usage of tables permits a set of tools to be devised and built, so that the transformations can be partially automated. These tabular representations constitute the main mechanism to automate a set of decision-assisted model transformation steps. Tabular transformations are supported in a table where the cells are filled with the set of decisions that were taken and made possible the derivation of a logical architecture for the cloud design. Each column of the table concerns a step/micro-step of the method execution. For readability purpose, the entire table was divided into five smaller tables (Tables 1 to 5). In the real context, we manipulate the entire table and not the smaller ones. The next sub-sections detail the extensions made to the process-level perspective of the 4SRS method and the added micro-steps (product-level 4SRS original steps are in [4]).

3.1   Step 1: Architectural Element Creation

This step regards the creation of AEs. The product-level 4SRS [4] rule of transforming each use case into three AEs is still valid in the process-level 4SRS. According to the MVC-like pattern applied in the product-level 4SRS, an interface, data and control AEs are created for each use case. *i-type*, *d-type*, or *c-type* stereotypes respectively are added to each AE and their names are prefixed with "AE" (the stereotypes definition will be detailed in micro-step 2i). No particular rationale or decision is required at this step since it concerns mainly the transformation of one use case into three specific AEs. This step is represented in the 1st and 2nd columns of Table 1.

An addition to this step is the identification of glue elements resulting from the textual descriptions associated with the use case under analysis. If the use case depicts pre- or post-conditions in the form of validations, those can be expressed in this step as a *Glue AE*. These AEs have the *c-type* stereotypes since they require decisions to be made with computational support, that is, they must be supported by the system architecture to be represented. A sequential number is added to each Glue AE. Those elements will be used as generic process interfaces between generated AEs and act as pre- or post-condition process validations. Other AEs are expressed as *Generated AE*.

For example, {AE1.9.c2} *Validate Business User* was created as a result of the analysis of the use case {U1.9.} *Send info to IBS* with the description *"[...] Before sending commands to an IBS, ISOFIN Customers must subscribe [...]"*.

Table 1. Step 1 of the 4SRS method

Step 1 -architectural element creation	
Use Case	**Description**
{U1.9.}	Send info to IBS
{AE1.9.c2}	Glue AE
{AE1.9.i}	Generated AE

3.2   Step 2: Architectural Element Elimination

In this step, AEs are submitted to elimination tasks according to pre-defined rules. At this moment, the system architect decides which of the original three AEs (i, c, d) plus any glue element are maintained or eliminated taking into account the entire system.

The original step 2 of 4SRS is divided into seven micro-steps. We added a new micro-step, 2viii: Architectural Element Specification. With this addition, step 2 becomes more robust and detailed. It provides information to the next steps that was hard to obtain in the original version.

Micro-step 2i: Use Case Classification. In this step, each use case is classified according to the nature of its AEs, previously created in step 1. The nature of an AE is defined according to the suffix the AE was tagged with. This classification is represented in the 2nd column of Table 2 (the 1st column regards the AE identification). In the process-level perspective more than one of each AE type can be generated according to the textual description and in the model of the use case. Each AE type must be interpreted as follows:

- *i-type* – refer to interface. These represent process' interfaces with users, software or other processes. An AE belonging to or being classified in this category is due to its ability interact with other AEs external to itself;
- *c-type* – refer to control. These represent a process focusing on decision making and such decision must have a computational support given from the overall intended system;
- *d-type* – refer to generic decision repositories (data), not computationally supported from the overall intended system. This repository stores information for a given period of time, regardless of duration, comprising decisions based on physical repositories (like documents or databases) or verbal decisions taken and transmitted between humans.

In the process-level perspective, *c-type* and *d-type* AEs are related to decision-making processes. The difference resides on the computational support of the AE by then under design overall intended system (in hypotheses).

Micro-step 2ii: Local Elimination. This micro-step refers to determining which AEs must be eliminated in the context of a use case, guaranteeing its full representation. This is required since micro-step 2i disregards any representativeness concerns.

There are cases when there is an explicit place for a *d-type* AE and it is admittedly eliminated. Reasons for this are due to the process-level perspective: there is no need for certain types of decision repositories that only regard information for the final product and not the process. This is the case, for example, in use case {U1.9.} *Send info to IBS*, where any possible repository (data object in the traditional 4SRS) that could exist would only reflect the product-level perspective and not the process. Other situation similar to the previous one is when a given *d-type* AE exists in the product-level perspective but also, and above it, exists in the process-level perspective. This is the case of {U1.6} *Instantiate IBS to Remote Business Program*, where {AE1.6.d} *IBS Configuration Decisions* represents the process for supporting the configuration process (process-level), not the configuration repository (product-level).

The 3rd column in Table 2 corresponds to the execution of micro-step 2ii. The cells are filled with "T" or "F". "T" means the AE is going to be eliminated and "F" that the AE is kept alive.

Micro-step 2iii: Architectural Element Naming. In this micro-step (4th column of Table 2), AEs that survived the previous micro-step are given a name. The name must reflect the role of the AE within the entire use case, in order to semantically give hints on what it represents and not just copy the original use case name. Usually, the AE name reflects also the use case from which the AE was originated.

For better understanding of the role of the AE, it is advisable that the name given reflects the type (c, d or i) of the AE. For instance, since *d-type* refers to decision-making, in our model, we decided to name "IBS Configuration Decisions" to {AE1.6.d}. In glue AE cases, the naming of the AE should reflect the pre- or post-conditions that are executed. For instance, {AE2.4.3.d} *ISOFIN Platform Supplier Policy*, reflects the pre-condition *"The ISOFIN Supplier must accept [...] to comply with the defined policy"*.

Table 2. Micro-steps 2i trough 2iv of the 4SRS method

	Step 2 - architectural element elimination			
	2i - use case classification	2ii - local elimination	2iii - architectural element naming	2iv - architectural element description
{U1.9.}	i			
{AE1.9.c2}		F	Validate Remote Business Program	Execute the necessary verification procedures to ensure that the Remote Business Program is ...
{AE1.9.i}		F	Send Commands to IBS	Send commands and associated information to the IBS in order to process a business request...

Micro-step 2iv: Architectural Element Description. This micro-step is represented in the 5th column of Table 2. The resulting AEs that were named in the previous micro-step must be described and the requirements that they represent must be addressed in the process-level perspective. This micro-step is where the transition is made from the problem domain to the solution domain, so the descriptions must detail, in process terms, how, why, when by whom that AE is going to be executed. This micro-step must explicitly describe the expected behavior of the AE execution, including which decisions will be made and how will they be supported.

Micro-step 2v: Architectural Element Representation. The purpose of this micro-step is to eliminate AE redundancy in the global process. In this micro-step, all AEs are considered and compared in order to identify if one AE is represented by any other one. The identification of AE representation is the most critical task in the 4SRS method application, because the elimination of redundancy assures a semantic coherence of the logical architecture and discovers anomalies in the use case model. Since the architecture being described concerns the process-level, the identification of AE redundancy takes in consideration facts like the execution context, actors involved, used artifacts, activities and tasks, among others. If all of these factors are similar, though the AEs are originated by different use cases, the given AE can be considered to represent another. Other cases when an AE is considered to represent another:

- In similar activities, if the same actor has the same role in the both AEs, despite different execution contexts (e.g., {AE2.4.1.i} *Perform ISOFIN Supplier Request Evaluation* is considered to be represented by {AE2.4.2.i} *Perform ISOFIN Customer Request Evaluation*, the IBS Business Analyst triggers both AEs – the first AE represents the second AE, because the actor interacts with the same type of information);

- In similar activities, different actors participate in the AE, but the execution context is the same (e.g., {AE2.1.c} *Access Remote Catalogs* and {AE1.11.i} *Browse ISOFIN Catalogs*, the involved actors are different, but the execution platform is the same – both of them execute in the ISOFIN Platform, in the SaaS layer).

These cases are only applicable for *i-type* and *c-type* AEs. This set of rules cannot be applied to *d-type* AEs since they represent the decisions that need to be taken and whose computational support is not assured by the scope of the project under analysis. Also, *d-type* AEs are usually input for other decision processes (*c-type* AEs) requiring computational support.

Despite the decision making process may be similar, *d-type* AEs differ in the decision making purpose. This difference is required to assure the process variability, when the execution contexts are similar but the involved actors and activities are different. For example, {AE1.5.d} *Consumer Subscription Requirements* and {AE3.3.d} *SBS Catalog Subscription Requirements* cannot be represented by one AE, although the *i-type* related AEs – {AE1.5.i} and {AE3.3.i} – are represented by the same AE. The decision making regarding a specific purpose viewed from different perspectives concerns different purposes, even if, at first sight, the interface seems to be the same.

A potential concern when executing this micro-step regards the number of AEs involved. Since all living AEs must be accounted in the analysis, it is hard to keep track of all the processes they refer to in order to know if one can be represented by other.

In the product-level perspective, this step concerns the analysis if a given AE is complex enough to exist by itself or if there is any other AE whose functionalities can be incorporated in the one under analysis. This rule also applies to the process-level perspective, if three questions are considered:

- Is the analyzed AE suitable to be represented by other in his entire functionality?
- Is the target AE suitable to incorporate the AE under analysis functionalities without losing any of its own characteristics?
- If the target AE is complex and the extra-functionalities to be added increase the complexity will it be in a degree where its maintenance, description or scope are compromised?

If the activities or processes executed within the context of a given AE are to be executed by another AE and the target AE is subject to change, no extra complexity should be added to that target AE nor its core specification change in order to full represent the source AE.

The execution of micro-step 2v is presented in Table 3 in the 2nd and 3rd columns. The 2nd column, "represented by", stores the reference of the AE that will represent the AE being analyzed. If the analyzed AE is going to be represented by itself, the corresponding "represented by" column must refer to itself. The 3rd column, "represent", stores the references of the objects that the analyzed AE will represent.

Micro-step 2vi: Global Elimination. This micro-step (4th column in Table 3) refers to determining which AEs must be eliminated in the context of the global model, similar to micro-step 2ii, since its execution is automatic.

The AE that is represented by itself or represents other AEs is maintained. The rest (i.e., AEs that are represented by other AEs) are eliminated. This is a fully "automatic" micro-step, since it is based on the results of the previous one. If the AE is represented by itself, cell is filled with "T", meaning that the AE is represented by other AE and thus, eliminated, and "F" if the AE is going to be kept alive.

Micro-step 2vii: Architectural Element Renaming. In this micro-step (5th column in Table 3), AEs that have not been eliminated in micro-step 2vi are renamed. In cases where the AE under analysis results of the representation of more than one AE, the new name must reflect the global execution of the AE in the project context.

Micro-step 2viii: Architectural Element Specification. This micro-step (6th column in Table 3) has never been considered in previous versions of the traditional 4SRS method. Though it is similar to micro-step 2iv, this micro-step intends to describe AEs that, in micro-step 2v, are considered to represent other AEs. The decision of creating this micro-step arises from the need to clearly define the proper behavior of the "new" AE in a way that is clear to system architects. Besides including the information regarding AEs eliminated in micro-step 2vi as a result of micro-step 2v, the AEs specifications must include the pre-conditions of the basic AEs, so it can properly support the associations to be established in step 4. For instance, if the extended description of {AE1.9.c1} does not include the conditions described in {AE1.1.c1}, that information would be lost since {AE1.1.c1} has been eliminated in micro-step 2vi and, as such, is not considered in step 4. If those references are not preserved in any surviving AEs, they will be permanently lost and thus, disregarded in the construction of the logical diagram model.

The specification must also include execution sequence references of the AEs. For instance, {AE2.9.i} must reference the ISOFIN Application catalog described by {AE1.3.d}, which is also eliminated in micro-step 2v, to create the association in step 4. The specification information is required in the transformation from the process-level approach to the product-level approach, to infer the necessary requirements of a given product based on the processes of which the product is composed.

This micro-step contributes to a better description of AEs that result from joining other AEs. By adding this information, the designer can clearly express their thoughts and decisions concerning the creation of the AE under analysis as a result of the potentially added extra-complexity resulting from micro-step 2v.

Table 3. Micro-steps 2v trough 2viii of the 4SRS method

	Step 2 - architectural element elimination				
	2v - architectural element representation		2vi - global elimination	2vii - architectural element renaming	2viii - architectural element specification
	represented by	represent			
{U1.9.}					
{AE1.9.c2}	{AE1.9.c2}	{AE1.1.c2}	F	Validate Platform Access	Execute the necessary verification procedures to ensure that subscribed ISOFIN Customers...
{AE1.9.i}	{AE1.9.i}		F	Send Commands to IBS	

It is necessary to pay a special attention to the AEs that represent other AEs in micro-step 2v. The specification must clarify system architects in what way the AE is executed and how its execution represents an eliminated AE.

3.3   Step 3: Packaging and Aggregation

Like in the traditional 4SRS method, in this step (2nd column in Table 4), the remaining AEs (those that were maintained after executing step 2), for which there is an advantage in being treated in a unified process, should give the origin to aggregations or packages of semantically consistent AEs. This step supports the construction of a truly coherent process-level model.

In order to correctly package AEs, it is necessary to consider the model as a whole, so that all relevant processes (in a high-level order of abstraction) are identified. Then, when justifiable, the AEs are associated to a package. The packaging technique contributes for a temporary obtainment of a more comprehensive and understandable process model. Typically, aggregation is used when there is a part of the process that constitutes a legacy sub-system, or when the design has a pre-defined reference architecture that constricts the model.

Table 4. Step 3 of the 4SRS method

	Step 3 - packaging & aggregation
{U1.9.}	
{AE1.9.c2}	{P6} ISOFIN Platform Management
{AE1.9.i}	{P2.4} IBS

3.4   Step 4: Architectural Element Association

Decisions on the identification of associations between AEs can be based in information contained in the use case model and in micro-step 2i. Thus, step 4 was divided in two micro-steps: micro-step 4i: Direct Associations and 4ii: Use Case Associations.

It is also important to point out that any textual references to eliminated AEs in micro-step 2vi, must be included in micro-step 2viii, making it another source of information for step 4.

In the traditional 4SRS application, this step is executed in a single step. We propose to do it in two micro-steps to easily identify unnecessary direct associations, as well as associations originated by textual description of eliminated AEs. This division, by separating the associations by its source, also helps to adjust the model when there are changes due to refinements or corrections in the previous steps execution.

Micro-step 4i: Direct Associations. Direct associations (2nd column of Table 5) are the ones that derive from AEs originated by the same use case. These associations are depicted from the classification given in the method micro-step 2i. For example, {AE1.6.d} *IBS Configuration Decisions* and {AE1.6.i} *Configure pre-runtime IBS* are directly associated since they are originated by the same use case, {U1.6} *Instantiate IBS to Remote Business Program*.

Micro-step 4ii: Use Case Model Associations. Use Case Model Associations are the ones that can be inferred from the textual descriptions of use cases, that is, when a use case description refers, implicitly or explicitly to another use case, the associations inferred imply that the use cases are connected. This micro-step is represented in the 3rd column of Table 5.

Table 5. Step 4 of the 4SRS method

	Step 4 - architectural element association	
	4i - Direct Associations	**4ii - UC Model Associations**
{U1.9.}		
{AE1.9.c2}	{AE1.1.i}, {AE1.9.c1}, {AE1.9.i}.	{AE3.3.i}.
{AE1.9.i}	{AE1.9.c1}, {AE1.9.c2}.	{AE1.7.i}, {AE2.9.i}, {AE3.3.i}.

As an example for these situations, the use case textual description of {U3.7.1.} *Publish in Platform Catalog* in the use case model refers that *"The SBS [...] is availa-ble for access to IBS Business Analyst (see use case {U2.2.} Choose SBS Specs, use case {U2.3.1.} Define IBS Internal Structure and use case {U2.5.} Choose SBS Im-plementation) and to the SBS Developer (see use case {U2.6.} Implement IBS)"*. Thus, the generated surviving AE – {AE3.7.1.i} *Remote SBS Publishing Interface* – is asso-ciated with {AE2.1.c}, {AE2.3.1.c}, and {AE2.6.1.i}.

4   The ISOFIN Process-Level Logical Architecture

The ISOFIN project [25] is executed in a consortium comprising eight entities (pri-vate companies, public research centers and universities). The initial request for the project requirements resulted in mixed and confusing sets of misaligned information. Even when a requirement found a consensus in the consortium, the intended behavior or definition was not easily understood by all the stakeholders. Our proposal of adopt-ing a process-level perspective was agreed on and, after being executed, resulted in a set of information that the consortium is sustainably using to evolve to the traditional (product-level) development scenario. Elicited requirements in a process-level perspective describe the processes in a higher level of abstraction, making them un-derstandable by business stakeholders. At the same time, definitions and intended behavior of the system, expressed in the architecture that results from the process-level 4SRS method, describe the system to technological stakeholders.

The turning point for eliciting requirements was the usage of the 4SRS method in the process-level perspective, which allowed the transformation of process-level re-quirements into the logical diagram. Due to size limitation for this paper and also to the diagram's complexity, we only present a subset in Fig. 3. This diagram represents the logical architecture of the process-level ISOFIN functionalities. The architecture is composed by the AEs that survived after the execution of step 2. The packaging executed in step 3 allows the identification of major processes. The associations iden-tified in step 4 are represented in the diagram by the connections between the AEs (for readability purposes, the "direct associations" were represented in dashed lines, and the "use case model associations" in straight lines).

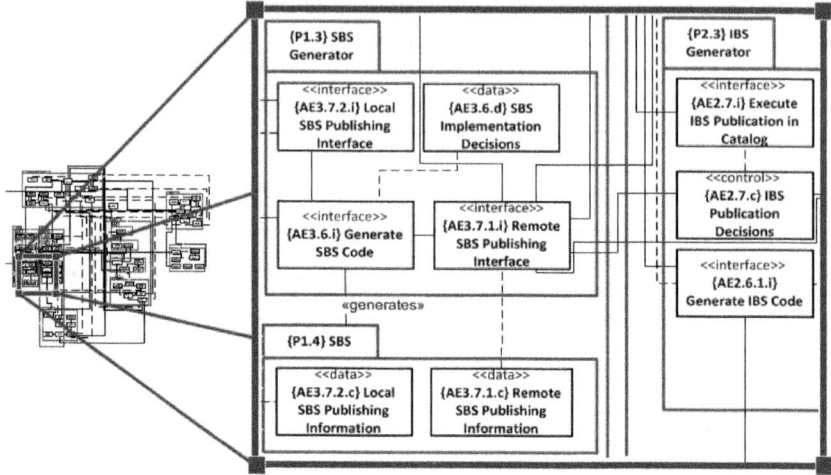

Fig. 3. Subset of the process-level logical architecture

As seen previously, the process-level architecture focuses on IBS and SBSs, acting as services in the cloud environment and allowing interoperability between the insurance domain business entities. In this context, there are two external business domain entities with access to the ISOFIN Platform: ISOFIN Customers and ISOFIN Suppliers. An ISOFIN Customer is an entity whose domain of interactions resides in the scope of consuming, for economic reasons, the functionalities exposed by IBSs. An ISOFIN Supplier is a company that interacts with the ISOFIN SaaS Platform by supplying the platform with functionalities (SBSs) that reside in their private clouds.

SBSs are made available in the ISOFIN Supplier private cloud by the use of generators ({AE3.6.i} Generate SBS Code) and are composed, in the public cloud where the ISOFIN SaaS Platform resides ({AE2.6.1.i} Generate IBS Code) to implement an IBS. Composition of basic SBSs into IBSs give origin to more powerful functionalities that are exposed by the platform.

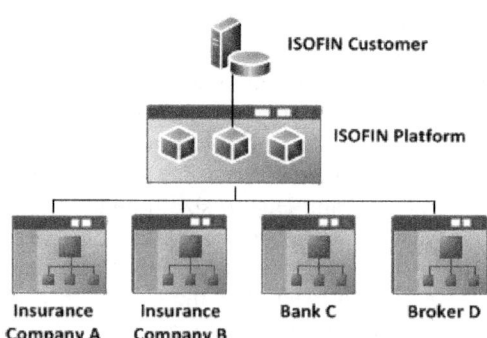

Fig. 4. Interoperability in ISOFIN

Due to the lack of consensus in the requirements elicitation in this "newfound" paradigm of IT solutions (Cloud Computing), our approach changed the traditional product-level perspective to the described process-level perspective. This new perspective allows the proper elicitation of requirements in Cloud Computing projects.

The ISOFIN project aims to deliver a set of functionalities that help forward interoperability in the Insurance application domain. The obtained process-level logical architecture is mainly devoted to be used by IT-professionals and not by business stakeholders. Based on the main constructors presented in the architecture (Fig. 3), Fig. 4 emerged with the aim to be presented to any technical role engaged in the ISOFIN project and be used to explain in a simple way that in the bottom layer there are SBSs that connect to IBSs in the ISOFIN Platform layer and that the later are connected to a ISOFIN Customer role.

5   Conclusion and Outlook

This paper presents the extensions to the traditional application of the 4SRS method, for creating context for requirements elicitation and later derivation of logical architectural diagrams from use cases in a process-level perspective. By using the proposed approach, we succeeded to define the requirements in such a way that they were understood by all the project stakeholders, uncovering more information: as an example, we started with 39 use cases and ended with 74 documented AEs (not counting associations). This means that we added more details to the problem description and that the information is understood by all involved. The process-level perspective allowed us to overcome difficulties when adopting a product-level perspective.

On the other hand, the manual execution of the method is prone to errors and very time consuming. Also, by adopting first the process-level perspective instead of the product-level perspective, time for delivering documentation to implementation teams increased. These are opportunities for improvement. We will address these drawbacks as future work. Additionally, we plan to study the required transformations to support the evolution of the process-level logical architecture into a product-level logical architecture that is needed to formally start the design phase of the cloud solution. We will also incorporate traceability features between process requirements, process-level logical architectures, product requirements and product-level logical architectures.

References

1. Davenport, T.H.: Process innovation: reengineering work through information technology. Harvard Business Press (1993)
2. Kruchten, P.: The 4+1 View Model of Architecture. IEEE Softw. 12, 42–50 (1995)
3. Machado, R.J., Fernandes, J.M., Monteiro, P., Rodrigues, H.: Transformation of UML Models for Service-Oriented Software Architectures. In: Proceedings of the 12th IEEE ECBS, pp. 173–182. IEEE Computer Society (2005)
4. Machado, R.J., Fernandes, J.M., Monteiro, P., Rodrigues, H.: Refinement of Software Architectures by Recursive Model Transformations. In: Münch, J., Vierimaa, M. (eds.) PROFES 2006. LNCS, vol. 4034, pp. 422–428. Springer, Heidelberg (2006)
5. National Institute of Standards and Technology, http://www.nist.gov/itl/cloud/upload/cloud-def-v15.pdf

6. Abran, A., Moore, J.W., Dupuis, R., Dupuis, R., Tripp, L.L.: In: Bourque, P., Dupuis, R., Abran, A., Moore, J.W. (eds.) Guide to the Software Engineering Body of Knowledge (SWEBOK). IEEE Press (2001, 2004)
7. Zowghi, D., Coulin, C.: Requirements elicitation: A survey of techniques, approaches, and tools. In: Engineering and Managing Software Requirements, pp. 19–46. Springer, Heidelberg (2005)
8. Cardoso, E.C.S., Almeida, J.P.A., Guizzardi, G.: Requirements engineering based on business process models: A case study. In: 13th Enterprise Distributed Object Computing Conference Workshops, EDOCW 2009, pp. 320–327 (2009)
9. Alter, S.: The work system method for understanding information systems and information systems research. Communications of the Association for Information Systems 9, 6 (2002)
10. Checkland, P.: Soft systems methodology: a thirty year retrospective. Systems Research 17, S11–S58 (2000)
11. Jacobson, I., Griss, M., Jonsson, P.: Software Reuse: Architecture, Process and Organization for Business Success. Addison Wesley Longman (1997)
12. Weiss, D.M., Lai, C.T.R.: Software Product-Line Engineering: A Family-Based Software Development Process. Addison-Wesley Professional (1999)
13. Kang, K.C., Kim, S., Lee, J., Kim, K., Shin, E., Huh, M.: FORM: A feature-oriented reuse method with domain-specific reference architectures. Annals of Sw Engineering (1998)
14. Bayer, J., Muthig, D., Göpfert, B.: The library system product line. A KobrA case study. Fraunhofer IESE (2001)
15. Matinlassi, M., Niemelä, E., Dobrica, L.: Quality-driven architecture design and quality analysis method. In: A Revolutionary Initiation Approach to a Product Line Architecture. VTT Tech, Research Centre of Finland (2002)
16. Castro, J., Kolp, M., Mylopoulos, J.: Towards requirements-driven information systems engineering: the Tropos project. Information Systems (2002)
17. Machado, R.J., Fernandes, J.: Heterogeneous Information Systems Integration: Organizations and Methodologies. In: Oivo, M., Komi-Sirviö, S. (eds.) PROFES 2002. LNCS, vol. 2559, pp. 629–643. Springer, Heidelberg (2002)
18. Hammer, M.: Beyond reengineering: How the process-centered organization is changing our work and our lives. Harper Paperbacks (1997)
19. Conradi, R., Jaccheri, M.L.: Process Modelling Languages. In: Derniame, J.-C., Kaba, B.A., Wastell, D. (eds.) Promoter-2 1998. LNCS, vol. 1500, pp. 27–52. Springer, Heidelberg (1999)
20. Azevedo, S., Machado, R.J., Muthig, D., Ribeiro, H.: Refinement of Software Product Line Architectures through Recursive Modeling Techniques. In: Meersman, R., Herrero, P., Dillon, T. (eds.) OTM 2009 Workshops. LNCS, vol. 5872, pp. 411–422. Springer, Heidelberg (2009)
21. Winter, R., Fischer, R.: Essential Layers, Artifacts, and Dependencies of Enterprise Architecture. In: 10th IEEE International Enterprise Distributed Object Computing Conference Workshops (EDOCW), p. 30 (2006)
22. Browning, T.R., Eppinger, S.D.: Modeling impacts of process architecture on cost and schedule risk in product development. IEEE Trans. on Eng. Management 49, 428–442 (2002)
23. Medvidovic, N., Taylor, R.N.: A classification and comparison framework for software architecture description languages. IEEE Trans. on Software Engineering 26, 70–93 (2000)
24. Kazman, R.: Tool support for architecture analysis and design. In: Sw Arch. Workshop (ISAW-2) and Intern. Workshop on Multiple Perspectives in Sw. Dev (Viewpoints 1996) on SIGSOFT 1996 Workshops, pp. 94–97. ACM, San Francisco (1996)
25. ISOFIN Research Project, http://isofincloud.i2s.pt

A Proposal for Simplified Model-Based Cost Estimation Models

Vieri del Bianco, Luigi Lavazza, and Sandro Morasca

Università degli Studi dell'Insubria
Dipartimento di Informatica e Comunicazione
Via Mazzini, 5 – 21100 Varese, Italy
{vieri.delbianco,luigi.lavazza,sandro.morasca}@uninsubria.it

Abstract. Most cost estimation models require a measure of the functional size of the application to be developed. To this end, FPA (Function Point Analysis) is one of the most used functional size measurement methods. FPA was originally proposed for traditional data processing systems, but it has been successfully adapted also to measure real-time and embedded systems. Since functional size measurement according to FPA can be quite expensive and time consuming, researchers have proposed "simplified" processes, which are expected to provide reasonably accurate measures, but require less effort and time. In this paper, we illustrate the application of these simplified techniques to UML models of software, via a precise mapping between UML elements and the so-called Basic Functional Components, upon which FPA measurement is based. As a result, it is possible to decrease the cost of modeling, and consequently the cost of measurement and estimation. The relatively low cost of the estimation models also allows developers to build different alternative models, to perform what-if analyses and choose the most economically sensible option.

Keywords: Functional Size Measurement, Function Point Analysis, Simplified functional size measurement, Model-based measurement, Measurement-oriented modeling.

1   Introduction

Cost estimation is one of the fundamental prerequisites for successful software development. Very important activities like feasibility analysis, pricing, and project planning depend on accurate and timely cost estimation.

Cost estimation techniques generally require a set of input data, the most important of which is the size of the software application to be developed [11][12].

Functional size measurement (FSM) is essential for cost estimation, since it measures requirements specifications, which are the only artifacts available when estimates are required. Older estimation methods were based on the expected size of the application to be developed expressed in Lines of Code (LOC) [11]. The problem with the size in LOC is that it can be measured only after the software has been developed,

O. Dieste, A. Jedlitschka, and N. Juristo (Eds.): PROFES 2012, LNCS 7343, pp. 59–73, 2012.

when there is no need for estimates. Also, estimating the size in LOC is not a good idea, since the size estimation error adds up to the inevitable effort estimation error. FSM solves these problems, as it applies to requirements specifications, which are available before the actual development starts.

To this end, Function Point Analysis (FPA) [3] was introduced to measure the size of data-processing systems, and thus estimate the development effort. FPA is today by far the most popular FSM method. Even though originally conceived for traditional data elaboration applications, it has been shown that FPA can be applied to real-time embedded software applications as well [1][2].

A first issue with FPA is that it can be subjective, hence it requires a precise representation of what needs to be measured, namely, a good representation of the software requirements, to lessen the measurement subjectivity. Though it has been proposed to base FPA measurement on UML models, it turned out that UML models not specifically conceived to support measurement may not provide the required information. A solution to this problem has been provided via measurement-oriented modeling [6]. Measurement consists in a quite deterministic counting of model elements. The subjectivity is thus moved from the measuring phase to the modeling phase. Modeling is generally done by people with a deep knowledge of the problem at hand, as opposed to traditional FPA, where measurement is performed by certified measurers that generally do not have good domain knowledge. This minimizes the possibility that requirements are omitted or not well represented. The cost of modeling can be very small if the organization that requires the measurement already uses UML for modeling requirements. If so, little effort is required for adapting existing models for measurement purposes.

Another problem with FPA is that the measurement of Function Points can be expensive and time consuming. To solve this problem, researchers have proposed "simplified" processes, which are expected to provide reasonably accurate measures, but require less effort and time. However, up to now, no guidelines have been provided for the application of such simplified measurement processes when requirements are described via UML models.

In this paper, we illustrate the application of these simplified techniques to UML models of software. This requires the establishment of a precise mapping between UML elements and the "Basic Functional Components" used to compute Function Points.

The presented approach combines the advantages of model-based measurement –in terms of little subjectivity of the measures– and of simplified measurement processes – in terms of shorter time and less effort required for measuring.

The paper is organized as follows. Section 2 briefly recalls the principles of FPA. Section 3 introduces measurement-oriented modeling and model-based measurement. Section 4 reports about the existing approaches to simplified FP measurement. Section 5 illustrates our proposals for basing simplified FP measurement processes on UML models. Section 6 accounts for related work. Section 7 draws some conclusions and outlines future work.

2   Function Point Analysis

Function Point Analysis was originally introduced by Albrecht [3] to measure the size of a data-processing system from the end-user's point of view, in order to estimate the development effort. FPA is maintained by the International Function Point User Group (IFPUG), which also publishes the official counting manual [4] and certifies counters. FPA is now an ISO standard [5]. Function Points aim at quantifying the 'amount of functionality' released to the user by taking into account the data that the application has to use in order to provide the required functions, and the transactions (i.e., operations that involve data crossing the boundaries of the application) through which the functionality is delivered to the user. Both data and transactions are considered only in that they are relevant to the user. Accordingly, FPs are counted on the basis of the specifications of the user requirements.

The core of the counting procedure consists in identifying and weighting data function types and transactional function types.

Data functions represent data that are relevant to the user and are required to perform some function. Data functions are classified into internal logical files (ILF), and external interface files (EIF). An ILF is a user identifiable group of logically related information maintained within the boundary of the application. The primary intent of an ILF is to hold data that are maintained by the application being counted and that are relevant with respect to the addressed problem. An EIF is similar to an ILF, but is maintained within the boundary of another application, i.e., it is outside the application being measured.

Transactional functions represent operations that are relevant to the user and cause input and/or output data to cross the boundary of the application. Transactional functions represent elementary processes. An elementary process is the smallest unit of activity that is meaningful to the user(s). The elementary process must be self-contained and leave the application being counted in a consistent state. An elementary process is counted only if it is different from the others.

Transaction functions are classified into external inputs (EI), external outputs (EO), external inquiries (EQ). An EI is an elementary process whose primary intent of is to maintain an ILF. EOs and EQs are elementary processes whose primary intent is to present information to a user. EOs perform relevant elaboration, while EQs simply retrieves data from ILFs or EIFs.

Every function (either data or transaction) contributes a number of FPs that depends on its "complexity".

The complexity of ILFs and EIFs is evaluated on the base of Data Element Types (DETs) and Record Element Types (RETs). A DET is a unique, non-repeated field recognized by the user. A RET is a subgroup of the information units contained in a file.

For transactions, the complexity is based on the number of DETs and File Type Referenced (FTRs). An FTR can be an ILF referenced or maintained by the transaction or an EIF read by the transaction. The DETs considered are those that cross the application boundary when the transaction is performed.

The weighting of function types on the basis of their complexity is done according to tables (not reported here). Finally, the FP number is obtained by summing the weighted function types, according to Table 1. For instance, the size of a system featuring 2 low complexity ILF, a high complexity EIF, 3 low complexity EI and a medium complexity EO is 2×7+1×10+3×3+1×5=38 FP.

Table 1. Function type weight according to complexity

Function type	Low	Medium	High
EI	3	4	6
EO	4	5	7
EQ	3	4	6
ILF	7	10	15
EIF	5	7	10

3   Measurement-Oriented Modeling

When measuring an artifact like software, which is complex, subject to many variability factors, and immaterial, a good idea is to start by building a model of the software to be measured. This practice is quite easy to adopt today, since many organizations routinely build software models as a part of their development process.

However, model-based measurement works well only if the given models incorporate all the required information at the proper detail level. To meet this requirement, measurement-oriented modeling has been proposed [6]. The idea is that, to build models that effectively support FPA, a set of modeling guidelines have to be followed, which take into account the relationships of UML elements with FPA concepts.

Moreover, basing the counting practices on a well defined model provides the necessary conditions to define precise and consistent rules, which are expected to make FP counting easier and affected by smaller variability.

The main points of measurement-oriented modeling and model-based measurement are reported below.

The technique described in [6] requires the analysis of a small number of UML diagrams:

— Use case diagrams (see Fig. 1) are used to: list the elementary processes as use cases; identify the boundary of the application precisely; identify the external elements with which the application interacts. Use case diagrams are not strictly necessary, as component diagrams provide the same type of information. However, they are generally useful to document the responsibilities of the system to be measured in a simple manner, before proceeding with building more detailed diagrams.
— Component diagrams (see Fig. 2) are used to classify external elements as <<LogicData>> (thus, EIFs) or as <<I/O>> elements that interact with the system. Logic data maintained within the boundary of the application (thus, ILFs) are also

identified. The internals of each <<LogicData>> component are specified in terms of classes (which represent the RET of the LogicData) and their attributes (the DET of the LogicData) as shown in Fig. 3.

— Finally, a sequence diagram (see Fig. 4) is built for each elementary process, to indicate: how it can be classified (EI, EO, or EQ); which DETs are exchanged through the boundary (they are the parameters of the messages that cross the boundary); which FTRs are involved (these are the internal component instances that appear in the diagram).

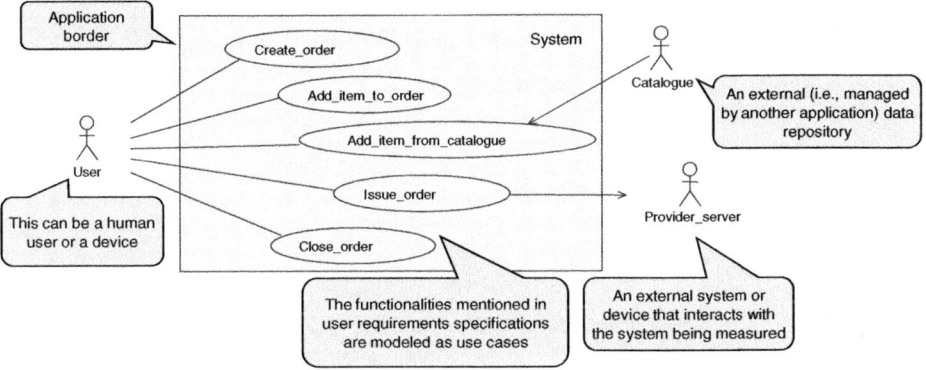

Fig. 1. Use case model of elementary processes

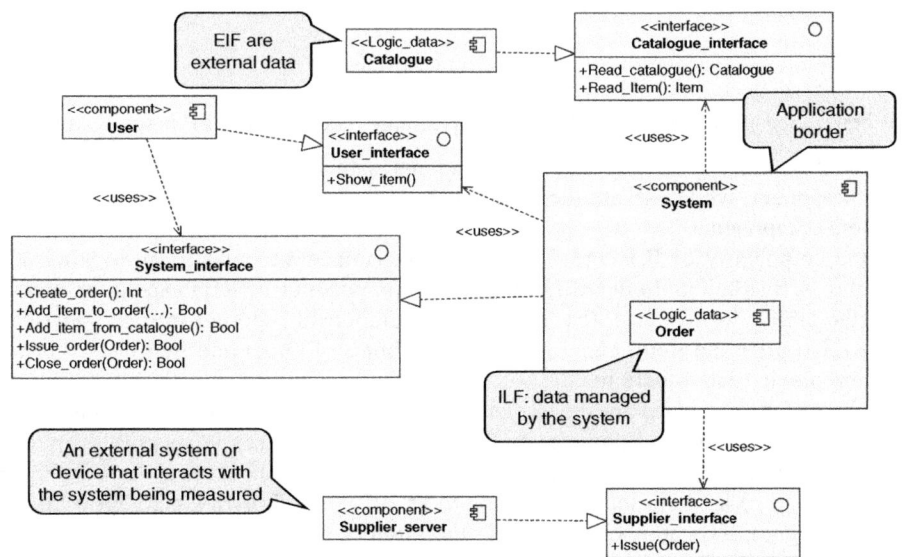

Fig. 2. Component diagram

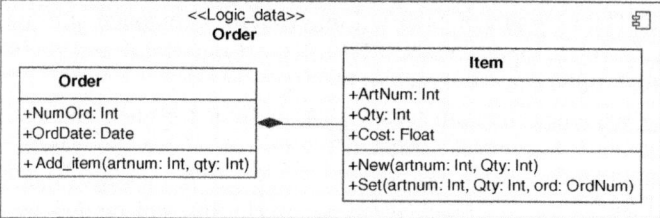

Fig. 3. Internals of a <<logic data>> component

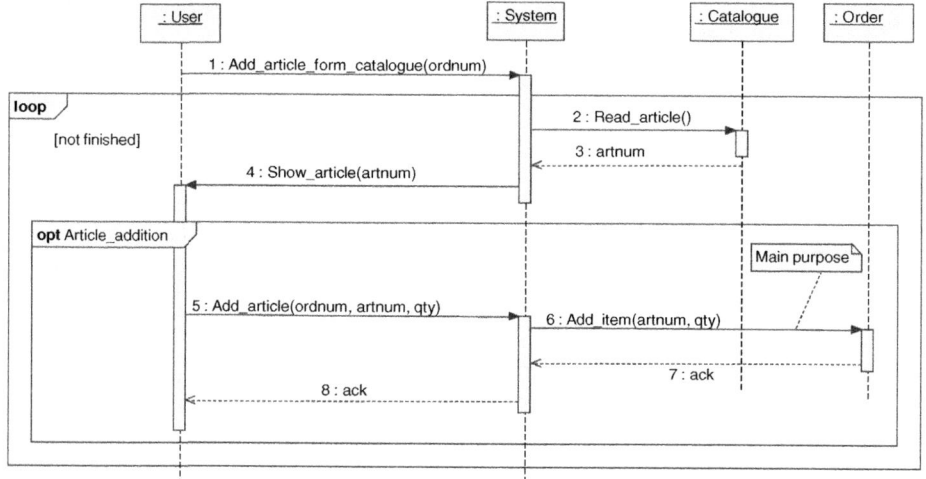

Fig. 4. Sequence diagram

When a measurement-oriented model is available, counting the FP is quite simple:

— the ILF are the <<LogicData>> components that are located within the system component, while EIF are the <<LogicData>> components located outside the system component;

— the complexity of ILF and EIF can be determined very easily by looking at the classes that belong to the <<LogicData>> component (the RET) and their attributes (the DET); for instance, the System data component reported in Fig. 3 involves 2 RET (Order and Item) and 5 DET (the attributes of Order and Item), so, it is a low complexity data function;

— elementary processes are the use cases that appear in the use case diagram;

— the classification and complexity of elementary processes is supported by the information provided in each sequence diagram. For instance, the process in Fig. 4 is an EI (since its main intent is writing to an ILF), and it involves 2 FTR (Order and Catalogue). The number of DET is the number of the elementary data types exchanged with the outside of the system (i.e., in Fig. 4 it is the number of parameter unique types carried by messages 1, 2, 3, 4, 5 and 8).

The principles of measurement-oriented modeling can also be applied to other Functional Size Measurement methods, like the COSMIC method [9], as described in [10].

4   Simplified FP Measurement Techniques

The most well-known approach for simplifying the process of FP counting is the Early & Quick Function Points (EQFP) method [7]. EQFP descends from the consideration that estimates are sometimes needed before the analysis of requirements is completed, when the information on the software to be measured is incomplete or not sufficiently detailed.

Since several details for performing a correct measurement following the rules of the FP manual [4] are not considered in EQFP, the result is a less precise measure. The trade-off between reduced measurement time and costs is also a reason for adopting the EQFP method even when full specifications are available, but there is the need for completing the measurement in a short time, or at a lower cost. An advantage of the method is that different parts of the system can be measured at different detail levels: for instance, a part of the system can be measured following the IFPUG manual rules, while other parts can be measured on the basis of coarser-grained information. In fact, the EQFP method is based on the classification of the processes and data of an application according to a hierarchy (see Fig. 5).

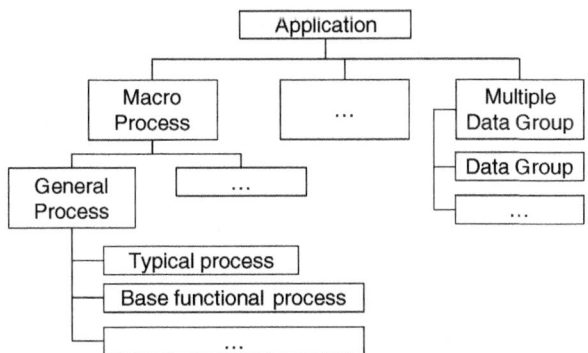

Fig. 5. Functional hierarchy in the Early & Quick FP technique

Base Functional Processes and Data Groups correspond to IFPUG's elementary processes and LogicData and the other elements are aggregations of processes or data groups. The idea is that if you have enough information at the most detailed level you count FP according to IFPUG rules; otherwise, you can estimate the size of larger elements (e.g., General or Macro processes) either on the basis of analogy (e.g., a given General process is "similar" to a known one) or according to the structured aggregation (e.g., a General process is composed of 3 Base Functional Processes and 2 Typical Processes). Therefore, by considering elements that are coarser-grained than the FPA BFC, the EQFP measurement process leads to an approximate measure of size in IFPUG FP.

Tables taking into account the previous experiences with the usage of EQFP are provided to facilitate the task of assigning a (minimum, maximum and most likely) quantitative size to each component. For instance, Table 2 provides minimum, maximum and most likely values for transaction functions.

Table 2. EQFP: function type weight according to complexity

Function type	Low	Likely	High
EI	3	4.3	6
EO	4	5.4	7
EQ	3	3.8	6

Methods for simplifying the counting of FP have also been proposed by NESMA [8]. The Indicative NESMA method simplifies the process by only requiring the identification of LogicData, from a data model. The Function Point size is then computed by applying predefined weights, whose value depends on whether the data model is normalized in 3rd normal form:

— Non normalized model: Function Points = Number of ILF × 35 + Number of EIF × 15
— Normalized model: Function Points = Number of ILF × 25 + Number of EIF × 10

It is quite clear that the Indicative NESMA method is quite rough in its computation. The official NESMA counting manual specifies that errors in functional size with this approach can be up to 50%.

The Estimated NESMA method requires the identification of each BFC, but does not require the assessment of the complexity of each component: Data Functions (ILF and EIF) are assumed to be of low complexity, while Transactions Functions (EI, EQ and EO) are assumed to be of average complexity. Accordingly, the Estimated NESMA method is more approximated than the EQFP method, which –as shown in Table 2– provides likely values for transactions of unknown complexity, derived from statistics.

5   UML-Based Simplified FP Measurement

This section shows that the simplified FPA techniques briefly presented in Section 4 can be easily applied on the basis of measurement-oriented UML-based modeling for simplified FPA techniques. Note that we do not change the simplified FPA techniques: we just use ad-hoc UML models to identify the elements upon which the simplified FP counting is performed.

The Indicative NESMA method just requires ILF and EIF to be identified, and the normalization level of the data model to be known.

The former requirement is satisfied by our method by the system-level component diagram (see Fig. 2): ILF are <<logic data>> in the system, while EIF are <<logic data>> located outside the system. Therefore, in our example we have one ILF (the Order) and one EIF (the Catalogue).

As for the evaluation of the normalization of the data model, it is clear that NESMA assumes that the data model is given by Entity/Relationship diagrams or as a set of relational tables and relationships. As a matter of fact, this is clearly not our case. However, we consider that the characteristics of a reasonably well written object-oriented model are close enough to those of a 3rd normal form E/R diagram. Accordingly, we may say that our UML-based modeling supports the Indicative NESMA method in the "normalized model" case. We can thus proceed to compute the size in FP according to the indicative NESMA method:

$$\text{Size} = \text{Number of ILF} \times 25 + \text{Number of EIF} \times 10 = 1 \times 25 + 1 \times 10 = 35 \text{ FP}$$

The estimated NESMA method requires the identification of each BFC, but does not require the assessment of the complexity of each component. Therefore, the system-level component diagram alone is sufficient, as it allows the measurer to identify processes from the operations contained in the interfaces and the ILF and EIF from <<LogicData>> components. In our example, the component diagram illustrated in Fig. 2 lets the measures identify Catalogue as an EIF; Order as an ILF; Create_order, Add_item, Add_item_from_catalogue, Issue_order, and Close_order as transactions.

To apply estimated NESMA method, transactions have to be classified into EI, EO and EQ. This operation is not directly supported by the component diagram (as it is delegated to sequence diagrams in our method). However, it is quite clear that in general, building sequence diagrams is excessively time and effort consuming for a simplified measurement method. There are a few possible ways to solve this issue:

- Annotating the component diagram with comments that make explicit the main purpose of each operation;
- Relying on the judgment of the modeler. This is somewhat not coherent with the goal of decreasing the subjectivity of FP counting, but may very well work in simple cases. For instance, in the example shown in most measurers would immediately conclude that Create_order, Add_item, Add_item_from_catalogue and Close_order are EI, while Issue_order is an EQ.
- Formalize the nature of operations by means of stereotypes which specify the nature of the operation and help the measurer classifying transactions correctly. For instance, stereotyping Add_article as <<update>> would leave little doubt about the transaction being an EI.

Therefore, the size of our example computed with the estimated NESMA method is 27 FP, as illustrated in Table 3.

Table 3. Computation of the example size using the estimated NESMA method

Function type	Number of functions in the model	Weight	Total
ILF	1	7	7
EIF	1	5	5
EI	4	3	12
EO	0	4	0
EQ	1	3	3
Total			**27**

To apply our model-based technique to EQFP, we need to represent the process and data composition hierarchies illustrated in Fig. 5. The example given in Section 4 is too simple to support EQFP, therefore here we propose an extended version of the example, to illustrate EQFP based measurement of the extensions.

Representing data composition hierarchies is not a problem: multiple data groups can be represented as components including <<Logic data>> components. For instance, Fig. 6 represents a "multiple data group" including three logical data groups, correspond exactly to IFPUG data functions. For clarity, multiple data groups are stereotyped as <<MultipleData>>.

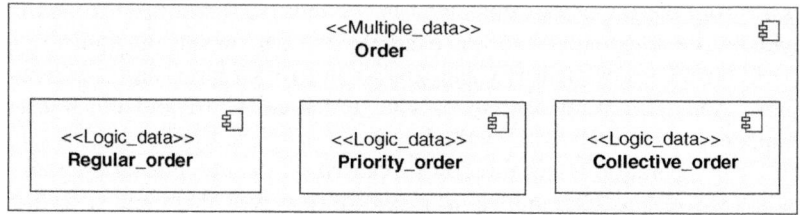

Fig. 6. Use case diagram representing Early & Quick data

The data structure illustrated in Fig. 6 suggests that following possibilities:

— We can estimate the size of the <<MultipleData>> component on the base of analogy, e.g., looking for previously measured data that contained similar data.
— We can measure precisely the size of Regular_order, Priority_order and Collective_order and then compute the size of <<MultipleData>> component as the sum of these. The sizes of Regular_order, Priority_order and Collective_order can be either properly measured or they can be estimated using analogy or any other method.

For instance, a possibility for the measurer is to consider that <<Multiple_data>> Order is composed of three ILF, whose complexity the measurer is not going to explore (either because details are not available, or because there is no time to do it). According to the EQFP indications, the three ILF are considered "generic", and their "most likely" complexity weight is 7.7. In conclusion, the size of <<Multiple_data>> Order is assumed to be $3 \times 7.7 = 23.1$ FP.

As to processes, we use the <<include>> relation among use cases in order to represent their composition. For clarity, we introduce stereotypes of the use cases, thus allowing the modeler to specify whether a given process is a <<MacroProcess>>, a <<GeneralProcess>>, or a <<TypicalProcess>>.

Fig. 7 illustrates the use case diagram of a software system at an early stage of requirements analysis, when it has not yet been understood in detail what processes are involved in Manage_order, but it has been discovered that Add_item_to_order and Add_item_from_catalogue belong to Add_item.

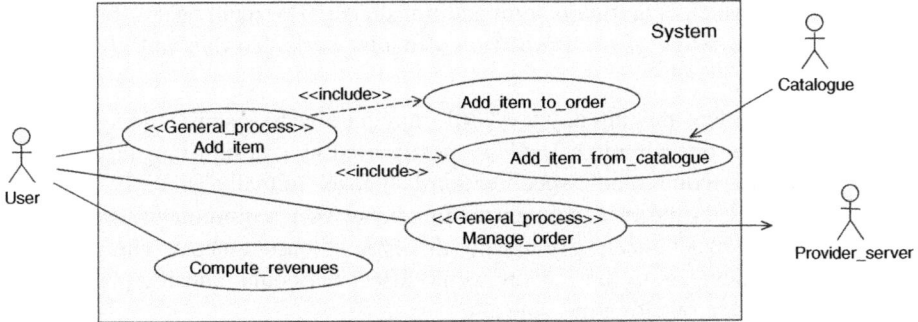

Fig. 7. Use case diagram representing Early & Quick processes

Some of the use cases appearing in Fig. 7 will be described by means of a sequence diagrams and sized as described in Section 3, while others will be evaluated according to the considerations advocated by the EQFP technique (analogy, structure, etc.). For instance, a possible scenario is:

- Add_item_from_catalog is measured on the basis of its sequence diagram (Fig. 4). Its size is that of an EI having 2 FTR and 4 DET, i.e., 3 FP.
- Compute_revenues is an EO. Its sequence diagram is not available, thus the measurer decides to base the sizing on the "most likely" complexity (as given in Table 2). Accordingly, the size of Compute_revenues is assumed to be 5.4 FP.
- Manage_order is assumed to be a large typical process (i.e., a collection of transactions), whose size is thus 26,3 FP, according to [24].

6   Applicability of the Proposed Approach: A Discussion

The adoption of the proposed approach has pros and cons. Among the pros are:

- measurement is based on explicit models that are easy to validate, therefore the result is more reliable;
- measures are better documented, as they are expressed with reference to models;
- the counting process is less subjective, as model construction by experienced analysts is inherently less subjective than the interpretation of informal documents by a measurer;
- the models used for counting can be used as a starting point for design;
- if software requirement specifications are described using UML, the models required for counting can be derived from specifications models.

The cons are essentially connected with the cost of the approach. One may also observe that poor knowledge of UML could also lead to wrong measures and consequently to huge costs (e.g., if effort estimation is based on size measures that on their turn are based on inaccurate UML models). However, this issue can be solved via

UML training which is an una-tantum additional cost. The main cost to be accounted for concerns the usage of the method on a regular basis. To this end, there are two cases to be considered:

a) Organizations that already use UML in requirements specification. We have to remember that although UML is mostly used as a design language, it can be used as a requirements specification language. Actually, since FSM methods are based on the measurement of functional user requirements, we need that UML models concern exclusively this type of requirements. The presence of design elements in the models would affect the count, causing possibly large errors in the resulting measures.

b) Organizations that do not use UML for requirements specification.

In case a), the cost of applying the proposed approach is little, since the information needed to apply the simplified FSM is a subset of the information already present in typical UML models. So, these organizations just need to extract the required information from the available models. This is expected to be a quite straightforward operation. However, it is possible that an organization uses a subset of the UML diagrams that is different from the one required by our method: for instance, an organization could use state diagrams instead of sequence diagrams. In such cases, the writing of the missing diagrams has to be considered. We should also consider that different simplified methods require different models or –more precisely– models having a different degree of detail and number of diagrams. So, an organization that does not use sequence diagrams would not need to write them anyway, if the estimated NESMA method is used.

Organizations that do not use UML on a regular basis would have to build models specifically for measurement.

Previous experiments with full-fledged measurement-oriented modeling performed by undergraduate students (e.g., the one reported in [ease 2008]) showed that the productivity of measurement ranged in the 35-120 FP/PersonDay. It is reasonable to expect that much higher productivity can be achieved by people that are more experienced with UML modeling than the students involved in the experiment, also considering that simplified measurement may require writing less diagrams per FP.

Further experimentation is needed to get accurate measurement productivity values. Once these values are known, each organization will be able to evaluate the convenience of the approach.

With respect to the accuracy level that can be achieved with the proposed approach, we have to consider that an accurate measure relies on two fact:

a)   We measure the right elements of the system;
b)   We measure the elements of the system right.

Our approach helps with point a), since the models make explicit and evident what are the elements of the system and what is their nature and role. Hence, it is less likely that some elements are missed, or that spurious elements are included in the model, or that elements are misinterpreted. On the contrary, the responsibility for point b) rests entirely on the simplified FSM technique used.

7   Related Work

Proposals for basing FSM on object-oriented models date back to the end of the 90's [18][19].

Fetcke [19] proposed rules and mapping steps to conform FPA to Object Oriented Software Engineering.

The demands that FSM methods (including FPA) pose to user requirements expressed in UML are studied by van den Berg et al. [16][17].

None of the mentioned approaches addresses the issue of defining guidelines for building UML models that convey the information required by the adopted FSM method, and that make it straightforward to identify and count BFC in the measurement phase.

Zivkovic et al. proposed a formal mapping of UML models into Function Points [22]. It was found that accuracy increases with the abstraction level of the description [23].

Concerning the simplification of the FP measurement process, other proposals have been made, in addition to those mentioned above. Forselius proposed a "Quick level" of the Kiss method [20] that requires the measurement of only a small subset of the functional components required by the FiSMA method (FiSMA is another FSM method [21]).

8   Conclusions

Function Point Analysis is by far the most used technique for functional size measurement. Nevertheless, it suffers from different problems: measures are to some extent subjective, while the measurement process can be lengthy and expensive.

In this paper we propose a manner to solve these problems by integrating two previously proposed techniques: model-based measurement and simplified FP measurement processes. Our proposal involves two phases. The first one involves modeling the software to be measured using UML and according to well defined guidelines that help the modeler including all the types of information that are required for FPA. In the second phase, thanks to a mapping between UML elements and the concepts of some well known simplified measurement techniques (namely those proposed by NESMA and the Early&Quick Function Points) a quick measurement can be obtained from UML models.

The proposed technique has the potential to provide reasonably approximated FP measures in very short time and at very little cost, especially if the measuring organization is already using UML for modeling, so that the measurement-oriented models do not need to be built from scratch, but can be derived from development oriented models.

The relatively low cost of the required models also allows developers to build different alternative models to perform what-if analysis and choose the most convenient option. Take for instance the estimated NESMA method: a manager could evaluate what set of use cases (i.e., functionalities) can be developed at a given maximum cost, or what is the best trade-off between produced value and development cost.

Future work involves the practical experimentation of the proposed technique on a set of real-life projects. Since cost estimation is more precise when complexity measures are used in conjunction with size measures [13][15], another interesting development is the exploration of applying complexity measures to UML models [14] in the context of simplified measurement processes. Finally, it will be possible to explore the application of model-based measurement to other FSM methods, like COSMIC.

Acknowledgments. The work reported here has been partially supported by project "Metodi e tecniche per l'analisi, l'implementazione e la valutazione di sistemi software" funded by Università degli Studi dell'Insubria.

References

[1] Lavazza, L., Garavaglia, C.: Using Function Points to Measure and Estimate Real-Time and Embedded Software: Experiences and Guidelines. In: ESEM 2009, 3rd Int. Symp. on Empirical SW Engineering and Measurement, Lake Buena Vista, Florida, October 15-16 (2009)

[2] Lavazza, L., Garavaglia, C.: Using Function Point in the Estimation of Real-Time Software: an Experience. In: Software Measurement European Forum – SMEF 2008, Milano, May 28-30 (2008)

[3] Albrecht, A.J.: Measuring Application Development Productivity. In: Joint SHARE/GUIDE/IBM Application Development Symposium (1979)

[4] International Function Point Users Group. Function Point Counting Practices Manual - Release 4.3.1 (2010)

[5] ISO/IEC 20926: 2003, Software engineering – IFPUG 4.1 Unadjusted functional size measurement method – Counting Practices Manual, ISO, Geneva (2003)

[6] Lavazza, L., del Bianco, V., Garavaglia, C.: Model-based Functional Size Measurement. In: ESEM 2008, 2nd International Symposium on Empirical Software Engineering and Measurement, Kaiserslautern, October 9-10 (2008)

[7] Santillo, L., Conte, M., Meli, R.: Early & Quick function point: sizing more with less. In: 11th IEEE International Symposium on Software Metrics, Como, September 19-22 (2005)

[8] ISO, Iec 24570: 2004, Software Engineering-NESMA Functional Size Measurement Method version 2.1 - Definitions and Counting Guidelines for the Application of Function Point Analysis. International Organization for Standardization, Geneva (2004)

[9] COSMIC – Common Software Measurement International Consortium. The COSMIC Functional Size Measurement Method - version 3.0.1 Measurement Manual (The COSMIC Implementation Guide for ISO/IEC 19761: 2003) (May 2009)

[10] Lavazza, L., del Bianco, V.: A Case Study in COSMIC Functional Size Measurement: the Rice Cooker Revisited. In: IWSM/Mensura 2009, Amsterdam, November 4-6 (2009)

[11] Boehm, B.W.: Software Engineering Economics. Prentice-Hall (1981)

[12] Boehm, B.W., Abts, C., Brown, A.W., Chulani, S., Clark, B.K., Horowitz, E., Madachy, R., Reifer, D.J., Steece, B.: Software Cost Estimation with COCOMO II. Prentice Hall Press (2009)

[13] Lavazza, L., Robiolo, G.: The Role of the Measure of Functional Complexity in Effort Estimation. In: PROMISE 2010, the 6th International Conference on Predictive Models in Software Engineering, Timisoara, Romania, September 12-13 (2010)

[14] Lavazza, L., Robiolo, G.: Introducing the Evaluation of Complexity in Functional Size Measurement: a UML-based Approach. In: 4th International Symposium on Empirical Software Engineering and Measurement – ESEM 2010, Bolzano, September 16-17 (2010)

[15] Lavazza, L., Robiolo, G.: Functional Complexity Measurement: Proposals and Evaluations. In: ICSEA 2011 – the 6th Int. Conf. on Software Engineering Advances, Barcelona, October 23-29 (2011)

[16] Oudshoorn, R.: Application of Functional Size Measurement on Requirements in UML, Ir.-degree Thesis, University of Twente (June 2005) (partly in Dutch)

[17] van den Berg, K., Dekkers, T., Oudshoorn, R.: Functional size measurement applied to UML-based user requirements. In: Software Measurement European Forum - SMEF 2005, Rome, March 16-18 (2005)

[18] Bévo, V., Lévesque, G., Abran, A.: Application de la méthode FFP à partir d'une spécification selon la notation UML: compte rendu des premiers essais d'application et questions. In: 9th Int. Workshop Software Measurement, Lac Supérieur, Canada (1999)

[19] Fetcke, T., Abran, A., Nguyen, T.: Mapping the OO-Jacobsen Approach into Function Points. In: TOOLS 23 – Technology of Object Oriented Languages and Systems, Santa Barbara, July 28-August 1 (1997)

[20] Forselius, L.: Faster and more accurate functional size measurement by KISS – keeping it simple. In: IFPUG FSS, Cambridge, MA, USA, March 28-29 (2006)

[21] FISMA (Finnish Software Measurement Association). FiSMA FSM Method 1.1 (2004)

[22] Zivkovic, A., Rozman, I., Hericko, M.: Automated software size estimation based on function points using UML models. Information and Software Technology 47(13) (2005)

[23] Zivkovic, A., Hericko, M., Brumen, B., Beloglavec, S., Rozman, I.: The impact of details in the class diagram on software size estimation. Informatica 16(2) (2005)

[24] Early & Quick Function Points for IFPUG method Release 3.0 Reference Manual 1.2, DPO (September 2009)

[25] del Bianco, V., Gentile, C., Lavazza, L.: An Evaluation of Function Point Counting Based on Measurement-Oriented Models. In: Evaluation and Assessment in Software Engineering – EASE 2008, Bari, June 26-27 (2008)

Estimating the Software Product Value during the Development Process

Oscar Castro[1], Angelina Espinoza[2], and Alfonso Martínez-Martínez[1]

[1] Universidad Autónoma Metropolitana, Electrical Engineering Department
Mexico City, 09340, México
{cloj,almm}@xanum.uam.mx
[2] Technical University of Madrid, E.U. Informática
Madrid, E-28051, España
a.espinoza@upm.es

Abstract. Nowadays software companies are facing a fierce competition to deliver better products but offering a higher value to the customer. In this context, software product value has becoming a major concern in software industry, leading for improving the knowledge and better understanding about how to estimate the software value in early development phases. Other way, software companies encounter problems such as releasing products that were developed with high expectations, but they gradually fall into the category of a mediocre product when they are released to the market. These high expectations are tightly related to the expected and offered software value to the customer. This paper presents an approach for estimating the software product value, focusing on the development phases. We propose a value indicators approach to quantify the real value of the development products. The aim is early identifying potential deviations in the real software value, by comparing the estimated versus the expected. We present an internal validation to show the feasibility of this approach to produce benefits in industry projects.

Keywords: Software Product Value, Software Value Estimation Method, Software Value Indicators, Software and Quality Metrics.

1 Introduction

For software products, as with every product, value is of great importance for development companies, as they invest large amounts of money in creating their products and positioning them in the market. Customers will always make a trade-off when buying a product, and they will prefer the one that meets all their requirements while offering a high value for their money. However, a main problem with the released software products is that companies do not have a solid understanding of their products value situation, at the end these products do not fulfill the company economical expectations. The problem is that these products are disproportionately expensive compared to the business level value that they produce. Even worse, companies draw funds and resources away from

O. Dieste, A. Jedlitschka, and N. Juristo (Eds.): PROFES 2012, LNCS 7343, pp. 74–88, 2012.

other higher value-producing opportunities [12], mainly because a deficient or lack of the product value estimation. Thus, the software companies that provide products to satisfy the customer needs, while offering a high value are more competitive in a value-consideration market as nowadays occurs. For reaching these goals, it is important that companies have the methods and knowledge to estimate and validate the software product value. To recollect and analyze quantifiable data, and to identify the factors that affect the software product value will allow managing it to meet the business goals. Thus, value must be taken in consideration when using software engineering techniques to develop software products, as cost, schedule, and other important aspects are often considered for development [3]. It is precisely in the software development tasks where technical issues are affecting the released products' value. Thus, companies need methods for estimating the software value during the development process, for getting a quantitative and real visibility about the product value that is going to be released to the market. However, value estimation is not an easy issue. It is easier to manage the development process of a new product with activity, effort or productivity metrics than product value metrics. There are some efforts for value estimation in Software Engineering, but they are mainly focused in the requirements phase such as Barney et al. who in [2] address a value-based approach in Requirements Engineering, which focuses on a process for creating product value through requirements selection for a software release. Ojala addresses in [15] an approach for product value assessment mainly through requirements prioritization and quality attributes, assigning percentages according to stakeholders' opinion. The main found limitation of these approaches is that they are not specifically focused on software product value estimation. They do not offer visibility in the value management, nor quantitative figures about the value estimation during the software development process. The Value-Based Software Engineering [3] is a promising approach but it is more process than product value focused. Thus, there are important gaps in value estimation for software products especially during the whole development life cycle. This is the focus of our approach; we address the software product value estimation focusing on the development process. We provide a method to quantitatively obtain a value estimation of the development work products, which directly affect the final product value. The main benefit pursued with our approach is to provide the involved stakeholder in the value management, with a tool to estimate the real value of such final product before is released to the market. The aim is to provide a deep insight into value figures, to be used for identifying deviations and correct decisions which affect the expected final product value. Our method is based on the value-indicators approach, and we use international standards for establishing an agreed development processes and their generated development work products. Similarly, the value indicators are determined according to international standards in quality for software products. The process model to determine the value estimation is also provided. An internal validation is included to show the feasibility and usage of our approach for producing benefits in industry projects. This paper is composed as follows: Section 2 covers the background; Section 3 introduces related literature on Software Value Estimation. Section 4 describes our approach for software product value estimation. Section 5 presents the internal validation case, and Section 6 the conclusion and future work.

2 Background

2.1 Value Definition in Software Engineering

Ojala defines value in [15] as: *"Value is a measure - usually in currency, effort or exchange or on a comparative scale - which reflects the desire to obtain or retain an item, service or ideal"*. Barney et al in [2] includes the value concept for software products, and this is as follows: *"Value constructions in economic theory are based on customer satisfaction, loyalty and re-purchasing behavior. By borrowing the economic theory, three aspects of value are addressed, namely product value, a customer's perceived value and relationship value. Product value is related to the product price and influenced by the quality attributes of the software product"*.

Finally, we propose our own software product value definition, which is based on [15] and [2]. The objective is to provide a complete definition according to our research goals, as follows: *"Value is a measure - usually in currency, effort or exchange, or on a comparative scale - of software (set of programs, procedures, algorithms and its documentation) goods or services that will meet the user's needs, desires, and expectations. All goods or services are being influenced by the quality attributes of the software product."*

3 Related Literature on Product Value Estimation

Even authors offer different approaches to estimate value, as it is shown in Table 1, they are using similar concepts. For instance, the quality factor has a strong relationship with value, as it is stated by Barney et al. in [2], and in the Ojala's formula in Table 1. One influential approach on value is provided in the *Value Standard of SAVE International* in [17]. This standard proposes a *value methodology*, which is applied to every kind of products, not only for software. The *value methodology* proposed by SAVE, is a systematic process that follows the *Job Plan*, consisting of the following phases [17]: 1) Information, 2) Function Analysis, 3) Creative, 4) Evaluation, 5) Development and 6) Presentation. The Evaluation Phase is particularly interesting to our research, since this phase is concerned on the value estimation for the products generated in the development process, and not only for final products. Specifically, the SAVE standard explains that through the Evaluation phase the value improvement is managed while delivering the projects function(s) and considering performance requirements and resource limits. Although the standard describes what must be done in the Evaluation phase, there is no a specific method to estimate the value neither how to next improve such value.

Table 1. Different approaches of value

Value Estimation	Description	Ref.
$\dfrac{Function}{Resources}$	Function: Is measured by the performance requirements of the customer. Resources: They are measured in materials, labor, price, time, etc. required to accomplish that function	[17]
$Bo - Re$	Bo: Benefits obtained. Re: Resources expended.	[5]
$\dfrac{Worth}{Cost}$	Worth: The least cost to perform the required function (product, service or process), or the cost of the least cost functional equivalent. If possible can also be the worth in money, what customer sees in a product, service or process. Cost: The life cycle cost of the object, product, service or process (price paid or to be paid).	[15]
$\dfrac{Function + Quality}{Cost}$	Function: The specific work that a design/item (product, service or process) must perform. Quality: The owner's or user's needs, desires, and expectations. Cost: The life cycle cost of the product, service or process.	[15]
$\dfrac{Benefits}{Price}$	Benefits: Total benefits derived from the product. Price: The amount a customer is willing to pay.	[2]

The Ojala's approach in [15] implements the SAVE International standard [17] in the Software Engineering field for software products assessment. Ojala in [14] also implements the Evaluation phase, giving the guidelines about how to perform a value assessment study on software products, as follows: 1) To discuss the criteria for the evaluation of improvement ideas, and the criteria on quality attributes, 2) to give a relative percentage (maximum 100%) for the criterion importance to the project, 3) to calculate averages for all the criteria (e.g. system stability 25%, safety 20% or ease of use 20%), 4) to give points to each improvement proposal on a scale of 1-6 (6 the better, 1 the worst). The points allocated are multiplied by the calculated weighting percentages. The Ojala's product value assessment has a good representation of business point of view and it offers worth and cost for components and requirements. However, those figures are mainly based on votes by stakeholders, and rely on the involved stakeholders' perception, and finally they do not offer a more direct evaluation of development products to estimate the value. Cerdegren et al in [4] propose a method called *Products in Development (PiD)* for integrating the perceived customer value as a performance measure during the new products development. The aim is to evaluate the value creation during the new product development. The main limitation according to our goals is that the PiD is strongly focused on estimating the value when requirements change and over those requirements. This is contrary to our goals about obtaining quantitative data on the software products value, but for the complete development process. Similarly, Barney et al [2] proposes a method mainly focused and based on requirements selection through a series of activities involving stakeholders and workshops to prioritize and validate requirements. Barney et al approach is not aligned with our main goal, as they focus on what they value based requirements selection; this approach does not estimate software product value during the development process.

4 Estimating the Software Product Value: An Indicators-Driven Approach

According to the value definitions provided in the Background section, value is closely related to the customer perception. Thus, the identification and quantification of elements which add or destroy value will provide a systematic and formal method for getting a more real perception of the value measure. Particularly for software products, the elements identification must be focused during the development process. The reason is that technical issues are strongly affecting the final product value, since the several development work products are used to build final software product that is released to the market. Thereafter, such work products must be subject to value estimation according to specific value indicators. As we identified in Section 3 the quality factor is closely affecting the value estimation, and this is happening even in software products. Thus the value indicators can be defined in terms of quality factors which are directly determining the value estimation. The aim is to get quantitative metrics on the work products in development phases in which the business criteria are barely involved. In this sense, the business perspective (such as customer preferences, competitors' features, and market position) can be lost if at least several important quality factors, besides obviously functionality, are missing. This section introduces our software value estimation approach, basing on the value indicators concept. Several metrics are also proposed in order to quantitatively measure the development work products value. We also proposed a general set of these work products and a general development process, together with a set of the possible development activities. For that we use international standards for software development life cycle' processes, activities and work products, as well as quality standards on Software Engineering, for determining the value indicators of such work products.

4.1 Value Indicator Definition

Firstly, we introduce our *Value Indicator* definition proposal (based on [16]) as follows: *"A device providing specific and quantitative information about the state or condition of the software product value"*. Therefore, indicators are developed based on quantitative measurements or statistics of the development work products value, which finally allow us to get visibility to the real offered value to the customer.

4.2 An Approach for Indicators-Based Value Estimation

A main issue is how to estimate the software work products value, thus as we reviewed in Table 1 (Section 3) there are several effort for measuring this concept.

The Ojala's formula [15] is based on the SAVE standard [17] and includes the quality factor in its metric, as well as this was defined for specifically measuring the software product value. Therefore, in our proposal we use the same estimation formula, but modifying the definition of its components, as follows:

$$Value = \frac{Function + Quality}{Cost} \tag{1}$$

Where: *Function* is the specific work that a design/item (product, service or process) must perform (example: function points needed to accomplish a software component). *Quality* is the owner's or user's needs, desires, and expectations (example: software quality attributes such as: usability, portability, security, traceability, etc.). *Cost* is the life cycle cost of the product, service or process (example: cost is normally expressed in man-hours). It is necessary to define how we will address each of these components. Thereafter, our proposal to estimate each component is described in Table 2.

Table 2. Measurement of the elements of the Ojala's formula according to our approach

Function	Cost	Quality
The function part is given by the development company through the project plan, since they state the functionality that the product must deliver. Therefore, for the purpose of calculating the Formula 1, we propose to use the project approach and its estimation figures, since this are designed together with all the involved stakeholders.	It is established by the development company, through the project plan estimation. This is a measure that commonly every software project estimate at least, therefore for the purpose of calculating the Formula 1, we propose to use the project estimation which is the closest to the reality.	This is the most difficult part to measure, as the quality attributes vary depending on the involved stakeholders' perception about the product quality. Quality attributes generally are very hard to measure, for example: usability, portability, integration, component reuse, performance, etc. Therefore, in our approach presented in this paper, we focus on defining the quantifiable indicators to get measures of quality (and therefore value). These indicators are then used to identify if the product is on the right way to accomplish the expected value according to the product designed plan by the business side.

4.3   Defining the Value Estimation Process Model

Figure 1 illustrates our process model workflow: 1) the Software Process Definition (SPD) is firstly performed, including the phases, activities that will be the focus during the value estimation process and the work products definition (WPD); 2) the Value Indicators Definition is the next phase, they are established according to the selected work products to be evaluated in the value estimation process; 3) the Quality Estimation (QE) is calculated using the information of phases 1) and 2), to be used it in the value equation(phase 6); 4) the function (FE) of the selected work products are estimated to be used in the equation of phase 6; 5) the cost (CE) is estimated to be used it in the equation of phase 6; 6) the value estimation (VE) is then performed using the data of phases 3, 4 and 5. Table 3 gives a deeper explanation about our process model for value

Table 3. Explanation of the process model steps for our value-indicators approach

Phase	Description
1. Software Process Definition (SPD)	The establishment of a series of phases and their respective activities, those are always present in every development project. For that we use the standards and SEI documents: Based on [9], [11] and [7]. A series of development work products (WPD) are defined and they are actually referred in this paper as outcomes of the development activities: based on [9], [11] and [13]. The establishment of the respective stakeholders (SE) involved in the creation and management of the outcomes (work products): based on [9], [11] and [7].
2. Value Indicators Definition (VID)	The assignment of a series of value indicators (VID) according to each outcome (work product) and its type. These indicators are based on [9], [1] and [10]. The assignment of a metric (or equation) for each value indicator (VIMD): based on [8].
3. Quality Estimation (QE)	The quality estimation based on the set of value indicators and their respective metric assigned.
4. Function Estimation (FE)	The establishment of the measurement functional size of the work product (expected and implemented).
5. Cost Estimation (CE)	The cost to accomplish the function of the work product (required and real).
6. Value Estimation (VE)	The definition of a value equation or formula based on the elements previously stated (function, quality and cost). The result of this value equation will determine the value of the development work products.

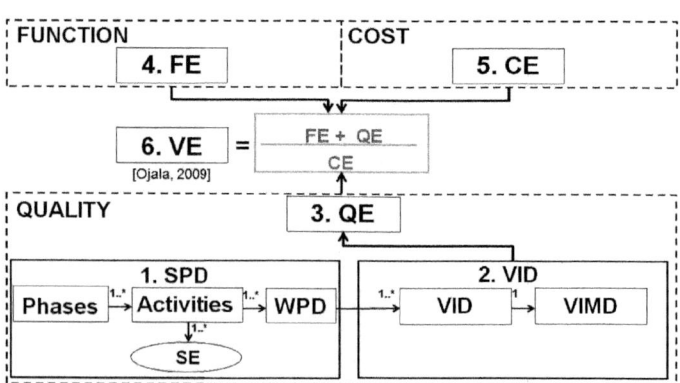

Fig. 1. Process model to estimate the software value, based on value indicators for development work products

estimation based on value indicators (centered on quality) and provides information on which standards and documents we used to define our approach. In this process, for each outcome (work product), all defined indicators to measure its quality are averaged for estimating the *Quality* figure in Equation 1. It is expected that the Function and Cost estimations are provided by the project plan, since our focus for value estimation is centered on quality. The final process step provides the value estimation for the development work products. We can see an example in Figure 2: WP1 has three value indicators, which are averaged to

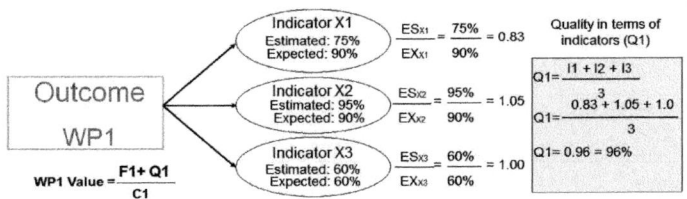

Fig. 2. The WP1 value indicators (centered on quality), are averaged for getting its quality estimation

get its quality estimation. This datum is next used in Equation 1, together with its *Function* and *Cost* estimations, for finally getting the value estimation for WP1. Table 4 shows an example excerpt of the process model execution: Phase: 1) Design Process; 2) Activity: Software Architecture Detailed Design; 3) Stakeholders: Developer, User-end; 4) Outcome: Software units defined by the design, 5) Value indicators: Performance Efficiency (PE) includes (a) Time behavior and b) Resource utilization), also the metrics to measure them are indicated in the table. It must be stated that these indicators have been previously defined, including their metrics, following our process model stated in Figure 1.In this example the value of the "Software units defined by the design" work product is only defined in terms of the *Performance Efficiency* quality category (*Time behavior and Resource utilization*). Thus, the *Quality* number that is required in Equation 1 is totally provided by PE. Therefore, for getting the final value estimation for this work product, the Formula 1 must be applied, where Quality = PE (as in Table 2).

5 Internal Validation

5.1 Scope

Several universities face the challenge to measure the academic level of incoming students for their undergraduate programs in engineering and science. Specifically, at the Universidad Autónoma Metropolitana this is important for making decisions about the inclusion of low profile students in preliminary courses. In this aim, a measurement instrument has been designed based on the institutional profile. Therefore, the proposed solution is to support those activities with a software system, whose development has been started last year with computer science students. A first system version, named Instrument System for Preparatory Courses (ISPC), is currently under development and some software components had been already tested.

5.2 Value Estimation for the Work Products

The aim of this internal validation is to analyze the benefits obtained with our Indicators-Based Value Estimation approach in real projects for the software products development. In this purpose, we focused the internal validation

Table 4. Excerpt of the process model execution example: Phase "Software Construction Process" and Activity "Develop and document each Software unit and database"

Outcome	Value Indicator & Metric	Quality Estimation
1. Software units defined by the design [9]	1. PE = Performance Efficiency (a) X1 = Time behavior $$X1 = t1 - t2/t3$$ t1 = Time of gaining the result. t2 = Time of a command input. t3 = Time of response expected. $$0 < T$$ The sooner is the better. (Metric based on [8]) (b) X2 = Resource utilization $$X2 = A/B$$ A = Estimated memory requirement for the component. B = Expected memory requirement for the component. $$0 <= X <= 1$$ The closer to 1, the better. (Metric based on [8])	$$PE = \frac{X1 + X2}{2}$$

Table 5. Project data for this internal validation (provided in the project documentation)

Functional Requirements	Release 1.0	Non-Functional Requirements	Assigned Measure
User Management	66%	1. Functional Suitability 2. Usability 3. Performance Efficiency 4. Portability 5. Maintainability 6. Security	100% 37% 62% 31% 33% 84%
Software Components		**Sub-Components**	
User Management		1. Add Group, 2. Add User, 3. User Query, 4. User Edit	

case in the ISPC system in Release 1.0 as follows: 1) from the Requirements Specification Document (RSD) and stakeholders interviews, we selected only one functional requirement, named "User Management"; 2) from the architecture documentation and the RSD, we selected a quality attributes set to be evaluated, these attributes determine the value indicators to be used; 3) the outcome (development work product) to be evaluated with the value indicators is the main ISPC's component named "User Management", which completely realizes the selected "User Management" functional requirement; 4) the "User Management" component is derived into several sub-components which we used for estimating this main component value, applying the selected indicators set. Table 5 summarizes the general project data that is used in this internal validation. Our approach comprises almost the whole software development process and defines value indicators for each outcome of the process's activities, however for this internal validation we focused in the context stated in Table 6 as follows: 1) Phase "Software Construction Process" [9], 2) Activity "Develop and Document each software unit and database" [9], 3) Stakeholders involved: product manager, end-user, developer, 4) Cost: 40 man-hour per "User Management" component (10 man-hour per sub-component), 5) for the Function estimation of Equation 1, we applied the Function Point metric for the "User Management" component, according to the function point manual [6]. The planning for performing the value estimation is also stated in Table 6. For performing the value estimation of the selected components, we firstly determined the Quality (QE), Function (FE) and Cost Estimation (CE), as it is specified in our process model (Figure 1).

Table 6. Planning and context of the internal validation

	Execution Time	Planned Value	Real Value
Planning	Internal validation performance	24 hours	30 hours
	Stakeholder Interviews	5 hours	5 hours
	Item	**Decision**	
Context	Phase	Software Construction Process	
	Activity	Develop and document each software unit and database	
	Stakeholders	Product Manager, Developer, End-User	
	Outcome	Component: "User Management" (completed at 66%)	
	Cost	40 Man/Hours for the component "User Management"	

Quality Estimation (QE). For each quality attribute of Table 5, we associate a value indicator which are stated in Table 7. The definition of these indicators was following our process model stated in Section 4.3 (see Figure 1). Then, for estimating the quality based on these indicators, we did the same as in the example (for Performance Efficiency estimation) showed in Table 4. That is for getting the Quality factor in Equation 1, for each indicator we got the real accomplished percentage (estimated number divided by the expected number), to next calculate the average of all involved indicators. Equation 2 shows the average among all value indicators of the "User Management" outcome for getting the *Quality (Q)* factor that is required in Equation 1, which is used for the final value estimation (VE).

$$Q = \frac{1 + 0.5 + 0.25 + 0.75 + 1.02 + 0.80 + 0.75 + 2.12 + 1.16}{9} = 0.93 \quad (2)$$

The value indicators X1, X2, X3 and X4 were associated to the Functional Suitability quality attribute (Table 5). The rest of the quality attributes (Security, Performance Efficiency, Maintainability, Portability and Usability) were associated to S, PE, M, P, and U respectively. Table 7 summarizes the results of the

Table 7. Value Indicators under study for the "User Management" component in Release 1.0: Expected Measure (by Project Team) vs. Estimated Measure (by our approach)

Value Indicator	Expected Measure (EX)	Estimated Measure (ES)	Ratio
X1: Traceability to the requirements and design of the software item	100 %	100 %	$\frac{ES_{X1}}{EX_{X1}} = \frac{100\%}{100\%} = 1$
X2: External consistency with the requirements and design of the software item.	100 %	50 %	$\frac{ES_{X2}}{EX_{X2}} = \frac{50\%}{100\%} = 0.5$
X3: Internal consistency between unit requirements	100 %	25 %	$\frac{ES_{X3}}{EX_{X3}} = \frac{25\%}{100\%} = 0.25$
X4: Appropriateness of coding methods and standards used	100 %	75 %	$\frac{ES_{X4}}{EX_{X4}} = \frac{75\%}{100\%} = 0.75$
S: Security	84 %	86 %	$\frac{ES_S}{EX_S} = \frac{86\%}{84\%} = 1.02$
PE: Performance Efficiency	62 %	50 %	$\frac{ES_{PE}}{EX_{PE}} = \frac{50\%}{62\%} = 0.80$
M: Maintainability	33 %	25 %	$\frac{ES_M}{EX_M} = \frac{25\%}{33\%} = 0.75$
P: Portability	31 %	66 %	$\frac{ES_P}{EX_P} = \frac{66\%}{31\%} = 2.12$
U: Usability	37 %	43 %	$\frac{ES_U}{EX_U} = \frac{43\%}{37\%} = 1.16$
Total of value indicators (Average of VI [$\Sigma VI/9$])			$\frac{8.35}{9} = 0.927 = 0.93$

indicators-based approach application to estimate the value of the "User Management" component in Release 1.0. Summarizing: The *Quality* factor is 0.93, meaning that the estimated Quality for User Management component in ISPC Release 1.0 reaches 93% of the expected quality.

Function Estimation (FE). The project did not have a measure of the software functional size. Thus, even it is not the focus of our research and in order to complete the internal validation, we carried ourselves out the task of estimating the functional size. For that, we used the Function Points counting method based on [6]. The function point metric is not mandatory to obtain the final value, but it is an alternative to measure the functional size of the development products. We use the RSD documentation to get the expected function points, and then we did a checklist to verify if our estimation was implemented on the Release 1.0. Table 8 exemplifies how we obtained the *Unadjusted Function Points (UFP)*.

After obtaining the UFP we applied the Value Adjustment Factor Calculation Table to obtain the Total Degree of Influence (TDI) explained in [6] resulting in 35. The next step is to apply the Formula 3 (stated in this section) to get the *Adjusted Function Points (AFP)*.

$$FP = UFP*[(TDI*0.01)+0.65] = 111*[(35*0.01)+0.65] = 111*[1] = 111 \quad (3)$$

This is the FPs for developing the "User Management" component with all the planned functionality. However in Release 1.0 is only required a 66% of

Table 8. Unadjusted Function Point Count Calculation Table for the entire "User Management". This calculation is based on the RSD documentaion.

Function Type	Functional Complexity (Count)x(Complexity)	Complexity Totals	Function Type Totals
EI (External Input)	(0)x(Low=3) = (6)x(Average=4) = (0)x(High=6) =	0 24 0	24
EO (External Output)	(9)x(Low=4) = (0)x(Average=5) = (0)x(High=7) =	36 0 0	36
EQ (External inQuiry)	(7)x(Low=3) = (0)x(Average=4) = (0)x(High=6) =	21 0 0	21
ILF (Internal Logical File)	(0)x(Low=7) = (2)x(Average=10) = (0)x(High=15) =	0 20 0	20
EIF (External Interface File)	(0)x(Low=5) = (0)x(Average=7) = (1)x(High=10) =	0 0 10	10
Total Unadjusted Function Point Count (Expected by the project)			111

this component functionality, this means that the required functionality for this component is of 73.26 FPs. We also applied this same method but for the real implemented functionality in Release 1.0, and we got 70 function points that were implemented. Summarizing: 70 FPs were implemented while the expectation was in 73.26 FPs, thus for the getting the Function Estimation, the implemented FPs are divided by the expected FPs (70/73.26) resulting in 0.955. Therefore, we got 95.5% of the expected functionality for the "User Management" component in release 1.0.

Cost Estimation (CE). The estimated cost for the development of the "user management" is 40, but the real development men-hours were 52 (which means it was required more men-hours than the expected ones). To get the Cost Estimation in Equation 1, these numbers are divided (real over expected) to finally get Cost = 1.3.

Value Estimation (VE). Summarizing: 1) Function = 0.955, 2) Quality = 0.93 and 3) Cost = 1.3, these numbers are substituted in Equation 1, with the aim of getting the value estimation for the "User Management" component of the ISPC Release 1.0, that has been developed in the activity "Develop and document each software unit and database" of the development phase "Software Construction Process". Equation 4 shows this calculation.

$$Value = \frac{0.955 + 0.93}{1.3} = \frac{1.885}{1.3} = 1.45 \tag{4}$$

5.3   Discussion and Limitations

The value indicators approach for product value estimation has shown their importance in this internal validation, since the stakeholders had a quantitative perspective based on the results. For this specific internal validation case the value was 1.45, his value result is not easy to interpret. However, if we go deeper verifying each element on the value equation we can get interesting information to get a better interpretation of the result. Specifically, *Function* and *Quality* were below the ideal but not by far, and costs were higher than the expected number. Thus, an immediate conclusion is that the larger cost estimation, the lower value of the work product, so costs must be corrected to assure the product value under the expected limits. Obviously, we rely on the product manager expertise for establishing the goals that the product must reach, in order to obtain the value needed for success against its competitors in the market. Also, for a better understanding of the Quality element in Equation 4 we can check the value indicators results to get a better understanding of the state of the product. For example, the *Value Indicator: External consistency with the requirements and design of the software item (X2)* in the internal validation case ratio is 0.5 (50% of accomplishment), therefore there are problems because the developed component does not follows the original design. In an ideal case (which is very rare) each element of the *Value* formula (Equation 1) should be 1 (which will end on a *Value* result of 2).

Analyzing the details of the value indicators approach application, we identify that one important aspect is that stakeholders claim that there is a bad transition from design to developed outcomes, due to changes in the development team and a poor members' expertise. This problem is obvious when we see that the consistency indicators had poor results (X3 and X4 in Table 7). Some value indicators had good results in spite of the transition problems addressed before (*Usability, Security and Portability*). Based on this information the project manager could change plans, for example re-writing some component parts for improving the compliance consistency to the described software architecture. Concluding, this approach was useful for providing a deep and quantitative visibility of specific value indicators, which revealed some hiding product quality issues. These issues must be corrected in order to meet the desired quality standards to finally meet the expected product value. Additionally, thanks to this internal validation, it was possible to understand how the software is going to be valuated before releasing that product to the market. This has been addressed thanks to the identification of the project planning deviations in terms of the costs, quality and functionality that were actually measured.

The main limitation in the application of our approach, is that for getting more accuracy in the results of this approach, full and clear documentation of the items to be evaluated is needed; as well as the stakeholders' feedback is a key element to get successful value estimation. It is also worthy to clarify that the stakeholders (specially the development team and product manager) must be experts on the matter to facilitate the application of the model, and for giving a more accurate perspective of the outcomes state. Thus, in a real case with a bad and disorganized documentation or with a team with a poor expertise on the project issues, it would not be feasible to apply this approach since the accuracy could not be assured. This is also true even if the code and working components are available, since both are required and fundamental for getting an accurate estimation of the software product value: 1) documentation and 2) the stakeholder's feedback.

6   Conclusion and Future Work

For a product manager a tool to model the product value, based on certain value indicators would be very useful for evaluating and managing the expected product value during the life-cycle development. This allows making better decisions when a new product is ready to be released, if it needs to be improved in certain aspects, or to evaluate if the product will reach the expectations compared to its competitors in the market. Also, decisions as to abandon a product release or to identify if the expected quality is feasible in a release can be analyzed with quantitative information.

There is specially an interesting aspect of our value indicator approach: it is very quantitative. However, if a company implements this approach, this will need to have certain prerequisites, such as owning the documental resources, experienced members, and analysts capable of answering the needs of the model metrics. Addressing this issue, then the benefits are obvious since the quantitative information will support a real management of the quality and at the end the value. Additionally, the application of our model in the internal validation gave us feedback for improving the model, in this stage of the research we are not still proven the complete set of value indicators that we already have for the whole software development process. Thus, it is part of the future work to perform full case studies, if possible in software product companies with real market targets. This will help in a better understanding on value results and will facilitate their interpretation. Also, to develop a prototype tool based in our approach to support the estimation in companies. Another important aspect of implementing this model is to determine the cost-benefit, since we must assure that it will be both feasible and useful for the companies.

Acknowledgements. This research is supported by The National Council on Science and Technology (CONACYT) of México and the Universidad Autónoma Metropolitana campus Iztapalapa.

References

1. Barbacci, M.R.: Software quality attributes and architecture tradeoffs. Tech. rep., Software Engineering Institute (2003)
2. Barney, S., Aurum, A., Wohlin, C.: A product management challenge: Creating software product value through requirements selection. J. Syst. Archit. 54, 576–593 (2008), http://portal.acm.org/citation.cfm?id=1374864.1375268

3. Boehm, B., Biffl, S., Aurum, A., Erdogmus, H., Grünbacher, P.: Value-Based Software Engineering. Springer (2006)
4. Cedergren, S., Larsson, S.: Improving traceability by focusing on value during development. In: de Madrid, U.P. (ed.) Proceedings of the 1st International Workshop on Value-Based Software Traceability (VALSOT 2011) in XP 2011 Conference (2011)
5. Day, E., Crask, M.R.: Value assessment the antecedent of customer satisfaction. Journal of Consumer Satisfaction, Dissatisfaction and Complaining Behavior 13 (2000)
6. International function point users group, T: Function Point Counting Practices Manual. The International Function Point Users Group, 191 Clarksville Road Princeton Junction, NJ 08550 U.S.A., release 1.4.1 edn. (April 2000)
7. IEEE: IEEE recommended practice for software requirements specifications (1998), http://ieeexplore.ieee.org/xpls/abs_all.jsp?arnumber=720574
8. International Organization for Standardization: ISO/IEC 9126 Information Technology - Software Product Quality (November 1999)
9. International Organization for Standardization: ISO/IEC 12207:2008 Systems and Software Engineering - Software life cycle processes (2008)
10. International Organization for Standardization: ISO/IEC FCD 25010: Systems and software engineering - Software product Quality Requirements and Evaluation (SQuaRE) - Quality models for software product quality and system quality in use (July 2009)
11. Jacobson, I., Booch, G., Rumbaugh, J.: The unified software development process. Addison-Wesley Longman Publishing Co., Inc., Boston (1999)
12. Keane: Application rationalization. Tech. rep., Keane (2011)
13. Kruchten, P.: Architectural blueprints: The "4+1" view model of software architecture. IEEE Software 12(6), 42–50 (1995)
14. Ojala, P.: Experiences of a value assessment for products. Softw. Process. 14, 31–37 (2009), http://portal.acm.org/citation.cfm?id=1507322.1507324
15. Ojala, P.: Value of project management: a case study. WSEAS Trans. Info. Sci. and App. 6, 510–519 (2009), http://portal.acm.org/citation.cfm?id=1553642.1553659
16. Oxford Dictionaries (2011), http://oxforddictionaries.com/definition/indicator
17. SAVE International: Value methodology standard and body of knowledge (June 2007)

Reusability Metrics for Program Source Code Written in C Language and Their Evaluation

Hironori Washizaki[1], Toshikazu Koike[2], Rieko Namiki[3], and Hiroyuki Tanabe[3]

[1] Waseda University, 3-4-1, Okubo, Shinjuku-ku, Tokyo, 169-8555 Japan
GRACE Center of National Institute of Informatics,
2-1-2, Hitotsubashi, Chiyoda-ku, Tokyo, 101-8430 Japan
washizaki@waseda.jp
[2] Yamaha Corporation, 10-1 Nakazawacho, Naka-ku,
Hamamatsu-shi, Shizuoka, 430-0904 Japan
toshikazu_koike@gmx.yamaha.com
[3] Ogis-RI Co., Ltd., MS-Shibaura Bldg., 13-23, Shibaura 4, Minato-ku, Tokyo, Japan
{Namiki_Rieko,Tanabe_Hiroyuki}@ogis-ri.co.jp

Abstract. There are various approaches to quantitatively and statically measuring the reusability of program source code; however, empirical demonstrations of the effectiveness of such approaches by considering actual reuse in actual development projects or of the magnitude of their effect on actual reusability have not been reported in depth. In this paper, we identified a set of metrics that are thought to be effective for measuring the reusability of C language program source code. Subsequently, for ten projects involved in development with existing software modification and adoption, during which conventional source code in an old project are extensively reused and adopted to a new project, we compared values of the static metrics identified and the reuse results before and after the development. Statistical analysis demonstrated that some of our metrics are effective for actual software development, and we accurately determined the magnitude of their effect on actual reusability. More concretely, it was found that when the percentage of files used outside the belonging directory is small and the number of function calls is small, the complexity of source code as the material of reuse and factors that are affected by the source code are limited, indicating high reusability.

1 Introduction

Reuse of common parts in some form (such as functions and directories) can reduce the development cost of new software[1]. Reusability is the extent to which a system or module-unit parts can be reused in a different environment. This quality characteristic is not regulated directly in the standard quality model specified in ISO9126-1[2]; however we have to consider its importance, particularly with respect to development efficiency within the same problem domain.

It has been said that you cannot control what you cannot measure[3]. A software metric is a measurement scale and the method used for measurement of

O. Dieste, A. Jedlitschka, and N. Juristo (Eds.): PROFES 2012, LNCS 7343, pp. 89–103, 2012.
© Springer-Verlag Berlin Heidelberg 2012

some property of software. Metrics for objectively evaluating the ease of reuse of target objects are essential for systematically controlling and conducting "development for reuse" and "development by reuse." Moreover, it is difficult to apply such reusability metrics in the actual development of software with satisfactorily high practicality, understandability, and persuasiveness unless the effectiveness of these metrics has been proven by accurate and empirical evaluation tests.

In this paper, we proposed a set of metrics for statically measuring (i.e., analyzing without executing programs) the reusability of C language program source code, and statistically evaluated the effectiveness of our metrics using a certain scale of actual metric values. The objective of our study is to provide a validated way for evaluating the ease of reuse of program source code accurately, without any other software materials such as documents and specifications.

The remainder of this paper is organized as follows. Next section introduces related works and problems in reusability measurement. Section 3 describes our reusability metrics and reuse rates for further evaluation. In section 4, we report on the results of empirical evaluations of our metrics by using ten projects data. In the last section, we draw a conclusion and state future works.

2   Problems of Reusability Measurement

Though many metrics have been proposed, it is generally difficult to select an appropriate one among them or to interpret the measurement results without appropriate models and goals[4, 5]. Various metrics for measuring the reusability of software have conventionally been proposed, mainly for program source code, including our previous researches[6–14].

In most cases, the effectiveness of metrics is evaluated by dividing a certain size of samples into a superior group and an inferior group from particular viewpoints (e.g., reuse results[8] and qualitative evaluation[14, 15]) and by comparing the distribution tendencies of the values of metrics between these groups.

However, data used in the evaluation by conventional metrics are based on the rough frequency of reuse of the partial or entire programs being examined and on qualitative evaluation, which inevitably depends on individuals. Therefore, whether the advantages of highly reusable program elements (or an entire program) are exploited in the programs being examined has not been accurately demonstrated through the consideration of concrete and detailed reuse results [Problem A].

In addition, for a similar reason, it has been difficult to analyze differences in the magnitude of the effect on reusability among individual metrics [Problem B]. Although there has been an approach to qualitative analysis and weighting, i.e., summarizing opinions from multiple specialists, when using multiple metrics[19], the effectiveness of this approach in actual software development has not yet been verified. Hence, the magnitude of the effects of individual metrics on reusability have not been quantitatively clarified.

3   Reusability Metrics and Reuse Results

We qualitatively identified multiple metrics considered to be effective for measuring reusability and compared their actual values with concrete and detailed reuse results. Thus, the effectiveness of individual metrics was accurately evaluated, resolving Problem A.

For the above comparison, regression analysis was carried out using reuse results as the objective variable and the actual values of individual metrics as explanatory variables, and the effect of individual metrics on actual reusability was accurately determined. As a result, Problem B was also resolved. In the following subsections, the proposed reusability metrics and reuse results are explained.

3.1   Definition of Reusability Metrics

Satisfactory understandability and persuasiveness cannot be obtained in the use of metrics unless the metrics themselves have been systematically derived following a particular policy and theory. In this paper, we adopted the Goal-Question-Metric (GQM) method[16]. The GQM method is a goal-oriented method for mapping a goal to a metric by using a question which must be evaluated in order to determine whether the goal has been achieved or not.

In working towards the goal of the accurate determination of reusability for supporting development for reuse and development by reuse, the questions to be examined were combined stepwise with the metrics used for projecting the properties of software to measures, thus obtaining multiple metrics. Although the process depended on human work, several specialists repeatedly reviewed and modified the hierarchy of the goal, questions, and metrics for as long as about one year, ensuring a reasonable certain level of plausibility and persuasiveness.

Table 1 summarizes the obtained metrics and the questions used to derive them. Seven metrics are derived from the four questions in the table. Each metric represents the complexity of the dependence or the complexity of the application programming interface (API) of the target itself.

For the six metrics other than MFl04, the smaller the value, the more positive the response to the corresponding question, which consequently indicates high reusability. For MFl04, it is considered that there is an appropriate range of values that give high reusability.

Because MFn05, MFn07, and MFn06 are metrics that evaluate functions, it is necessary to summarize measurement results by summation or other means in the case of evaluating upper unit levels, such as modules and the entire system. MFl and MMd are intended for source code files and modules (directories for C language), respectively, and similarly to MFn, these metrics require the summarization of results when upper unit levels are targeted.

MMd03 and MFn07 could be interpreted as variations of conventional information flow-based complexity metric called "fan-out"[17]; however MMd03 and MFn07 provide concrete ways to measure external dependencies at the module level and the function level, respectively. Similarly, MMd01, MFl02, MFn05 and

Table 1. List of reusability metrics obtained by qualitative identification

Question	Metric		
	ID	Name	Definition and interpretation
Is not API too complex?	MMd01	Percentage of externally used files	**Definition:** The percentage of files used outside the belonging directory among all files within the directory (module). $$\frac{\text{Number of files used outside the belonging directory}}{\text{Number of all files in the directory}}$$ **Interpretation:** The smaller the value, the more limited the use of API by external modules, indicating high reusability of the directory (module).
	MFl02	Number of externally used functions	**Definition:** The number of functions defined within the file and used outside the directory (module) to which the file belongs. Even when the same function is used multiple times, it is counted as 1. **Interpretation:** The smaller the value, the more limited the use of API by external modules, indicating high reusability of the file.
Is not the module dependent on too many other modules?	MMd03	Number of dependent modules	**Definition:** The number of modules on which the target module depends. When the target module uses functions of other modules, the former is considered to depend on the latter. **Interpretation:** The smaller the value, the smaller the number of dependent modules, indicating high reusability of the module.
Is the division and allocation of responsibilities appropriately?	MFl04	Percentage of functions without parameters	**Definition:** The percentage of functions without parameters among all functions in the file. **Interpretation:** The greater the value, the smaller the amount of (dependent) data required for use, indicating high reusability of the file. Note that a too high value (e.g., 1.0) indicates difficulty in providing data from outside and thereby difficulty in setting, which may decrease reusability.
Are external components that affect functions appropriately limited?	MFn05	Number of parameters	**Definition:** The number of parameters declared within the argument list of the function. **Interpretation:** The smaller the value, the smaller the amount of (dependent) data required for use, indicating high reusability of the function. Note that a too small value (e.g., 0) indicates difficulty in providing data from outside and thereby difficulty in setting, which may decrease reusability.
	MFn06	Number of readings of external variables	**Definition:** The number of readings of external variables (for C language, external global variables) by the function. When the same single variable is read twice, it is counted as 2. **Interpretation:** The smaller the value, the more limited the dependent external variables, indicating high reusability of the function.
	MFn07	Number of function calls	**Definition:** The number of function calls **Interpretation:** The smaller the value, the more limited the dependent functions, indicating high reusability of the function.

MFn06 are somewhat related to conventional complexity metrics "fan-in"[17] and IF4[18]; however these metrics derived in our study are fine-grained and specific to answer corresponding questions in the obtained GQM model.

3.2 Definition of Reuse Rate

A specific and detailed analysis of the extent of reuse can be accurately performed by evaluating the reuse rate, i.e., the percentage of components reused without modification (or completely reused) out of the entire adopted components, rather than simply by evaluating the frequency and amount of reuse. Here we define "reuse" and "adopt" in the followings.

- "Reuse" means the use of original components without any modification in the development of other programs.
- "Adopt" means the use without modification, the use with modification, or the use of extracted components; therefore conceptually, "adopt" includes "reuse".

On the basis of the above concept, we defined the reuse rate that can be measured in the context of development with software modification and adoption, and used it to represent the reuse results.

In our study, the reuse rate is defined as the ratio of the number of components reused without modification to that of components adopted in some way during the development of a new project by adopting the entire product of an existing project. A higher reuse rate indicates that the reuse of the product of the original existing project as the reuse source was much easier in such reuse and modification-based new development (i.e. derivative development).

In Figure 1, for example, an existing project as the reuse source is composed of several components, such as A, B, C, D, and E, among which, A, B, and C are assumed to be reused in a new project. Whereas A and B are adopted with some modification, for example, because of a difference in functional or nonfunctional requirements, C is reused without modification; therefore, C is counted in calculating the reuse rate in accordance with the definition of reuse. D and E in the existing project are not adopted at all and are excluded from the calculation of the reuse rate because it is difficult to specify the reason for not adopting D or E, i.e., whether it is because functional or nonfunctional requirements differ in the new project and the existing project (namely, reuse itself is not needed) or because D and E are difficult to adopt in the new project.

On the basis of the above concept, we defined the following three reuse rates: line, function, and file.

$$\text{Line reuse rate} = \frac{\text{Total number of lines in the files reused in the new project from the existing project}}{\text{Total number of lines in the files adopted in the new project from the existing project}}$$

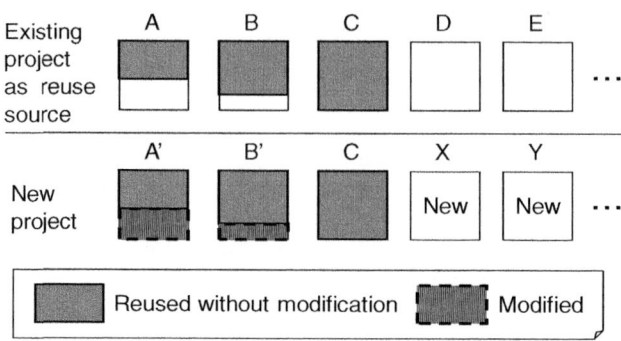

Fig. 1. Concept of reuse rate

$$
\text{Function reuse rate} = \frac{\text{Total number of functions in the files reused in the new project from the existing project}}{\text{Total number of functions in the files adopted in the new project from the existing project}}
$$

$$
\text{File reuse rate} = \frac{\text{Total number of files reused in the new project from the existing project}}{\text{Total number of files adopted in the new project from the existing project}}
$$

Given that component in Figure 1 denote files, three files are adopted in the new project, one of which is reused without modification. Therefore, the file reuse rate is 1/3.

4   Evaluating Effectiveness of Reusability Metrics

We statistically evaluated whether the above-mentioned seven reusability metrics were effective for the actual measurement of reusability using a certain size of obtained values and reuse results.

In the following subsections, we explain the projects used to obtain the values of the metrics and reuse results, the process of evaluation based on the comparison of the obtained values and reuse results, and the obtained results.

4.1   Target Projects

Data on metrics and reuse results were selected. Specifically, ten existing projects on embedded software development for some instruments (P1–P10) in the same domain were first selected from various projects in a company, in which corresponding succeeding developments (P1'–P10') based on P1–P10 were conducted and from which the above-mentioned three reuse rates (as reuse results) could be obtained. In the company, Px' could be recognized as an extension and new release of corresponding Px. There was no significant and architectural change between Px' and Px; however it can be said that the software environment of Px' is changed from that of Px because these are different projects with different functional and non-functional requirements. These projects contain relatively recent and reliable data and were selected so that the greatest reuse rate differences could be obtained with the aim of acquiring statistically significant results.

The reuse rates from the above existing projects, P1–P10, to the new derivative projects P1'–P10', respectively, were calculated and used as reuse results. Program source code of P1–P10 were used as the target of application of the reusability metrics. Our expectation is that the higher the reusability of P1–P10, the more components of P1–P10 have been reused in P1'–P10'.

Here, the files of the existing projects include files that were not reused at all in the new projects subsequently developed. Table 2 summarizes the project data. The directories, files and lines that were not reused in the subsequent developments were excluded from evaluation targets because it was unclear whether the reason for the lack of reuse was the difference in the dynamic/static characteristics of the target projects or because reuse was not needed in the functional requirements.

Table 2. Data on scale of ten projects (P1–P10)

	N. directories	N. files	N. effective LOC
Total amount	213	10,298	5,291,096
Reused	173	7,940	3,734,614

4.2 Evaluation Process

The process and result of evaluation are chronologically described below. Because there were many parameters that affected the results of our statistical analysis, we carefully examined each step as follows: 1) selection of measurement level, 2) selection of reuse rate and data format of metric value, and 3) selection of explanatory variables (metrics).

Selection of Measurement Level. First, multiple linear regression analysis using the reuse rate as the objective variable and all our metrics as the explanatory variables was carried out for all the reuse rates and the different three measurement levels: file, directory, and system. In this analysis, the objective variable was subjected to the logit transformation[20] because it was proportional data originally so that it is preferable to average the roughness of variation in raw data. For the explanatory variables, three types of data, i.e., raw data, proportional data, and log data, were used, as described later.

For the measurement levels of file and directory, no statistically significant differences were observed regarding all the reuse rates. This implies that the features that affect the reusability of the developed projects exist at the level of the project itself (namely, the entire system) and that no features that can be observed as statistically significant differences exist in the levels of file and directory.

New projects may require the addition of functions and other items. Therefore, it is appropriate to measure the reusability of the entire system rather than that of some component levels, which depend on individual requirements.

Selection of Reuse Rate and Data Format of Metric Value. From the above results, the measurement level was fixed at the system, and multiple regression analysis was carried out for all combinations of the reuse rate and the actual metric value in each data format. The following three types of metric data format were examined:

- Raw data
- Proportional data obtained by normalizing the raw data using an appropriate parameter
- Log data obtained by a log transformation to average the roughness of variation in raw data.

The analytical results revealed that the combination of the function reuse rate and the proportional data of metric values has the highest contribution rate that is adjusted for degrees of freedom and therefore this combination is valid. This is considered to be because raw data are strongly affected by the scale of the project, whereas proportional data have been normalized in accordance with the scale.

Table 3 shows correlation coefficients for all of combinations among the proportional data of seven metric values and the three reuse rates. In the table, it can be seen that the correlation coefficients between the function reuse rate and several metrics proportional data are high compared with other combinations.

Figure 2 shows scattergrams for the function reuse rate and each of seven reusability metrics. From the figure, it is thought that MMd01 and MFn07 are strongly correlated to the function reuse rate compared with other five metrics.

Selection of Explanatory Variables (Metrics). In the above analyses, all seven metrics were used as the explanatory variables; however, the number of target projects is ten, which is small relative to the number of explanatory variables (the number of target projects should preferably be at least double the number of explanatory variables). Therefore, the reliability of the regression equation obtained by multiple regression analysis may be low.

When all seven metrics were used as the explanatory variables, the contribution rate after adjustment for degrees of freedom was 0.812, and the obtained regression equation had positive partial regression coefficients for five of the seven explanatory variables.

Table 3. Correlation coefficient for each combination among the proportional data of seven metric values (MMd01, MFl02, MMd03, MFl04, MFn05, MFn06 and MFn07) and the three reuse rates (LR, FnR and FlR)

	MMd01	MFl02	MMd03	MFl04	MFn05	MFn06	MFn07	LR	FnR	FlR
MMd01	1									
MFl02	0.693	1								
MMd03	0.332	-0.012	1							
MFl04	0.744	0.429	0.491	1						
MFn05	-0.719	-0.354	-0.586	-0.956	1					
MFn06	0.538	0.968	-0.15	0.299	-0.19	1				
MFn07	0.518	0.733	-0.177	-0.11	0.163	0.721	1			
LR	-0.792	-0.561	0.009	-0.328	0.299	-0.446	-0.699	1		
FnR	-0.792	-0.768	0.125	-0.357	0.275	-0.693	-0.792	0.944	1	
FlR	-0.761	-0.715	0.14	-0.38	0.328	-0.639	-0.701	0.915	0.964	1

LR: Line reuse rate after the logit transformation
FnR: Function reuse rate after the logit transformation
FlR: File reuse rate after the logit transformation

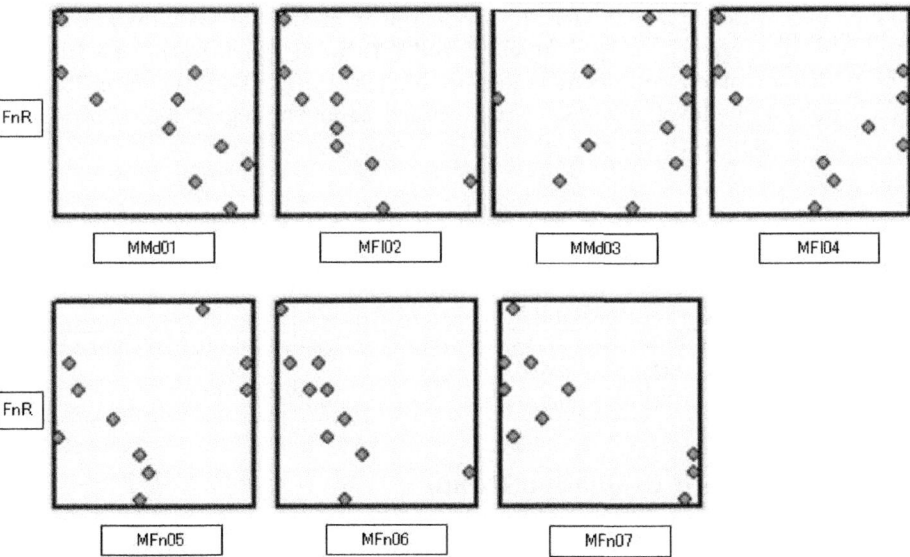

Fig. 2. Scattergrams of the function reuse rate and the seven metrics

As explained above, the six metrics other than MFl04 shown in Table 1 were derived by assuming that the smaller the value, the higher the reusability. The above analytical result was in disagreement with this assumption. This may be because there was originally some correlation among the seven metrics we adopted. As a result, multicollinearity occurred in the multiple regression analysis.

To solve this problem, appropriate explanatory variables were interactively selected using a statistical analysis tool so that no multicollinearity was observed, and we obtained the combination that gave the highest contribution rate after adjustment for degrees of freedom. It was clarified that the best regression equation with a contribution rate of 0.827 after adjustment for degrees of freedom was obtained when MMd01, MMd03, and MFn07 were selected.

Tables 4 and 5 summarize the basic statistics of the analysis and the statistics for each explanatory variable selected, respectively. In Table 4, the variance ratio is high and the level of significance is 1%, indicating that the obtained regression equation is valid. From Table 5, the partial regression coefficients are negative for MMd01 (proportional data) and MFn07 (proportional data), which is in agreement with the initial assumption that the smaller the metric value, the higher the reusability.

Here, the partial regression coefficient for MMd03 (proportional data) is positive. This may be because the three explanatory variables used in multiple regression analysis were not completely independent. However, MMd03 has the smallest standardized partial regression coefficient among the three explanatory variables and thereby has the smallest effect on the objective variable; hence, its effect is considered to be negligible.

Figure 3 shows a scattergram of the function reuse rate estimated from the obtained regression equation with three reusability metric values (MMd03, MMd01 and MFn07), and the actual function reuse rate for ten projects. In Figure 3, the multiple correlation coefficient is as high as 0.941. The estimated function reuse rate at the level of the system obtained using the regression equation is in good agreement with the actual function reuse rate.

Table 4. ANOVA table of basic statistics after selecting explanatory variables

Factor	Sum of squares	Degree of freedom	Dispersion	Dispersion ratio	Test
Regression	10.713	3	3.571	15.34	Level of significance = 1%
Residual error	1.397	6	0.233		
Total	12.11	9			

4.3   Summary of Evaluation Results

The results of the evaluation of effectiveness are summarized below.

1. Program source code are reused at the level of function.

   For reuse results based on the reuse rate, the function reuse rate was most strongly related to the values of reusability metrics. This is considered to be because C language program source code are mostly reused at the level of function.

2. Ease of reuse can be estimated from the data at the level of the entire system. As the level of reusability measurement, the entire system is more suitable for the evaluation of reuse rate than individual components. This is probably because the features and tendencies that affect the reusability of projects are at the level of the entire project.

Table 5. Statistics for each explanatory variable selected

Variable	Partial regression coefficient	Standard error	t-value	Standard partial regression coefficient	Tolerance
Constant term	3.446	1.769	1.948		
MMd03 (proportional data)	0.362	0.207	1.744	0.284	0.723
MMd01 (proportional data)	-8.453	2.31	-3.66	-0.687	0.546
MFn07 (proportional data)	-1.029	0.48	-2.14	-0.386	0.594

In other words, such features and tendencies do not necessarily exist in individual files or directories of the entire system; in the experiments such features and tendencies are not concentrated in particular files and directories of the system.

3. The more limited the externally used files, the higher the reusability (MMd01). Multiple regression analysis and the correlation analysis shown in Figure 2 revealed that when the percentage of externally used files in the directories of the system is smaller, namely, the API and interfaces that are used externally at the level of directory are more limited, the function reuse rate at the level of the system tends to be higher.

   For example, let us consider directories Ma and Mb, as shown in Figure 4. The values of MMd01 are $3/5 = 0.6$ and $1/5 = 0.2$ for Ma and Mb, respectively. In this case, the number of externally used files in Mb is smaller, or more limited, than that in Ma; a system composed of such directories with limited entrance will be more reusable. A directory in which only one file is used by external modules, similarly to Mb, is considered to be a result of applying the Facade pattern[21], which defines an unified and higher-level interface to a set of interfaces in a subsystem.

4. The smaller the number of function calls, the higher the reusability (MFn07). Multiple regression analysis and the correlation analysis shown in Figure 2 also revealed that when the number of function calls in each function is smaller, namely, the function under evaluation is called more often than it makes calls, and is closer to the end of call, the function reuse rate at the level of the system tends to be higher.

   In Figure 5, for example, the values of MFn07 are 3, 1, and 0 for `fa()`, `fb()`, and `fc()`, respectively. In this case, `fa()` mainly has the role of calling other functions, whereas `fc()` is just called by other functions. Therefore, a system having more such `fc()` end functions in the call chain has greater reusability.

5. Ease of reuse is more significantly affected by the percentage of files used by external modules (MMd01) than by the number of function calls (MFn07). Furthermore, multiple regression analysis revealed that the percentage of files used by external modules significantly affects reusability.

   On the other hand, the effect on reusability of the number of dependent modules (MMd03) remains unclear and will be examined in the future; currently we cannot find any significant correlation between MMd03 and the function reuse rate.

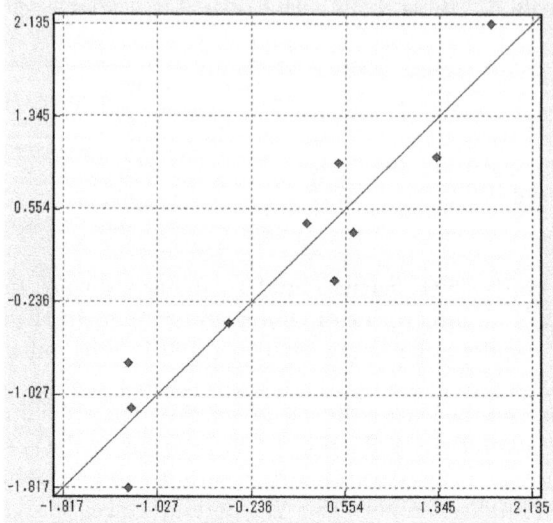

Fig. 3. Scattergram of function reuse rate at the level of the system for 10 projects after the logit transformation (X-axis, estimated values obtained using regression equation; Y-axis, metric values); multiple correlation coefficient = 0.941

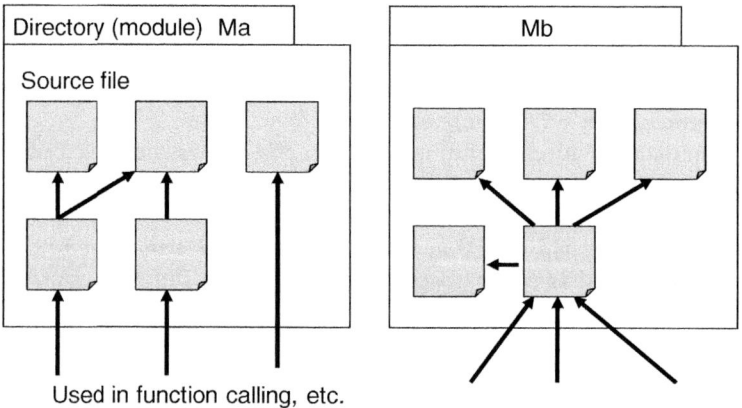

Fig. 4. Example of measuring MMd01 (percentage of externally used files)

As mentioned above, these evaluations were carefully carried out through several regression analyses, in which three types of detailed data were used for reuse results as the objective variable. Therefore, the validity of the proposed reusability metrics was accurately evaluated, thus resolving Problem A. In addition, the magnitude of effect on reuse results was individually analyzed and determined for three reusability metrics, thus resolving Problem B.

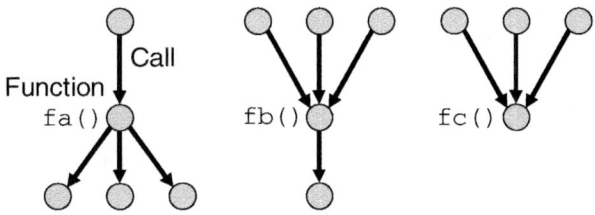

Fig. 5. Example of measuring MFn07 (number of function calls)

According to the above-mentioned goal, these validated metrics could be used for supporting development for reuse and development by reuse, such as estimating the effort necessary for reusing existing source code.

4.4   Threats to Validity

We used the reuse rate between corresponding two projects as a proxy for reusability of original program source code. We believe that the reuse rate defined in the subsection 3.2 reflects the reusability; however there might be several other factors affecting the reuse rate, such as requirement changes. It could be a threat to internal validity; in the future, we will inspect the similarity of requirements among target 20 projects.

Regarding threats to external validity, the evaluation was done on projects on embedded software development for some instruments in the same domain. We expect that the characteristics of all projects used in our experiments, such as the data on scale shown in Table 2, could help readers utilize the evaluation results. Moreover the evaluation was limited to derivative developments involving the reuse of entire architecture; in the future we will consider the generalizability of the obtained results by applying the metrics to completely new developments involving reuse of existing components.

5   Conclusion and Future Work

For C language program source code, a set of metrics considered to be effective for measuring reusability were qualitatively identified. Through accurate analyses using several types of data on reuse results, it was statistically clarified that three of the identified metrics tend to have different effects on actual reusability. In these analyses, we defined the reuse rate, which can more accurately reflect the actual state of reuse than the frequency of reuse.

The main contribution of this paper is the development of procedures for accurately evaluating the validity and effectiveness of reusability metrics and for analyzing the magnitude of their individual effects on actual reusability. As a result, a set of reusability metrics, the effectiveness of which has been evaluated and which can be used for C language program source code, were proposed together with an evaluation of the magnitude of their individual effects on reusability.

The followings are future works.

- Further review and expand the metrics (particularly MMd03) by increasing the number of project data and repeating the analysis, and analyze the generality of the metrics. Moreover it is necessary to consider the effect of various files (such as XML files[22]) on implicit module dependencies.
- Expand the definition of the reuse rate, which is used for comparison with metric values during the evaluation of their validity, so that the reuse rate can be applied even when original existing projects do not necessarily correspond to new derivative projects on a one-on-one level (e.g., the reuse rate when a project product is reused by various new projects).
- Analyze the relationship between metric values and other reuse result data such as the frequency of reuse in a certain time frame.
- Examine the applicability of the metrics, the validity of which has been verified, to source code written in other program languages considering that the questions used to derive the reusability metrics are independent of the program language.
- The reusability metrics proposed in this paper could constitute part of a practical framework (such as [6, 7]) for measuring the internal quality including reusability.

References

1. Poulin, J.S.: Measuring Software Reuse: Principles, Practices, and Economic Models. Addison-Wesley (1996)
2. ISO/IEC 9126-1: 2001, Information technology – Software product evaluation: Quality Characteristics and Guidelines for their use (2001)
3. DeMarco, T.: Controlling Software Projects: Management, Measurement & Estimation. Yourdon Press (1982)
4. Fenton, N., Whitty, R., Iizuka, Y.: Software Quality Assurance and Measurement: A Worldwide Perspective. Thomson Computer Press (1995)
5. Laird, L.M., Carol Brennan, M.: Software Measurement and Estimation: A Practical Approach. John Wiley & Sons (2006)
6. Washizaki, H., Namiki, R., Fukuoka, T., Harada, Y., Watanabe, H.: Practical Framework for Evaluating Quality of Program Source code. IPSJ Journal 48(8), 2637–2650 (2007)
7. Washizaki, H., Namiki, R., Fukuoka, T., Harada, Y., Watanabe, H.: A Framework for Measuring and Evaluating Program Source Code Quality. In: Münch, J., Abrahamsson, P. (eds.) PROFES 2007. LNCS, vol. 4589, pp. 284–299. Springer, Heidelberg (2007)
8. Kanno, A., Yoshizawa, T.: Techniques for Assuring Software Quality towards 21st Century. JUSE Press, Ltd. (1994)
9. Sindre, G., Conradi, R., Karlsson, E.-A.: The REBOOT Approach to Software Reuse. Journal of Systems and Software 30(3) (1995)

10. Frakes, W., Carol, T.: Software Reuse: Metrics and Models. ACM Computing Surveys 28(2), 415–435 (1996)
11. Etzkorn, L.H., Hughes, W.E., Davis, C.G.: Automated Reusability Quality Analysis of OO Legacy Software. Information and Software Technology 43(5), 295–308 (2001)
12. Nakajima, S., Suguta, S., Hotta, Y.: Evaluation of Metrics for Reuse of C++. In: Object-Oriented Symposium (1998)
13. Washizaki, H., Yamamoto, H., Fukazawa, Y.: A Metrics Suite for Measuring Reusability for Software Components. In: Proc. of the 9th IEEE International Symposium on Software Metrics (Metrics 2003), pp. 211–223. IEEE CS (2003)
14. Hirayama, M., Sato, M.: Evaluation of Usability of Software Components. IPSJ Journal 45(6), 1569–1583 (2004)
15. Inoue, K., Yokomori, R., Yamamoto, T., Matsushita, M., Kusumoto, S.: Ranking Significance of Software Components Based on Use Relations. IEEE Transactions on Software Engineering 31(3), 213–225 (2005)
16. Basili, V.R., Weiss, D.M.: A Methodology for Collecting Valid Software Engineering Data. IEEE Transactions on Software Engineering 10(6) (1984)
17. Henry, S.M., Kafura, D.G.: Software Structure Metrics Based on Information Flow. IEEE Transactions on Software Engineering 7(5) (1981)
18. Shepperd, M., Ince, D.: Metrics, outlier analysis and the software design process. Information and Software Technology 31(2) (1989)
19. Lee, K., Lee, S.J.: A Quantitative Software Quality Evaluation Model for the Artifacts of Component Based Development. In: Proc. 6th International Conference on Software Engineering, Artificial Intelligence, Networking and Paralle/Distributed Computing, and 1st ACIS International Workshop on Self-Assembling Wireless Networks (2005)
20. Ashton, W.D.: The logit transformation with special reference to its uses in bioassay. Hafner Pub. Co. (1972)
21. Gamma, E., Helm, R., Johnson, R., Vlissides, J.: Design Patterns: Elements of Reusable Object-Oriented Software. Addison-Wesley (1994)
22. Karus, S., Gall, H.: A study of language usage evolution in open source software. In: 8th Working Conference on Mining Software Repositories, MSR (2011)

Modeling the Effects of Project Management Strategies on Long-Term Product Knowledge

Martin Höst

Department of Computer Science
Lund University
Sweden
martin.host@cs.lth.se

Abstract. In a team, people sometimes leave the team and become replaced by new persons with less experience, and sometimes people participate in new activities and thereby obtain new knowledge. Different processes, in terms of different management strategies, can be followed, e.g., to introduce people to new tasks so they get new knowledge. There is a need to investigate the long term effects of different strategies on a team's software product knowledge. This paper presents an initial approach for how this type of knowledge can be modeled as a stochastic process. Metrics representing the long term effects on knowledge are derived, and two different example strategies are investigated numerically. Based on this it is discussed how the model can be further elaborated and evaluated.

Keywords: software process modeling, product knowledge, learning, truck factor.

1 Introduction

The relation between the software process and the product is of interest in order to be able to define a suitable process under a certain condition. In this paper the effects of the process in terms of how people are assigned to different tasks are investigated with respect to a team's long term knowledge of the product.

In software maintenance and evolution, teams are responsible for working with a rather large amount of software. The team is composed of a number of different engineers with different competencies, and the software consists of different modules, which means that different engineers can have knowledge about different modules. It is, of course, positive if many engineers have experience of many modules and if there for every module is several engineers that have experience of it.

In many cases there may be only few persons with experience of some modules even if there in an initial phase were several persons with knowledge about every module. Reasons for this might be that people leave the team. That is, the number of people with experience of a certain module is changing according to a dynamic process. A situation that is not attractable is when there are very few people with experience of a module, or when there are no people at all

O. Dieste, A. Jedlitschka, and N. Juristo (Eds.): PROFES 2012, LNCS 7343, pp. 104–115, 2012.

with experience of it. Staffing and assigning tasks to engineers is a typical task for management which can affect the knowledge of people in the team. People working with a module gain experience from working with it, but it is in many cases less expensive to have a person who already have experience of the module working on it.

One reason for working in groups with a shared responsibility of the product is that the knowledge about the code can be spread among several engineers, and the risk that certain parts of the code is only known by a single engineer is lowered. The term "collective code ownership" was coined as part of agile software development, meaning that anyone can change any code anywhere in the system at any time [1]. It is argued that this means that knowledge about the code is spread among the engineers and that code that is not well structured or too complex will be improved since many people are working with it.

The overall objective of this paper is to present a model for how the dynamic changes of knowledge about a module in a team can be modeled, taking into account that people sometimes leave the team and experience is lost and that people sometimes gain new knowledge. The objective is also to illustrate how the model can be used by showing the results for a number of example situations.

The outline of this paper is as follows. In Section 2 related work is presented and in Section 3 the analysis model is presented. The model is presented for two example strategies. In Section 4 the numerical results of the model for the two example strategies are presented. The results of using the model is discussed in Section 5, and conclusions and further research are presented in Section 6.

2   Related Work

Ricca and Marchetto [2] investigated if there are "heroes" in empirical studies of open source projects, where they with the term heroes mean people who are the only ones who have contributed to different files. In a set of studied open source projects it was found that heroes are common in open source projects, and that they are faster in development than non-heroes.

In their work on formulating approaches for analysis of process compliance, Zazworka et al. [3] defined and studied a metric of "truck factor". They evaluate the approach for analysis of non conformance in a case study on XP, where non conformance can be detected through a metric for truck factor. They define the truck factor as the maximum number of developers that could leave the team, and still at least a certain percentage of the modules would be known by at least a certain number of people. That is, they define the metric as one single number for a whole project. The formula for calculating the truck factor they define is

$$tf_{x,c} = \max\{n \mid \mathrm{cov}_x(n) \geq c\} \tag{1}$$

where c is a percentage, and $\mathrm{cov}_x(n)$ is the coverage, defined as the percentage of components that would still be known by the developers if n developers were absent according to different types of situations, x, as worst case, average case, or best case.

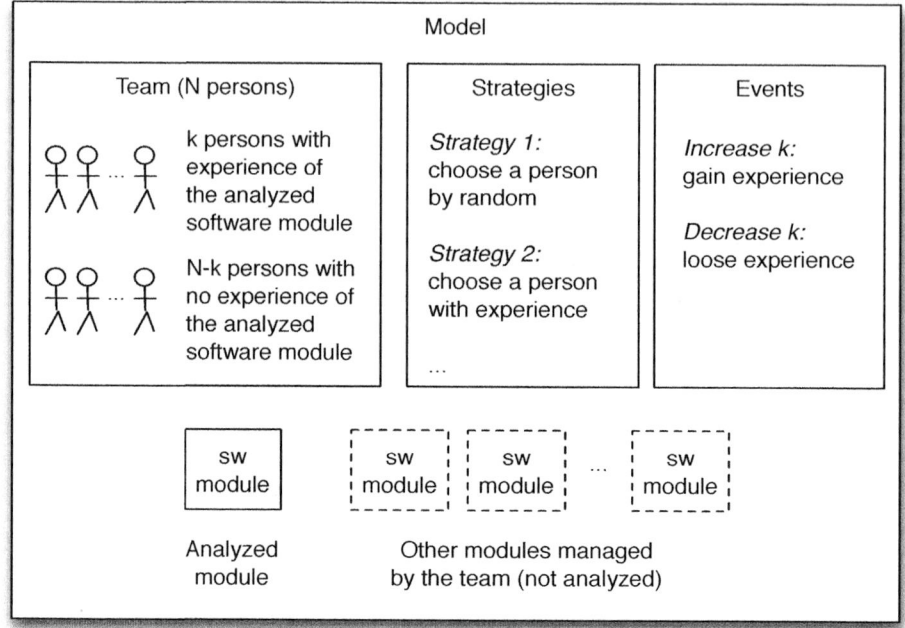

Fig. 1. Overview of the model

Torchiano et al. [4] build on the work by Zazworka et al. [3] and investigate threshold values for the truck factor, and they look at data from a set of 20 open source projects. Ricca et al. [5] continue this work and present a tool for calculating the truck factor and investigate the sensibility of the truck factor metric. They conclude that the metric is sensible, but that more research is needed on how it is calculated and that there may be scaling problems for large projects.

Compared to related work on knowledge about software in teams, the model presented in this paper focuses more on the dynamic changes of knowledge than existing models. This is done at the cost of focusing on only a single module at a time of the software, instead of at the whole software system.

3   Model

3.1   General Overview

The model is outlined in Figure 1. It is based on the following assumptions:

– The model describes the experience of one code module in the product. The size or type of the code module is not described by the model, but the basic idea is that a person in the team either has experience and knowledge about the module or not.

- The team consists of N engineers. That is, the team size is constant. When one person leaves the team, that person is replaced by a new person.
- When a new person is introduced in the team, that person does not have experience of the code module.
- When a person in the team gets an assignment to work with the code module it is assumed that the person during this work obtains experience and knowledge about the module. When this happens it can be assumed that the person obtains experience. If there are other people in the team who have experience of the code it is probably easier for a novice to work with the code since there are other people to ask for example when the documentation is hard to understand.
- In the team there are k persons that have experience and knowledge about the code module under study. k can take any value from 0 to N and is used to model how the knowledge changes over time.
- How people are assigned to maintenance tasks are decided by the strategy of the management and the team. One strategy could be to always let a person with experience of the module work with the task, and another strategy could be to always let a person with no experience of the module work with the task. The strategy affects how how often people in the team get new experience of the module under study.

It is assumed that new maintenance jobs arrive to the organization with intensity λ. The intensity of people leaving the team and thereby being replaced by someone else without any knowledge about the module is μ. The time between new assignments is exponentially distributed with mean value $1/\lambda$, and the time between people leaving the team is exponentially distributed with mean value $1/\mu$. Define ρ as $\rho = \lambda/\mu$.

Altogether this means that the model describes how k varies between 0 and N over time. This is modeled as a stochastic Markov process with discrete levels in continuous time (e.g. [6]). This type of model is used to model a wide spectrum of processes and systems in the literature, e.g. in different areas like performance behavior in telecommunication systems and user behavior in software testing. They provide a well known and easy way to derive mathematical expressions, and on the same time the possibility to model a level of detail that is sufficient in many situations. The Markov model that is used in this paper is outlined in Figure 2. This model shows that there are transition intensities between adjacent states, and the states represent how many people in the team that have experience of the module. In this model, λ_k denotes the transition rate from state k to state $k + 1$, and μ_k the transition rate from state k to state $k - 1$.

It is, of course, possible to define more complex models with transition rates between more than adjacent states, e.g. if two novice programmers work together with a module. However, for the strategies presented in this paper the model presented in Figure 2 is enough, and there is no difference between this model and a more complex model when it comes to how the metrics presented below are calculated.

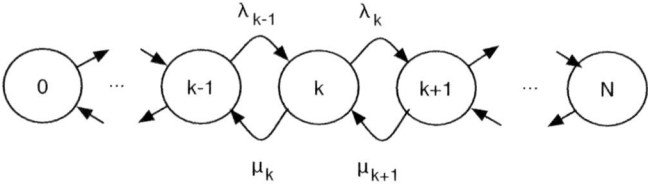

Fig. 2. Markov model

The number of people in the team with experience can be affected by management through applying different *strategies*. Strategies may concern both how people who not yet have experience can get experience through involvement in projects and in other ways affecting how people leave the team and how they get new experience. The transition rates between different states (i.e. λ_k and μ_k) can then be estimated based on the strategies. In this paper two different example models based on two different strategies are presented. In the example strategies presented below it is shown how the transition rates can be decided from the strategies.

The fact that knowledge is gained by working with the code module deserves a discussion. There are, of course, other ways to obtain knowledge, such as through training, participating in inspections, or other ways. However, contributing to the code has been used as an indication of knowledge in other studies ([2,3,4]), and it is at least an intuitive indication of knowledge. Fritz et al. [7] investigated the relationship between activity for a piece of code and knowledge about it and found that activity could be used as an indicator, although additional factors could also be considered such as role and professional work experience. Of course, all tasks are not large enough to give experience enough for a person to obtain knowledge. As part of using the model the type of task that is assumed to give experience must be defined. A factor that is not considered in the model presented in this paper is the fact that people forget their knowledge after some time and that knowledge about a module may be outdated after some a longer time when a module has been extensively modified. This is a result of a trade-off between having a simple and a complete and detailed model.

The model that is presented is analytical, but it would of course also be possible to define a simulation model for this purpose. The advantage of an analytical model is that it is possible to investigate more values for different parameters in a certain amount of time, and when formulas can be derived they ca give a knowledge as such of the relations between different factors. Simulation-based analyses require longer execution times, although they make it possible to analyze more complex processes. In this research we have seen that it is possible to define an analytical model which answers the basic questions that are of interest.

3.2   Metrics Based on the Model

The goal of the analysis is to investigate which strategy helps maintaining knowledge about each code module as long as possible. Then, we want to know the answer to questions about the risk of loosing all people with that knowledge, and how long it would take to come into that situation. Based on this, two metrics are investigated in this paper:

p_0: The probability that the team at a random point in time will be in the state that no one has knowledge about the module.

t_i : If there are i persons in the team with experience of the module, t_i is the mean time it takes until the first time that no one has experience of the module.

These metrics can be derived and calculated from the model as follows. Let $(q_{ij}) = Q$ denote the $(N + 1) \times (N + 1)$ transition rate matrix for the process with $N + 1$ states $(0, 1, \ldots N)$. Let the rates in the first row denote the rates from state 0, the rates in the next row denote the rates from state 1, etc. i.e. a traditional transition rate matrix as described e.g. by Cox and Miller [6].

The calculation of p_0 is based on calculating the steady state probabilities $p = (p_0, p_1, \ldots p_N)$, that is the probabilities that the process will conform to after an infinite amount of time. We use this as an indication of the state probability at a random point in time. The probabilities p can be found by solving

$$0 = pQ \qquad (2)$$

with the normalization condition $\sum_i p_i = 1$ (see e.g. [6]).

In order to determine t_i, state 0 is defined as absorbing, by adapting the Q-matrix by setting the first row to zeros:

$$Q = \begin{pmatrix} 0 & 0 \\ \hat{q}_0 & \hat{Q} \end{pmatrix}, \qquad (3)$$

i.e. there are no transition rates from state 0, otherwise Q is not changed. This means that $\hat{q}_0$ is a vector with the transition rates to state 0 and $\hat{Q}$ is an $N \times N$ transition rate matrix for the transitions between states 1 to N. Then the mean times t_{ij} that the process stays in state j before absorption if it starts in state i can be derived as

$$(t_{ij}) = T = -\hat{Q}^{-1} \quad \begin{matrix} 1 \le i \le N \\ 1 \le j \le N \end{matrix} \qquad (4)$$

A proof of this is presented by Tavere [8]. Actually that proof is presented for two absorbing barriers, but it easily follows that it is valid also for one absorbing barrier as in this case. From this it follows that the mean time until the process reaches state 0 if it is in state i is

$$t_i = \sum_{j=1}^{N} t_{ij} \quad 1 \le i \le N \qquad (5)$$

That is, in order to calculate the metrics (p_0 and t_i) the following factors must be known, measured or estimated: λ (i.e. how often new maintenance tasks for the module arrives), μ (i.e. how often people leave the team), and what strategy is applied.

It should be noted that it is easy to define other metrics in the same way as p_0 and t_i. For example, a measure of few (≤ 1) persons with experience could be defined as $p_0 + p_1$.

3.3   Strategies

Two strategies for how people are assigned to tasks are defined and analyzed in this paper.

- *Strategy 1:* A person is chosen for the task by random. That is, all persons in the team are equally likely to work with the task.
- *Strategy 2:* If there are persons in the team with knowledge about the task, one of them will be chosen. Only if no one has experience of the task, someone without experience will be chosen.

The two strategies are further presented below.

Strategy 1. According to this strategy, every time a new job arrives a person in the team is chosen by random. This means that the probability that a person without experience of the module is chosen in state k is $(N-k)/N$, which means that the intensity of an increasing the number of people with experience is

$$\lambda_k = \frac{N-k}{N}\lambda \tag{6}$$

When people leaves the team and are replaced by someone with no experience then the probability that the person had experience of the module is k/N. That is,

$$\mu_k = \frac{k}{N}\mu \tag{7}$$

The state probabilities can be found through equation (2), but it is also possible to decide an expression for p_0 as (see Appendix A.1):

$$p_0 = 1/(1+\rho)^N \tag{8}$$

For this strategy, formula (8) can be used instead of formula (2), which is valid for any strategy.

Strategy 2. This strategy is to always choose a person who has experience of the code if such person is working in the team. This means that the intensity of people with experience leaving the team is the same as in model 1, i.e. formula (7), but the intensity of acquiring experience is

$$\lambda_k = \begin{cases} \lambda, & k = 0; \\ 0, & 1 \leq k \leq N; \end{cases} \tag{9}$$

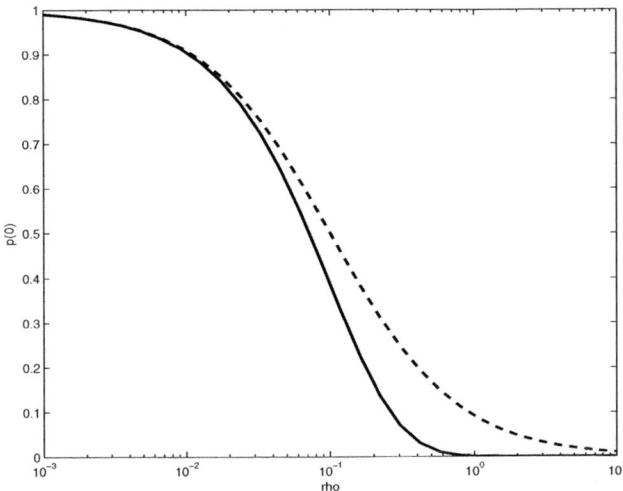

Fig. 3. p_0 as function of ρ with $N = 10$. The solid curve is for strategy 1 and the dashed curve is for strategy 2.

Note that when calculating the stationary probabilities, p, only p_0 and p_1 will have values larger than zero for this strategy. It can easily be shown that the p_0-probability is (see Appendix A.2)

$$p_0 = 1/(1 + N\rho) \tag{10}$$

In the same way as in strategy 1, formula (10) can be used instead of formula (2), which is valid for any strategy.

4   Model Results

In this section it is shown what the results of the model are for a set of different values. In Figure 3 it is shown how p_0 varies for different values of ρ with the two strategies. The solid line shows strategy 1 and the dashed line strategy 2. Note that p_0 depend only on the relation between λ and μ, i.e. ρ. For example, if $\lambda = 1$ month^{-1} and $\mu = 0.1$ month^{-1} this means that $\rho = 10$.

Figure 4 shows how t_i varies for different values of i. The three solid curves show the results for three different values of ρ for strategy 1. The dashed curve shows the results for strategy 2. Note that for strategy 2 the time to absorption is independent of λ, which is why only one curve for strategy 2 is shown.

As expected, strategy 1 is better than strategy 2 when it comes to the investigated metrics. For example, comparing the two curves in Figure 3 for $\rho = 1$, p_0 is very small for strategy 1 ($1/2^{10}$), while it is quite significant for strategy 2 ($1/11$).

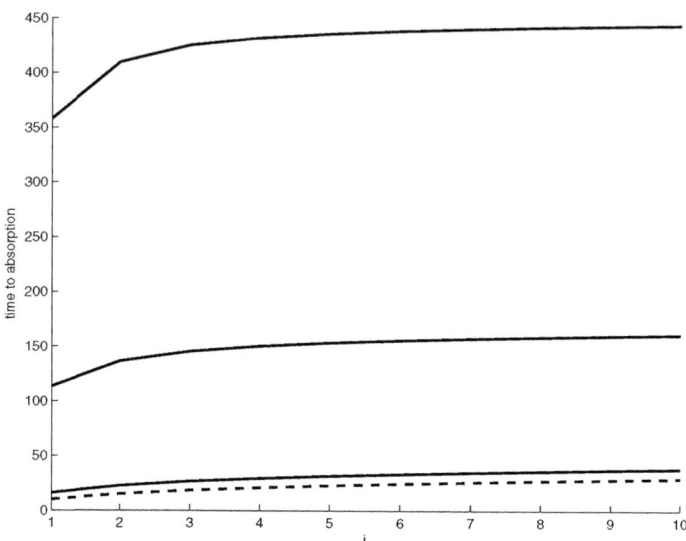

Fig. 4. t_i for $\mu = 1$ and $N = 10$. The three solid curves show the results for strategy 1, where $\rho = 0.1$ in the lower curve, $\rho = 0.5$ in the middle curve, and $\rho = 0.75$ in the upper curve. The dashed curve shows the results for strategy 2.

5   Discussion

A model like this can not be expected to present values that perfectly correspond to actual values. One reason is that the input parameters can not be known in detail. Instead, estimates of values must be used. It is the same for the definition of strategy. In most cases it is not possible to formulate exactly what strategy is used, only to describe what overall strategy that is most similar to the actual strategy that is likely to be followed in a team. It is also worth noting that it is not probable that the results will be valid when very long times are predicted, e.g. as in the upper curve in Figure 4 where times longer than 400 months are predicted if, for example, $1/\mu = 1$ month. This type of result should more be seen as the model does not predict any problem with respect to knowledge over time. It should also be noted that, since the result of the model is the result of many events in a stochastic process, the variation of the results may be large. Especially the actual variation around the mean value t_i may be large. To illustrate how large the variations can be, a team with with strategy 1, $N = 10$, $\lambda = 0.75$, and $\mu = 1$ has been simulated 200 times with a discrete event simulator. The resulting measures of t_5 are illustrated in the histogram in Figure 5. It can be seen that the variations are large. When the results of this kind of model are used it should be known that the actual results in reality will not be exactly as the mean value is predicted.

An assumption in the model concerns the distribution of times between assignments and the times between people leaving the team. The model assumes

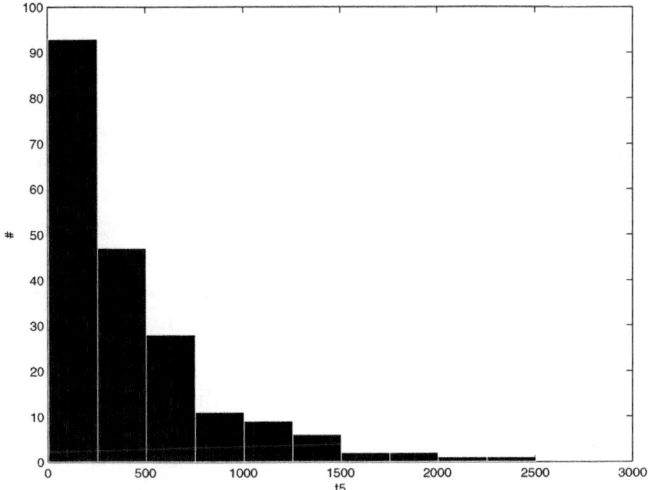

Fig. 5. Simulation results, where a team with $N = 10$, $\lambda = 0.75$ and $\mu = 1$ is simulated and the time t_5 is measured 200 times

that these times are exponentially distributed with different mean values. In reality it is of course not certain or even likely that this is true. However, in order to derive a model certain assumptions and simplifications of the reality must be made and the exponential distribution do not have to bee too far from reality. There are other aspects that the specific distribution that can be discussed, such as if events are independent o not. A realistic situation that is not modeled is that an external event, such as the start of another large project, could mean that several people left the team simultaneously. When models are formulated, simplifications must be made, and it is important to be aware of this when the results are used. We believe that the model represent a reasonable trade-off between simplification and inclusion of details.

The realism of the two formulated strategies can also be discussed, although they should be seen more as examples of strategies than actual strategies. However, the two strategies can be seen as two basic ways of assigning people to tasks, where strategy 1 is more focused on assigning people to new tasks than strategy 2, which is intended to model a very "short sighted" management strategy. Concerning strategy 1, people are not assigned to tasks by random in reality. However, people in the team are in a real situation working with several different tasks, which means that it is not possible to assign any person to any task at any time. This means that someone else than would initially be seen as most suited for a task may have to be chosen. Even if this is not the same as strategy 1, it may be nearer to the reality than for example strategy 2.

The proposed usage of the model is not to use it to derive definite and exact figures of future results. It is more to follow a procedure where a process is modeled as good as possible with respect to parameters and strategy. This probably involves formulating a strategy in the same way as was presented in Section 3, but it may also be possible to choose one of the two models that are presented in this paper. Based on this it is then possible to investigate different "what-if"-scenarios by changing parameters and/or strategy and to compare the results in order to get an understanding of the effects of different types of changes. That is, when processes and management strategies are improved, different alternatives can be evaluated with this type of model. For example, a manager responsible for a team can investigate the implications of different strategies on the product knowledge. Then the results of his model could, in combination with other factors, such as estimated cost of different strategies and the impact of delivery date, be used when processes and strategies are defined.

6   Conclusions and Further Research

The presented model can be used to get an indication of the long-term effect on knowledge in teams for different types of strategies. That is, it is one example of a model that can be used to analyze the effects of different processes on product. In this model the process aspect concerns the strategies for staffing in projects, and the product aspect is the team's knowledge of the product.

The model can likely be used when different strategies are compared and the likely effects of changing parameters are studied. It can be used as one source of information when different strategies are considered. Other sources of information can for example be estimates of the costs of different strategies. However, this should be seen as a first attempt to formulate a model, and a number of areas for further research remain.

There is a need to formulate and investigate more strategies than the two investigated in this paper. Strategies based on "pair-programming" [1] may for example be investigated. The model needs to be further evaluated by comparing the results of it to empirical measurements. This could, for example, be carried out in the form of surveys with real industrial projects. There is also a potential possibility to investigate knowledge about other factors than code modules, e.g. treating "system knowledge" as one unit of analysis.

A   Appendix

A.1   Derivation of (8)

Equilibrium gives that

$$p_{k-1}\lambda_{k-1} = p_k\mu_k \qquad 0 < k \leq N \tag{11}$$

which is the same as

$$p_{k-1}\lambda\frac{N-(k-1)}{N} = p_k\mu\frac{k}{N} \tag{12}$$

that is

$$p_k = \rho\frac{N-(k-1)}{k}p_{k-1} = \rho^k\binom{N}{k}p_0 \tag{13}$$

The normalization condition means that

$$1 = \sum_{k=0}^{N} p_k = \sum_{k=0}^{N} \rho^k \binom{N}{k} p_0 = (1 + \rho)^N p_0 \tag{14}$$

which means that $p_0 = 1/(1 + \rho)^N$.

A.2   Derivation of (10)

Since $\lambda_k = 0$ for $k > 0$, equilibrium means

$$p_0 \lambda = p_1 \mu \frac{1}{N} \tag{15}$$

which means that
$$p_1 = N \rho p_0 \tag{16}$$
Since the sum of p_0 and p_1 is 1, $p_0 = 1/(1 + N\rho)$.

Acknowledgment. This work was funded by the Industrial Excellence Center EASE – Embedded Applications Software Engineering, (http://ease.cs.lth.se).

References

1. Beck, K.: Extreme Programming Explained. Addison Wesley (2000)
2. Ricca, F., Marchetto, A.: Heroes in FLOSS projects: An explorative study. In: 17th Working Conference on Reverse Engineering, pp. 155–159 (2010)
3. Zazworka, N., Stapel, K., Knauss, E., Shull, F., Basili, V.R., Schneider, K.: Are developers complying with the process: An XP study. In: Proceedings of the 2010 ACM-IEEE International Symposium on Empirical Software Engineering and Measurement, ESEM (2010)
4. Torchiano, M., Ricca, F., Marchetto, A.: Is my project's truck factor low? theoretical and empirical considerations about the truck factor threshold. In: WETSoM (2011)
5. Ricca, F., Marchetto, A., Torchiano, M.: On the Difficulty of Computing the Truck Factor. In: Caivano, D., Oivo, M., Baldassarre, M.T., Visaggio, G. (eds.) PROFES 2011. LNCS, vol. 6759, pp. 337–351. Springer, Heidelberg (2011)
6. Cox, D., Miller, D.: The Theory of Stochastic Processes. Chapman & Hall (1965)
7. Fritz, T., Murphy, G.C., Hill, E.: Does a programmer's activity indicate knowledge of code? In: Proceedings of the the 6th Joint Meeting of the European Software Engineering Conference and the ACM SIGSOFT Symposium on the Foundations of Software Engineering, ESEC-FSE, pp. 341–350 (2007)
8. Tavere, S.: A note on finite homogeneous continouos-time Markov chains. Biometrics 35(4), 831–834 (1979)

Growing into Agility: Process Implementation Paths for Scrum

Kevin Vlaanderen[1], Peter van Stijn[1],
Sjaak Brinkkemper[1], and Inge van de Weerd[2]

[1] Utrecht University, Department of Information and Computing Sciences,
P.O. Box 80.007, 3508 TA, Utrecht, The Netherlands
{k.vlaanderen,s.brinkkemper}@uu.nl, pcestijn@cs.uu.nl
[2] Vrije Universiteit Amsterdam, Faculty of Economics and Business Administration,
De Boelelaan 1105, 1081 HV Amsterdam, The Netherlands
i.vande.weerd@vu.nl

Abstract. Background: Many organizations struggle with the implementation of agile methods. Such methods pose considerable challenges related to organizational demand and process configuration. **Goal:** In this paper, we analyze the introduction of Scrum in the development organization in order to determine distinct approaches to its implementation. **Approach:** We compare the Scrum introduction paths of four case companies. **Results:** This results in a discussion of implementation paths ranging from gradual to disruptive introduction of Scrum. **Contribution:** The description of these paths provides insight into process improvements. We demonstrate how a structured description of process improvements can improve understanding of process improvement paths.

Keywords: software process improvement, Scrum, product software, incremental, process implementation.

1 Introduction

Since the publication of the Agile Manifesto in 2001 [3], agile software development methods have become an ever-increasing part of the software development industry. The Agile Manifesto, but also the period before its publication, gave rise to several agile software development methods [1]. Examples of such methods are DSDM [24], Extreme Programming [2] and Scrum [20]. The principles of such methods are that by employing them, the development process becomes more responsive to a changing environment, working software is chosen over extensive documentation, individuals and interactions are considered more important than tools and processes, and customer collaboration is valued more than contract negotiation [3]. In the last few years, these agile methods have proven to be successful in a large number of cases [17].

Scrum is one of the agile methods that is gaining popularity [9]. The Scrum development method was proposed by Ken Schwaber [20], at a time when it became clear to most professionals that the development of software was not something that could be planned, estimated and completed successfully using

O. Dieste, A. Jedlitschka, and N. Juristo (Eds.): PROFES 2012, LNCS 7343, pp. 116–130, 2012.
© Springer-Verlag Berlin Heidelberg 2012

the common 'heavy' methods. Therefore, the Scrum method adheres to the principles of agile software development. Companies that have put Scrum to practice range from small companies as described by Dingsøyr et al. [8] to large multinationals [10]. Research has shown that the use of Scrum within a company can lead to significant benefits [10].

In its purest form, Scrum provides a rather simple approach to agile, iterative software development. Although various additions have been made during the years, the process boils down to a planning phase, a closure phase, and several iterations, or sprints, during which the software is developed by one or more development teams. No new requirements can be introduced during these sprints. This ensures that the final product is being developed with a high probability of success, even within a constantly changing environment. This environment, which includes factors such as competition, time and financial pressure, maintains its influence on development until the closure phase. Sprints are structured according to a set of recurring activities. These basic, relatively fixed activities are the sprint planning meeting, the daily Scrum meeting, the sprint review meeting, and the retrospective meeting. The essential deliverables within Scrum are the sprint backlog, the product backlog, and the increment of potentially shippable product functionality [20].

Although Scrum can provide significant benefits, implementing it in an organization is not a trivial task. Many authors have described the risks and critical success factors of Scrum implementations in various (types of) organizations [23,21]. Not only for bespoke software development but also for product software development organizations, as recognized by several authors, including one of the founders of the Agile Alliance [7,15]. While agile methods can provide significant advantages to a software producing company, there are many challenges that can inhibit a successful move from traditional software development approaches to an agile environment, such as developer resistance, challenges in decision making, and the need for increased customer involvement [5,14]. From a questionnaire on the subject conducted by Livermore [13], it becomes clear that knowledge sharing is one of the most important factors in the success of implementation projects, followed by management support.

Process improvements can intrinsically be performed according to two main types. On the one hand, process improvements can be implemented in a revolutionary manner. In such a case, large changes are introduced to a process at once. On the other hand, process improvements can be cut into smaller chunks, causing a more step-wise evolution of the process. This distinction has been discussed quite frequently in literature [19,16,12,28] for various domains. The approaches are visualized in Figure 1.

Scrum comprises a fairly simple, iterative process model, which is to a large extent adaptable by the organization. The fact that it does not entail many constraints [4] makes Scrum suitable to many types of organizations. However, this also implies that their specific approaches, and consequently the path to reach agility, can vary considerably. During recent year, a decent body of knowledge has been built regarding agile software development in the context of software

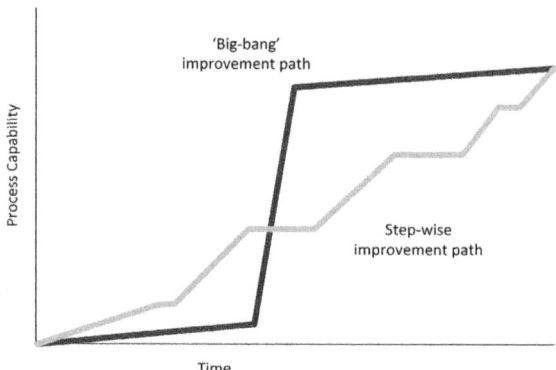

Fig. 1. Generic Process Improvement Paths

process improvement [6,18,22]. In this paper, we relate different styles of process improvement to the introduction of Scrum. We present a multiple case study, using the data from the case studies to discuss the introduction of process improvements in general, and the introduction of Scrum specifically. As such, our analysis discusses the question *'Acccording to which paths can Scrum be implemented?'* In the context of this question, we define a path as a series of changes to a process.

A description of the research approach is provided in Section 2. In Section 3, we provide a description of the four case studies in which we outline the approach that was taken to implement Scrum in the organizations. Based on the case studies, we analyze the implications for the implementation paths in Section 4. We briefly reflect on the research project in Section 5. Conclusions and further research are described in Section 6.

2   Case Study Research Approach

The research presented in this paper is part of a series of case studies that is performed with the aim of improving our knowledge of incremental method evolution. Out of the seven case study companies that are part of the overall research, four have implemented Scrum during the past few years. The implementation of Scrum is interesting from the perspective of software process improvement, as it is clearly defined in literature and it is a rather confined process. The case study companies selected for this research displayed different approaches to the implementation of Scrum, which makes the Scrum implementation approach an interesting unit of analysis. Each case company is briefly introduced throughout Section 3. For the sake of confidentiality, company names have been pseudonymised.

Data gathering was partly performed on-site, and partly through internet research, telephone calls, and e-mails. For each case, between three and five stakeholders were selected and interviewed. Roles that were suitable for interviews included (depending on the specific situation) the product manager, manager product management, general manager (in small companies), development manager, lead developer, senior consultant, and support managers. In addition, data was gathered through analysis of relevant documents. These documents included, if available and not limited to, requirements databases, internal communication regarding process changes, process descriptions, templates, change-plans, presentations regarding the Scrum process and other documents that describe changes in the process. All data collected either through interviews or through documents were included in a case study database.

3   Case Studies

Each section below gives an account of the evolution of Scrum per organization. Each case study is described according to three stages; *preparation* describes the process up to the start of the Scrum implementation, *implementation* describes the actual process changes related to the generic Scrum activities, and *customization* describes additional changes to the process.

3.1   ChatComp

ChatComp is a privately-held company, which develops two product lines; instant messaging, and real-time messaging for smartphones, serving approximately 100 million users (within a growing market). ChatComp develops its products for multiple platforms, including the Android, Windows Mobile and BlackBerry platforms. As a consequence, it has to deal with constantly changing development platforms. Its products are released in cycles of 4 weeks. The organization deals with a large number of incoming wishes that vary significantly in nature, resulting in approximately 500 distinct product requirements per year. Within three years, the company has grown from 20 employees to over 100 employees. This was accompanied by several extensive changes to the development and product management processes.

Preparation - The introduction of Scrum in ChatComp started around August 2008, based on the initiative of the development manager. The aim of introducing Scrum was to improve the company's ability to deal with an increasing amount of requirements and a quickly growing development team. In order to determine how Scrum was supposed to be implemented, an external consultant was hired. Once the idea was concrete enough, the company received an in-house training regarding the workings of Scrum.

Implementation - After the training, the entire development department started working according to the process of Scrum. During the first six months, the management team was strongly involved in the Scrum process. Once the teams became more adept at Scrum and the company started to grow, this involvement steadily decreased. The initial implementation was rather standard. This means that the sprint planning, daily standup, demo meeting and retrospective meeting all were in place, and the product managers have taken the role of product owners. The organization did make changes to the parameters of the process (such as sprint duration and team size) several times, causing a series of minor process changes.

Customization - Initially, the sprints lasted two or three weeks, depending on the team, causing a discrepancy between the sprint durations of some of the teams. At the same time, interdependencies started to become more of an issue as the amount of teams grew. This caused problems when, for instance, front-end teams needed functionality in the back-end that was not yet developed. These problems, which consisted mainly of delays, were solved by fixating sprint duration at two weeks for all teams.

The sprint planning meeting initially took approximately one day, because all the user stories had to be discussed, estimated and planned at once. This was considered too long to be effective. Therefore, story estimation is now done regularly throughout the sprints. This requires shorter bursts of attention, which eases the process. On the day of the sprint planning, the product owners present the user stories to their own team(s), followed by the selection and planning of user stories by the development teams. The process of selection and planning now takes approximately one hour, instead of one day.

Interesting in this light has been the introduction of the kick-off week. The kick-off week was an attempt to streamline the Scrum development process by dividing the year into four quarters of 13 weeks, each starting with a kick-off week during which all the user stories for the remainder of the quarter were identified, estimated and planned. Although the idea of a detailed roadmap per quarter seemed useful, the approach turned out to be problematic in practice. Developers were kept an entire week from developing their products, spending one entire week one estimating and planning is an exhausting activity, and the workload turned out to be too high for the product owners. Quickly after the first quarter, ChatComp decided to cancel the kick-off week.

Due to the quick growth of the organization, internal communication of the product plan became increasingly important. For this reason, the product owners have changed the original schedule of the sprint planning meeting. The meeting now starts out with a presentation on the roadmap, the development focus, and the target market segment, in order to make sure that all internal stakeholders have the same objective and are aware of the context in which they are working. After this presentation, selection and planning continues as usual.

When Scrum was just implemented in ChatComp, IM was the only product line. Initially, there were three teams with a specific functional focus. After approximately eight months, one platform specific team was extended with a developer for another platform, making it a cross-platform team. The team quickly realized that this was not an ideal situation, as it inhibited collaboration. Once enough developers were available, the team was split into two teams, each focusing on their own platform. This process has recurred several times during the past few years. Each time, the organization moved back to platform specific teams to increase effectiveness of the teams. Currently, seven teams are active, each with a specific focus.

Other changes, less related to the interface between Scrum and product management, include the introduction of a Scrum of Scrums in order to facilitate inter-team communication, and a similar ScrumMaster counsil in which all ScrumMasters briefly meet to discuss any problems they encountered, things they learned or questions they have. The focus of this meeting is process-oriented instead of development-oriented.

3.2   FacilityComp

FacilityComp is an international software vendor that produces a total of five facility management and real estate management software products for medium to large organizations (Integrated Workplace Management Systems). Founded in 1984, it currently has a customer base of over 1300, supported by more than 325 employees. The company's products are marketed through multiple, international subsidiaries, and a worldwide network of partners. FacilityComp releases its products bi-yearly.

Preparation - Until 2004, product development at FacilityComp was based on the Prince2 method. New functionality for each product was fully described and planned upfront, after which it was developped in a waterfall approach. As the organization became larger and the products more complex, it became increasingly difficult to manage the development activities. Release cycles could take up to one or one and a half year and release dates were difficult to predict. Additionaly, many changes were requested during a project. The Prince2 method did not offer sufficient support for this, resulting in a lot of calculations that caused a large share of the product managements time to be put into these tasks instead of in product value. Based on these issues, the chief technology officer decided to change the development process to Scrum. He was also the person responsible for the actual introduction of Scrum. After he studied Scrum, he performed several internal sessions to explain the process. In addition, several persons took an external course to familiarize them with the method.

Implementation - Once a sufficient knowledge level was reached, the development team switched to Scrum completely. In principle, all basic Scrum activities were introduced at once. Initially, Scrum was only utilized for the new products, and the organization kept managing its cash-cow product using the old waterfall development method. One after the other, all products where then switched to the new Scrum process. Along the way, minor adjustments were often made. The teams were constantly searching for the right balance between sprint duration, size estimation, requirement size, and time spent on backlog administration. Changes to the process were initially often managed by the the CTO. However, they were increasingly delegated to the appropriate ScrumMasters.

Customization - Until 2007, agile product development was accompanied by non-agile product management. Although several stages of elaboration were employed, no fixed cycles were used. This caused that product managers did not manage to provide development with sufficiently detailed requirements before the start of each sprint. To improve this, the product management team adjusted their process to the Scrum principles as well. This implied a continuous adaptation of the product backlog to a changing environment. Since Scrum itself does not provide guidelines for effectively managing large amounts of requirements of different granularity, a set of stages has been introduced, called the *Agile Requirements Refinery* [26]. Within the agile requirements refinery, an idea will generally move through the stages *vision, theme, concept*, and *requirement definition*. During these stages, requirements are refined with details and specifications. This has resulted in a new categorization on the product backlog.

3.3 SocialComp

SocialComp is a large social networking site in the Netherlands, focusing mainly on Dutch visitors and members. It was founded in 2004, and since then it has built a user base of over eleven million accounts and serves over 5,8 billion page views per month. Even though its active user base is declining in the past few years, it potential market, consisting of individual users, is growing. Social-Comp releases updates to its platform once per week. The organization has a very low level of organizational policy and does not need to deal with a high number of standards or a high level of legislation. However, it does receive many product requests directly from its users.

Preparation - SocialComp is a very young company, despite the fact that it was founded in 2004. Many of the employees are below the age of 35, and this is reflected in a very creative and informal setting. This setting has always resulted in a development environment without strict processes and, consequently, without a strong structure. This attitude is seen throughout the organization. However, the considerable growth during the past few years has forced the organization to apply some structure to its internal processes. The move to Scrum should therefore be seen in the context of a larger movement within the organization.

During the period between 2009 and late 2010, the organization moved away from its 'startup structure' and added a clearer division of responsibility. During this time, Scrum is mentioned several times, and requirements are from that time on written in the form of user stores. However, new functionality was still developed in the form of waterfall projects, where all functionality was designed upfront. Requirements prioritization and selection was still done based on 'fingerspitzen-gefühl'. Real improvements were made in the end of 2010, when a clear product vision and strategy were defined. The previous 15 focus areas were reduced to 6, with one responsible product manager per area. The choice to implement Scrum was made by the CTO at that time, based on earlier, positive experiences with it. He felt that it offered advantages to SocialComp as well in the form of improved backlog management and scope change management. Scrum's team-based approach seemed like it would respect the independence of the programmers while providing a scalable structure.

Implementation - The introduction of Scrum was performed gradually. The first step towards agile development was the creation of fixed teams that were located in one room. Each team was assigned a team lead and a ScrumMaster. Through several internal presentations, all stakeholders were taught the workings of Scrum. During the first period, the teams got used to the process by working with a product backlog in fixed teams.

After some time, daily standups were introduced. These standups were performed in the original sense as described by Schwaber et al. [20]. Each day, teams would come together to discuss work performed the day before, work planned for the current day, and any problems that were experienced. The introduction of daily standups was gradually followed by other essential elements of Scrum. Rather quickly, a definition of done was introduced. This definition has changed somewhat throughout the last two years, and basically states that functionality is done when it is developed, verified and prepared for automated testing. Soon after the introduction of the definition of done, the first demo meetings were organized. Such meetings were initially only held when important features were finished. Later, demo's became a regular part of the Scrum process. Retrospective meetings were introduced gradually. Initially, only a few developers would discuss a sprint after it had finished. After some time, other teams started to hold retrospective meetings as well.

Customization - The gradual introduction of Scrum seems to correlate with the acceptance of Scrum within the organization. Initially, many developers were rather skeptical due to the changed responsibilities, more formal processes and reduction in freedom. During the past two years, approximately 20% has come to actively support Scrum, and 60% does not have a strong opinion about it. The final 20%, mainly developers that have been at the company for a long time, actively resists a full Scrum implementation. Due to the informal setting within Social-Comp, this resistance is not seen as a huge problem. If a developer fails to comply to the process but maintains a good rate of productivity, this is accepted as well.

3.4   TimeComp

TimeComp is a small independent Dutch software company, founded in 1992. The organization provides qualitative software applications and accompanying services to fulfil the need of achieving a higher efficiency from the utilization of human resources. TimeComp currently has two software products in its portfolio: one for time resource management, and one for printing and copying facilities for organizations. Its market consists of small to medium enterprises, and its size is fairly stable. It serves approximately 400 organizations within Europe. It releases its products twice per year, based on a steady inflow of customer requests. As TimeComp is a fairly small organization, with approximately 25 persons, it has a fairly loose internal structure with low internal policy.

Preparation - Until 2010, TimeComp worked in a non-agile and non-iterative manner. The product planning and development processes were not officially structured. Development was performed ad hoc and little overview existed on the features that were currently requested, worked on, or implemented in the latest release. The development process was not formally structured. Functionality was built as it was made up, and new releases were delivered when enough improvements had been implemented.

Due to a sudden demand increase and rise in customer wishes, the old development approach of the company was not suitable any more. The management team and employees started to realize that a more reliable requirements management process and a more predictable release heartbeat were needed in order to stay competitive. This awareness was strengthened by the recognition of increased communication problems in the development department. There was little teamwork among the developers, and a great deal of expertise resided with specific employees.

The first suggestion to use Scrum in the company was opted by the former head of product development (now product manager). He explicitly pointed out these issues to the internal stakeholders, and introduced Scrum as a possible solution. The introduction of Scrum was accompanied by a change of management, change of organizational structure and an improved requirements management approach. It took more than a year before Scrum was actually picked up by some of the developers.

Implementation - Scrum was formally introduced in 2010. This introduction was performed within one single meeting with the management team and development employees together. The meeting was held in a Scrum-like fashion, i.e., everybody was standing and the presentation progress was captured with a burn-down chart. During this meeting, the Scrum method was explained briefly to the audience again. Before this meeting, the new product manager together with the managing director, created a first product backlog from a large list of customer wishes. During the meeting, user stories that would be implemented in the next sprint were chosen, story points were assigned and the tasks were divided. These actions initially took a lot of time and discussion. This especially applied to the estimation of story points; the developers were not used to predicting what time they would need to spend on a feature implementation.

All meetings prescribed by the Scrum methodology were included and planned for this new agile development method, and the first three-week sprint was started. The scrum team consisted only of the five developers, the role of Scrum Master was occupied by the development manager and the role of the Product Owner was occupied by the product manager. The Scrum process elements were followed as strictly as prescribed. To facilitate the Scrum process and to store user stories, a Scrum specific tool was employed.

Customization - During the initial period, the developers showed a lot of resistance towards Scrum. One effort to undermine the Scrum process was to cancel the daily Scrum meeting. However, once the product manager discovered this, it was quickly reinstated. Another example is the introduction of a refactoring sprint, which was mainly used as 'slack time' to perform miscellaneous tasks and bug fixes, instead of actual refactoring. This sprint type was also quickly cancelled. Instead, developers now have a 'delay-day' before the start of a new sprint, during which outstanding issues can be resolved that would otherwise disrupt the next sprint.

An important addition to the process has been the introduction of grooming sessions. At first, these grooming sessions strongly resembled the usual sprint meetings. The meetings were still very long, and many developers still did not understand the user stories after the explanations. After a while, these sessions were timeboxed to one hour and much more visualizations (e.g. adapted screenshots) were used to clarify user stories. Very complex user stories (which could not be cleared with one short meeting) were first attended in a work group.

4   Scrum Implementations Paths

The case companies show a high degree of variation in their specific implementation of Scrum, as well as the path that they have followed in order to reach that situation. The cases have shown that a Scrum implementation path is highly dependent on the context of the organization, including its internal culture and the implementation strategy, i.e. top-down or bottom-up. Although the case study research presented in this paper is not suitable for quantitative analysis regarding the relation between situational factors and implementation paths, we can make several important observations.

Table 1. Characteristics of the Scrum Implementation

Overarching process improvement framework	
ChatComp	None
FacilityComp	None
SocialComp	None, but part of a larger professionalization effort
TimeComp	None
Main drivers for the implementation of Scrum	
ChatComp	Increasing amount of requirements; Quickly growing development team
FacilityComp	Increasingly complex development setting
SocialComp	Unprofessional and unstructured product development process
TimeComp	Low development productivity; Unclear product definition process
Initiator for implementing Scrum	
ChatComp	Chief Technology Officer
FacilityComp	Chief Technology Officer
SocialComp	Development Manager
TimeComp	Development Manager / Product Manager
External advice	
ChatComp	Initial Scrum training
FacilityComp	Initial Scrum training
SocialComp	External advice after implementation
TimeComp	None

First of all, we observe that only one case company implemented Scrum as an explicit part of a larger process improvement strategy. In most cases, the drivers were similar to the advocated and well-known advantages of agile software development methods, such as quicker time-to-market, less process overhead, and scalability. However, opposite to what is often stated in literature, the implementation of Scrum was in all cases initiated by the management team instead of the developers. In one of these cases, at TimeComp, Scrum was actually forced onto the developers.

All managers responsible for the introduction of Scrum have indicated that the initiation period took a significant amount of time. A large share of this time was spent on familiarization with the method, either through available literature or with the help of an external advisor. This process was never steered using existing process improvement frameworks or knowledge databases, leaving room for improvement in the areas of process selection and knowledge acquisition.

Table 2 provides an overview of the paths that the case companies followed during the implementation of Scrum. The first column shows all basic elements of Scrum as described by Schwaber [20], in addition to the additional activities found throughout the cases. For each activity, the table indicates the implementation order. The arrows indicate where multiple elements were introduced at the same moment. Such collections of changes are named increments, which are defined as the collection of changes to a method between two points in time [29]. The bottom row summarizes the style of the process improvement effort.

Table 2. Increment Sequence of Scrum Elements

	Scrum elements	ChatComp	FacilityComp	SocialComp	TimeComp
Generic Scrum Elements	Product Backlog			Increment1	
	Fixed Teams				
	Sprint Backlog				
	Product Increments			↓	
	Sprints			Increment2	
	Sprint Planning Meeting			Increment3	
	Daily Scrum Meeting				
	Sprint Review Meeting			Increment4	
	Definition of Done				
	Retrospective Meeting	Increment1	Increment1	Increment5	Increment1
Additional Scrum Elements	Agile SPM	-	Increment2	-	-
	Requirements Refinery	-	Increment3	-	-
	Scrum of Scrums	Increment2	Increment4	-	-
	ScrumMaster Counsel	Increment3	-	-	-
	Kick-Off Week	Increment4	-	-	-
Improvement style		Disruptive & Incremental	Disruptive & Incremental	Incremental	Disruptive

We can see a clear distinction in the approaches that were taken to implement Scrum. In three of the case, the implementation path mostly resembles that of disruptive or revolutionary process improvement. In these cases, an initial training period was followed by a sudden switch to Scrum. At this time, a large, high-impact change to the development process is made, changing the way of working radically. Such a process improvement path has a high impact on the organization, and can cause considerable resistance among the employees, such as in the case of TimeComp.

In the case of SocialComp, we see a different approach. During the introduction of Scrum at this organization, a range of small process changes is made with some time in between, applying the Scrum constructs in an iterative manner. SocialComp has applied a more step-wise approach to move towards the desired process state. New activities and deliverables were introduced in small bundles, and refinements were constantly performed.

In all cases, the process is constantly being adjusted based on internal feedback. This constant change is an inherent aspect of Scrum, which advocates continuous improvement. Interesting in this regard is that such changes are not always an improvement. In the case of TimeComp, the removal of the daily Scrum meetings from the process was quickly reversed, once it became clear that this would jeopardize the quality and stability of the process.

Once a certain part of Scrum has been implemented, all organizations demonstrate a trial-and-error approach to reach the desired process state. These trials can consist of additional Scrum activities (shown in the bottom section of Table 2), or configurations of the already implemented process (e.g., changes in the team size or sprint duration). With disruptive improvement paths, the introduction of Scrum and the fine-tuning are two separate processes. With gradual implementation paths, a continuous improvement can be observed.

The four case indicate that the style of the process improvement path is highly dependent on the context of the organization, including amongst others its drivers, size, culture, and products. One approach to create a better insight into the drivers behind a specific process improvement effort and the possible issues related to certain process improvements, and to provide a direct link between specific goals, detailed process attributes, pre-conditions and post-conditions, is by describing process improvements in a structured manner. Ultimately, it facilitates knowledge sharing by standardizing the gathering of relevant process improvement information.

Table 3. Structured process improvement description for SocialComp

Name	Implement Scrum
Goal in context	# Improve the effectiveness of the development team
Scope	Development process
Primary and Secondary Stakeholders	# Head of product # Developers # Product manager
Trigger	The development organization resembles that of a 'startup' organization. Due to growth, there is a need to apply some structure to the internal processes.
Pre-Conditions	# Unstructured software development process
Post-Conditions	# Full initial implementation of Scrum

Increment Path	1. Assign Scrum roles
	  - *Driver: Get people involved*
	  - *Stakeholders: Head Of Product, product managers*
	2. Implement product backlog
	  - *Driver: Clarify the work to be done, improve uniformity of requirements, provide a way of work planning, improve communication*
	  - *Stakeholders: Head of Product, product managers*
	Further details omitted due to space limitations

Unordered Increments	# Increments not part of the sequence or executed during multiple steps. *None*
Failed Paths	# Steps that were undone afterwards. *None*

In order to provide the insight described above, we have partially described the implementation of Scrum at SocialComp using a structure called the *method increment case description* in Table 3. This structure has been proposed in an earlier paper, with the aim of providing a concise description of improvement paths that allow organizations to reflect on their implementation and to guide similar improvement efforts [25].

Sharing detailed experience related to process improvement in a structured manner such as demonstrated above can aid in the prevention of repeating mistakes in similar contexts. Method increment case descriptions can be used to either describe improvement paths at organizations that have already implemented a certain process, or to prescribe a process improvement path for an organization, taking into account its specific context and goals.

5 Discussion

In order to ensure the quality of our work, we have followed the guidelines that have been defined for performing multi-case study research [30,11]. Interviews were held with several people in order to cross-check documentation found and to confirm facts stated in other interviews. Concerning the ability to generalize the results, we cannot make quantitative statements about the general population based on the findings in this paper. Generalizability is partially ensured by the analysis of four separate cases. However, we expect that the qualitative results are applicable in other, similar situations.

A threat to the validity of the research is that not all case studies were performed by the same persons. However, the first author of this paper was present at each interview. In addition, a case study protocol has been written prior to the start of the case studies. This protocol has been used during each case. The findings of the case studies have been stored in a case study database [11].

6 Conclusions and Future Research

The multiple case study research presented in this paper shows distinct approaches for the implementation of Scrum. Three of the organization initially followed a disruptive path which, in one case, led to significant resistance from developers. In two of these cases, the basic Scrum process was extended with additional activities in an incremental manner, such as a Scrum of Scrums and a Kick-Off Week. The fourth organization followed a gradual implementation path for the entire introduction of Scrum.

On the scale of revolutionary versus evolutionary process improvement, the position of the cases varies considerably. In neither of the cases, we can speak of a completely 'big-bang' approach to the implementation of Scrum. In all cases, the process is implemented or altered in an iterative manner to some extent. In the case of TimeComp, the implementation can be classified as fairly disruptive. However, given the state of the development team at the time of implementation, this could not be avoided. Once the team had accepted Scrum as a new development process, it started improving it iteratively.

Situational factors have highly influenced the parameters of Scrum in all organizations. Based on organizational properties such as company policy and business unit size, the organizations have implemented different sprint lengths and Scrum activities, and have employed different implementation styles. However, the manner in which these choices were made was in most cases rather unstructured. The link between context and decision is rather unclear, and trial-and-error approaches often resulted in unwanted results and lost resources. Based on this observation, we think that further research into the relationship between situational factors and the 'parametrization' of methods would be very valuable.

In order to provide more insight into the change process, we have demonstrated how a structured approach can be used. Such structured process improvement descriptions aid in sharing knowledge related to the individual steps within a process improvement effort, using attributes such as stakeholders, drivers, and improvement steps. However, further research into evolutionary process improvement and more insight into the structure of improvement steps is required. This is in line with the statement that "incremental policies are anxiously required by the industry" [12]. Essential in this light is a better linking between situational factors, available knowledge, and process needs. A knowledge infrastructure for incremental process improvement is currently being developed [27].

References

1. Abrahamsson, P., Warsta, J., Siponen, M.T., Ronkainen, J.: New directions on agile methods: a comparative analysis. In: Proceedings of the International Conference on Software Engineering, pp. 244–254. IEEE (2003)
2. Beck, K.: Extreme programming explained: embrace change. Addison-Wesley Longman Publishing Co., Inc., Boston (1999)
3. Beck, K., Beedle, M., van Bennekum, A., Cockburn, A., Cunningham, W., Fowler, M., Grenning, J., Highsmith, J., Hunt, A., Jeffries, R., Kern, J., Marick, B., Martin, R.C., Mellor, S., Schwaber, K., Sutherland, J., Thomas, D.: Agile Manifesto (2001), http://www.agilemanifesto.org
4. Boehm, B., Turner, R.: Balancing agility and discipline: a guide for the perplexed. Pearson Education, Boston (2004)
5. Boehm, B., Turner, R.: Management Challenges to Implementing Agile Processes in Traditional Development Organizations. IEEE Software 22(5), 30–39 (2005)
6. Borjesson, A., Mathiassen, L.: Successful process implementation. IEEE Software 21(4), 36–44 (2004)
7. Cohn, M., Ford, D.: Introducing an Agile Process to an Organization. Computer 36(6), 74–78 (2003)
8. Dingsøyr, T., Hanssen, G.K., Dybå, T., Anker, G., Nygaard, J.O.: Developing Software with Scrum in a Small Cross-Organizational Project. In: Richardson, I., Runeson, P., Messnarz, R. (eds.) EuroSPI 2006. LNCS, vol. 4257, pp. 5–15. Springer, Heidelberg (2006)
9. Dyba, T., Dingsøyr, T.: Empirical studies of agile software development: A systematic review. Information and Software Technology 50(9-10), 833–859 (2008)
10. Fitzgerald, B., Hartnett, G., Conboy, K.: Customising agile methods to software practices at Intel Shannon. European Journal of Information Systems 15(2), 200–213 (2006)
11. Jansen, S., Brinkkemper, S.: Applied Multi-Case Research in a Mixed-Method Research Project: Customer Configuration Updating Improvement. In: Cater-Steel, A., Al-Hakimi, L. (eds.) Information Systems Research Methods, Epistemology, and Applications, pp. 120–139. IGI Global, Utrecht (2007)

12. Krzanik, L., Jouni, S.: Is my software process improvement suitable for incremental deployment? In: Proceedings of the International Workshop on Software Technology and Engineering Practice, London, UK, pp. 76–87 (2002)
13. Livermore, J.A.: Factors that Significantly Impact the Implementation of an Agile Software Development Methodology. Journal of Software 3(4), 31–36 (2008)
14. Moe, N.B., Aurum, A.: Understanding Decision-Making in Agile Software Development: A Case-study. In: Proceedings of the Conference on Software Engineering and Advanced Applications, pp. 216–223. IEEE (September 2008)
15. Nerur, S., Mahapatra, R., Mangalaraj, G.: Challenges of Migrating to Agile Methodologies. Communications of the ACM 48(2), 72–79 (2005)
16. Pettersson, F., Ivarsson, M., Gorschek, T., Ohman, P.: Packaging software process improvement issues: a method and a case study. Software Practice and Experience 34(14), 1311–1344 (2004)
17. Salo, O., Abrahamsson, P.: Agile methods in European embedded software development organisations: a survey on the actual use and usefulness of Extreme Programming and Scrum. IET Software 2(1), 58 (2008)
18. Salo, O.: Enabling Software Process Improvement in Agile Software Development Teams and Organisations. VTT Publications 618(618), p. 153 (2006)
19. Sawyer, P., Sommerville, I., Viller, S.: Requirements process improvement through the phased introduction of good practice. Software Process: Improvement and Practice 3(1), 19–34 (1997)
20. Schwaber, K.: Agile Project Management with Scrum. Microsoft Press, Redmond (2004)
21. Scotland, K., Boutin, A.: Integrating scrum with the process framework at yahoo! europe. In: Proceedings of the AGILE Conference. pp. 191–195. IEEE (2008)
22. Sidky, A.S.: A Structured Approach to Adopting Agile Practices: The Agile Adoption Framework (June 2007)
23. Smits, H., Pshigoda, G.: Implementing Scrum in a Distributed Software Development Organization. Management, 371–375 (2007)
24. Stapleton, J.: DSDM: Dynamic Systems Development Method. In: Proceedings of the Technology of Object-Oriented Languages and Systems, p. 406. IEEE Computer Society, Washington, DC (1999)
25. van Stijn, P., Vlaanderen, K., Brinkkemper, S., van de Weerd, I.: Documenting Evolutionary Process Improvements with Method Increment Case Descriptions (submitted for publication, 2012)
26. Vlaanderen, K., Jansen, S., Brinkkemper, S., Jaspers, E.: The Agile Requirements Refinery: Applying SCRUM Principles to Software Product Management. Information and Software Technology 53(1), 58–70 (2011)
27. Vlaanderen, K., van de Weerd, I., Brinkkemper, S.: Improving Software Product Management: a Knowledge Management Approach. International Journal of Business Information Systems (in print, 2012)
28. van de Weerd, I.: Advancing in software product management: An incremental method engineering approach. Ph.D. thesis, Utrecht University (2009)
29. van de Weerd, I., Brinkkemper, S., Versendaal, J.: Concepts for Incremental Method Evolution: Empirical Exploration and Validation in Requirements Management. In: Krogstie, J., Opdahl, A.L., Sindre, G. (eds.) CAiSE 2007 and WES 2007. LNCS, vol. 4495, pp. 469–484. Springer, Heidelberg (2007)
30. Yin, R.K.: Case Study Research - Design and Methods. SAGE Publications (2003)

Differences between Traditional
and Open Source Development Activities

John Wilmar Castro Llanos and Silvia Teresita Acuña Castillo

Departamento de Ingeniería Informática, Universidad Autónoma de Madrid
Calle Francisco Tomás y Valiente 11, 28049 Madrid, Spain
john.castro@estudiante.uam.es, silvia.acunna@uam.es

Abstract. The growing importance of open source software (OSS) has led researchers to study how OSS processes differ from traditional software engineering processes. The aim of this study is to determine the differences and similarities between development process activities (requirements, design, and implementation) enacted by the OSS community and established by IEEE Standard 1074:2006. We conducted a systematic mapping study to find out which activities are part of the OSS development process. We identified a total of 22 primary studies. Of these, 46% described activities related to the requirements process, just over 60% reported activities related to design and almost all accounted for activities related to implementation. The OSS community does not enact prescriptive software engineering models. OSS requirements are evolved using several different web artefacts, as well as through continual interactions in forums and via messaging. Requirements are asserted rather than elicited. A common feature of all OSS projects is that software system design and implementation is modular. The priority in the OSS community is implementation. Anyone, developers or users, can make contributions, including designs and code.

Keywords: Systematic Mapping Study, Software Development Process, Open Source, Requirements Engineering.

1 Introduction

The growing importance of OSS in recent years has led researchers to study how OSS processes differ from traditional software engineering processes. The context, structure and activities of software development processes applied in practice have not been and are not easy to understand [1].

Some studies have shown that many aspects of OSS project development processes differ [1], [2], [3]. Studies conducted by Scacchi on requirements engineering software processes enacted in OSS development projects across different domains (such as astrophysics, networked computer games and software design systems), for example, have found that there are generally no specified software requirements documents [4], [5], [6]. Yet, as reported by Mockus et al. [7], [8], examples of successful OSS systems abound. Therefore, although different from the standard model, the requirements

O. Dieste, A. Jedlitschka, and N. Juristo (Eds.): PROFES 2012, LNCS 7343, pp. 131–144, 2012.

engineering process would appear to work, as it results in internationally recognized quality products. Authors, like Fuggetta [9] and Godfrey and Tu [10], however, claim that this is not so. They suggest that the OSS development model is not really a new process description; it is just an alternative view of software engineering activities applied in traditional commercial development models.

Can the software development process enacted by the OSS community really be said to be different from the orthodox model established by IEEE Std. 1074 [11]? The aim of this paper is to determine the differences and similarities between the software development processes enacted by the OSS community and established by IEEE Std. 1074 [11]. We have compared the OSS development process with IEEE Std. 1074 [11]. IEEE Std. 1074 is our baseline process model, as it has a bearing on many development processes and is what we refer to here as traditional development. To do this, we first need to determine which activities are part of the development process enacted by the OSS community. We conducted a systematic mapping study (SMS) for this purpose. We then focused on activities that are part of the requirements, design and implementation processes, which, taken as a whole, make up the development activity group in the IEEE Std. 1074 [11].

This paper is organized as follows. Section 2 describes the research method. Section 3 discusses the match between the software development (requirements, design and implementation) process activities in the IEEE Std. 1074 and similar activities of the process enacted by the OSS community. These activities are compared in Section 4. Section 5 discusses the OSS requirements process. Finally, Section 6 outlines the conclusions.

2   Research Method

The research method applied in this paper is a SMS conducted to select the applicable primary studies [12]. The aim of the SMS is to answer the following research question.

RQ: What activities do OSS process models contain?

We started our mapping study by identifying keywords and search terms that we put together from the research question. We then ran a traditional search. This search returned some papers that were examined to determine the best search strings for the SMS. These search strings were Okayed and rounded out by two expert software engineering researchers. The search strings used were:

- OS-SPM: **O**pen **S**ource AND **S**oftware **P**rocess **M**odel
- OS-SDP: **O**pen **S**ource AND **S**oftware **D**evelopment **P**rocess
- OS-DP: **O**pen **S**ource AND **D**evelopment **P**rocess
- FS-SPM: **F**ree **S**ource AND **S**oftware **P**rocess **M**odel
- FS-SDP: **F**ree **S**ource AND **S**oftware **D**evelopment **P**rocess
- FS-DP: **F**ree **S**ource AND **D**evelopment **P**rocess

The electronic databases (DB) used in the mapping study were: IEEE Xplore, ACM Digital Library, SpringerLink, Science Direct and Scopus. We applied the six defined search strings to each of the selected DBs. We set 31 March 2010 as the publication deadline for the search. The inclusion and exclusion criteria that we used to determine which primary studies had a bearing on our research question were as follows.

Inclusion Criteria

- Paper title must contain the words open source or free source,
- Keywords refer to the open source software development process,
- Abstract alludes to open source software development process issues,
- Paper describes the open source software development process,
- Paper lists open source software development process activities,
- Paper lists free source software development process activities,
- Paper discusses the development process enacted in a particular open source software project,
- Paper presents an open source software development process proposal.

Exclusion Criteria

- Paper does not discuss the open source software development process,
- Paper does not present open source software development process activities,
- Paper does not present free source software development process activities.

Table 1 shows the number of articles located by applying the six search strings, as well as the number of selected candidate papers. The candidate papers are all studies that comply with the inclusion/exclusion criteria applied to the title and keywords only. Applying this strategy, we were able to quickly screen the search results by reducing the number of papers for thorough examination from 12,269 to 621 (just 5% of the total). This set of candidate papers does not contain duplicates.

Finally, we applied the inclusion and exclusion criteria scrupulously and selected 19 primary studies. We then inspected the references of these primary studies and located another eight studies that were not stored in any of the five DBs used. The total number of primary studies amounted to 27. Of these 27 primary studies, five were removed because the authors failed to define activities, which ruled out their analysis. Finally, we selected the 22 primary studies that are listed in Appendix A. Each primary study has an ID for reference purposes.

Table 1. Total number of articles located in each DB

Search Term	Retrieved	Candidates	Primary Studies
IEEE Xplore	387	89	7
ACM Digital Library	6.118	282	8
SpringerLink	2.459	147	3
Science Direct	199	21	0
Scopus	3104	80	1
Total	**12.267**	**619**	**19**

The SMS reported here includes only English papers, as all the search terms are defined in that language. This poses a potential threat to its validity. In this case, however, there is no risk of primary studies being biased or rejected as the results of the selection process were checked by an expert in the area.

3   Mapping OSS Process Activities to IEEE Std. 1074 and SWEBOK Activities

Of the activities identified within the OSS development process, we have mainly analysed activities related to requirements, design and implementation processes, as, taken as a whole, they make up the IEEE Std. 1074 development activities [11]. Of all the identified primary studies (22), about half (10) describe development processes with activities related to the requirements process, 64% include activities related to design and almost all the primary studies account for activities related to implementation.

As described above, the activities that are part of the development process enacted by the OSS community were elicited using a SMS. To do this, we analysed each primary study retrieved paying special attention to the sections describing the development process enacted by the OSS community. This analysis output the name (if any) and description of the activity given by each author. According to its description, each activity was matched to its equivalent IEEE Std. 1074 [11] activity according to what developers did in the activity. In the particular case of OSS requirements process activities, we split the IEEE Std. 1074 *"Define and Develop Software Requirements"* activity into SWEBOK [13] activities to facilitate mapping and make up for an IEEE Std. 1074 [11] deficiency.

At the end of this process, we built a table in which each OSS process activity related to the development activity group was matched with an IEEE Std. 1074 activity [11] or with a SWEBOK activity [13]. This is called the instantiation table and contains the name and author's description of the activity, as well as a comment. For reasons of space, Table 2 illustrates just a fragment of this instantiation table.

As Table 2 shows, there is a line through some of the activity names given by authors, as the name does not serve the purpose of the activity or mapping. There is also a line through fragments of the definition of some activities, because they either add nothing to the definition of the activity or simply define another activity, that is, the author has grouped more than one activity under the same name. The comments column is designed to help to identify such circumstances. This column specifies whether the activity in question has been mapped to another activity. We have drawn a line through the text inapplicable definitions because colour coding is not an option in black and white print.

Mapping was labour intensive, as the primary study authors did not always divide the description of the development process enacted by the OSS community into activities. Most gave a narrative description, which we had to divide for analysis and later mapping purposes. When authors did divide the process into activities, the activity names sometimes did not match the specified definitions. On this ground, we decided to match activities based on the activity description rather than the activity name. Moreover, some definitions listed under a single activity name had to be processed separately because the author was really defining more than one activity.

The problems encountered were typed as follows:

- **EN-EC**: Equivalent Name, Equivalent Content;
- **IN-EC**: Inequivalent Name, Equivalent Content;
- **UN-EC**: Unnamed Name, Equivalent Content;
- **NA:** New Activity (not equivalent to any traditional software engineering activity).

Table 2. Fragment of Instantiation Table

IEEE Std. 1074 – SWEBOK Activity Name	Activity as Named by Author	Activity as Defined by Author	Comment
Requirements Elicitation	1. Developer driven requirements [Simm03]	~~Since a lack of domain knowledge is frequently a problem in large software projects [5], one of the main sources of error is eliminated when domain experts write the code. Open source projects do not typically produce formal requirements specifications rather requirements are continuously changing and being debated in public via the use of Internet technology such as mailing lists.~~ As requirements are asserted rather than elicited, feature creep can be a problem, therefore once asserted requirements must be justified to the project leadership before being adopted.	Also listed in: - Requirements Specification
:	:	:	:
Requirements Specifications	1. ~~Developer driven Requirements~~ [Simm03]	Since a lack of domain knowledge is frequently a problem in large software projects [5], one of the main sources of error is eliminated when domain experts write the code. Open source projects do not typically produce formal requirements specifications rather requirements are continuously changing and being debated in public via the use of Internet technology such as mailing lists. ~~As requirements are asserted rather than elicited, feature creep can be a problem, therefore once asserted requirements must be justified to the project leadership before being adopted.~~	Also listed in: - Requirements Elicitation
:	:	:	:
:	:	:	:

We analysed the above instantiation table to determine whether each author named and described the activities suitably. As a result of this process, we built another table called analysis table. We built this table using the above four typologies. Table 3 illustrates a fragment of this analysis table. We used the same activities as in Table 2 to illustrate how the information evolves from table to table and depict the enacted process.

Table 3. Fragment of Analysis Table

IEEE Std. 1074 – SWEBOK Activity Name	Activity as Named by Author	Activity as Defined by Author	Typology
Requirements Elicitation	1. Developer-driven requirements [Simm03]	As requirements are asserted rather than elicited, feature creep can be a problem, therefore once asserted requirements must be justified to the project leadership before being adopted.	Equivalent name and equivalent content (Stage matches more than one SE stage activity)
:	:	:	:
Requirements Specifications	1. ~~Developer driven Requirements~~ [Simm03]	Formal requirements specifications rather requirements are continuously changing and being debated in public via the use of Internet technology such as mailing lists.	Inequivalent name, equivalent content (Stage matches more than one SE stage activity)
:	:	:	:
:	:	:	:

Table 4 shows how OSS development process activities match with IEEE Std. 1074 [11] development process activity groups. Each activity is assigned its respective type as explained above and the ID of the primary study referencing the activity. For reasons of space, Table 4 does not include the definitions given by each author.

Table 4. Mapping of IEEE Std. 1074/SWEBOK and OSS Process Activities

	IEEE Activity Name	OSS Activity Name	Typology	ID
SOFTWARE REQUIREMENTS	Requirements Elicitation	Marketing requirements	IN-EC	[Vixi99]
		Requirements	EN-EC	[Reis02]
		Requirement	EN-EC	[Seny04]
		Requirements	EN-EC	[Seny04]
		Developer driven requirements	EN-EC	[Simm03]
		Requirements are strongly user-driven	EN-EC	[John01]
		Requirements analysis and verification	IN-EC	[Ezea08]
		Requirements analysis and specification	IN-EC	[Scac04]
		Requirements	EN-EC	[Erdo09]
		Rough specifications	UN-EC	[Yama00]
	Requirements Analysis (Requir. Negotiation)	Marketing Requirements	IN-EC	[Vixi99]
		Requirements	IN-EC	[Reis02]
		Analysis	EN-EC	[Fitz06]
	Requirements Specifications	Developer driven requirements	IN-EC	[Simm03]
		Requirements are strongly user-driven	IN-EC	[John01]
		Requirements analysis and verification	IN-EC	[Ezea08]
		Requirements analysis and specification	EN-EC	[Scac04]
		TODO list	UN-EC	[Yama00]
	Prioritize and Integrate Software Requirements	TODO list	UN-EC	[Yama00]
DESIGN	Perform Architectural Design	System-level design	EN-EC	[Vixi99]
		Design	EN-EC	[Reis02]
		Good programmers know what to write	IN-EC	[Raym99]
		Identifying a solution	IN-EC	[Mock00]
		Design	EN-EC	[Seny04]
		Design and the importance of modularity	EN-EC	[Seny04]
		Design and the concept of modularity	EN-EC	[Schw03]
		Identify a solution	UN-EC	[Mock02]
		Initial design	EN-EC	[Simm03]
		Modular design	EN-EC	[Simm03]
		Development operates concurrently at many levels	IN-EC	[John01]
		Architectures are designed for modularity	EN-EC	[John01]
		Design, implementation and testing of new functionality	EN-EC	[Ezea08]
		Design	EN-EC	[Erdo09]
		Communication and documentation	IN-EC	[Mart07]
		Design	EN-EC	[Fitz06]
		Analysis and design	EN-EC	[Fitz06]
	Perform Detailed Design	Detailed design	EN-EC	[Vixi99]
		Design and the importance of modularity	EN-EC	[Seny04]
IMPLEMENTATION	Create Executable Code	Implementation	EN-EC	[Vixi99]
		Distributed development	EN-EC	[Reis02]
		Good programmers know what to write	EN-EC	[Raym99]
		Development and testing the code	EN-EC	[Mock00]
		Code	EN-EC	[Jorg01]
		Parallel debugging	EN-EC	[Jorg01]
		Implementation	EN-EC	[Seny04]
		Concurrent development	EN-EC	[Seny04]
		Parallel implementation and debugging	EN-EC	[Seny04]
		Introduction Phase	EN-EC	[Wynn04]
		Growth	EN-EC	[Wynn04]
		Development of an initial product	EN-EC	[Schw03]
		Assigning and performing development work	EN-EC	[Mock02]
		Prototype implementation	EN-EC	[Simm03]

Table 4. *(Continued)*

	IEEE Activity Name	OSS Activity Name	Typology	ID
IMPLEMENTATION –Cont'd–	Create Executable Code -Cont'd-	Iterative concurrent development	EN-EC	[Simm03]
		Prototyping is closed	EN-EC	[John01]
		Implement change	EN-EC	[John01]
		Development operates concurrently at many levels	EN-EC	[John01]
		~~Design,~~ implementation ~~and testing~~ of new functionality	EN-EC	[Ezea08]
		Build management	EN-EC	[Mart07]
		~~Assigning and~~ performing development work	EN-EC	[Dinh05]
		Phase I: Initial development	EN-EC	[Gurb06]
		Phase III: Establishing open source development project	EN-EC	[Gurb06]
		Debian Distributions	EN-EC	[Mong04]
		Implementation	EN-EC	[Yama00]
		~~Fixing bugs or~~ implementing the proposals	EN-EC	[Yama00]
		Make the code understandable by others	EN-EC	[Lell09]
		Planning	IN-EC	[Fitz06]
		Code	EN-EC	[Fitz06]
		Parallel debugging	EN-EC	[Fitz06]
		Writing your first patch	EN-EC	[Egan04]
	Create Operating Documentation	~~Design~~	IN-EC	[Reis02]
		~~Communication and~~ documentation	EN-EC	[Mart07]
	Manage Software Releases	~~Distributed development~~	IN-EC	[Reis02]
		Release early, release often	EN-EC	[Raym99]
		~~Development and testing the code~~	IN-EC	[Mock00]
		~~Iterative concurrent development~~	IN-EC	[Simm03]
		~~Development operates concurrently at many levels~~	IN-EC	[John01]
		~~Design, implementation and testing of new functionality~~	IN-EC	[Ezea08]
		~~Assigning and performing development work~~	IN-EC	[Dinh05]
		~~Debian Distributions~~	IN-EC	[Mong04]

Finally, we compared the IEEE Std. 1074 [11] (or SWEBOK [13]) definition with the author's definition according to the above mapping. This comparison shows up the differences and similarities of each activity described in the analysed primary studies. These differences and similarities are described in Section 4.

4   IEEE Std. 1074 and SWEBOK Process Activities vs. OSS Development Process Activities

In this section, we describe each of the activities involved in the development process enacted by the OSS community, which we compare with comparable activities in the traditional development process by means of the analysis procedure described in Section 3.

4.1   Requirements Process Activities

Table 5 illustrates just a fragment of the comparison of the requirements process activities. We also built tables comparing the design and implementation processes. The full comparisons of all the above processes are omitted for reasons of space.

Table 5. Fragment of the Comparison of IEEE Std. 1074/SWEBOK and OSS Process Requirements Activities

IEEE Std. 1074 – SWEBOK Activity Name	Activity as Named by Author	Traditional Process Activity and Activity Defined by Author	
		Differences	Similarities
Requirements Elicitation	1. Developer driven requirements [Simm03]	In the OSS community, requirements are asserted. According to SWEBOK, requirements are elicited.	The result is the same: requirements.
	⋮	⋮	⋮
Requirements Specifications	1. ~~Developer driven Requirements~~ [Simm03]	OSS projects do not usually have formalized requirements specifications, as requirements change continually and are discussed publicly. According to SWEBOK, there is a formalized requirements specification. Changes to specified requirements are an exception.	
⋮	⋮	⋮	⋮

In the OSS community, it is the users that request the functionalities or features that the software system should have; OSS users know exactly what they want. An OSS project is motivated by a specific requirement. In traditional software development, the software engineer has to follow a procedure to elicit requirements, for example, by interviewing project stakeholders. There is a controlled procedure for adding new requirements.

There is a procedure for determining the requirements that the software system must satisfy in both traditional software and OSS development, but requirements are asserted rather than elicited in the OSS community.

Requirements negotiation in the OSS community involves a large number of developers who are often system users, too. The participants in traditional software development analysis are clearly separate: software engineer/project stakeholders. Conflicting requirements are negotiated in both traditional software and OSS development.

In traditional software development process, the requirements specification is a deliverable required by contract. Once specified, changes are an exception. In most OSS projects, there are no contractual obligations and no formal requirements specification documents, save in the case of [Ezea08]. OSS community requirements are specified as narrative descriptions posted on message boards, emails and websites.

None of the primary studies analysed in this research included activities related to requirements validation. These findings suggest that the OSS community does not conduct validation in the manner of traditional software development.

Some OSS projects have to-do lists, and each task on the list has a priority and difficulty level. In traditional software development, these tasks are known as requirements. They are also assigned priorities.

4.2   Design Process Activities

Only two of the IEEE Std. 1074 [11] activity groups within the design process are present in the OSS community: perform architectural design and perform detailed design. As a general rule, software system architecture design in the OSS community is implicit and evolves over time [Vixi99]. In some OSS projects, design is based on a similar OSS software system [Raym99]. IEEE Std.1074 [11] establishes that the architecture design should be explicit and designed based on software requirements.

Clean or elegant design is not always a practice in OSS projects. Design is secondary, and implementation takes priority [John01]. For IEEE Std. 1074 [11], design is just as important as implementation.

Any developer or user in the OSS community can contribute to and participate in the discussion of designs via mailing lists [Seny04], [Mock02]. Developer preferences are decide what they choose to design. In traditional development, users do not participate in design, and developers have defined work allocations.

In the OSS community, detailed design does not come before coding; it is a by-product of the implementation which is reported in API documentation [Vixi99]. Developers discuss and test different alternative designs simultaneously. System users may also contribute designs [Seny04]. These detailed designs compete with each other. In IEEE Std. 1074 [11], detailed design is a specific activity performed before implementation [Vixi99].

Both in the OSS community and in traditional software development, the software system is designed modularly, defining components with a specific scope.

4.3   Implementation Process Activities

OSS community developer teams are distributed and developers do not have personal (face-to-face) contact with each others [Reis02]. Developers select the functionalities that they want to implement, according to their tastes, preferences and knowledge [Seny04]. In traditional development, development teams are centralized, and developers are allocated the functionalities that they are to implement previously by team managers.

In the OSS community, everyone has access to freely available code, and anyone, including users, can contribute code [Schw03], [Dinh05]. Code is debugged by people with more technical knowledge, that is, not all code contributors (including some users) are allowed to do this job [Seny04]. In traditional development, only developers are allowed write code, and this code is only available to development team members. Any developer is qualified to do this job.

In the OSS community, operational documentation is generally based not on detailed design but on source code [Reis02]. Documentation on how to operate the software is distributed via user lists, as user questions and answers [Mart07]. There are no structured documents. IEEE Std. 1074 [11] establishes structured documents specifying how to install and operate the system.

In OSS projects, minor version updates are released on a regular basis [Raym99], [Simm03]. Frequency is lower in traditional development, where versions are released according to a set schedule, which does not exist in the OSS community.

As established in IEEE Std. 1074 [11], developers of some OSS projects comply with a coding standard [Jorg01], create modular code and debug the created code [Seny04]. Different versions of the software are administered and correct versions of software items are compiled in both the OSS and conventional developer communities.

5   Discussion of the OSS Development Process

The traditional software development process starts by defining and specifying requirements. These requirements are vague; developers are unfamiliar with real needs and have to interview project stakeholders to elicit requirements. On the other hand, OSS development is launched for the purpose of satisfying clear requirements, as developers are well acquainted with their needs (well-defined need).

OSS software systems requirements are asserted, analysed, specified, negotiated and prioritized using a range of web-based artefacts. In OSS software systems development, requirements emerge from interactions between developer-users and the artefacts (discussion forums, emails, newsgroups) and software systems that they use-develop instead of requirements being elicited before the software system is in use.

There is no formalized requirements analysis in OSS projects, and they do not have conventional requirements documents. In their place, requirements are posted in e-mails, on message boards or emerge from discussions among users and developers about what the software should and should not do. These discussions take place in a web scenario.

OSS community developers are generally also the end users of the software systems that they develop (well-understood need). Thanks to this, there are fewer misunderstandings or communication gaps in this community. OSS developers are not under any contractual obligation to document software functionalities before they are implemented. In the traditional requirements process, either the need is not well defined or the need is not well understood, or both.

Modularity is an important concept in the OSS community, as it means that many people can work in parallel. As a general rule, no structured design documents are drafted. The only project in which design was documented was Mozilla, studied by [Reis02]. Users can help developers with designs, which they discuss to gather feedback.

The opportunity to write code is the main motivation for almost all the OSS development projects [vixi99]. The development effort focuses on package production. A package is the smallest unit that can be installed or removed from a software system [Mong04]. As many different types of people can contribute code, the OSS community has guidelines that describe the programming style and standards [seny04]. Version control tools are used in most OSS projects, except [Ezea08] because not many (only two) developers participated in the project.

6   Conclusions

This research reports a study of the requirements process enacted by the OSS community, compared with the process prescribed by traditional software requirements engineering. To find out which activities are part of the OSS requirements process, we have conducted a SMS. The aim of this SMS was to answer the research question, What activities do OSS process models contain? We located a total of 22 primary studies, of which about half included development processes with activities related to traditional requirements engineering. These primary studies were useful as a starting point for later analysing the OSS development process and proposing a process model enacted by this community.

Traditional software engineering assumes that the requirements can be elicited, analysed, specified and managed as centrally controlled resources by an administrative agency that has to meet contractual requirements. The OSS community does not adhere to software engineering prescriptive models and standards. OSS requirements evolve through a series of different web artefacts, online conversations, as well as interactions emerging continually in discussion forums and emails. There can be conflicting requirements, where negotiation is required to reach agreement. If no agreement is reached, the project is divided into separate forks. OSS projects are representative of an alternative paradigm to the one long defended by traditional software engineering and by the software requirements engineering community.

In general terms, the OSS community enacts a semi-formalized requirements process, composed of activities equivalent to traditional requirements engineering prescriptions, but developed differently. For example, requirements are recorded in discussion forums or emails rather than in a software requirements specification document or requirements are asserted instead of elicited.

A common factor in all OSS projects is the modularity with which software systems are designed and implemented, as this means that multiple programmers can work together to build new functionalities. Designs are discussed through mailing lists, and it is the developers that choose what they want to design or implement. The priority in the OSS community is implementation. Design is a secondary concern and is often a by-product of source code. In other cases, designs take a similar obsolete software system as the baseline.

Requirements Analysis, Requirements Specification, Perform Architectural Design and Manage Software Releases are the OSS development process activities reported in primary studies where the names and definitions referred by authors were least consistent. This suggests that there are contradictions with respect to each author's understanding of OSS process activity naming conventions. These contradictions have been removed by the systematic mapping procedure enacted in this paper.

Acknowledgments. This work has been funded by the Spanish Ministry of Science and Innovation *Tecnologías para la Replicación y Síntesis de Experimentos en IS* (TIN2011-23216) and *Go Lite* (TIN2011-24139), and by Community of Madrid R&D program *e-Madrid* project (S2009/TIC-1650).

References

1. Scacchi, W., Jensen, C., Noll, J., Elliott, M.: Multi-Modal Modeling of Open Source Software Requirements Processes. In: First International Conference on Open Source Systems, Genova, Italy, pp. 1–8 (2005)
2. Tian, Y.: Developing an Open Source Software Development Process Model Using Grounded Theory, Universidad of Nebraska – Lincoln, NB, USA, 143 p. (2006)

3. Potdar, V., Chang, E.: Open Source and Closed Source Software Development Methodologies. In: 26th International Conference on Software Engineering, pp. 105–109 (2004)
4. Scacchi, W.: Understanding the Requirements for Developing Open Source Software Systems. IEE Proceedings-Software 149(1), 24–39 (2002)
5. Scacchi, W.: Free and Open Source Software Development Practices in the Computer Game Community. IEEE Software 21(1), 59–67 (2004)
6. Scacchi, W.: Socio-Technical Interaction Networks in Free/Open Source Software Development Processes. In: Acuña, S.T., Juristo, N. (eds.) Software Process Modeling, pp. 1–27. Springer, New York (2005)
7. Mockus, A., Fielding, R.T., Herbsleb, J.: A Case Study of Open Source Software Development: The Apache Server. In: 22nd International Conference on Software Engineering, Limerck, Ireland, pp. 263–272 (2000)
8. Mockus, A., Fielding, R.T., Herbsleb, J.: Two Case Studies of Open Source Software Development: Apache and Mozilla. ACM Transactions on Software Engineering and Methodology 11(3), 309–346 (2002)
9. Fuggetta, A.: Open Source Software: An Evaluation. Journal of System and Software 66, 77–90 (2003)
10. Godfrey, M.V., Tu, Q.: Evolution in Open Source Software: A Case Study. In: International Conference Software Maintenance (ICSM 2000), San José, CA, pp. 131–142 (2000)
11. IEEE Std 1074:2006: IEEE Standard for Developing Software Life Cycle Processes. IEEE Computer Society (2006)
12. Petersen, K., Feldt, R., Mujtaba, S., Mattsson, M.: Systematic Mapping Studies in Software Engineering. In: 12th International Conference on Evaluation and Assessment in Software Engineering, pp. 71–80 (2008)
13. IEEE Computer Society Professional Practices Committee: Guide to the Software Engineering Body of Knowledge (SWEBOK, version 2004). IEEE Computer Society. Los Alamitos (2004)

Appendix A: Primary Studies

This appendix contains the references to primary studies identified by the SMS. Each primary study has been assigned an ID for reference purposes.

[Dinh05]: Dinh-Trong, T., Bieman, J.M.: The FreeBSD Project: A Replication Case Study of Open Source Development. IEEE Transactions on Software Engineering 31, 481--494 (2005)

[Egan04]: Egan, S.: The Open Source Development Process. In Open Source Messaging Application Development: Building and Extending Gaim, ch. 2, pp. 23--36. Apress (2004)

[Erdo09]: Erdogmus, H.: A Process That Is Not. IEEE Software 26(6), 4--7 (2009)

[Ezea08]: Ezeala, A., Kim, H., Moore, L.A.: Open Source Software Development: Expectations and Experience from a Small Development Project. In Proceedings of the 46th Annual Southeast Regional Conference on ACM-SE 2008, Auburn, AL, USA, pp. 243--246 (2008)

[Fitz06]: Fitzgerald, B.: The Transformation of Open Source Software. Forthcoming in MIS Quarterly 30(3), 1--26 (2006); Including subseries Lecture Notes in Artificial Intelligence and Lecture Notes in Bioinformatics - 3840 LNCS

[Gurb06]: Gurbani, V.K., Garvert, A., Herbsleb, J.D.: A Case Study of a Corporate Open Source Development Model. In: Proceedings of the 28th ACM International Conference on Software Engineering (ICSE 2006), pp. 472--481 (2006)

[John01]: Johnson, K.: A Descriptive Process Model for Open-Source Software Development. Master. Thesis in Computer Science. Department of Computer Science. University of Calgary, 156 p. (2001), http://sern.ucalgary.ca/students/theses/KimJohnson/thesis.htm

[Jorg01]: Jorgensen, N.: Putting It All in the Trunk: Incremental Software Development in the FreeBSD Open Source Project. Information Systems Journal. 11(4), 321--336 (2001)

[Lell09]: Lelli, F., Jazayeri, M.: Community Support for Software Development in Small Groups: The Initial Steps. In: Proceedings of the 2nd International Workshop on Social Software Engineering and Applications (SoSEA 2009), pp. 15--22 (2009)

[Mart07]: Martin, K., Hoffman, B.: An Open Source Approach to Developing Software in a Small Organization. IEEE Software 24, 46--53 (2007)

[Mock00]: Mockus, A., Fielding, R.T., Herbsleb, J.: A Case Study of Open Source Software Development: The Apache Server. In: Proceedings of the 22st International Conference on Software Engineering (ICSE 2000), Limerck, Ireland, pp. 263--272 (2000)

[Mock02]: Mockus, A., Fielding, R.T., Herbsleb, J.: Two Case Studies of Open Source Software Development: Apache and Mozilla. ACM Transactions on Software Engineering and Methodology 11(3), 309--346 (2002)

[Mong04]: Monga, M.: From Bazaar to Kibbutz: How Freedom Deals with Coherence in the Debian Project. In: Proceedings of the 4th Workshop on Open Source Software Engineering Engineering – 26th International Conference on Softtware Engineering (ICSE 2004), pp. 71--75 (2004)

[Raym99]: Raymond, E.S.: The Cathedral and the Bazaar. In: Cathedral and the Bazaar: Musing on Linux and Open Source by an Accidental Revolutionary, pp. 19--64. O'Really, Sebastapol (1999)

[Reis02]: Reis, C.R., Mattos Fortes, R.P.: An Overview of the Software Engineering Process and Tools in Mozilla Project. In: Proceedings of the Workshop on OSS Development, Newcastle Upon Tyne, UK, pp. 162--182 (2002), http://opensource.mit.edu/papers/reismozilla.pdf

[Scac04]: Scacchi, W.: Free and Open Source Development Practices in the Game Community. IEEE Software 21(1), 59--66 (2004)

[Schw03]: Schweik, C.M., Semenov, A.: The Institutional Design of Open Source Programming: Implications for Addressing Complex Public Policy and Management Problems. Revista First Monday 8(1) (2003), http://firstmonday.org/issues/issue8_1/schweik/index.html

[Seny04]: Senyard, A., Michlmayr, M.: How to Have a Successful Free Software Project. In: Proceedings of the 11th Asia-Pacific Software Engineering Conference (APSEC 2004), pp. 84--91. IEEE Computer Society, Busan (2004)

[Simm03]: Simmons, G.L., Dillon, T.: Open Source Development and Agile Methods. In: Proceedings of the 7th IASTED International Conference Software Engineering and Applications, Marina del Rey, CA, USA, pp. 523--527 (2003)

[Vixi99]: Vixie, P.: Software Engineering. In: de DiBona, C., Ockman, S., Stone, M. (eds.) Open Sources: Voices from the Open Source Revolution, ch. 6, 1st edn., pp. 91--100. O'Reilly Press: Sebastopol, CA (1999)

[Wynn04]: Wynn Jr., D.E.: Organizational Structure of Open Source Projects: A Life Cycle Approach. In: Proceedings of the 7th Annual Conference of the Southern Association for Information Systems, Georgia, pp. 285--290 (2004)

[Yama00]: Yamauchi, Y., Yokozawa, M., Shinohara, T., Ishida, T.: Collaboration with Lean Media: How Open-Source Software Succeeds. In: Proceedings of the ACM Conference on Computer Supported Cooperative Work (CSCW 2000), pp. 329--338 (2000)

Analyzing the Drivers of the Combination of Lean and Agile in Software Development Companies

Pilar Rodríguez[1], Jouni Markkula[1], Markku Oivo[1], and Juan Garbajosa[2]

[1] University of Oulu, Department of Information Processing Sciences,
P.O. Box 3000, 90014 University of Oulu, Finland
{Pilar.Rodriguez,Jouni.Markkula,Markku.Oivo}@oulu.fi
[2] Technical University of Madrid (UPM) SYST Research Group E.U. Informática
Ctra. Valencia Km. 7. E-28031 Madrid
jgs@eui.upm.es

Abstract. Agile software development has been widely accepted by the software industry as a means for improving flexibility and innovation capabilities. More recently, lean thinking has emerged as a new paradigm to make software development more efficient. In practice, quite often lean is seen as an evolution of agile when agile is not considered to be *enough*. However, how they can relate to each other is not clearly understood. This paper presents the results of a survey study conducted among 408 software practitioners of 200 software intensive companies in Finland, which is one of the early adopters of lean for software development. The results highlight the interest of software professionals in adopting a combination of agile and lean paradigms, to achieve both flexibility and economical efficiency. Unlike manufacturing, the transformation is being actually conducted as a single trip where the borders between agile and lean are not clearly defined.

Keywords: Agile software development, agile manufacturing, lean software development, lean thinking, agility, leanness.

1 Introduction

Methodologies labelled as *agile* appeared as a way to provide flexibility to software development processes over a decade ago [1]. Nowadays, the trend towards agile is a fact in software development [2]. More recently, and mainly motivated by the advent of the agile community, the lean paradigm has been highlighted as an alternative to make the software development processes more efficient. Based on fundamental industrial engineering principles, lean is steeped in a philosophy of maximizing value and minimizing waste [3]. In practice, in the field of software development, lean is often seen as a continuation of agile when agile is not considered sufficient [4]. However, differently from other software engineering topics conceived in the academia and then transferred to the industry, agile and lean are mainly growing up directly in the industry. As a consequence, existing theories on this research topic are scarce [5] and the meaning of agile and lean in a software context and the differences between both paradigms are not clearly understood yet [6].

O. Dieste, A. Jedlitschka, and N. Juristo (Eds.): PROFES 2012, LNCS 7343, pp. 145–159, 2012.
© Springer-Verlag Berlin Heidelberg 2012

To improve our understanding and provide first-hand industrial insight on how agile and lean are being understood in the real-world industry, a web-based survey study was conducted among 408 software development practitioners belonging to 200 companies of the software intensive industry in Finland. The goal of the survey was to identify the adoption level of agile and lean in the Finnish software industry as well as the companies' goals driving towards processes based on these paradigms. Since the Finnish software industry can be considered as one of the early adopters of agile and lean methods for software development, Finnish companies represent a suitable population for the study [7]. Moreover, the results are especially relevant if it is considered that Finland takes up the second position in the *IT Industry Competitiveness Index 2011* of the BSA/Economist's report [8].

The results of the survey show the interest of software professionals towards combining agile and lean. It is remarkable that agile is not thought of as just "*another disposable method tried before*", but it is deliberately maintained when moving towards lean. Regarding the goals on adopting agile and lean in software development, the paper presents a comparison between companies following a combination of agile and lean methods and companies following only agile or only lean. The results indicate that software development companies usually use a combination of agile and lean to achieve the best from both paradigms, i.e. flexibility and economical efficiency.

One of our concerns was the characterization of agile and lean and their relationship. Both agile and lean principles are essential part of the corresponding body of theory. However, agile and lean have followed different paths for software development. Agile was characterized in the Agile Manifesto [1]; lean emerged in a manufacturing context [3] and its initiation has suffered multiple adaptations, being often over simplified as a search for value removing waste. We felt the need to go back to the sources of lean to analyze the goals in adopting lean for software development since the original lean thinking. Supported by the results of the survey and considering the differences between software and manufacturing disciplines, the possibility of using a combination of agile and lean paradigms at the same time in the same space in software domain, considered as not viable in manufacturing [9], is pointed out in this paper. A clear understanding of the requests/constrains of the organization business environment is seen fundamental to be able to develop the agile/lean combination that best meets the organizational needs in terms of flexibility and economical efficiency.

The rest of the paper is organized as follows: Section 2 reviews the relevant literature on agile and lean. Section 3 defines the research design. Section 4 presents the results of the study and in section 5 these results are discussed. Finally, section 6 concludes the paper and espouses the limitations of the study as well as future research.

2   Overview of Agile and Lean Paradigms

This section provides an overview of agile and lean paradigms, analyzing how they have been consolidated in manufacturing with regard to software development. Although previous adaptations of lean principles to software domain are valuable contributions, we consider the original works from lean manufacturing, taking into account also space and time dimensions, may provide new insights in Lean Software Development.

2.1   Agile and Agile Software Development

Although the problem of how to successfully deal with changing environments has been studied for a few decades, agile appeared in manufacturing at the beginning of the 1990s as a solution to satisfy fluctuating demand, in terms of both volume and variety [9]. However, just a few years ago, there was not seen to be a commonly accepted definition of agility in manufacturing [10].

In software development, the term *agile* was coined in 2001 when the *Agile Manifesto* was formulated [1]. Abrahamsson et al. defined agile method as the method used *"when software development is incremental (small software releases, with rapid cycles), cooperative (customer and developers working constantly together with close communication), straightforward (the method itself is easy to learn, to modify, and well documented), and adaptive (able to make last moment changes)"* [11]. Under the umbrella of Agile Software Development (ASD), there is a group of methods such as eXtreme Programming [12], Scrum [13] and Feature-Driven Development [14]. Even when agility is also a confusing and multi-faceted concept in software development [15], the Agile Manifesto has been generally accepted as a body of theory [1].

Despite the different ways of defining agile [15, 16, 17], there seems to be an agreement that speed and flexibility to adapt and take advantage of business changes are the primary attributes of agile [10, 15]. It is remarkable that, while agile in manufacturing emphasize flexibility and speed in both capabilities to adapt changes in volume (close related to agile workforce) and variety, agile in software development mainly refers to flexibility and speed to adapt to changing requirements (variety). This is quite understandable since the entire product creation process fabricates a single copy of the software product that can be easily replicated.

2.2   Lean and Lean Software Development

Lean is the English name that western researchers (from the Massachusetts Institute of Technology, MIT) used to describe the system of organization created by Toyota in Japan. Lean is a management philosophy focused on providing maximum customer value through an end-to-end focus on delivering to customer needs, efficient work streams, empowered teams and continuous improvement initiatives [3]. Five principles constitute its backbone: value, value stream, flow, pull and perfection [18]. *Value* is everything for which a customer is willing to pay. Understanding value from the customer perspective is the central focus of lean. *Waste*, defined as everything that absorbs resources but outputs no value, is also an important concept of lean. Lean seeks the complete elimination of waste in all aspects of production.

Lean paradigm has revolutionized manufacturing worldwide in companies from diverse industries, such as 3M, Boeing Corporation, Zara, and General Electric [19]. In software development, the discussion about lean started as early as the 1990s [20] well before the *Agile Manifesto* was formulated. While the progress toward Lean Software Development (LSD) has been mainly driven by industry pioneers, there is a growing body of literature not only documenting case studies such as [21], but also investigating specific elements of lean, e.g., flow [22, 23]. Currently, universal application of lean principles to knowledge work such as software development is under debate [24]. A widely acknowledged adaptation of lean principles with respect to software was proposed by Poppendieck and Poppendieck [25] including: eliminate waste, amplify learning, decide as late as possible, deliver as fast as possible, empower the team, build in integrity and see the whole.

2.3   "Agile or Lean" or "Agile and Lean"?

Business needs, especially in the software development industry, demand to operate at high levels of customer responsiveness. Moreover, keeping cost efficiency is also important. Consequently, ways in which hybrid agile/lean approaches can be taken into practice have received attention for a long time, even when, as philosophies, lean and agile have different origins and some intertwined ideas [9]. As stated above, while agile focuses more on flexibility and the capacity to rapidly embrace change, lean focuses on overall economic contribution. Marso-Jones et al.' matrix [26], shows graphically how whilst in agile it is highly desirable to have low cost, it is not essential if it puts the capability to respond quickly to changes at risk (see Fig. 1).

Fig. 1. Market Winners-Market Qualifiers Matrix for Agile vs. Lean[1]. Source: [26]

Although Marson-Jones et al.'s matrix designates cost as the market winner of lean, it is important to remember that lean is not just about reducing costs, as it is occasionally misinterpreted, but it is more about providing value to the customer in a way that every company activity does contribute valuably to the ultimate customer.

It is commonly argued that a combination of agile and lean might work well in operational terms as lean capabilities can contribute to agile performance [27]. In manufacturing, there is a tendency to suggest that although agile and lean can be combined,

---

[1] Market winners refer to those attributes that dominate the paradigm as the prime requirement. Market qualifiers point to those attributes that although are highly desirable are not strictly requested. The matrix emphasizes those attributes that must be excelled as market winners and be highly competitive as market qualifiers.

they cannot be employed at the same time in the same space. The main reason is that it is not possible to deal with the unstable demand, that characterizes environments where agile is used, in a levelled schedule as requested by lean [9]. Thus, although the combination, labelled as *"le-agility"*, is recognized in a manufacturing context, lean and agile can coexist in manufacturing only in separate processes, different products or using de-coupling strategies [16].

The combination of agile and lean has been interpreted in the field of software development without considering space or time restrictions. This is demonstrated by the fact that, in software development, lean thinking was one of the inspiring sources of the Agile Manifesto [28]. Furthermore, in the context of Information Systems and Software Engineering, Conboy [15] has defined agility as *"the continual readiness of an Information System Development to rapidly or inherently create change, proactively or reactively embrace change, and learn from change while contributing to perceived customer value (economy, quality, and simplicity), through its collective components and relationships with its environment"*. This definition roots in the concepts of flexibility and leanness, considering therefore leanness as an underlying notion of agility. Poppendieck [29] considers lean thinking as a *"platform upon which to build agile software development practices"*, so lean could work as a platform for scaling agile. Coplien and Bjornwig [30] argue that although agile and lean have fundamental differences, yet they complement each other by addressing different "components" of systems development. Consequently, software development is interpreting the combination of agile and lean in a different way than in manufacturing.

3   Study Design

In this study, based on a descriptive web survey research [31] and considering the discussion in section 2, we focus our attention on two research questions: 1) What is the level of using lean, agile or a combination of both methods in the software development industry? 2) What are the reasons why agile, lean or a combination of both methods are being adopted in some software development organizations?

Many organizations in Finland are showing interest in adopting lean, emerging major initiatives such as the Lean Software Enterprise initiative inside Cloud Software Program [7]. Therefore, Finnish software intensive industry can be considered as one of the early adopters of lean in software development, constituting a suitable study population. The membership registry of *The Finnish Information Processing Association* (FIPA), which is a major Finnish organization that has 16 000 professionals and more than 500 companies as members, was used as a sampling frame [32]. For the survey sample, FIPA provided the e-mail addresses of a subset of 4950 professionals whose background was relevant to software development [31]. This can be considered as a very large and representative sample of the population of software professionals and companies in Finland. After piloting the questionnaire for checking its consistency and legibility, it was e-mailed to individual software practitioners. The name of the company was collected allowing the analysis of the results also at company level. A total of 408 responses from 200 companies were collected (response rate was 8,2%).

The background information of the sample is shown in the following tables. Table 1 presents the positions of the respondents in their organization, Table 2 the size of the organizations and Table 3 the respondents' experiences in software development.

Table 1. Positions in organization

Position	n	Position	n
Developer	113	Scrum master	33
Project manager	99	Process manager	31
IT staff	79	Product owner	25
Architect	63	Product manager	23
Consultant/Trainer	52	President/VP/CEO/COO/CIO/CTO	22
Quality assurance/Tester	38	Sales/Marketing personnel	10
Operations/Support staff	35	Other	48

Table 2. Size of the organizations

Employees	n	%
1-10	34	8,3
11-50	38	9,3
51-250	50	12,3
251-1000	95	23,3
1001-10 000	97	23,8
More than 10 000	89	21,8
Missing information	5	1,2
Total	408	100,0

Table 3. Experience in software development

Years of experience	n	%
More than 20	55	13,5
10-20	144	35,3
5-10	80	19,6
2-5	56	13,7
Less than 2	31	7,6
None	42	10,3
Total	408	100,0

The roles of the respondents were mainly developers (n=113) and project managers (n=99). Most of the organizations were big (45%, more than 1000 employees) and middle size (45%, number of employees between 10-1000). Respondents were mainly very experienced in software development (48%, more than 10 years of experience).

4   Results

The survey previously introduced was a wide explorative survey, including almost fifty questions. In this paper, in order to answer the research questions presented earlier, we focused only on two sets of questions of the survey. The first set is related to the level of agile and/or lean methods adoption and the second set to goals in adopting agile and/or lean methods. The results are presented in the following subsections.

4.1   Level of Agile and Lean Adoption in the Finnish Software Industry

The level of adoption of agile and/or lean methods was studied using three variables. The first variable is Agile and/or Lean usage, which has four categories (*Only Agile, Agile and Lean, Only Lean, No Agile or Lean*). The two other variables are Agile methods usage time and Lean methods usage time, which have five categories (*Less than 1 year, 1-2 years, 2-5 years, 5-10 years, More than 10 years*).

Of the 408 responses, agile and/or lean methods usage was reported by 58% (n=236) of the respondents and the rest (42%, n=172) are applying neither agile nor lean methods. Further analyses were carried out within the first group, i.e. agile and/or lean methods users group. From this group, 58% (n=137) were using only agile methods, 37% (n=88) both agile and lean methods and 5% (n=11) only lean. Among the agile and/or lean methods users, in general, agile methods have been used mostly 2-5 years (Median=Mode="2-5 years") and lean methods 1-2 years (Median=Mode="1-2 years"). According to the data, 51% (n=115) have been using agile more than two years, in comparison to 25% (n=27) of lean usage more than two years. The distribution of both methods usage time, separated by single and joint methods usage groups, is presented in Fig. 2.

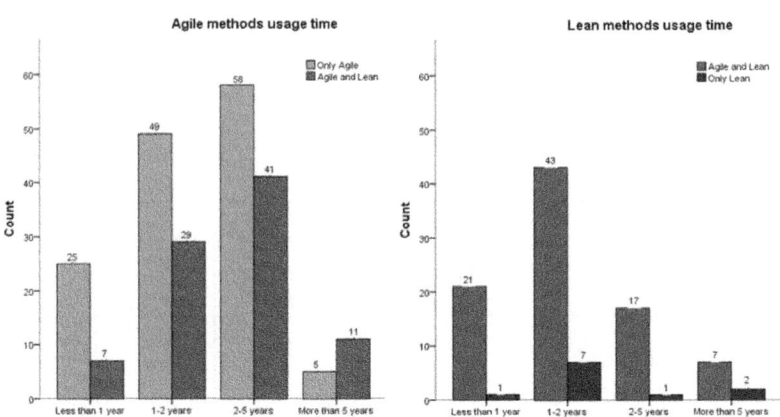

Fig. 2. Time of using agile and lean methods in the organizations

Based on the analysis, the average usage time is longer in agile methods than in lean methods, i.e. agile has been adopted usually earlier than lean. When considering the order of adoption, in Agile and Lean adopters (n=88) exactly half has been using agile and lean the same time (50%, n=44), and the reported usage time is different in the other half of the cases. From the later group, only 2 respondents (2% of all Agile and Lean adopters) report having been using lean longer time than agile. The rest

(47% of all Agile and Lean adopters) have been using agile longer time than lean. This shows clearly that lean methods have been in almost always adopted later than agile methods, if they have not been adopted around the same time.

4.2   Companies' Goals Driving towards the Adoption of Agile and/or Lean Methods

Goals in adopting agile and/or lean methods were studied based on goal importance variables. The importance of different goals was measured in the survey by asking the respondents which of the specified goals were their organizational unit's goals when adopting agile and/or lean methods. Respondents were requested to indicate all of the valid goals from a given list of eighteen goals, and there was also an option to indicate other goals.

In the first phase of the analysis, we wanted to identify those goals of which importance is varying depending on the adopted methods (variable *Agile and/or Lean usage*). For this purpose, we analyzed the association of the goal importance and method adoption with Chi Square test of independence. For the following analysis, we chose those goals that had a statistically significant association ($p<.05$) with the method adoption group. This leads us to seven goals, which are presented in Table 4 below. In the table, the order of importance of the goals is presented for the agile and/or lean methods usage groups. The goals are ordered according the importance priority in agile and lean group. The numbers indicate the priority of the goals, combined within the percentage of the respondents identifying it as a goal when adopting agile and/or lean methods. The Chi Square test of independence results in the table present Cramer's V value as a measure of association between the goal and methods adoption group, and p the statistical significance of the association.

Table 4. Importance of goals in adopting agile and/or lean

Goal	Importance priority			χ^2 Test of Independence	
	Only Agile (n=137)	Agile and Lean (n=88)	Only Lean (n=11)	Cramer's V	p
To reduce development cycle times and time-to-market	1 54 %	1 69 %	5 18 %	,232	,002
To improve process quality	2 39 %	2 59 %	1 73 %	,224	,003
To remove waste and excess activities	3 20 %	3 48 %	3 45 %	,287	,000
To improve organizational learning	5 12 %	4 27 %	4 45 %	,240	,001
To improve our understanding of the whole value stream	6 8 %	5 22 %	7 9 %	,193	,012
To improve the management of business/product value	4 12 %	6 22 %	2 55 %	,241	,001
To achieve success others have achieved using lean methods	7 6 %	7 19 %	6 18 %	,207	,006

The variation of importance of the goals by the three different methods adoption groups are presented below in two figures. The figures show the percentage of respondents in each group who indicated the goal as their unit's goal in adopting agile and/or lean methods. Fig. 3 shows those goals that appear to be more important in adopting lean and less important in adopting agile. *Agile and Lean's* users goal importance in this goal group appears to be between *Only Agile* and *Only Lean* adopters' group. The rest of the goals are presented in Fig. 4. Those goals appear to be most valued in the *Agile and Lean* group, and less important in *Only Agile* and *Only Lean* groups.

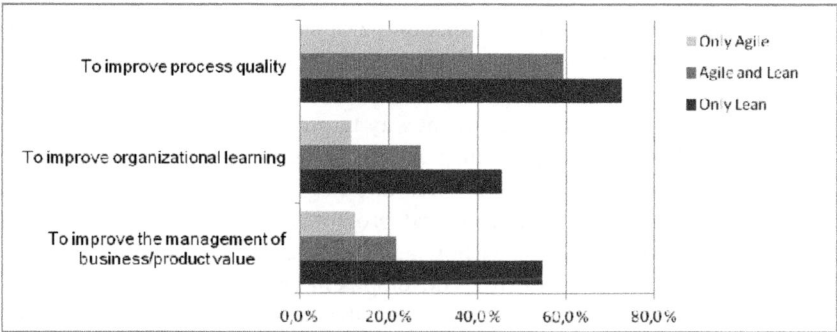

Fig. 3. Importance of goals by methods adoption groups – most important for lean

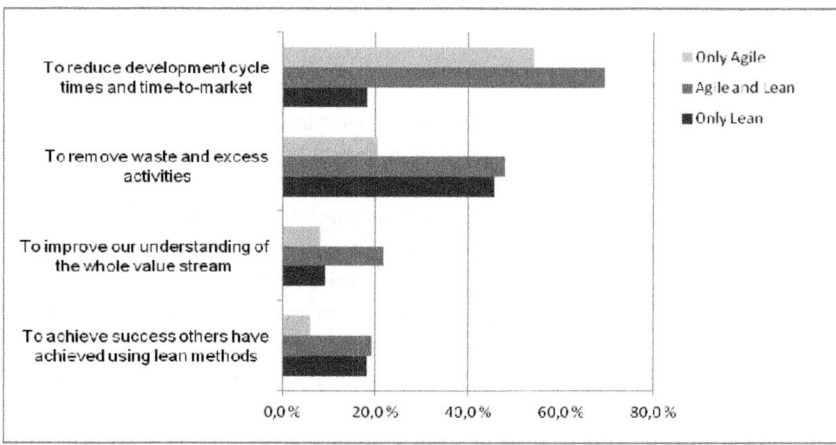

Fig. 4. Importance of goals by methods adoption groups – most important for agile and lean

5   Discussion of the Results

This section discusses the results of the study in the light of how agile and lean paradigms have been applied in manufacturing, where these concepts are more mature.

5.1   Agile and Lean Origins

The results of the survey confirm the interest of software development organizations using agile and lean methodologies. Majority, 58% of respondents reported that they were following either agile or lean in isolation, or a combination of agile and lean. Although the use of agile in isolation was the most popular approach (58% of agile and/or lean methods users), a tendency towards developing software in a combination of agile and lean is also emerging (37% of agile and/or lean methods users).

One interesting difference appears in the chronological order in which agile and lean have been adopted in manufacturing and software. We think the chronological order may be impacting the perceptions of the market winners and market qualifiers when adopting lean in manufacturing and software. The survey results show that lean adoption is following agile in software development (see Fig. 2). In manufacturing, lean production emerged years before agile methods appeared. First manufacturing industry adopted lean paradigm as a more efficient way to produce large quantities of products. After that, when lean was already in place, manufacturers realized that they needed more flexibility in their production process to satisfy the fluctuating demand that characterized their business environment, and promoted Agile manufacturing [33]. The different adoption order may impact how agile and lean methods have been viewed in both domains. In fact, while software development emphasizes on operating with the leanest agile system, manufacturing focus on the most responsive lean system. This can also explain to some extent the stronger focus on reducing costs when combining agile and lean paradigms in manufacturing as opposed to a stronger focus on flexibility in the case of the software development industry (see Sections 5.2 and 5.3).

5.2   Combining Agile and Lean Methods in Software Development

There is emerging a trend towards adopting a combination of agile and lean. Based on the data, using lean in isolation is quite uncommon (only 5% of users of agile and/or lean reported to be using only lean, compared to 37% that are using both agile and lean). It can be also seen that agile is not abandoned when lean is adopted.

Literature on how to apply lean paradigm in software development suggests that, although with some fundamental differences, agile and lean can be combined complementing each other and achieving therefore an improved paradigm [15, 29, 30]. Thus, authors in the field commonly propose integrated processes for an agile/lean combination. A clear example representing this approach is the use of kanban systems by agile teams [34].

This alternative of combining agile and lean paradigms in the same products at the same time has been considered invalid in manufacturing according with the theory of *le-agility* [16]. The reasoning behind that assertion is justified by the levelled schedule that lean requests. It is argued that lean manufacturing avoids the requirement of flexibility by calling for a stable demand and forward planning [9]. In consequence, it is unfeasible to use both paradigms in integrated processes. According to Towill and Christopher [16], the alternatives for adopting a combination of agile and lean paradigms in manufacturing are limited to:

1. *Same times, different space*: To use both paradigms in separate processes by using agile and lean for delivery in different value streams. This strategy is used when it does not make business sense to pull all the products through an agile channel.
2. *Same space, different times*: To use both paradigms in the same product but at different points of the time, where agile and lean are seasonally separated.
3. *Different space, different times*: To use both paradigms at different points of the value stream using de-coupling strategies [9].

Due to the singular characteristics of software development, a fourth alternative could be discerned in a software context:

4. *Same space, same time*: To use a mixing of agile and lean techniques in the same product at the same time.

Although this alternative has been claimed to be invalid in manufacturing, it is seen as the approach that software companies are currently choosing for carrying out the combination in a real world. It is a long known fact that software production is very different compared to manufacturing physical goods. Software production is basically a design process that ends up in a product that can be very easily replicated. Flexibility requirement is not coming from the production volume but from changing customer needs. Consequently, a smooth demand or levelled schedule is not impacted by a variable demand in terms of volume, which according to Naylor [9] could lead to waste either in not producing near capacity or keeping larger buffer stocks.

These particularities of software product and development processes compared with manufacturing open new possibilities to combine agile and lean methods in ways that has not been considered previously. Although, as discussed in the next subsection, agility and flexibility can be associated with higher costs, they are needed in some business environments to provide what customers really want. If software development looks for operating with the leanest agile system, this fourth alternative could be suitable.

5.3 Goals of Software Development Companies Driving towards Combined Agile and Lean

Goals for adopting agile and lean methodologies in isolation or combination are presented in Table 4. Overall, the goals of the organizations of those respondents adopting either agile or a combination of agile and lean paradigms are quite similar. Only the position of *"To improve organizational learning"*, *"To improve the understanding of the whole value stream"* and *"To improve the management of business/product value"* are slightly alternated. However, they differ considerably from the goals of those applying only lean. Again, this result could be interpreted as a trend of transforming the processes from basic agile software development principles towards complementing them with lean principles following similar purposes.

"To reduce development cycle time and time to market" is the main goal of both respondents using only agile and respondents using an agile and lean combination. The unpredictability that characterize the software industry have forced organizations

developing software to look for mechanisms that provide more flexibility, reduce development cycles times and enable to adapt to the real customer demand. While leanness may be an element of agility in certain circumstances, it will not enable the organization to be agile [27]. Therefore, software organizations deliberately maintain agile when transforming towards lean. As depicted in Fig. 4, to reduce development cycle times and time-to market is not a main goal for those organizations adopting only lean methods. On the other hand, "*To improve process quality*" is shared as an important goal for all of them, users of only agile, agile and lean, and only lean.

It is significant that the goal "*To remove waste and excess activities*" had similar importance in organizations using a combination of agile and lean methods and in those applying only lean (see Fig. 4). As argued by some authors on manufacturing, agile could endanger the target of complete elimination of waste in all aspect of production. In this line, van Hoek [27] affirms that if lean refocuses around responsiveness, it might sacrifice its foundations in efficiency. He goes so far as to say "*If lean thinking is the relevant approach in the operational environment of a company, it can better focus around that solely and not mess up its underlying principles by adding different dimensions* [such as flexibility]*, given that the concept centre around effective waste elimination*". Our position is that while waste is an important concept of lean, the first principle of lean stresses the concept of value. Lean is not just about reducing cost but it is about providing customer value in an economically efficient way. In a dynamic business environment, as is the case of software development, to have adaptation capabilities is needed for providing real customer value. The time spent in developing a product that finally will not meet the real customer demand is a clear source of waste from a lean perspective.

Therefore, the issue is not lean or agile; rather it is the judicious selection and integration of appropriate aspects of both paradigms appertaining to the particular company strategy [16]. For example, if the business environment of the software company is turbulent, higher levels of flexibility will be needed to provide what the customers really want. As a result, higher costs will be needed such as costs on creating flexible architectures or costs coming from refactoring [35, 36]. As lean realizes, waste exists in even the best processes. Further, lean separates waste with a two-type classification: waste originates from activities that do not provide value, but are necessary to be performed, and waste arises from activities that create no value and are avoidable. The second type of waste has to be immediately eliminated. The cost associated with providing flexibility can be considered as a type of the first waste. While they don't provide direct customer value, due to the business environment, they are needed to provide what the customer really wants more quickly.

Therefore, the organization needs to understand the requirements and constraints of its business environment and balance the cost associated with the use of techniques that provide flexibility with the value that the flexibility is going to provide to its customers. However, according to the results of the survey, it is not fully clear whether software companies are paying attention to these issues when deciding their agile and/or lean transformation, since "*To achieve success others have achieved using lean methods*" appears also as a goal guiding the transformation (see Fig. 4).

Finally, *"To improve organizational learning"* and *"To improve the understanding of the whole value stream"* seem also to be important goals for transforming software companies according to agile and lean paradigms.

6   Conclusions, Limitations of the Study and Future Work

This paper presents the results of a web based survey study conducted among 408 software development practitioners belonging to 200 companies of the software intensive industry in Finland. Given the reported performance of Finnish IT industry (e.g. second highest productivity in the world according to *The Economist Intelligence Unit* [8]), the conclusions can have interest and applicability to most of the existing software development communities. Two main goals drive the research: i) adoption level of agile and/or lean in software developing companies, and ii) companies' goals driving towards agile and lean processes. Three main results are highlighted in the study:

1. The interest of professional in developing software in a combination of agile and lean approaches, where agile is not abandoned when lean is adopted.
2. The possibility of combining agile and lean in an integrated way in software development. This approach has been considered unviable in manufacturing so far. However in software development, agile and lean methods seem to be combined and integrated in the same processes (same products at the same time). The particularities of software development compared to manufacturing may open new possibilities for using lean in different ways than those known in manufacturing.
3. The importance of a careful selection and integration of appropriate aspects of both paradigms appertaining to the particular organization strategy, in terms of flexibility and economical efficiency.

The results of the survey provide a good preliminary and evidence based analysis of agile and lean methods adoption in Finland. However, some limitations should be taken into account when considering the results: i) The survey was conducted mainly as an exploratory descriptive study of the current state of agile and lean adoption in software intensive companies. It has certain limitations in its usage for company level analysis such as the varying role of the respondents from one company to another. This can affect the perspectives that the respondents may have of the companies, ii) in the survey, the importance of the goals was not differentiated when adopting agile and lean methods in combination (which goals are driving lean and which are driving agile), iii) in addition, it should be noted that even if the number of observations is relatively high, more than four hundred respondents, there is still some groups of analysis that have rather limited number of observations, e.g. the only lean adopters including eleven respondents.

As future work, a study focussed on specific roles in the company (transformation responsible, software development departments heads, software developers/engineers with specific roles such as testers or architects, and so on) would help to get a deeper understanding of the picture. Second, it would be interesting to clarify the influence of the interaction of the customer with the team; in manufacturing this interaction has clearly different objectives. A third issue could be to get a better understanding of how innovation is perceived and could be introduced systematically in the software development lean context, similarly as it happens in manufacturing quality circles.

Acknowledgements. This article is based on the work carried out in the ICT SHOK Cloud Software program financed by the Finnish Funding Agency for Technology and Innovation (Tekes) and Tivit OY. The graduate school on Software Systems and Engineering (SoSE) funded by the Ministry of Education in Finland and by the Academy of Finland, and the Spanish Ministry of Science and Innovation under the project INNOSEP TIN2009-13849 have also partially supported the work. We are especially grateful to FIPA (Tietotekniinan Liitto) for kindly helping us to distribute the survey to their members.

References

1. Beck, K., Beedle, M., van Bennekum, A., Cockburn, A., Cunningham, W., Fowler, M., Grenning, J., Highsmith, J., Hunt, A., Jeffries, R., Kern, J., Marick, B., Martin, R.C., Mellor, S., Schwaber, K., Sutherland, J., Thomas, D.: Manifesto for Agile Software Development (2001), http://www.agilemanifesto.org/
2. West, D., Grant, T.: Agile Development: Mainstream Adoption Has Changed Agility. Trends in Real-World Adoption of Agile Methods. Forrester Research (2010)
3. Womack, J.P., Jones, D.T., Roos, D.: The Machine that Changed the World: The Story of Lean Production. HarperPerennial, New York (1990)
4. Vilkki, K.: When Agile Is Not Enough. In: Abrahamsson, P., Oza, N. (eds.) LESS 2010. LNBIP, vol. 65, pp. 44–47. Springer, Heidelberg (2010)
5. Dyba, T., Dingsøyr, T.: Empirical Studies of Agile Software Development: A Systematic Review. Inf. Softw. Technol. 50, 9–10 (2008)
6. Wang, X., Conboy, K.: Comparing Apples with Oranges? Perspectives of a Lean Online Community on the Differences between Agile and Lean. In: Thirty Second International Conference on Information Systems, Shanghai (2011)
7. Cloud SW Research Project (2010-2013), http://www.cloudsoftwareprogram.org/
8. Business Software Alliance: Investment for the Future Benchmarking IT Industry Competitiveness Report (2011)
9. Naylor, B.J., Naim, M.M., Berry, D.: Leagility: Integrating the Lean and Agile Manufacturing Paradigms in the Total Supply Chain. Int. J. Production Economics 62, 107–118 (1999)
10. Sherehiy, B., Karwowski, W., Layer, J.K.: A Review of Enterprise Agility: Concepts, Frameworks, and Attributes. International Journal of Industrial Ergonomics 37(5), 445–460 (2007)
11. Abrahamsson, P., Salo, O., Ronkainen, J., Warsta, J.: Agile software development methods: review and analysis, VTT Technical report (2002)
12. Beck, K., Andres, C.: Extreme Programming Explained: Embrace Change, 2nd edn. Addison-Wesley, Boston (2004)
13. Cohn, M.: Succeeding with Agile: Software Development Using Scrum, 1st edn. Addison-Wesley Professional (2009)

14. Palmer, S.R., Felsing, J.M.: A Practical Guide to Feature-Driven Development. Prentice Hall PTR (February 2002)
15. Conboy, K.: Agility from First Principles: Reconstructing the Concept of Agility in Information Systems Development. Infor. Systems Research 20(3), 329–354 (2009)
16. Towill, D., Christopher, M.: The Supply Chain Strategy Conundrum: To Be Lean or Agile or To Be Lean and Agile? International Journal of Logistics Research and Applications: A Leading Journal of Supply Chain Management 5(3), 299–309 (2002)
17. Sharafi, H., Zhang, Z.: A method for achieving agility in manufacturing organisations: An introduction. Internat. J. Production Econom. 62, 7–22 (1999)
18. Womack, J.P., Jones, D.: Lean thinking. Simon and Schuster, New York (1996)
19. Ransom, C.: Don't Give Up On Good Industrial (Lean) Companies; Take Advantage of The Long-Term Up-Cycle. Manufacturing News 14(13), July 17 (2007)
20. Freeman, P.: Lean Concepts in Software Engineering. In: IPSS-Europe International Conference on Lean Software Development, Stuttgart, Germany, pp.1–8 (1992)
21. Mehta, M., Anderson, D., Raffo, D.: Providing Value to Customers in Software Development Through Lean Principles. Software Process Improvement and Practice 13(1), 101–109 (2008)
22. Mandić, V., Oivo, M., Rodríguez, P., Kuvaja, P., Kaikkonen, H., Turhan, B.: What Is Flowing in Lean Software Development? In: Abrahamsson, P., Oza, N. (eds.) LESS 2010. LNBIP, vol. 65, pp. 72–84. Springer, Heidelberg (2010)
23. Petersen, K., Wohlin, C.: Measuring the Flow in Lean Software Development. Software: Practice and Experience 41(9), 975–996 (2011)
24. Staats, B., Brunner, D., Upton, D.: Lean Principles, Learning, and Knowledge Work: Evidence from a Software Services Provider. Journal of Operations Management 29(5), 376–390 (2011)
25. Poppendieck, M., Poppendieck, T.: Implementing Lean Software Development: From Concept to Cash. Addison-Wesley, cop., Upper Saddle River (2007)
26. Mason-Jones, R., Naylor, J.B., Towill, D.: Engineering the Leagile Supply Chain. International Journal of Agile Management Systems 2(1), 54–61 (2000)
27. van Hoek, R.I.: The Thesis of Leagility Revisited. International Journal of Agile Management Systems 2(3), 196–201 (2000)
28. Highsmith, J.: Agile Software Development Ecosystems. Addison-Wesley, Boston (2002)
29. Poppendieck, M.: Principles of Lean Thinking (2002), http://www.leanessays.com/2002/11/principles-of-lean-thinking.html (last accessed January, 30, 2012)
30. Coplien, J., Bjornwig, G.: Lean Architecture for Agile Software Development. John Wiley & Sons Ltd., West Sussex (2010)
31. Turula, K.: Ketterien menetelmien ja Lean-menetelmän käyttö Suomessa. Master thesis, University of Oulu (November 2011) (in English: Agile and Lean Adoption in Finland)
32. The Finnish Information Processing Association (FIPA), Tietotekniinan Liitto, http://www.ttlry.fi/english
33. Booth, R.: Agile Manufacturing. Engineering Management Journal 6(2), 105–112 (1996)
34. Kniberg, K.: Kanban and Scrum – Making the Most of Both (2010), http://Lulu.com
35. Erdogmus, H.: Architecture Meets Agility. IEEE Softw. 26(5), 2–4 (2009)
36. Pérez, J., Díaz, J., Garbajosa, J., Alarcón, P.P.: Flexible *Working Architectures*: Agile Architecting using PPCs. In: Babar, M.A., Gorton, I. (eds.) ECSA 2010. LNCS, vol. 6285, pp. 102–117. Springer, Heidelberg (2010)

Fostering and Sustaining Innovation
in a Fast Growing Agile Company

Nils Brede Moe[1], Sebastian Barney[2,3], Aybüke Aurum[2], Mahvish Khurum[3],
Claes Wohlin[3], Hamish T. Barney[2], Tony Gorschek[3], and Martha Winata[2]

[1] SINTEF ICT, NO-7465 Trondheim, Norway
nilsm@sintef.no
[2] Information Systems, Technology and Management,
UNSW, Sydney NSW 2052, Australia
{s.barney,aybuke}@unsw.edu.au, hamish@hbarney.com,
m.winata@unswalumni.com
[3] Blekinge Institute of Technology, 37179 Karlskrona, Sweden
{mahvish.khurum,claes.wohlin,tony.gorschek}@bth.se

Abstract. Sustaining innovation in a fast growing software development company is difficult. As organisations grow, peoples' focus often changes from the big picture of the product being developed to the specific role they fill. This paper presents two complementary approaches that were successfully used to support continued developer-driven innovation in a rapidly growing Australian agile software development company. The method "FedEx™ Day" gives developers one day to showcase a proof of concept they believe should be part of the product, while the method "20% Time" allows more ambitious projects to be undertaken. Given the right setting and management support, the two approaches can support and improve bottom-up innovation in organizations.

Keywords: agile software development, innovation, scrum, XP, FedEx Day, 20% Time, empirical, case study.

1 Introduction

For a company to be successful it needs to promote innovation [19]. An innovation is the implementation of a new or significantly improved product (goods or service), or process, a new marketing method, or a new organisational method in business practices, workplace organisation or external relations [31]. Innovation is something that comes naturally for a start-up, but becomes harder as a company grows. Managers have identified insufficient innovation as a crucial problem, however, successfully implementing good innovation management practices is difficult [17]. Start-up software companies are creative by nature and their success heavily depends on executive managers, who are responsible for developing and implementing the company's technical strategy [9]. In a start-up, it is crucial to create and stimulate a culture where developers are encouraged to participate in all aspects of development and are allowed to have significant influence over the their work [9]. Innovation may also occur when knowledge from different areas is combined, and shouldering multiple roles

O. Dieste, A. Jedlitschka, and N. Juristo (Eds.): PROFES 2012, LNCS 7343, pp. 160–174, 2012.

forces developers to become accustomed to formerly unfamiliar areas. Everyone working on the product must internalize the company's strategy and work to realize the goals for the product and the goals for the company as a whole. In addition, the effect an individual developer can have on the bottom line is much more substantial in a start-up, and developers often have a personal stake in the company.

Growth makes enabling and managing innovation harder [17]. This creates a problem for companies as they make the transition from start-up to a larger company with entrenched products and processes. Implementing innovative products and processes often becomes more challenging. One of the challenges that hinders innovation as a company grows is greater specialization, as employees move from cross-functional positions where innovation can be spurred by the diverse responsibilities and information, into more traditional job roles where responsibilities and information are typically narrower. While specialization confers many advantages, it often comes at the cost of innovation capacity originally afforded by the multifunctional work performed by the handful of 'all-doers'. Specialization in-the-best-of-cases allows people to focus on what they do best, but it can also result in a loss of the broader vision of what made the start-up successful to begin with. The concept of developing visually impressive features and providing support by fixing problems on the fly is transformed into turning requirements obtained from someone else into code. The understanding of the overall purpose of the product, as well as customer proximity is greatly diminished.

Motivated by the challenge of maintaining a capability to undertake innovation while growing, our research question has been: *How can a former software start-up maintain innovation capability while growing its workforce?*

To investigate this research question we conducted a case study at Atlassian. Atlassian, facing this challenge of growth, has taken steps to ensure that developer initiated innovation remains one of the foundations of the organization.

The main contribution of this paper is an empirical investigation of two complementary approaches Atlassian has used to empower its developers to innovate, called *FedEx™ Day* and *20% Time* respectively. This paper also contributes to the literature of innovation and agile development. While many of the agile methods explicitly state that facilitating innovation is a key motivation underpinning the emergence and use of agile approaches, rigorous research evaluating innovation in an agile context is lacking [1, 40].

The remainder of this paper is organized as follows. Section 2 gives an overview of the research on innovation. Section 3 defines and describes the case study. Section 4 describes our findings. Finally, our discussion and conclusions are presented in Sections 5 and 6 respectively.

2   Innovation in Software Development

2.1   The Concept of Innovation

Innovation is a synonym for change [7]. To create an environment that supports innovation, we must understand what innovation is and how it arises. Innovation is commonly categorized into four types [31]:

- **Product innovation:** the development of new products and new features that significantly improve an existing product.
- **Process innovation:** new or significantly improved changes to working processes.
- **Market innovation:** significant changes to product design or packaging, product placement, product promotion or pricing through new marketing methods.
- **Organization innovation:** (or business model innovation) encompasses changes to the company's business practices, workplace organization or external relations.

Each of the above four types of innovation can be further categorized into one of four levels of innovation impact [16, 20]:

- **Incremental innovations:** relatively minor changes in technology normally based on an existing platform. The innovation delivers relatively low value to customer benefits.
- **Really new (Market breakthroughs):** based on core technology that is similar to existing products, but that provide substantially higher customer benefits per dollar.
- **Really new (Technological breakthroughs):** substantially different technology than existing products, but do not provide superior customer benefits per dollar.
- **Radical innovations:** or disruptive innovations, which introduce first time features or exceptional performance using substantially different technology at a cost that transforms existing markets or creates new markets and delivers novel utility.

The process for innovation involves searching for and selecting ideas, implementing them and learning from the innovation process. Literature identifies several drivers or determinants of innovation within an organisation (see Section 2.2).

Software product innovation is differentiated from other product innovation, with relatively low start-up costs and short lead-time. It is possible to write, compile and test code all in one day, and the only resource consumed is time. Physical products, however, may require machining, molding, prototypes and by their nature will consume physical resources to test and produce.

Creating an environment that fosters innovation and creativity requires employees to feel motivated, capitalizing on their interests, and enabling satisfaction through the challenge of the work [6].

In addition to motivational factors, management needs to provide time and space for innovation to occur [6]. Google™ does this most visibly through their *20% Time* program. This has lead to many product innovations, including Gmail®, Google News®, Orkut®, and AdSense®. However, Google™ provides little information on how *20% Time* has been operationalized. A similar strategy was adopted much earlier at 3M™, where the "15-percent rule" gives technical staff six hours per week on projects of their own choosing. This strategy led to ScotchTape® and Post-it Notes®.

Innovation management and practices are implicit and a part of every-day-work in start-ups, which are, almost by definition, doing something new. As organizations grow, enabling and managing innovation becomes harder [17], and risk increases as dedicated resources have to be spent on new ideas in parallel with maintaining the incremental development of the present offering.

2.2   Internal Determinants of Innovation

The authors undertook a review of the literature to identify internal determinants of innovation. A snowball sampling strategy was used to identify the relevant literature. A summary of the findings is presented in Table 1 and reflected upon in Section 4. The list of determinants given below is not exhaustive as the purpose of the review was to find determinants in literature that illustrate and support the relevance of innovation related activities at Atlassian.

Table 1. Internal innovation determinants

Determinants of Innovation		Reference
1. Organization Culture	1.1 Risk taking culture	Aiman-Smith et al. [2]
	1.2 Entrepreneurial culture	Sjoerd et al. [34]
	1.3 Creative stimulants	Fagan [13]
	1.4 Open Communication	Aiman-Smith et al. [2]
	1.5 Incentive provision	Fitzgerald et al. [14]
	1.6 Encouragement of initiatives	Kivimaki et al. [25]
	1.7 Supportive climate	Jong et al. [24]
2. Empowerment	2.1 Job challenge	Jong et al. [24]
	2.2 Agile decision making	Aiman-Smith et al. [2]
	2.3 Autonomy	Jong et al. [24]
	2.4 Meaningful tasks	Aiman-Smith et al. [2]
3. Customer-related	3.1 Customer acceptance	Dunphy et al. [10]
	3.2 Customer orientation	Aiman-Smith et al. [2]
	3.3 Recognizing user need	Voss [17, 37]
4. Inter Collaboration	4.1 Multifunctional teams	Gebauer et al. [18]
	4.2 Technology transfer	Love et al. [27]
	4.3 Team work quality	Hoegl et al. [22]
	4.4 Interaction of human and social capital	Subramaniam et al. [35]
	4.5 Inter-functional coordination	Akman et al. [3]
5. Trust	5.1 Trust to be heard	Clegg et al. [8]
	5.2 Belief to have an impact	Clegg et al. [8]
	5.3 Openness	Prather [32]
6. Knowledge management	6.1 Knowledge sharing	Zhu et al. [39]
	6.2 Organizational learning abilities	Aiman-Smith et al. [2]
	6.3 Organizational capital	Antonio et al. [5]
	6.4 Variety of knowledge sources	Amara et al. [4]
	6.5 Knowledge diffusion	Tseng [36]
	6.6 Training and education of staff	Gebauer et al. [18]
	6.7 Idea generation	Koc [26]
7. Champions	7.1 Innovation catalyst	Freeman et al. [15]

3   Research Method

We choose a case study to investigate our research question: How can a former software start-up maintain innovation capability while growing its workforce?.

3.1   Study Context

Atlassian Software Systems is an agile company selling software to support software development. It began its operations in 2002 in Sydney, Australia and has since opened offices in San Francisco, Gdansk, Kuala Lumpur, Porto Alegre and Amsterdam.

Atlassian sells products aimed at facilitating collaboration and supporting software development. Products include: issue tracking software, enterprise wiki and collaboration software, online source code review and source code repository management. The software developed by Atlassian is also used internally, which means that the developers are also users of the software.

Atlassian has recently started making a push to transform itself from a more traditional software company to a software-as-a-service company. To this end, Atlassian has been focusing resources on making sure that its existing and new products are delivered as services. Its product sales figure was AU$35.5 million for 2008 with more than 12,000 customers in 104 countries.

Since its inception the company has used a combination of XP and Scrum (for an overview of agile methods see e.g. [12] and [11]), and has undergone rapid growth; approximately doubling the number of staff in each year of its ten year existence. By 2010 Atlassian had more than 275 employees.

Atlassian is an open company with important company details being available to all employees. Internal and external wikis and blogs are used heavily and these often host lively discussions about the company. As one of the managers commented, *"everything gets documented on the [intranet], everyone has buy in and everyone has a say in everything so that's why it's such a cool place to work"*.

The founders of the company were responsible for the initial development of some of Atlassian's products. They still play a role in software development and are well known within the company for quickly developing prototypes of new features. When interviewed, the head of engineering commented on this practice: *"Yes, especially [one of the founders]. But he's prototyping, he'll be: I can't tell you what I want, so let me code it real quick, then I'll show you, that's [one of the founders]. Yeah it's scary."*

The attitude displayed by the founders towards prototyping has translated itself throughout the company to a preference for action rather than just words or ideas. One of the core company values is for individuals within the company to be proactive, not just to *have* ideas but to *do* something about them. A tech lead discussed this aspect of Atlassian's culture: *"it's just ideas and I have ideas and I want other people to see my ideas, our company isn't as big on it. It's basically do it. Don't just tell me about some great dashboard, show me a prototype, do something, make it happen in the product or something."*

3.2   Data Sources and Analysis

We relied mainly on semi-structured interviews as these provide a rich picture of the internal workings of the company in general and the specifics of the *FedEx™ Day* and *20% Time*, the development practice under investigation. In total 17 employees were interviewed: 2 executives and 15 team members, tech leads, and team leads from three product teams. Each of the semi-structured interviews took approximately one hour. All interviews were recorded and transcribed. The interview schedule and questionnaire are available online (http://sebseb.info/publications/profes2012/). The results have been presented to the management at Atlassian. Author number six, who worked at Atlassian for over five years, helped ensure that our findings were consistent with his experience as a software developer at the company.

To be able to address a broader range of historical and behavioral issues [38], we used multiple sources of evidence. In addition to interviews, we conducted a small survey on the use of *FedEx™ Day* and *20% Time* and we collected data from Atlassian's internal and external websites, which host information and discussions about Atlassian's development practices and the company's structure and culture. These sites are updated frequently and all employees are encouraged to participate in these forums. Data were then categorized and coded. Observations were also made in-situ by attending meetings and observing the operation of *FedEx Day* and *20% Time*.

By combining the data from interviews with the information from the websites, we were able to develop a converging line of inquiry [38] and form a rich and accurate picture of the company in general and the practice of FedEx Day and 20% Time in particular. Our main analysis technique was to combine pattern-matching logic with explanation building [38]. That is, we compared empirically based patterns with the patterns predicted by the theory, while at the same time building an explanation of the case. This strategy also helped us to strengthen the internal validity of the case study.

4   FedEx Day and 20% Time at Atlassian

4.1   Task Allocation at Atlassian

The way tasks are allocated normally at Atlassian is crucial to understanding *FedEx Day*, *20% Time* and their effects. Each team has a product backlog that is updated regularly based on *releases*. A release includes major feature improvements that can be marketed and distributed to all customers. Features in the release backlog are divided into sprints and each sprint produces a point release – a smaller product release. At the beginning of each sprint, the list of features is presented to the developers.

Identifying and allocating tasks/features affects how specialised developers become since this defines what the developer will do. This is done differently in the various teams at Atlassian. We found that in some teams there were limited possibilities for individuals to choose the tasks they wanted, because there was little redundancy in the teams. One developer said: "*A lot of the time it is based on whoever can do the tasks because we've got all very different skill sets*". One team leader said: "*People do volunteer, but there's never a surprise on what they volunteered for.*" Another said: "*we don't share what everyone's working on and how it works. That's why if someone gets sick, it can take longer time to pick up the stuff after them*"

Another team leader, responsible for 15 developers in 4 sub-teams, said: "*We found with XP, the whole approach of not doing a lot of planning up front gives us a lot of trouble ... a lot of people get frustrated because the release takes longer than the original plan*". This team leader pre-planned the sprint with management and with some input from developers. Then, during the Scrum planning meeting, the team leader assigns tasks to developers.

The introduction of story cards into one of the development teams was seen as a reason for developers not being able to focus on innovation. Story cards are a standard XP practice. Requirements are broken up into short user stories, which are written on small cards. A developer is assigned (or chooses) one or more story cards to work on. Estimated and actual time spent is also tracked on the story card. In this team, story cards were assigned to developers in the fortnightly planning meetings or by the team leader. While story cards were selected and prioritised by the whole team during their planning meetings, many developers commented on the feeling that, with their time being tracked, they no longer had the freedom to experiment and play with new features.

The developers are encouraged to suggest features that should be in the product backlog. However, resource limitations led upper management to reduce the number of features the teams could develop for a release, since resources are allocated according to the revenue generated. In terms of prioritising the features, a developer explained how he influenced the direction of the product: "*[The CEOs] do kind of get a higher priority when we're making our decisions. But in the end it's really the developers and our product manager that decide what goes in and what goes out and have full control over what we do*". Only a few developers reported having this kind of influence on the product, mostly those in the smaller teams.

4.2   FedEx™ Day

Like express couriers, each *FedEx™ Day* gives developers at Atlassian one day to deliver a software product improvement of their choice (Table 1: 1.6, 2.4). The rotating *coordinator* starts organizing the next *FedEx™ Day* several weeks in advance. It is held "during a calm time," three-to-four times per year, to help ensure that most developers will be able to participate.

Most developers at Atlassian know in advance what they want to do on *FedEx™ Day*, but there is support for those who are unsure. A couple of weeks prior to the *FedEx™ Day*, the coordinator organises a series of voluntary lunchtime meetings to discuss possible options. Developers attend not only to seek inspiration, but also to share and discuss ideas.

As *FedEx™ Day* approaches the developers write *delivery orders*, detailing what they hope to achieve on the day. Other employees write comments on these orders, offering hints, tips and ideas. This collaboration occurs between different teams, products and roles (Table 1: 4.5, 6.1, 6.2).

FedEx™ Day itself has been described as a "*rush of adrenaline*," providing a sense of exhilaration. Developers said that the pace within the organization changes considerably: "*You don't write unit test. You just blast out the feature, hack it out however you want because it doesn't matter*." One team leader estimated that "*people get about three days of work done in just that one day, it's amazing*."

All the projects are presented at the end of the day (Table 1: 6.1, 6.7). The participants vote to select a winner. Experienced *FedEx™ Day* developers know that the presentation makes or breaks the project. As a result, they always set time aside to make their presentation, even if it means presenting incomplete functionality. The winner receives a trophy and, more importantly bragging rights.

4.3   Experiences with FedEx™ Day

Experience has shown that *FedEx™ Day* projects generally deliver product innovations, and provide incremental innovations and technological breakthroughs. The projects generally fit into one of four categories:

* Features/improvements that a developer wanted, but that never made it onto the roadmap;
* Architectural improvements and bug fixes that were bothering the developer;
* Integration of some new technology with the existing product; and
* Novel and unexpected features that had not previously been discussed with any of the development teams.

The survey results indicate that 80% of the developers use *FedEx™ Day* to work on unscheduled features for the product on which they normally work. The others work on other products at the company, or improving features already scheduled for development.

People within Atlassian clearly see *FedEx™ Day* as satisfying its aim of support innovation. All survey respondents who had participated in *FedEx™ Day* believed it encouraged innovation. During interviews, a number of developers and managers stated that developers are encouraged to *"think differently," "do stuff that is a little unusual"* and *"try new technologies"* and *"collaborating with colleagues from other parts of the company that they wouldn't normally work with"* (Table 1: 4.5, 6.2). Also we found that many of the innovations trialed during FedEx Days have been incorporated into the Atlassian products.

FedEx™ Day is clearly enjoyed by the participants. A number of developers stated in the interviews that *FedEx™ Day* was one of the factors that encouraged them to seek employment at Atlassian.

4.4   The 20% Time Program

As the company grew the Atlassian founders realized that developers' time was increasingly being filled with daily tasks, to the detriment of free time previously used to tackle things judged important by the individual developers. The introduction of *20% Time* program reflected the fact that free-time problem solving had been behind many of the company's most successful products (Table 1: 1.6, 7.1).

The goal of *20% Time* is *"to encourage innovation in products, development techniques and the Atlassian development ecosystem"* (Table 1: 1.3). The "rules" of the program, designed to ensure that the program provides value for the company, emphasize the broad range of work that can fit into *20% Time*, and acknowledge that innovation requires experimentation and tolerance of failure.

1. Any 20% project that has consumed more than five days effort requires sign-off – that it is both viable and a good idea – from three developer colleagues not involved in the project, and
2. Any 20% project that has consumed more than 10 days requires sign-off from one of the company founders.

The decision to require only developer sign-off to pass the five-day mark was a conscious one to allow developers to take risks with new ideas (Table 1: 1.1). Presenting ideas and work to senior management is intimidating. Given that developers have an interest in the product as a developer, maintainer and user; it is believed they will have the best interests of the product at heart.

20% projects can either graduate from *20% Time* onto a product roadmap, or be retired. Upon graduation the project is put into a virtual *"Hall of Fame"* and the remainder of the project is funded from the appropriate product budget – freeing up the developers' *20% Time* for new projects.

4.5   Experiences with the 20% Time Program

After one year with the program, Atlassian found the projects making it onto a product roadmap typically lasted only one to five days. In total 48 projects were tracked during the first year: 16 made the Hall of Fame, seven were retired, and the remaining 25 were in-progress. The longest project was 18 days.

Development managers noted that developers used *20% Time* "*to work on things that they really, really want to do*" (Table 1: 2.4). One added that the developers who made contributions to a product could "*identify with the product a lot more*".

The survey and interviews show that developers use this time to work on problems similar to what they focus on for *FedEx™ Day*. Part of the complementary nature of *FedEx™ Day* and *20% Time* is that developers often start a project for *FedEx™ Day* and continue working on it with *20% Time*.

Around 85% of the developers use *20% Time* to work on unscheduled features for the product with which they primarily work. However, some people seek to improve scheduled features, or to work on other products. One developer was even working on an open source project that had benefits to Atlassian.

One of the managers discussed the key differences between the types of innovation seen from *FedEx™ Day* and *20% Time*. "*FedEx™ Day is a competition that developers try to win with flashy presentations and features. 20% Time is different because developers have more time to work and do not need to win over their teammates in a short presentation. Thus they can also focus on backend changes, and software product quality.*" These differences mean that a wider variety of ideas are tried, some better fitting *FedEx™ Day*, while some are more likely to be done in *20% Time*.

The greatest challenge developers faced with *20% Time* was allocating time. Managers were initially concerned that the program would consume more than the allocated number of hours. This fear was unfounded. In the first year only 6% of the hours allocated to the program were used. It is likely more time was taken, as these projects are not formally tracked; however, the actual time is below the program's maximum. Detailed tracking of innovation projects was avoided; managers feared this could stifle creativity, as developers felt compelled to deliver results (Table 1: 1.1).

For this reason developers are entrusted with the responsibility of tracking their own time, and seeking approvals.

All developers interviewed said they had nothing but support and encouragement from their managers, although many admitted feeling guilty when using *20% Time*. Developers worried about the impact this had on the rest of their team, especially those from smaller teams.

Development teams tested different ways of allocating time to *20% Time* to minimize disruptions. This included having a 20% week between development cycles, and giving people blocks of time. These tests received mixed reactions; the general sentiment was that it is not always possible to schedule innovation. Some prefer an extended break from their daily work, while others prefer taking a day here and there.

After a yearlong trial, *20% Time* was deemed a success. All *20% Time* participants surveyed felt that it encouraged innovation. *20% Time* is also a successful recruiting tool; a number of employees cited this as one of their reasons for joining the company. One newly hired developer said FedEx and 20% Time *"are pretty much the reason why I applied for a job in Atlassian. For me, it's about innovation. I personally need a creative outlet. Now I have every Friday to look forward to, to do my 20% project which I love doing because it is something that I thought of myself and it's something that hasn't really been done before."*

4.6   Innovation Practices Supported by the Development Process

The way Atlassian works, utilizing the complementary nature of their innovation tools *FedEx™ Day* and *20% Time*, makes the company attractive as an employer as demonstrated by the reactions of many of the developers that were interviewed. Many cited these initiatives as reasons why they chose to work for Atlassian.

Experimental Culture

The company's founders see innovation as an important part of Atlassian's every-day business. It permeates everything from strategies to ways of working. The company has focused on entrepreneurial innovation (Table 1: 1.2), and continues to try new practices to remain innovative. The founders and directors are also still actively involved in product development. The attitude towards trying new things through prototyping has permeated the company's culture, which is an important internal innovation determinant (Table 1: 1.3)

Direct Customer Contact

All developers at Atlassian regularly complete stints in technical support, putting them in direct contact with customers. One aim of this strategy is for developers to understand the products from their customers' perspective – to understand users' problems and get developers to prioritize fixes for the most troublesome bugs (Table 1: 3.2, 3.3). One of the technical managers at Atlassian said that their developers are *"the best people to evaluate which internal improvements need immediate attention"*.

The high level of customer interaction also helps ensure that feature development is aligned with actual and potential customers' needs (identified as important for success in many case studies [17]).

"Dogfooding" (Developers Use the Products)

Atlassian is in a different position to most development companies as it makes tools that support software development. These tools are used extensively within the company. The developers are users of the products, and can understand and evaluate their products from a customers' perspective. This practice is widely known both inside the company and in the wider developer community as "dogfooding". This gives them a strong understanding of a product's strengths, weaknesses and opportunities.

The program manager stated, *"the fact that we use our own products ... is a really cool reinforcing kind of loop and it means that everyone owns their own products and we all use internally, so it means you can be really proud of a product ... In some of the companies I previously worked at I've had no idea how to use our products or what the typical users' problems might be."*

"Dogfooding" mean the Atlassian developers have a deep understanding of their products from the perspective of a user, a developer and technical support (Table 1: 6.4). This knowledge empowers the developers to make development decisions that benefit all of these groups. This set of incentives has clear commercial benefits. Developers can build features that users want (users perspective), that make sense for the system (developers perspective) and that are intuitive reducing the need for technical support (technical support perspective) (Table 1: 3.3).

One of the managers noted that people use *FedEx™ Day* and *20% Time* to address issues that people identified from their time as users of the products in combination with knowledge acquired during customer interactions.

Agile Development Practices

In areas where rates of technological change are high and development cycles are short, being a "fast innovator" is increasingly seen as an important determinant of competitiveness [33]. The use of agile development methods, like those used at Atlassian, help support fast product innovation. For example, agile development methods support collaboration and improve information exchange between management, developers, and existing and potential customers [21].

At Atlassian innovation is supported through the use of agile practices such as daily stand-up meetings and job rotations (for example working in support). These practices empower the stakeholders to make better trade-offs as they have a richer understanding of the product (Table 1: 2.2, 2.3). Scrum style retrospectives are also used to support innovative process improvements, because they result in new or significantly improved changes to the working processes.

Information Sharing

Atlassian is an open company. Company information is made available to all employees through blogs and wikis hosted on the company's intranet (Table 1: 6.1). This information includes strategic plans, sales figures and targets and discussions about the future of the products and the company. This value is also reflected in one of the core company values, which they aspire to and advertise throughout the company offices: "Open company, no bullshit". Further, much information is made available to the general public through the company website. For example, they provide open access to the bugs that customers have logged about their products.

5   Discussion

In this article we present how Atlassian has addressed the challenge of maintaining innovation capacity while growing. We now discuss the case in light of our research question: *How can a former software start-up maintain innovation capability while growing its workforce?* From conducting a single case study, we found the following:

The agile team is often given authority and responsibility for many aspects of their work, and it was important for the innovation capacity of that the team to have direct customer contact. This is consonant with Gassmann et al., who found that a significant proportion of innovative product development ideas come directly or indirectly from the specific needs and requests of customers [17]. Also, Atlassian develops its software using short iterations, which is recognized to support innovation by allowing an organization to be responsive to changing consumer demands [21].

While Atlassian uses Scrum in combination with XP, and the founders encourage people to try out new things, we found that adopting agile practices alone is not enough to foster innovation. Agile development practices alone were found to only support two of the seven categories of innovation determinants, empowerment and knowledge management. Simply adopting agile development practices on their own is insufficient to ensure that a company remains innovative. This is consistent with Hosbond and Nielsen [23]. Developers need to feel that the environment supports and is open to innovation before they will make a contribution [8, 32]. Further, people working on the product need to share information and collaborate so they are sufficiently informed [2, 28, 39]. Due to specialization in teams and iteration pressure (the constant pressure of delivering what has been promised for the next iteration), the individual developer had little freedom. The fact that tasks were often assigned based on skills rather than preferences was the main reason for this. Morgan [30] refers to this as lack of redundancy, and it often leads to little flexibility within agile teams [29].

To conquer the above-mentioned challenges, to give developers time and space to explore and make mistakes and to help them maintain their innovation capacity, Atlassian implements *FedEx™ Days* and *20% Time*. Activities and incentives used to foster innovation require thought, planning and evolution, as these shape the types of innovations that are created. *FedEx™ Day* leads to flashier, user orientated innovation, while *20% Time* provides an opportunity to work on a broader range of improvements. Ultimately these two processes are complementary and bring about different types of innovations that are important to the company.

We also found that Atlassian adopted a suite of development practices that support all seven categories of innovation determinants found in literature (see Table 1). *20%*

Time and an experimental culture support an organisational culture that supports innovation. *FedEx™ Day* and *20% Time* lead to further worker empowerment than agile development practices alone. Direct customer contact and "dogfooding" lead to customer-related orientation that also encourages innovation. *Fedex™ Day* also encourages inter-collaboration between people across diverse areas of the company.

Further we found that *20% Time* addresses two of the three innovation drivers (Section 2.1) – individual champions can drive innovation and organisational support for innovation, and *FedEx™ Day* exploits all three innovation-drivers (Section 2.1). It supports individual champions within the company to drive innovation; it provides a process to support innovation; and through the *FedEx™ Day* planning sessions, developers discuss and share ideas. We found many benefits of fostering developer-driven innovation within a company including:

- Improving developer's morale; developers want to say: "that was my feature, that was my idea". Employees that feel valued are more likely to stay.
- Increasing developers' ownership of the product and getting them "thinking about what's relevant to customers." The benefits of this type of thinking extend beyond innovation, to all work done by the developers.
- The successful implementation of an innovation strategy will attract great people.

Based on these results from this single case study, it seems worthwhile for companies to examine the development practices that they have adopted and the categories of innovation determinants that these development practices support. Adopting practices like *FedEx™ Day* or *20% Time* may allow companies to overcome shortcomings in their current innovation strategy and pave the way for long-term growth.

6   Conclusion

By observing, interviewing, conducting a survey, and reading company documents, we found that for a software development company to compete it needs strategies to sustain the development of new products, processes and features. The successful implementation of an innovation program requires the work environment to support and encourage creativity and innovation.

Simply adopting agile development practices was found to be insufficient to maintain innovative edge. In Atlassian, agile development practices alone only supported two of the seven categories of innovation determinants. In order to support all seven categories, alternative development practices needed to be adopted. Of these some of the most interesting included *FedEx™ Day* and *20% Time*, which can also be seen as organisational innovation methods.

Further, a successful approach to innovation will ensure that innovators understand the product from a range of perspectives, and have the freedom to experiment and make mistakes. It is also crucial to motivate developers by celebrating the use of ideas included in the product. Encouraging and supporting innovation will help attract and retain great people – and with great people follow great ideas. Innovation implies not only generating great ideas, but also taking advantage and capitalizing on those ideas – turning them into innovation.

References

1. Abrahamsson, P., Conboy, K., Wang, X.F.: Lots done, more to do': the current state of agile systems development research. European Journal of Information Systems 18, 281–284 (2009)
2. Aiman-Smith, L., Goodrich, N., Roberts, D., Scinta, J.: Assessing your organization's potential for value innovation. Research Technology Management 48, 37–42 (2005)
3. Akman, G., Yilmaz, C.: Innovative Capability, Innovation Strategy And Market Orientation: An Empirical Analysis In Turkish Software Industry. International Journal of Innovation Management (IJIM) 12, 69–111 (2008)
4. Amara, N., Landry, R.J., Doloreux, D.: Patterns of innovation in knowledge-intensive business services. The Service Industries Journal 29, 407–430 (2009)
5. Antonio, C.L., Gloria, C.R., Carmen, C.M.: Social and organizational capital: Building the context for innovation. Industrial Marketing Management 39, 681–690 (2010)
6. Bonn, I.: Developing strategic thinking as a core competency. Management Decision 39, 63–71 (2001)
7. Christensen, C.M., Anthony, S.D., Roth, E.A.: Seeing What's Next: Using Theories of Innovation to Predict Industry Change. Harvard Business School Publishing Corporation, Boston (2004)
8. Clegg, C., Unsworth, K., Epitropaki, O., Parker, G.: Implicating trust in the innovation process. Journal of Occupational and Organizational Psychology 75, 409–422 (2002)
9. Coleman, G., O'Connor, R.: An investigation into software development process formation in software start-ups. Journal of Enterprise Information Management 21, 633–648 (2008)
10. Dunphy, S., Herbig, P.A.: Acceptance of innovations: The customer is the key! Journal of High Technology Management Research 6, 193–209 (1995)
11. Dybå, T., Dingsøyr, T.: Empirical Studies of Agile Software Development: A Systematic Review. Information and Software Technology 50, 833–859 (2008)
12. Erickson, J., Lyytinen, K., Siau, K.: Agile Modeling, Agile Software Development, and Extreme Programming: The State of Research. Journal of Database Management 16, 88–100 (2005)
13. Fagan, M.H.: The influence of creative style and climate on software development team creativity: an exploratory study. Journal of Computer Information Systems 44, 73–80 (2004)
14. Fitzgerald, C.A., Flood, P.C., O'Regan, P., Ramamoorthy, N.: Governance structures and innovation in the Irish Software Industry. Journal of High Technology Management Research 19, 36–44 (2008)
15. Freeman, J., Engel, J.S.: Models of innovation: Startups and mature corporations. California Management Review 50, 94-+ (2007)
16. Garcia, R., Calantone, R.: A critical look at technological innovation typology and innovativeness terminology: a literature review. Journal of Product Innovation Management 19, 110–132 (2002)
17. Gassmann, O., Sandmeier, P., Wecht, C.H.: Extreme customer innovation in the front-end: learning from a new software paradigm. International Journal of Technology Management 33, 46–66 (2006)
18. Gebauer, H., Krempl, R., Fleisch, E., Friedli, T.: Innovation of product-related services. Managing Service Quality 18, 387–404 (2008)
19. Gorschek, T., Fricker, S., Palm, K., Kunsman, S.A.: A Lightweight Innovation Process for Software-Intensive Product Development. IEEE Software 27, 37–45 (2010)

20. Herrmann, A., Tomczak, T., Befurt, R.: Determinants of radical product innovations. European Journal of Innovation Management 9, 20–43 (2006)
21. Highsmith, J., Cockburn, A.: Agile software development: The business of innovation. Computer 34, 120–122 (2001)
22. Hoegl, M., Gemuenden, H.G.: Teamwork Quality and the Success of Innovative Projects: A Theoretical Concept and Empirical Evidence. Organization Science 12, 435–449 (2001)
23. Hosbond, J.H., Nielsen, P.A.: Misfit or misuse? Lessons from implementation of scrum in radical product innovation. Agile Processes in Software Engineering and Extreme Programming 9, 21–31 (2008)
24. de Jong, J.P.J., Kemp, R.G.M.: Determinants of Co-workers' Innovative Behaviour: An Investigation into Knowledge-intensive Services (2003)
25. Kivimaki, M., Lansisalmi, H., Elovainio, M., Heikkila, A., Lindstrom, K., Harisalo, R., Sipila, K., Puolimatka, L.: Communication as a determinant of organizational innovation. R & D Management 30, 33–42 (2000)
26. Koc, T.: Organizational determinants of innovation capacity in software companies. Computers & Industrial Engineering 53, 373–385 (2007)
27. Love, J.H., Roper, S.: The Determinants of Innovation: R&D, Technology Transfer and Networking Effects. Review of Industrial Organization 15, 43–64 (1999)
28. Moe, N.B., Aurum, A., Dybå, T.: Challenges of Shared Decision-Making: A Multiple Case Study of Agile Software Development. Information and Software Technology (2012)
29. Moe, N.B., Dingsøyr, T., Dybå, T.: Overcoming Barriers to Self-Management in Software Teams. IEEE Software 26, 20–26 (2009)
30. Morgan, G.: Images of Organizations. SAGE publications, Thousand Oaks (2006)
31. OECD, Oslo Manual - Guidelines for Collecting and Interpreting Innovation Data (2005)
32. Prather, C.W.: Use mistakes to foster innovation. Research Technology Management 51, 14–16 (2008)
33. Rothwell, R.: Towards the Fifth-generation Innovation Process. International Marketing Review 11, 7–31 (1994)
34. Sjoerd, B.: Entrepreneurial Culture, Regional Innovativeness and Economic Growth. European Regional Science Association (August 2004)
35. Subramaniam, M., Youndt, M.A.: The influence of intellectual capital on the types of innovative capabilities. Academy of Management Journal 48, 450–463 (2005)
36. Tseng, C.-Y.: Technological innovation and knowledge network in Asia: Evidence from comparison of information and communication technologies among six countries. Technological Forecasting and Social Change 76, 654–663 (2009)
37. Voss, C.A.: Determinants of success in the development of applications software. Journal of Product Innovation Management 2, 122–129 (1985)
38. Yin, R.K.: Case study research: design and methods. Sage, Thousand Oaks (2009)
39. Zhu, Y., Wang, Y., Lan, H.: Innovative capabilities in the process of knowledge sharing to firm performance, Piscataway, NJ, USA, pp. 5394–5397 (2007)
40. Ågerfalk, P.J., Fitzgerald, B., Slaughter, S.A.: Flexible and Distributed Information Systems Development: State of the Art and Research Challenges Introduction. Information Systems Research 20, 317–328 (2009)

Software Architecture as a Means of Communication in a Globally Distributed Software Development Context

Richard Berntsson Svensson[1], Aybüke Aurum[2], Barbara Paech[3],
Tony Gorschek[4], and Devesh Sharma[2]

[1] Department of Computer Science School of Lund University Lund, Sweden
richard.berntsson_svensson@cs.lth.se
[2] School of Information Systems, Technology and Management,
University of New South Wales Sydney, Australia
aybuke@unsw.edu.au, d.sharma@unswalumni.com
[3] Institut fur Informatik University of Heidelberg, Heidelberg, Germany
paech@informatik.uni-heidelberg.de
[4] School of Computing Blekinge Institute of Technology Karlskrona, Sweden
tony.gorschek@bth.se

Abstract. The management and coordination of globally distributed development poses many new challenges, including compensating for informal implicit communication, which is aggravated by heterogeneous social and engineering traditions between development sites. Although much research has gone into identifying challenges and working with practical solutions, such as tools for communication, little research has focused on comparing communication mechanisms in terms of their ability to provide large volumes of rich information in a timely manner. Data was collected through in-depth interviews with eleven practitioners and twenty-eight responses through a web-based questionnaire from three product lines at an international software development organization. This paper assesses the relative importance of ten commonly used communication mechanisms and practices across local and global development sites. The results clearly indicate that some communication mechanisms are more important than others in providing large volumes of rich information in a timely manner. The prevalence of architecture in providing rich information in large volumes for both local and global communication can be clearly observed.

Keywords: Global Software Engineering, Communication, Case Study, Software Product Lines, Software Architecture, Product Management.

1   Introduction

Software product development and software product management have emerged as ways of developing software as a product for the mass-market [27], rather than for a specific customer [26]. Software product managers steer software product development towards a beneficial direction for the company by selecting requirements for the coming releases of a product and creating business objectives [19], while the

O. Dieste, A. Jedlitschka, and N. Juristo (Eds.): PROFES 2012, LNCS 7343, pp. 175–189, 2012.
© Springer-Verlag Berlin Heidelberg 2012

development teams formalize the product's functionality and assure its quality [17] to increase the likelihood of market success. Although a software product's functionality and quality are important for the success of the product, the collaboration between software product management and the development team is crucial for product success [8]; however, the collaboration requires a handle of communication and coordination challenges [9].

However, large-scale software development can be complicated, expensive and unpredictable [3]. For software companies to succeed in the global markets of software-intensive products, shortened cycle time of product development and improved product quality are essential. To achieve shortened cycle time and improved quality, two internal strategies can be used, namely software product lines (SPL) and global software engineering (GSE). Potential advantages of GSE include "round-the-clock" development, access to global markets, and reduced development time and cost [11]. However, SPL and GSE are further accelerating the complexity of software product development [3]. Furthermore, when a product line is adapted to GSE, processes, tools, and organizational structure changes [2], and has significantly more difficulties to implement the necessary coordination [3].

One key factor of the software product development process is the process of communication, coordination, and collaboration [4, 6, 12, 25]. However, it is not only the formal communication process that impacts the development. Several studies [7, 13, 16] observe that developers rely on informal and ad-hoc communication. Lack of, or problems in the informal communication channels may lead to increased development time [16]. Communication issues in GSE have been addressed by other studies; see e.g. [6, 11, 16], while communication in new product development has been addressed by, e.g., [8]. However, none of these have focused on comparing local peer-to-peer (e.g. face to face meetings), long-distance peer-to-peer (e.g. electronic chat, including instant messaging) and technical (e.g. architecture) communication tools in GSE, for their ability to provide information in a timely manner, with richness and with large volumes of information.

This paper presents the result of an empirical study that includes data collected through in-depth interviews with eleven practitioners and twenty-eight responses through a web-based questionnaire from three product lines in one international software development organization operating in over one hundred countries around the world. The case organization uses SPL in a GSE context. The main objective of this study is to assess the relative importance of ten commonly used communication mechanisms and practices from three different aspects, for their ability to transmit information quickly, transmit rich information, and to transmit large volumes of information across local and global development sites. The study incorporates two main perspectives with regards to communication mechanisms through the study of local and global development sites.

The reminder of this paper is organized as follows. In Section 2, background and related work are presented. The case organization is described in Section 3, and Section 4 describes the research methodology. Section 5 presents the results, while the results are discussed in Section 6. Validity threats are discussed in Section 7, and Section 6 gives a summary of the main conclusions.

2   Background

In SPL, software development is coordinated between teams in several different ways, during the front-end of the development, during the development, and during the end of the development [3]. During the front-end of the development, roadmaps need to be shared, discussed, and agreed upon. During the development phase, new components and interfaces need to be coordinated, while in the end of the development phase integration needs to be coordinated.

Over the last few decades, the software industry has been exposed to a steady and irreversible trend towards the globalization of business [25]. The global expansion of software organizations has made companies aware of the potential advantages that GSE has to offer, such as capitalization of global resources pools, "round-the-clock" development and access to global markets, reduced development time and cost [11]. On the other hand, these benefits are not clear-cut and should not be taken-for-granted [5]. Ó Conchuir et al., concluded that overall development costs might not be reduced due to the introduction of higher managerial complexities [5]. Furthermore, "round-the-clock" development seemed unrealistic, and companies may prefer to modularize work [5]. In addition, there are a number of challenges introduced by GSE, such as communication, coordination, and control of the development process [5].

There exists no shortage of studies relating to communication in a GSE context. Herbsleb and Grinter showed the importance of informal communication and the difficulties in communicating across global sites [10]. In fact, a major challenge in GSE is the lack of informal communication [7]. Herbsleb and Mockus further found that cross-site work takes longer than same-site work [11]. In addition, cross-site teams seem to have relatively little understanding of the overall context compared to same-site teams [11].

As for same-site development, the communication process, particularly informal communication [11], is an important factor for success in GSE [4, 6, 12]. According to Curtis et al., communication barriers in cross-site teams can be mitigated by an architect who acts as a boundary spanner between the teams [7]. Most, if not all, stakeholders in the software development can use software architecture as a basis for mutual understanding, negotiation, consensus, and communication. Bass et al. point out that the architecture provides a common language in which different concerns can be expressed, negotiated, and resolved at a level that is intellectually manageable, even for complex systems [1]. Ovaska et al., found that in a multi-site development environment, developers coordinate their work through the use of well-defined interfaces and an appropriate architecture description [16]. Using such an approach also means that components can be developed separately and the impact of distance, language and culture are minimized.

Furthermore, it is important how communication tools are utilized. Niinimäki and Lassenius conducted a multiple case study to investigate how instant messaging was used [15]. The results show that instant messaging was used to communicate simple questions and clarifications, as well as technical decisions and solutions. Šmite found that the communication channels used by a GSE organization were mainly email and telephone [24]. Very seldom was communication conducted through meeting in person, while videoconferences were never used. In McDonough et al., eight different communication tools were assessed based on speed, richness, and volume [14]. The results show that e-mail and company databases in the organization were the fastest communication tools; face-to-face meetings provided the richest information, while email and databases were viewed as providing a large volume of information.

3   Case Description

Data was collected from an international software development organization operating in over 100 countries around the world. The organization primarily specializes in database management systems, enterprise resource planning, customer relationship management and other industry-tailored products targeting government, finance and healthcare sectors. Based in the USA, it employs over fifty thousand workers around the world, with more than 25% of its workforce involved in software development. For the purposes of confidentiality, this organization will be simply referred to as "the company" throughout this paper. All of the company's products stem from its four major software product lines (SPL). The company has a few teams actively involved in the development of its software in Australia, and a larger research and development base in India. The company had four individual SPL at the time this research was conducted. However, development in Australia was only conducted for three of the SPL. Hence, only three SPL could be examined in this study.

Product line A (PLA) comprises enterprise resource planning, supply chain management, customer relationship management, human resources and industry-specific applications targeting banking and healthcare. This is the company's original product line and has been undergoing iterative development for over ten years. It now boasts a large product mix, but has an aging core asset base with slow evolution of components and architecture. The products in PLA are currently in their 12th major release.

Product line B (PLB) consists of a collection of products offering solutions for human resource management, customer relationship management, manufacturing, and student administration software for large corporations and government sectors. The company acquired this product line in 2005 through a takeover of its parent organization. PLB has a relatively well maintained core asset base, and has a proprietary integrated development environment which forces developers to reuse core assets. The products in PLB are currently in their ninth major release, and its architecture is built around the company's own proprietary development platform.

Product line C (PLC) is the company's latest collection of products aimed at unifying the best-of-business capabilities offered by its applications and other product lines. Through the use of an open, service oriented architecture, PLC is used as a standards-based technology blueprint that enables effective, predictable business process changes through standards-based integration of applications developed as web services. Developers and managers in PLC follow strict standards that do not allow for the duplication of core assets, and encourage evolution of existing assets. To date, most PLC products are still undergoing development and have yet to be released.

4   Methodology

The main objective of this research is to examine commonly used communication mechanisms and practices across local and global development sites. The research questions, in Table 1, provide the focus for the empirical investigation. RQ1 is a macro question that is broken down into three discrete sub-questions, each addressing the separate aspects of timeliness, speed, information richness and scalability of information load. To address the research questions an exploratory case study was undertaken. This study was built on semi-structured interviews [20] with a high degree of discussion between the interviewer and the interviewee, complemented with a questionnaire. This study was conducted purely from the perspective of the software organization, i.e. customers were not involved in this research. The study consisted of two steps, described in the following section.

Table 1. Research questions

Research Questions
RQ1: What communication mechanisms are central to a distributed SPL environment in order to provide large volumes of rich information in a timely manner?
RQ1.1: What communication mechanisms are central to a distributed SPL environment in terms of speed?
RQ1.2: What communication mechanisms are central to a distributed SPL environment in terms of providing rich information?
RQ1.3: What communication mechanisms are central to a distributed SPL environment in terms of providing large volumes of information?

4.1   Step 1: Interview Study

Planning: The first part of the study involved brainstorming and planning to design the study and to identify different areas of interest. The contact person at the company assisted in the identification of appropriate participants to be interviewed. The interview instrument was designed with respect to the different areas of interest i.e. company and personal background details, product and SPL background, requirements engineering process, architecture design, and impact of GSE. In addition, the interview instrument examined coordination issues in a global setting, and the communication mechanisms used by the company to communicate, both locally and globally. The interview instrument is available in [21]. To test the interview instrument, pilot interviews were carried out. Some questions were clarified and the structure of the interview instrument was improved before interviewing proceeded.

Data Collection: The study involved eleven interview participants in the roles of product managers (PM) and development managers (DM). The distribution of participants among the three SPL are displayed in Table 2. All interviews were attended by one interviewee and one interviewer. Each interview took approximately an hour. The interviews from Australia were recorded, while notes were taken at interviews involving Indian participants. Transcripts of all interviews were made in order to facilitate and improve the analysis process.

Analysis: An interpretive analysis of the interview data was conducted to address the research objective [23]. Content analysis of the transcribed interview data was also conducted using the Leximancer content analysis software. The interviewer examined the transcripts from different perspectives. In addition, another researcher, who did not attend the interviews, also analyzed the transcripts to enhance validity. Preliminary results from Step 1 are presented in [22].

Table 2. Distribution of Participants in Interviews

	Interviews	
Country	Australia	India
PLA	4 (2 PM, 2 DM)	0
PLB	4 (3 PM, 1 DM)	0
PLC	1 (1 PM)	2 (1 PM, 1 DM)
Total	9	2

Table 3. Distribution of Participants in Questionnaire

	Questionnaire	
Country	Australia	India
PLA	6	7
PLB	2	6
PLC	2	5
Total	10	18

4.2   Step 2: Questionnaire

Planning: The aim of the questionnaire was to understand the importance of different communication practices used in local and global communication by development teams, and to confirm the findings from the interviews. The questionnaire[1] was adopted from McDonough et al. who systematically studied eight different communication mechanisms, including phone calls, fax, e-mail, teleconference, face-to-face meetings, mail, company databases, and videoconferencing, in terms of their unique information transmission capabilities [14]. The communication mechanisms were rated with respect to their ability to transmit information quickly (speed), to transmit rich information (richness) and to transmit large volumes of information (volume). The questionnaire was modified by replacing the original communication mechanisms with ten communication practices that were commonly used in the company. The communication practices were identified through the study of process and project management documentation at the company and the initial interviews as follows (for explanations of the ten communication mechanisms see footnote 1): software architecture, code walkthroughs, visiting engineer, regular meetings, change management processes, discussion forums, electronic chat, face-to-face communication and process walkthroughs. The participants rated the communication mechanisms for their ability to transmit information quickly (speed), to transmit rich information (richness) and to transmit large volumes of information (volume). The rating mechanism used in the original questionnaire was also modified from independently ranking communication mechanisms, to the ranking of relative importance of different mechanisms when compared to each other. Participants were required to compare the different communication mechanisms against each other and attach a weighting to the importance of different communication mechanisms. This was enabled through the distribution of a

---

[1] http://serg.cs.lth.se/research/experiment_packages/GSE

thousand 'points' across the ten different communication mechanisms. To test the questionnaire, two pilot studies were carried out. Some questions were clarified and improved.

Data Collection: The questionnaire targeted employees involved in the development of products within each of the studied SPL. The company contact assisted with the identification of appropriate software developers within Australia to participate in the questionnaire. In order to obtain a balanced perspective on the use of communication practices in the global environment, the questionnaire was also distributed to the Indian branch of the company. Participants in India were selected through the identification of Indian counterparts of participants in Australia.

In total, 28 of 53 participants completed the questionnaire, yielding a response rate of 53%. Participants were mainly project and product managers, application architects and application engineers. The distribution of participants among the three SPL, and between Australia and India, are displayed in Table 3.

Final Analysis of All Data: The questionnaire results were analyzed for each PL individually. The importance of each criterion, at both local and global level, was analyzed by summing all the points for the respective criterion, followed by normalizing the result for each criterion to a percentage. Since a comprehensive view of the complete data set was sought, the data from the first part of the study was re-analyzed together with the data from the questionnaire.

5   Results and Analysis

The following sub-sections present and discuss one research question each, corresponding to the research questions in Table 1.

5.1   Most Suitable Communication Mechanism (RQ1)

This section examines the relative importance of the most suitable communication mechanisms to deliver large volumes of rich information in an effective timeframe.

The different communication mechanisms are divided into three main categories: (1) *local peer-to-peer*, which includes face-to-face, regular meetings, and visiting engineer, (2) *long distance peer-to-peer*, which includes electronic chat and forums, and (3) *technical*, which includes architecture, code walkthrough, process walk through, progress report, and change management. We calculated the average relative importance of speed, richness, and volume for each of the ten communication mechanisms. In addition, to understand what communication mechanism provides large volumes of rich information in a timely manner, we summed all points from all three aspects at local and global levels, and calculated the average relative importance of the combined total sum for each SPL individually. The result is shown in Table 4.

The results clearly indicate that some communication mechanisms are more important than others in local and global site communication. It is worth noting the difference in the top communication mechanisms when compared for their ability to provide information in a timely manner, with richness and with large volumes of information.

Table 4. Local vs. global distributed communication mechanisms

	PLA		PLB		PLC	
	Local	*Global*	*Local*	*Global*	*Local*	*Global*
Technical communication mechanisms						
Architecture	12.13%	**17.53%**	**15.90%**	**16.73%**	11.93%	**15.97%**
Change Management	6.87%	7.43%	7.20%	5.47%	7.20%	6.97%
Code Walkthrough	11.03%	9.57%	9.00%	7.27%	9.13%	7.70%
Process Walkthrough	7.23%	6.80%	13.13%	8.30%	7.57%	11.53%
Progress Report	7.00%	8.53%	4.93%	6.10%	6.63%	8.10%
Local peer-to-peer communication mechanisms						
Face-To-Face	**14.80%**	8.70%	**15.40%**	8.50%	**14.77%**	7.20%
Regular Meeting	10.80%	8.50%	7.07%	9.53%	11.20%	10.83%
Visiting Engineer	10.50%	14.00%	7.20%	16.17%	9.73%	12.63%
Long distance peer-to-peer communication mechanisms						
Forums	8.53%	5.80%	7.60%	5.00%	11.50%	13.47%
Electronic Chat	11.10%	13.17%	12.57%	**16.90%**	10.43%	5.60%

For local communications, face-to-face was seen by participants from PLA as a communication method that delivered large volumes of rich information in an effective timeframe in PLA. Other important communication mechanisms were architecture, followed by electronic chat. The result (the order of communication mechanisms) for PLC was exactly the same as for PLA, with the difference that forums replaced electronic chat as the third preferred communication method. For PLB, the result was similar; architecture was seen as the most suitable criterion, followed by face-to-face and process walkthrough. One major difference was that participants from PLC perceived all technical communication mechanisms, with the exception of architecture, as providing small volumes of less rich information in a relatively slow manner. This result was not consistent with the result from PLA and PLB, where, for example, participants viewed code walkthrough as a better alternative to regular meetings and visiting engineers.

Looking at global communication sites, architecture and the presence of a visiting engineer were perceived as delivering large volumes of rich information in an effective timeframe. In PLA and PLB, electronic chat was viewed as almost equally important, and again, participants from PLC preferred forums over electronic chat. It is interesting to note, for global communication, the participants from all three SPL prefer either electronic chat or forums, never both. The less preferred one was seen as the least effective communication method that delivered the smallest volume of less rich information. One interesting finding was the view of technical communication mechanisms in PLB. All of the technical communication mechanisms, except for architecture, were perceived as the least suitable communication methods, together with forums. This result is not consistent with PLA and PLC. It is surprising to note that participants from PLC viewed electronic chat as delivering relatively large volumes of rich information in an effective timeframe for local site communication, but not in communication with offshore teams.

Despite participants from PLA considering architecture to be the most suitable communication mechanism to deliver large volumes of rich information in an effective timeframe, the interviews revealed that the used mechanism when communicating with offshore teams were conference calls, group meetings, review tools and documentation. In addition, the main constraints imposed in communication with offshore teams in PLA participants were the inability to have in-depth discussions and the lack of body language.

Similar to PLA participants, PLC participants considered architecture as the most suitable communication mechanism for offshore communication. Despite electronic chat being considered by PLC participants as the least suitable mechanism for communication, several interviewees' explained that this was one of the tools used in PLC. Other communication mechanisms used in PLC were telephone and web conferences, documents, and electronic mails. Furthermore, according to PLC participants, the main constraint of offshore communication was the lack of face-to-face meetings. The lack of face-to-face meetings may have an impact on the decision-making process because *"when people do not meet face-to-face, they face a lack of understanding of capability and abilities"*.

PLB participants had a different view than PLA and PLC participants on which communication mechanism was the most suitable for offshore communication. For PLB participants, electronic chat was the mechanism that provided large volumes of rich information in a timely manner. However, electronic chat was not used in PLB, instead, offshore communication involved web and telephone conferences and documents. According to one interviewee in PLB, *"nothing beats face-to-face meetings. Meetings are conducted a lot easier, and in a more understanding manner when done face-to-face"*. However, PLB participants only considered a visiting engineer as the third most suitable communication mechanism.

For all three SPLs, the perceived most suitable communication mechanism was not used in practice. Instead, less effective mechanisms were used when communicating with offshore teams. No further elaboration was given on the topic by participants.

5.2   Communication in a Timely Manner (RQ1.1)

In analyzing Research Question 1.1, this section examines which communication mechanism provides information in a timely manner. Among PLA participants, for local site communication, all *local peer-to-peer* communication mechanisms and electronic chat were perceived as the fastest methods to distribute information (see Table 5), meaning that peer-to-peer communication mechanisms were the perceived as faster than technical communication mechanisms. For PLB participants, there was a mix of mechanisms that were perceived as the fastest. The two quickest communication mechanisms were face-to-face and electronic chat, however code walkthroughs and process walkthroughs were also perceived as relatively quick. The result for PLC is similar to PLA and PLB where face-to-face communication was the fastest communication mechanisms. In addition, regular meetings, electronic chat, and code walkthroughs were perceived as quicker than other communication mechanisms in distributing information.

For local site communications, all three SPL viewed face-to-face and electronic chat communication as the fastest methods to distribute information. In PLA, all *local peer-to-peer* communication mechanisms and electronic chat were perceived to be faster than any of the technical communication mechanisms. Unlike PLA, both PLB and PLC participants perceived the *technical* criterion code walkthrough to be faster than a visiting engineer. In addition, PLB participants perceived process walkthrough to be quicker than regular meetings and visiting engineer.

The results for communication between global sites evidently show that distributed teams, in terms of fast methods to distribute information, rely heavily upon a mix of *local* and *long distance peer-to-peer* communication, such as visiting engineers, electronic chat, and forums. The only other communication criterion, across all three SPL, that was perceived as being quick was architecture. In addition, PLC viewed process walkthrough as a fast method. One main difference between the three SPL was that PLA and PLB participants viewed electronic chat as one of the fastest criterion, while PLC participants preferred forums.

Table 5. Relative importance of speed

	Speed					
	Local			*Global*		
	PLA	PLB	PLC	PLA	PLB	PLC
Technical communication mechanisms						
Architecture	7.8%	9.5%	8.4%	14.2%	12.1%	12.3%
Change Management	7.4%	4.4%	7.5%	8.1%	5.2%	7.5%
Code Walkthrough	9.4%	10.2%	11.6%	7.9%	6.5%	6.1%
Process Walkthrough	8.3%	13.3%	9.0%	7.1%	8.9%	11.7%
Progress Report	7.2%	4.6%	6.4%	8.2%	5.1%	8.2%
Local peer-to-peer communication mechanisms						
Face-To-Face	**17.1%**	**20.6%**	**16.7%**	10.8%	9.0%	8.6%
Regular Meeting	11.0%	8.5%	10.3%	9.5%	11.8%	11.2%
Visiting Engineer	11.3%	6.9%	9.0%	12.9%	**19.6%**	**14.4%**
Long distance peer-to-peer communication mechanisms						
Forums	8.4%	4.9%	8.3%	5.8%	4.2%	14.0%
Electronic Chat	12.2%	17.1%	12.9%	**15.5%**	17.5%	6.0%

5.3   Communication Rich Information (RQ1.2)

In terms of providing rich information for local site communication, a mix of *technical* (architecture) and *local peer-to-peer* (face-to-face) communication mechanisms were perceived to provide the richest information (see Table 6). For PLA and PLC, face-to-face provided the richest information, while PLB participants viewed architecture as the richest source. It is interesting to note that PLB participants viewed process walkthrough as a criterion that provided rich information, while PLA and PLC participants perceived process walkthrough among the least effective communication mechanism for providing rich information. For global sites communication, all three SPL agreed that architecture provided the richest information. Moreover, a visiting engineer was viewed, by all three SPL, to be a good communication method for rich information. The main difference between the three SPL related to how long distance peer-to-peer provided rich information. PLA and PLB participants perceived electronic chat as a good source of rich information, while PLC participants viewed forums as a good source.

Table 6. Relative importance of richness

		Richness				
	Local			*Global*		
	PLA	PLB	PLC	PLA	PLB	PLC
Technical communication mechanisms						
Architecture	12.6%	**18.2%**	14.4%	**17.7%**	18.1%	17.4%
Change Management	6.7%	7.9%	7.0%	7.6%	5.3%	6.2%
Code Walkthrough	11.6%	9.7%	8.2%	10.0%	8.5%	8.8%
Process Walkthrough	6.7%	14.1%	7.3%	6.5%	8.6%	11.3%
Progress Report	6.4%	4.4%	5.6%	8.7%	6.1%	7.5%
Local peer-to-peer communication mechanisms						
Face-To-Face	**17.7%**	17.5%	**16.3%**	9.7%	7.9%	6.2%
Regular Meeting	9.7%	5.7%	10.3%	6.9%	8.2%	9.7%
Visiting Engineer	10.0%	6.5%	9.0%	15.5%	14.6%	13.6%
Long distance peer-to-peer communication mechanisms						
Forums	8.0%	6.1%	12.1%	5.7%	5.6%	13.3%
Electronic Chat	10.5%	9.9%	9.9%	11.8%	17.1%	6.0%

5.4   Communicate Large Volume of Information (RQ1.3)

Looking at which communication mechanism provides the largest volume of information, both PLA and PLB participants viewed *technical* communication mechanisms as providing the largest volume of information. Architecture was perceived as the preferred criterion when sharing large volumes of information. PLA participants viewed code walkthrough and PLB participants viewed process walkthrough as the second most suitable criterion respectively. Unlike PLA and PLB participants, PLC participants viewed forums (*long distance peer-to-peer*) as the criterion that provided the largest volume of information, which is a surprising finding. Moreover, regular meetings were perceived as equally good as architecture for distributing large volumes of information. For global sites communication, the results with regards to providing large volume of information were similar to the results of providing rich information. Architecture was viewed by all three SPL as the preferred criterion for sharing large volumes of information. Moreover, PLA and PLB participants perceived electronic chat as a way of sharing large volumes, while PLC preferred forums. In addition, PLA and PLB participants identified visiting engineers, while PLC participants viewed regular meetings, as other good communication methods for sharing large volumes of information.

6   Discussion

The result of the survey shows that a number of communication mechanisms are more important than others in local and global environments. While no single mechanism meets all three needs of speed, richness and volume perfectly, when examining the results across the three product lines, the prevalence of architecture in providing rich information in large volumes, for both local and global communication, can be clearly observed. This has important implications for SPL engineering, which uses product line architecture as a driving force in developing software products. It indicates that traditional SPL engineering practices and artifacts have the ability to act as reusable items, reused as a communication mechanism enabler. This finding is expected as architecture establishes a method of effective communication through a common vocabulary [1]. Not only does architecture make large-scale reuse possible, by establishing component definitions and proper interfaces, it also provides for orientation of different development teams systematically producing different parts of the system [15], while the impact of distance, language, and culture are minimized [16]. This provides a potential solution for a fundamental challenge for GSE: the communication and coordination between distributed teams working on different areas of product development. This also implies that SPL engineering can be used efficiently and effectively in organizations that have globally distributed teams.

Further examination of the results by product lines show that, communication between development teams, locally or globally, is also dependent on their development practices. Taking the communication practices for local sites into consideration, it was mostly peer-to-peer communication methods, such as face-to-face conversations and electronic chat that provided information in a relatively fast manner across all product lines. Communication mechanisms that allow for mass distribution of information, such as forums and architecture, generally rated lower in terms of speed of distribution. This may be attributed to the fact that such mechanisms were generally qualitative and textual in nature, requiring time to comprehend. In the case of global communication, face-to-face conversations were replaced by an equivalently fast communication mechanism, a visiting engineer. This indicates that personal contact is largely associated with faster dissemination of information. However, the importance of a visiting engineer is not consistent with the findings of Smite, which found that communication conducted through meeting in person was very seldom used [24]. In addition, McDonough et al. found that email and databases were the fastest communication tool, while face-to-face was considered as providing the richest information [15].

The importance of local peer-to-peer communication mechanisms is not surprising; however, having regular meetings (part of local peer-to-peer communication mechanisms) was not viewed as being among the top three fastest communication mechanisms. This indicates that the participants referred to informal and ad-hoc communication when talking about face-to-face communication. This result is consistent with several studies [4, 6, 10, 12] that point out the importance of informal communication for the success of GSE. One reason why regular meeting was not viewed in the top three fast communication mechanisms may be the difficulties of using formal communication channels to handle unexpected events [10].

The influence of development practices on the communication mechanisms used was more evident in the criteria of richness and volume. In particular, electronic forums were rated considerably lower in PLA due to developers working more closely on their own products, rather than relying on shared artifacts. Greater use of shared artifacts correlates with an increase in the use of mechanisms that provide large volumes of rich information. This was evident in PLC, which heavily utilizes shared artifacts, where electronic forums and architecture were ranked higher when compared to other mechanisms.

In summation, the prevalence of architecture in providing rich information in large volumes, both for local and global communication can be observed. This may indicate that software architecture can enable communication in SPL in a globally distributed software development context.

7   Threats to Validity

In this section, threats to validity are discussed. We consider the four perspectives of validity and threats [28], i.e. construct, conclusion, internal and external validity.

Construct validity is concerned with the relation between theories behind the research and the observations. The variables in our research are measured through interviews, including open-ended aspects where the participants are asked to express their own opinions, and a questionnaire. To avoid evaluation apprehension [28], complete anonymity from other participants, and researchers was guaranteed. Another validity threat lies in the questionnaire that asked the participants to rank communication practices and include additional practices if the list provided to them was inadequate. Participants may have thought that it was easier to rank the provided factors than propose new factors. Hence, important communication practices may be missing.

Threats to *conclusion validity* arise from the ability to draw accurate conclusions. The interviews were conducted at different branches and each interview was done in one work session. Thus, answers were not influenced by internal discussions. To obtain highly reliable measures and to avoid poor question wording and poor layout, several pilot studies were conducted.

Internal validity is related to issues that affect the causal relationship between treatment and outcome. Threats to internal validity include instrumentation, maturation and selection threats. In our study, the research instruments were developed with close reference to literature relating to GSE, and influenced by a previously administrated and validated research instrument [14], which mitigates instrumentation threat. Maturation threats are handled by keeping the interview session to 60 minutes.

External validity is concerned with the ability to generalize findings beyond the actual study. Qualitative studies rarely attempt to generalize beyond the actual setting since it is more concerned with explaining and understanding the phenomena. The nature of qualitative designs also makes it impossible to replicate since identical circumstances cannot be recreated. However, understanding the phenomena may help in understanding other cases and situations. The participants selected may not adequately reflect the diversity of opinion on current practice communication mechanisms. The small sample size used in this study may also indicate that conclusions made may not be generalized across the software industry. Hence, the results of the study must be interpreted with caution when moving away from the characteristics of the studied case organization.

8   Conclusion

This paper presents the results of an empirical study that examines the importance of commonly used communication mechanisms across local and global development sites. To the best of our knowledge, there is no empirical study that specifically examines the aspects of communication mechanism, in product lines, for their ability to transmit information quickly, to transmit rich information and to transmit large volumes of information.

This study has shown that some communication mechanisms are more important than others in a local and global environment. While there are some differences between the three product lines, peer-to-peer communication mechanisms are perceived to be particularly important at a local level, and to provide a faster speed of communication at a global level. Software architecture was generally perceived to communicate large volumes of rich information at both a local and global level. Participants across all three product lines understood the relative importance of architecture in the global environment when compared to other communication mechanisms. This indicates that SPL engineering has the ability to utilize a globally distributed development environment and that a heavy reliance on software architecture can enable communication in SPL in a globally distributed software development context.

This study is only a first step in understanding commonly used communication mechanisms in SPL in a global development context. Given the limitations with the sample size, there is opportunity for future research to replicate this study across various cases and across different industries. Future work should focus on the detailed utilization of software architecture or other SPL engineering assets for GSE. This could provide improvements for these artifacts to be more useful in a global context. It also could provide ideas for improving the global SPL engineering process in terms of work distribution and management.

References

1. Bass, L., Clements, P., Kazman, R.: Software Architecture in Practice. Addison-Wesley Professional (2003)
2. Berenbach, B.: An Introduction to Global Product Line Requirements Engineering. In: Proc. of the Second Int. Conference on Global Software Engineering, pp. 300–301 (August 2007)
3. Bosch, J., Bosch-Sijtsema, P.: From integration to composition: On the impact of software product lines, global development and ecosystems. Journal of Systems and Software 831, 67–76 (2010)
4. Carmel, E., Agarwal, R.: Tactical approaches for alleviating distance in global software development. IEEE Software 18, 22–29 (2001)
5. Conchuir, E.O., Ågerfalk, P.J., Olsson, H.H., Fitzgerld, B.: Global Software Development: Where are the benefits? Communications of the ACM 52, 127–131 (2009)
6. Deridder D.: A concept-oriented approach to support software maintenance and reuse activities. In: Workshop on Knowledge-Based Object-Oriented Software Engineering (2002)
7. Falbo, R.A., Menezes, C.S., Rocha, A.R.: Using ontologies to improve knowledge integration in software engineering environments. In: Proc. of the 4th Conference on Information Systems Analysis and Synthesis (1998)
8. Fricker, S., Gorschek, T., Glinz, M.: Goal-Oriented Requirements Communication in New Product Development. In: Proc., Second Int. Workshop on Software Product Management (2008)

9. Griffin, A., Hauser, J.: Integrating R&D and Marketing: A Review and Analysis of the Literature. Journal of Product Innovation Management 13, 191–215 (1996)
10. Herbsleb, J.D., Grinter, R.E.: Architectures, Coordination, and Distance: Conway's Law and Beyond. IEEE Software 16, 63–70 (1999)
11. Herbsleb, J.D., Mockus, A.: An Empirical Study of Speed and Communication in Globally Distributed Software Development. IEEE Transactions on Software Engineering 29, 481–494 (2003)
12. Herbsleb, J.D., Mockus, A., Finholt, T.A., Grinter, R.E.: An Empirical Study of Global Software Development: Distance and Speed. In: Proc. 3rd International Conference on Software Engineering. Inst. of Elec. and Elec. Eng, pp. 81–90 (May 2001)
13. Kraut, R.E., Streeter, L.A.: Coordination in software development. Communications of the ACM 38, 69–81 (1995)
14. McDonough, E.F., Kahn, K.B., Griffin, A.: Managing Communication in Global Product Development Teams. IEEE Transaction on Engineering Management 46, 375–386 (1999)
15. Niinimäki, T., Lassenius, C.: Experiences of Instant Messaging in Global Software Development Projects: A Multiple Case Study. In: Proc. IEEE International Conference on Global Software Engineering, pp. 55–64. IEEE (August 2008)
16. Ovaska, P., Rossi, M., Marttiin, P.: Architecture as a coordination tool in multi-site software development. Software Process: Improvement and Practice 8, 233–247 (2004)
17. Paech, B., Dörr, J., Koehler, M.: Improving Requirements Engineering Communication in Multiproject Environments. IEEE Software 22, 40–47 (2005)
18. Perry, D.E., Staudenmayer, N.A., Votta, L.G.: People, organizations and process improvement. IEEE Software 11, 36–45 (1994)
19. Regnell, B., Brinkkemper, S.: Market-Driven Requirements Engineering for Software Products. In: Aurum, A., Wohlin, C. (eds.) Engineering and Managing Software Requirements, pp. 287–308. Springer (2005)
20. Robson, C.: Real World Research. Blackwell, Oxford (2002)
21. Sharma D.: Blueprint of Success: Creating Software Product Value through Product Line Engineering, Honours Thesis, School of Information Systems, Technology and Management, University of New South Wales, Australia (2007)
22. Sharma, D., Aurum, A., Paech, B.: Business Value through Product Line Engineering – An Empirical Study. In: Proc., 34th Euromicro Conference on Software Engineering and Advanced Applications, pp. 167–174 (September 2008)
23. Silverman, D.: Interpreting Qualitative Data. Sage Publication, London (2001)
24. Šmite, D.: Global Software Development Projects in One of the Biggest Companies in Latvia: Is Geographical Distribution a Problem? Software Process Improvement and Practice 11, 61–76 (2006)
25. Šmite, D., Wohlin, C., Gorschek, T., Feldt, R.: Empirical Evidence in Global Software Engineering: A Systematic Review. Empirical Software Engineering 15, 91–118 (2010)
26. Ullah, M.I., Ruhe, G.: Towards Comprehensive Release Planning for Software Product Lines. In: Proc. of the 1st International Workshop on Software Product Management (ISPM 2006). Inst. of Elec. and Eng. Computer Society, pp. 51–55 (September 2006)
27. Van De Weerd, I., Brinkkemper, S., Nieuwenhuis, R., Versendaal J., Bijlsma, L.: A Reference Framework for Software Product Management, Technical Report UU-CS-2006-014, Department of Information and Computing Sciences Utrecht University (2006)
28. Wohlin, C., Runeson, P., Höst, M., Ohlson, C., Regnell, B., Wesslén, A.: Experimentation in Software Engineering: An Introduction. Kluwer Academic, Boston (2000)

Socio-technical Congruence Sabotaged by a Hidden Onshore Outsourcing Relationship: Lessons Learned from an Empirical Study

Darja Šmite[1,2] and Zane Galviņa[2]

[1] Blekinge Institute of Technology, Karlskrona, Sweden
[2] University of Latvia, Riga, Latvia
Darja.Smite@bth.se, Zane.Galvina@lu.lv

Abstract. Despite the popularity of outsourcing arrangements, distributed software development is still regarded as a complex endeavor. Complexity primarily comes from the challenges in communication and coordination among participating organizations. In this paper we discuss lessons learned from participatory research carried out in a highly distributed onshore outsourcing project. Previous research established that socio-technical congruence principles alleviate distributed work. In practice we have found that alignment between the systems structure and organizational structure can be studied from different abstraction levels and also during different phases of project lifecycle. We have found that official organizational structure differed from the applied one, which meant that the planned alignment in task allocation strategies was broken. Our findings indicate that the lack of socio-technical congruence caused several implications, including unclear responsibilities, delays in problem turnaround, conflicting changes, and non-delivered parts.

Keywords: Distributed software development, onshore, outsourcing, socio-technical congruence, Conway's law.

1 Introduction

The topic of distributed software development emerged with the popularity of globalization. Distributed projects involve geographically dispersed team members and despite the widespread utilization empirical studies show that distributed teams are far less productive than co-located teams [1]. The majority of the studies focusing on distributed software development investigate offshore outsourcing projects [2], which means that the work is performed in a sub-contracting relationship among companies from different countries. This is also the main focus in global software projects [3]. However, not all distributed software projects are necessarily global. While multinational organizations perform on a global arena, it is not uncommon that small and medium software development companies team up locally to be able to compete for larger contracts. Furthermore, Balajiand and Brown claim that current trends in outsourcing are moving toward a multi-vendor arrangement, in which

O. Dieste, A. Jedlitschka, and N. Juristo (Eds.): PROFES 2012, LNCS 7343, pp. 190–202, 2012.
© Springer-Verlag Berlin Heidelberg 2012

multiple vendors are pooled together to achieve and exceed the overall expertise required for a project [4]. If distributed projects are challenging due to communication, coordination and control among the partners [1], it is fair to assume that the more participating companies, the more challenging is their collaboration. In fact, an empirical investigation demonstrated that increase in the number of sites decreased quality and profits for the company leading distributed software development projects [5].

In this paper we investigate a highly distributed project that involves four different companies involved in software development. The collaboration studied is onshore outsourcing — physically local companies, which are distinct entities [2]. The rest of the paper is organized as follows: in Section 2 we present related work. Section 3 describes research methodology. Findings are presented in Section 4 and discussed in Section 5. Section 6 concludes the paper with the answers to research questions and outline of future work.

2   Related Work

While distributed work requires new process models for managing team relationships to deliver software on time and within budget, such dedicated models are yet to be developed [2]. Nonetheless, different aspects of distributed work are widely discussed in the research literature. Among the most popular are the topics related to coordination of work and task allocation in particular [1, 6, 7, 8], and difficulties regarding team efficiency [9]. It was found that coupling between tasks decreases productivity [1]. Empirical evidence also suggests that communication and coordination across different locations usually requires more people and thus results in overhead [10]. One way of reducing this overhead is to modularize development and minimize technical and thus social dependencies [6]. If the work is partitioned into autonomous units without any complex dependencies, it might enable concurrent development and might not necessarily result in lower performance [5]. This line of research applies the principles of the Conway's law, which suggests that software design mirrors communication structure of the organization that builds it [9].

In the light of distributed software development the importance of Conway's law and its implications grows. The harmony between the organizational and architectural structures, which is often referred to as the socio-technical congruence, is not always easy to establish. One of the reasons for this is the rapidly changing nature of the organizations already discussed by Conway [9]. In distributed projects task allocation can be driven by on demand availability of resources, and change in the course of the project. Therefore, predicted inefficiency caused by coordination and communication breakdowns becomes evident. However, there is another important challenge. To reduce the costs even further some outsourcing service suppliers start delegating tasks to their subsidiaries or third parties. Thus, organizations who initially establish the project structure might not be aware of the true social structure, and thus fail to comply to the rules of socio-technical congruence.

In this paper we study the implications of an unintentionally non-congruent socio-technical structure of a highly distributed software development project. Social structures in distributed teams are represented by organizational units and distributed developers as suggested by [6, 11]. While the most studied technical structures are usually related to source code or development tasks [6, 11], these are not the only artifacts by which articulation of work can be carried out. Similarly to de Souza et al. who suggest that software artifacts can reveal the relationship between technical and social structure of large-scale development projects [11], in this paper we aim at exploring the socio-technical relationship using a number of different work products during the life cycle of a highly distributed software development project. Our case sheds the light on potential challenges for task allocation introduced by the differences between the planned and the actual social-technical structures.

3   Research Methodology

Research reported in this paper was participatory in nature — the second researcher (Zane Galviņa) was directly involved in an industrial software development project, in which she participated as a system analyst. Participatory research method addresses the gaps between the researchers and the researched people, and provides a great potential for rich empirical observations. In particular, participant observation are said to be useful for gaining a deeper understanding of the physical, social, and cultural contexts, relationships, ideas, norms, and events; and people's behaviors and activities, which were not necessarily included in the study design from the very beginning [12].

The research focused on investigating a highly distributed onshore outsourcing project and collaboration among four software companies which we for confidentiality reasons refer to as D1, D2, D3 and D4 (see also Figure 1). Due to a complex organizational structure and social relationships the project coordination was challenging. These challenges triggered an exploratory study and motivated us to seek the answers to the following research questions:

RQ1: Does the studied highly distributed project follow socio-technical congruence principles?
RQ2: What are the consequences of non-congruence?

The data was collected from a variety of sources (see Table 1). Official project plans were used to outline the planned social structures, while observations from participatory research activities formed the basis for identifying the actual social relationships. These were further supplemented by an analysis of different project artifacts that formed the basis for studying the technical structures and relationships. The socio-technical links were established through the task allocation strategies outlined in the project plans, and compared with those suggested by the Conway's principles. The socio-technical relationships are visualized with the help of diagrams that follow original Conway's notations [9]. In particular, we have created diagrams for planned and actual social structures, technical structures, which are further linked through the socio-technical structures.

Table 1. Data collection

Project phase	Artifacts collected	Observations
Requirements analysis and design	• Project Management Plan • Software Requirement Specification • Software Design Specification • Problem reports	• Interviews with users • Weekly meetings with D4 and D3 • Participation in two meetings among D1, D3, D4 to finalize the requirements and design documentation
Development	• Problem reports	• Participation in the virtual weekly meetings at D4 • Participation in demo sessions at D1
Testing	• Problem reports	• Participation in the weekly virtual meetings with D4 • Participation in demo sessions regarding fixes

Our research has several limitations. First of all, the focus of this exploratory study is to illustrate only one plausible challenge in coordinating work in a highly distributed project and by no means implies that similar socio-technically non-congruent projects would suffer from the same consequences discussed in this paper. Secondly, our findings may be affected by a single researcher's bias, since the case description is based on observations from the participatory research. This was mitigated through triangulation of the observations with the actual project documentation.

4   Results

In this section we present the results and lessons learned from the study. We start by describing the project background and socio-technical structures that we have found in different phases of the project life cycle. Our results illustrate how even having best intentions to comply with the rules of socio-technical congruence the project may suffer from inefficient structure due to unforeseen circumstances.

4.1   Project Overview: Social and Technical Structures

The project discussed in this paper was a bespoke software development project for two customer organizations, which started in the beginning of 2011. The aim of the project was to move an existing software system to a new platform and significantly enhance its functionality. The project was motivated by the necessity to comply to the new legal requirements as well as technical obsolescence, while the platform change was necessary to enable complex integration with the other systems existing in the organizations. Customer organizations organized a tender and contracted development to the winning organization. Unfortunately, the winning software company neither possessed required experience and expertise in all knowledge domains nor had sufficient number of on demand available developers to fulfill the requirements on their own. Therefore the development in practice was performed by a network of small software companies collaborating on a joint project (see Fig. 1).

The project team consisted of 21 employees from all participating organizations. Organization D1 was the prime contractor who has won the tender and contributed with the largest share in the project. At the time of the study D1 was an SME employing approx. 140 employees; ten of them were involved in this project. D2 was a small company with only 16 employees and involved five developers in the project. Even smaller organizations were D3 and D4, each employing approx. ten people. Three employees from each of the latter organizations were involved in the project. It is worth noting that the customer organizations engaged 13 employees in the project, who were available during different phases of the lifecycle.

Fig.1 is created on the basis of official project management plan and supplemented with our observations. It demonstrates the organizational structure and contractual relationships made by the prime contractor (D1). The entity D4 is added to reflect the actual structure that was discovered through observations and participatory involvement in D3 activities. In particular, we have found that D3, one of the direct sub-contractors of D1, further outsourced parts of the work to another company (D4). However, the existence of this outsourcing relationship was hidden from the prime contractor (indicated by the dashed line in the figure) and the employees from D4 were presented as the employees from their contractor's company (D3). Conway in his proposition did not address hidden structures and their implication and we found politically flavored relationships and its implications interesting to explore.

The technical structure of the system that was developed comprised of two separate sub-systems, which utilize the same data for different purposes. Sub-system 1 allowed users to enter the data, while Sub-system 2 was developed for dissemination purposes.

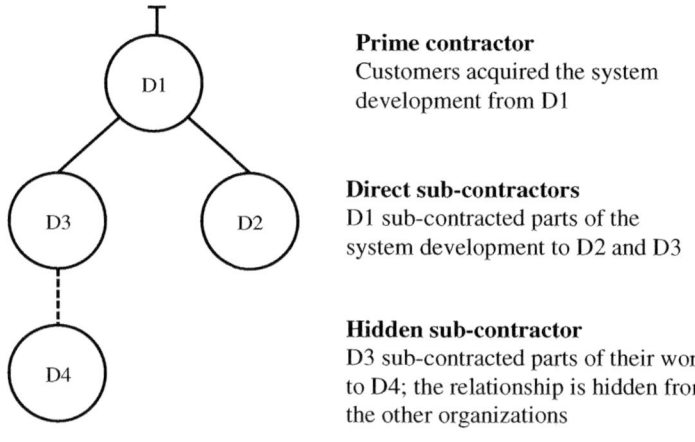

Prime contractor
Customers acquired the system development from D1

Direct sub-contractors
D1 sub-contracted parts of the system development to D2 and D3

Hidden sub-contractor
D3 sub-contracted parts of their work to D4; the relationship is hidden from the other organizations

Fig. 1. Organizational structure

In this paper we focus our attention on exploring the socio-technical dependencies within Sub-system 1. An overview of the technical system's structure is given in Figure 2. The figure also outlines the integration requirements to support internal and external interfaces. In the figures we use original notations proposed by Conway [9].

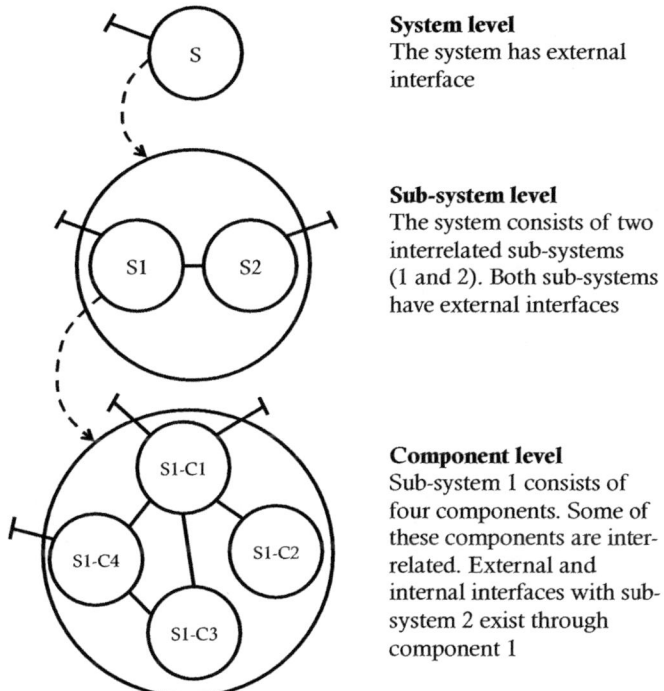

System level
The system has external interface

Sub-system level
The system consists of two interrelated sub-systems (1 and 2). Both sub-systems have external interfaces

Component level
Sub-system 1 consists of four components. Some of these components are inter-related. External and internal interfaces with sub-system 2 exist through component 1

Fig. 2. Product structure

The project was broken into sub-projects and further managed applying Rational Unified Process (RUP). The delivery was expected by December 2011, however due to a three month delayed iteration in one of the sub-projects, the whole project was significantly delayed. To understand the reasons for the failure of this distributed project to meet the deadline we investigate the socio-technical congruence through studying the task allocation strategies in this onshore outsourcing network for different project artifacts.

4.2   Task Allocation: Socio-technical Links

As mentioned earlier, modularization on the sub-system level motivated division of the project into two sub-projects. Due to unavailability of resources in one place, the work on Sub-system 1 was further split into four components, which were assigned to different organizations. According to Conway's law, the task allocation shall follow a homomorphic approach [9]. In other words, each organizational unit can work on several components, while each component must be assigned to only one unit. From the task allocation strategy we can easily see that system development in the project studied did not fully apply the congruence principles proposed by Conway. In practice, Sub-system 2 was developed by two organizations (D1 and D2), three different organizations were involved in developing Component 1 for Sub-system 1, and while Component 2, 3 and 4 were allocated solely to a single organization, some of the social links necessary to support the technical dependencies did not exist. In particular, the interface between Components 1 and 4 was not supported by the links between D1 and D4.

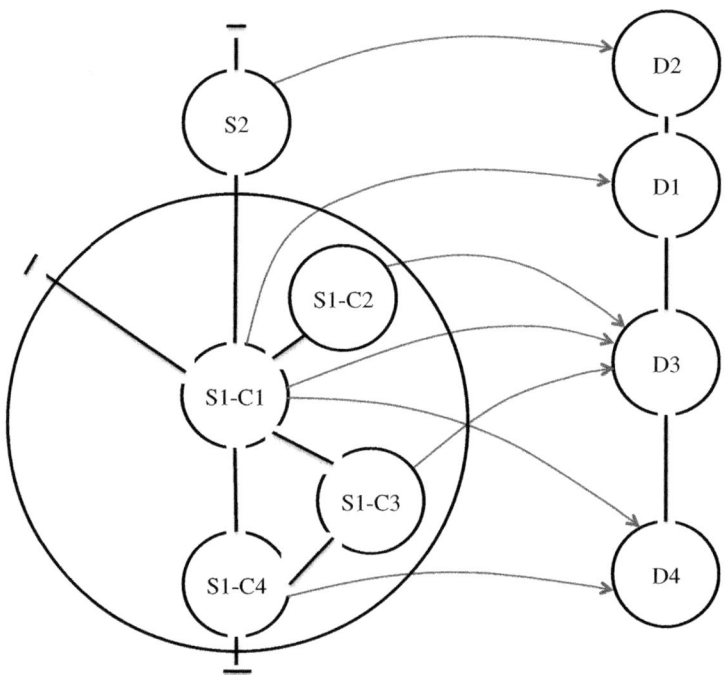

Fig. 3. Task allocation illustrates socio-technical non-congruence in Sub-system 1

Lessons Learned: Work on Component 1 aimed at developing the database solution for the Sub-system, and the tasks were shared between D1, D3 and D4. It was decided that each organization would develop the part that represents and communicates with the other components that are developed by respective organizations. This however breaks the homomorphic principle of task allocation. In practice, the three organizations shared the work on the same component level and notably two of them did not have any direct contact (see Figure 4). The missing link in this case impacted the way changes were handled. When D1 implemented the changes necessary for supporting the interface between sub-systems, they impacted the parts that were responsible for supporting the interface between Component 1 and Component 4. Since no direct communication was established between D1 and D4, and in the light of poorly documented interface specifications, the changes remained unnoticed until it caused a failure when D4 tested their parts of the sub-system. In result, it took approximately two weeks for D4 to find the cause of this failure. Thankfully their solution to the problem did not cause another loop of errors.

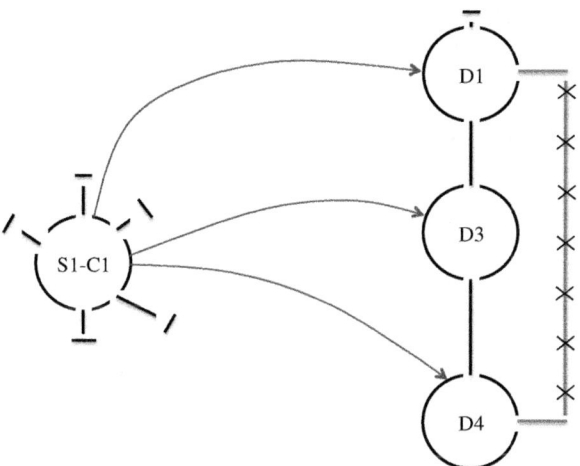

Fig. 4. Missing relationship between organizational units working on Component 1

Significant challenges were introduced by the work on Component 4, which was assigned to organization D4. The component has one external and two internal interfaces. Since the prime organization (D1) was formally responsible for the integration tasks, communication was required between D1 and D4 to effectively handle these tasks. This link was, however, not established (see Figure 5).

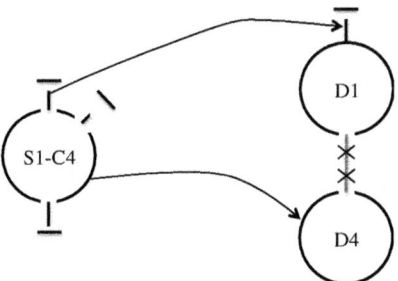

Fig. 5. Missing relationship between organizational units working on Component 4

In practice, interface specifications were poorly documented and since D4 was not involved in specifying these requirements they assumed that all integration would be solved by D1. Due to missing direct contact between the two organizations, and misunderstood responsibilities, the integration part was missing. This was discovered one week before the delivery deadline and caused a loop of blaming between D1 and D3, which was formally responsible for the work.

4.3   The Impact of Socio-technical Non-congruence during Requirements Analysis and Design

In order to get a better understanding of the task allocation problems and project coordination breakdown, we further illustrate the responsibilities shared by the four organizations in the requirements analysis and design phases. During systems analysis each organization (except for the hidden organization D4) interacted with the customers in order to elicit requirements for the system parts within their responsibility. Each organization contributed in development of the software requirement specification (SRS) and software design specification (SDS), which were finally reviewed and integrated into one package by D3.

Lessons Learned: Fragmentation during the requirements elicitation led to dissatisfaction of the customers, since different organizations contacted the same prospective users and often asked the same questions.

Most importantly, the reasons of failure in delivering the integration parts could be traced back to requirements analysis and design phases. Since formally each organization focused on specifying the functionality of their respective components and sub-systems, integration parts were poorly documented. Organizational dispersion resulted in limited social interaction, and confusion regarding the interfaces remained unsolved. While formal responsibility for integration, as well as the overall project coordination, was assigned to the prime organization (D1), hidden parts of the organizational structure were invisible. Therefore threats to coordination of work on Component 4 and related interfaces were not foreseen.

4.4   The Impact of Socio-technical Non-congruence during Testing

Testing activities were performed stepwise. First of all, responsibility for testing the developed parts was assigned to each respective organization (D1, D2, D3, and D4). Then an additional systems testing was performed by the prime organization (D1). This included testing systems integration, during which a missing interface was detected.

Later acceptance testing was coordinated by D1. Trouble reports from the customers were gathered centrally by D1, and then assigned to responsible organizations (D2 or D3 by the D1, and further to D4 by D3, if necessary).

Lessons Learned: From this study we learned that strict modularization of work and isolated functional testing that excluded testing the interfaces prevented early identification of the missing integration links.

Additionally, coordination of trouble report resulted in significant time overhead. Mediation of problems prolonged communication paths and therefore resolution intervals. The delay was especially noticeable in coordination of changes in Component 4, for which reports were reassigned twice. Direct interaction between D1 and D4 would have shortened the turnaround paths of the tasks and potentially communication overhead in case of misunderstandings and clarifications.

5   Discussion

Related studies suggest that distributed projects shall have a clear distribution rationale and only consider well structured, well understood and stable projects, decomposable into discrete tasks [7]. This is in line with the socio-technical congruence principles proposed by Conway [9] who promoted the alignment, or a homomorphic relationship, between the tasks and organizational units. To understand the existence and impact of these relationships we have performed a study of a highly distributed onshore outsourcing project. We have found that identification of the socio-technical congruence requires careful attention, as parts of the organizational structure can be hidden. The project described in this paper involved a hidden outsourcing relationship between two organizations (D3 and D4), which the prime contractor, who is responsible for responsibility allocation, was not aware of. The implication of this is that the socio-technical congruence was significantly affected.

When studying the degree of alignment to understand the reasons for poor task allocation, we also noticed that different levels of abstraction provide us with a different view (see Fig. 6).

- From the customers' perspective the system and its developing organization are perfectly aligned, since the development of the system is assigned by the contract to the prime contractor (D1).
- When studying the prime contractor's perspective, we see a strict decomposition of the system with only one shared component. The technical structure of the system contains the database in Sub-system 1, which is usually difficult to isolate, as it is used by other components. Also the social structure is simple — D1 communicates directly with D2 and D3. We therefore conclude that the socio-technical structure was designed to ensure homomorphic relationship between the organization (social structure) and the system (technical structure) with one exception.
- However, our findings indicate that the actual socio-technical structure was different from that planned by D1. When adding D4 into the social structure, the homomorphic socio-technical relationship breaks significantly. We observe that one component is now assigned to three organizations, two of which are not socially linked. Isolation of problems and coordination of responsibilities for this vulnerable component (the database in Sub-system 1) was thus problematic, as could be predicted by the Conway's proposition.

The misalignment identified had an impact on the way the work was coordinated, and also resulted in several misunderstandings. The missing link between D1 and D4 meant that there was no direct communication and thus all the necessary clarifications or problem escalations were organized through D3. This caused delays in problem turnaround and inability to react on the changes during the course of the project, which confirms existing findings from studying speed and communication in distributed teams [10]. At the same time, we have found that some of the interfaces were not developed on time due to confusion regarding responsibilities, and that shared components caused misunderstandings when implementing the changes to

Customers' perspective

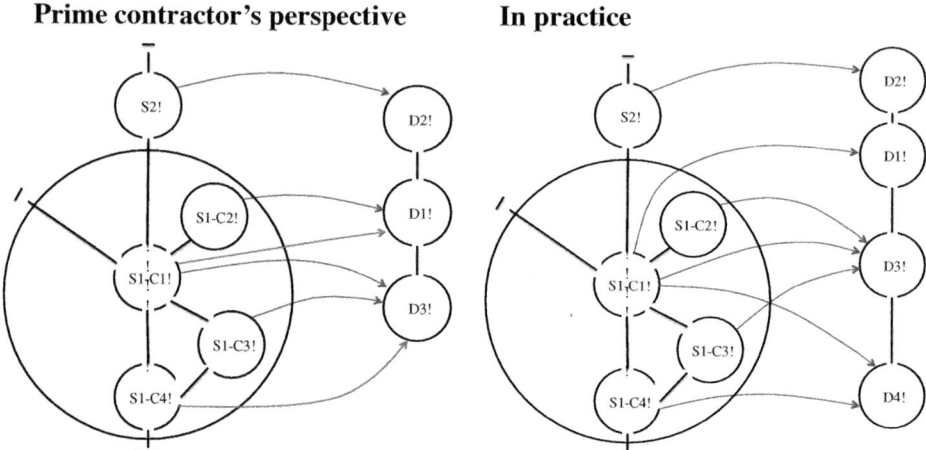

Fig. 6. Task allocation illustrates socio-technical non-congruence in Sub-system 1

existing working parts of the system. The problem of unclear roles and responsibilities is also discussed in existing research on global teams. For example, Kotlarsky et al. [13] found that participants of a global software development project often had different views on their own or their colleagues' responsibilities.

We believe that many of these problems could be avoided, if the interfaces between the system's components and sub-systems would be well documented, and if the organizational structure would have been clear.

Lings et al. suggest that a distributed project can be partitioned functionally according to organizational and systems structure or by process during other life-cycle phases prescribing natural divisions of work in relatively small bundles [7]. We have found that the work allocation strategies during requirements analysis, development and testing did not follow the same pattern. Notably, the major challenges in this respect can be related to documenting requirements for, developing and testing of interfaces among the systems components.

Although it has been noted that increase in the number of sites usually results in the increase productivity (since the development capacity grows) [5], the same study demonstrates that the quality of the developed software decreases. Our observations indirectly support this view, as the growing complexity of coordination development of interfaces between the components that were allocated to different sites, resulted in a missing interface.

6   Conclusions and Further Research

In this paper we have discussed lessons learned from a highly distributed project. Our observations indicate that distribution makes projects more complicated, and we have traced the major sources of complexity to be triggered by the missing communication links between the participating organizations. One of the most interesting findings is related to the fact that the official organizational structure differed from that in practice. In particular, a hidden outsourcing relationship existed, which the prime contractor, who was responsible for task allocation, was not aware of. The lack of awareness of the true organizational structure and missing direct communication between the prime contractor and the hidden organization propagated into all phases of the project lifecycle.

In response to **RQ1** we have studied the task allocation strategies from a socio-technical congruence perspective, and realized that the answer to the research question is not trivial. We learned that the project was designed to comply with the homomorphic principles proposed by Conway [9] and discussed by other researchers [6, 7], but in practice failed to follow the plan. The congruence was sabotaged by the hidden onshore outsourcing relationship.

In response to **RQ2** our findings suggest that although the project task allocation followed modularization, several important practices were missing. Incompliance resulted in unclear responsibilities assigned for documenting, developing and testing the interfaces among the modules that were further complicated by the missing communication links between the prime contractor and the hidden supplier. This caused delays in problem turnaround, conflicts with change implementation and non-delivered parts.

In conclusion we expect that a task allocation strategy that is compliant with the Conway's proposition is more likely to minimize similar problems.

Our findings are based on qualitative analysis of the gathered material. Further work will focus on qualitative measurements of the lead times for change requests during the development phase. We also hope to have insights into the destiny of the project during its maintenance.

Acknowledgement. We thank our industrial partners for the opportunity of following the project.

This work has been supported by European Social Fund project No. 2009/0216/1DP/1.1.1.2.0/09/APIA/VIAA/044, as well as BESQ+ (20100311) grant from the Knowledge Foundation in Sweden, and Center Of Nordic Excellence in Software Engineering (CONES) grant from NordForsk.

References

1. Lamersdorf, A., Münch, J., Rombach, D.: A Decision Model for Supporting Task Allocation Processes in Global Software Development. In: Bomarius, F., Oivo, M., Jaring, P., Abrahamsson, P. (eds.) PROFES 2009. LNBIP, vol. 32, pp. 332–346. Springer, Heidelberg (2009)

2. Prikladnicki, R., Audy, J.L.N., Shull, F.: Patterns in Effective Distributed Software Development. IEEE Software 27, 12–15 (2010)
3. Šmite, D., Wohlin, C., Feldt, R., Gorschek, T.: Empirical Evidence in Global Software Engineering: A Systematic Review. Journal of Empirical Software Engineering 15(1), 91–118 (2010)
4. Balajiand, S., Brown, S.A.: Strategic IS Sourcing and Dynamic Capabilities: Bridging the Gap. In: Proc. of the 38th Hawaii Int. Conf. on Systems Sciences (HICSS) — Track 8, p. 260. IEEE CS Press (2005)
5. Ramasubbu, N., Cataldo, M., Balan, R.K., Herbsleb, J.D.: Configuring global software teams: a multi-company analysis of project productivity, quality, and profits. In: Proceedings of the 33rd International Conference on Software Engineering (ICSE 2011), pp. 261–270 (2011)
6. Cataldo, M., Herbsleb, J.: Socio-Technical Congruence: A Framework for Assessing the Impact of Technical and Work Dependencies on Software Development Productivity. In: Proceedings of the Second ACM-IEEE International Symposium on Empirical Software Engineering and Measurement (ESEM 2008), pp. 2–11 (2008)
7. Lings, B., Lundell, B., Ågerfalk, P.J., Fitzgerald, B.: A reference model for successful Distributed Development of Software Systems. In: Proceedings of the 2nd International Conference on Global Software Engineering (ICGSE), Munich, Germany, pp. 27–30 (2007)
8. Avritzer, A., Paulish, D., Cai, Y.: Coordination Implications of Software Architecture in a Global Software Development Project. In: Proceedings of the Seventh Working IEEE/IFIP Conference on Software Architecture (WICSA), pp. 107–116 (2008)
9. Conway, M.: How do Committees Invent? Datamation 14, 28–31 (1968)
10. Herbsleb, J.D., Mockus, A.: An empirical study of speed and communication in globally distributed software development. IEEE Transactions on Software Engineering 29(6), 481–494 (2003)
11. de Souza, C., Froehlich, J., Dourish, P.: Seeking the Source: Software Source Code as a Social and Technical Artifact. In: Proceedings of the International ACM SIGGROUP Conference on Supporting Group Work, pp. 197–206 (2005)
12. Mack, N., MacQueen, C.W.K.M., Guest, G., Namey, E.: Qualitative Research Methods: a data collector's field guide. Family Health International (2005)
13. Kotlarsky, J., van Fenema, P.C., Willcocks, L.P.: Developing a knowledge-based perspective on coordination: The case of global software projects. Inf. Management 45(2), 96–108 (2008)

Providing Training in GSD
by Using a Virtual Environment

Miguel J. Monasor, Aurora Vizcaíno, and Mario Piattini

Alarcos Research Group, Institute of Information Technologies & Systems,
Escuela Superior de Informática, University of Castilla-La Mancha,
Paseo de la Universidad 4,
13071, Ciudad Real, Spain
MiguelJ.Monasor@gmail.com,
{Aurora.Vizcaino,Mario.Piattini}@uclm.es

Abstract. In Global Software Development (GSD) the human factor is one of the main assets for the companies. Their efficiency in communication and collaboration, as well as their knowledge of the processes applied in GSD, can lead the companies to be more competitive.

Participants require knowing the customs and culture of other participants. Moreover they need to improve their social and interpersonal competencies such as: negotiation, teamwork, conflict resolution, time management, leadership, and communication skills using a common language.

In this paper we present a simulation-based approach for training GSD with which users can train by interacting with Virtual Agents which play a role in the development process. These Virtual Agents textually interact with users by means of a chat by simulating being people with different personalities, experiences, skills and culture.

The lessons learned in a feasibility study carried out with a group of practitioners and PhD students are also analyzed in this paper.

Keywords: Global Software Development, Engineering Education, Educational Environment, Teaching Model, Virtual Agents.

1   Introduction

In Global Software Development (GSD) the human factor is one of the main assets for the organizations [1]. Their productivity, the effective use of communication and collaboration tools and their knowledge of the processes can lead the companies to be more efficient than their competitors [2]. Because face-to-face contact is restricted in GSD, human relations and attitudes towards distant participants become a key factor.

Therefore, participants must not only focus on technical aspects, but also in social and interpersonal and intercultural competencies such as: negotiation skills, teamwork skills, conflict resolution, time management skills, leadership, decisions making, reasoning skills, knowledge of communication protocols and customs, communication skills using a common terminology in a second language, ability to motivate others and

O. Dieste, A. Jedlitschka, and N. Juristo (Eds.): PROFES 2012, LNCS 7343, pp. 203–217, 2012.

create trust, information management, ambiguity and uncertainty management and knowledge of tools and processes used in GSD [3, 4].

Personality dimensions such as extroversion, anxiety, self-control, sensitivity, independence, emotional stability, reasoning or dominance also influence in software activities success [2, 5].

In terms of cultural boundaries, there is also a need for cultural understanding and sensitivity. Participants require knowing the customs and culture of other project members, as this factor significantly influence the performance and quality of their work [6]. For instance, in some cultures participants tend to not to speak during team meetings until invited to do so, because it would be considered impolite in their culture. Therefore, a software engineer should be trained to detect what problems can arise in this type of development and for instance to know how to confront situations to kindly encourage such participants to discuss a certain issue.

On the other hand, English is used more and more in international collaboration, gaining importance in applied linguistics research given the challenges for non-native speakers. Lack of fluency is a common problem which produces hesitancy or delay [7]. Native speakers have a natural tendency to assume facts that can negatively affect the project and eventually damage the team relationships. However, non-native speakers must improve their language proficiency and learn common expressions that could allow them to participate in a more dynamic way.

Our goal is to help software engineers (practitioners or students) to develop all these skills necessary for GSD. Thus, first of all we carried out a systematic literature review [4] were we found that the main difficulty for providing an adequate training on these skills consists of setting up realistic settings that could allow the students to tackle representative problems. Therefore, the current educational programs rarely organize collaborative activities with other institutions, because of scheduling differences and coordination problems [8].

To tackle that problem we propose a simulation-based approach for training some of the problems that often take place in GSD. Therefore, users can train at any moment by interacting with Virtual Agents which play a role in the software development process. These Virtual Agents interact textually with user by means of a chat by simulating being people with different personalities, experiences, skills and culture. In this way, it is possible to design rigorous training scenarios for dealing with specific problems and skills required in GSD.

The architecture of the simulator is integrated into an e-learning platform and it has also been designed to ease the design of the simulation scenarios. The definition of the simulation scenarios is based on a metadata language defined for this purpose. The scenarios designer permits to drag and drop the different phases in which the simulation is composed by defining a sequential workflow that will guide the conversation. Each phase contains the conversational knowledge required for such specific context as well as cultural and linguistic rules that will allow correcting the users' interactions by means of a special virtual agent called virtual colleague that will help the users during the simulation.

The execution engine is responsible for interpreting the defined information and executing the different phases of the conversation within the time limit. For that purpose it uses a chatbot system that responds to the users. The students' goal is to confront situations in which they could appreciate typical problems, detecting cultural differences and trying to obtain as much information as possible during the conversation, as well as minimizing the cultural and language errors made during the interaction.

Other advantages of the proposal are that it provides an independent and controlled training, the rapid reception of feedback by means of the virtual colleague, the rigor of the training in cultural issues and the reduction of the instructors' effort.

A feasibility study was carried out in a presentation of the tool that served to analyze the first impressions of experts of multinational companies as well as of a set of PhD students that provided feedback to improve several aspects of the architecture and the training scenarios.

This paper is organized as follows: Section 2 explains the context of this research. The influence of personal aspects in GSD is explained in Section 3. The proposal in which is focused this work is detailed in Section 4. Section 5 provides an example of its use. Finally, Section 6 provides some concluding remarks and future work.

2   Context of Current Research

In the context of our research, the main focus is around the influence of social factors and cultural and linguistic differences in GSD. According to a systematic literature review on the field of teaching and training GSD [4], the strategies that have been applied in academic courses, mainly consists of replicating the conditions of real environments by collaborating in software developments with other universities [9]. GloSE-Lab [8] is an example including theory and practice in collaboration with distant universities.

The main problems of these approaches are given by the difficulty of creating settings that suits the teaching goals of each university, which moreover, can have different schedules. The lack of knowledge and experience in the development of big projects, the unequal workload of the participants, communication problems and conflicts among partners are common problems.

Blended learning environments [10] and e-Learning platforms [11] are commonly used in these approaches in order to facilitate the collaboration among students from distant universities, while other approaches are focused on games and simulation, placing the users in scenarios in which they have to cope with specific problems of GSD. As the context of our research is in this last field, the following subsection details the related state-of-the-art.

A.   Games and Simulation

Learning happens most easily when the students actually need the knowledge of how to do something for a reason. Feedback reception is an important factor to enhance knowledge and skills of the student [12]. Games and simulation have been applied in many fields of software engineering because these approaches are among the most motivating for the students.

An example of on game-based approaches is IT Billionaire [13]; a turn based board game designed to teach dynamics of GSD in order to discover the many variables involved in these environments. The players must attempt to become billionaire by running a company that applies GSD. However these kinds of approaches are limited to develop a reduced set of skills mainly related to management tasks.

In terms of simulation, the SESAM project [14] is a representative example intended for investigating and comparing different strategies for software development. Students use a textual interface in which they read and type text for training in project management activities.

M. Samejima et. al [15] address situation-dependent scenarios, in this case for simulating project management activities, specifically covering generation of scenarios for the progress management phase.

The use of augmented spaces like iBistro [10], based on the 'learning by doing' approach are also used as a way to enable distributed members to collaborate during the development so that can be used to learn project management, software development and social skills.

Social aspects are a key factor for improving the development process [2], and in this field, M. Yilmaz and R. V. O'Connor [16] propose a framework for modeling development activities, serving for the research of several social issues in software development, such as team formations, interpersonal conflicts or social loafing.

In a related vein, C. Pelachaud [17] has worked on behavior expressivity, presenting an affective embodied conversational agent which is able to display communicative and emotional signals. Expressive qualifiers are used to modulate the expressivity of lip movement [18].

An embodied conversational agent is presented by M. Kavakli et. al [19] with the aim of counseling neglected aborigines in Australia, who have problems of poverty and disease as a consequence of past neglect and torture. The agent plays the role of sociologist in advising on strategies to overcome their addiction to alcohol problems. It can also represent protocols to express social relations between humans.

In the field of GSD, [20] explores the interaction with avatar-based humans in virtual collaborative projects, in order to train collaboration skills and intercultural competences. Configurable avatars are also used in Teamlink [21]; a collaborative 3D virtual environment conceived to support icebreaking activities with the aim of establishing trust between virtual team members.

B.   Teaching Cultural Aspects

GSD is recognized as a sociotechnical activity in which cultural play an important role. Practitioners cannot ignore the impact of cultural diversity and the barriers and problems it can create [22]. Educators must prepare the students, at undergraduate and postgraduate level to tackle the problems in these environments, paying special attention to the impact in computer mediated communication, which is particularly affected by this aspect [23].

Many organizations try to minimize this impact by implementing strategies in order to foster an organizational culture trying to set up a set of norms, values, objectives and beliefs that are touch to their members [23]. However, many aspects of the national culture are difficult to change, and participants must learn to understand each other character, philosophy and mindset [24]. The following authors propose different ways in which to classify cultural aspects:

- **Hofstede** [25]: defines a classification focused on the values and culture of computer professionals, considering five value dimensions in which countries differ: power distance, uncertainty avoidance individualism/collectivism, masculinity/femininity and long-term/short-term orientation.
- **House et al.** [26]: is a more recent classification focusing on culture and leadership in 61 nations, defining the following dimension: uncertainty avoidance, power distance, societal collectivism, in-group collectivism, gender egalitarianism, assertiveness, future orientation, performance orientation and humane orientation. The first six dimensions have their origins in the Hofstede dimensions.
- **Trompenaars and Hampden-Turner** [27]: compare culture to an onion made up of layers that can be peeled to be understood. They outline seven dimensions of culture: universalism versus particularism, individualism versus communitarianism, "specific" versus diffuse, affective versus neutral, achievement versus ascription, sequential versus synchronic, internal versus external control.
- **Hall** [28]: for whom culture is equated to communication, which is made up of three elements: words, material things and behavior. He defined seven relevant concepts to study national and corporate culture: speed of messages, context, space, time, information flow, action chains and interfacing.

By considering these dimensions it is possible to quantify the probability that certain cultural patterns could occur during the interaction, and this may serve to focus the training for confronting specific patterns. As an example, E. MacGregor et. al [29] present a set of cultural patterns in GSD: yes (but no) pattern, proxy pattern, we'll-take-you-literally (anti) pattern, we're-one-single-team (anti) pattern, the-customer-is-king (anti) pattern.

For example the "Yes (but no) pattern" consists in the fact that individuals in some cultures tend to respond requests by saying "yes". As a consequence, problems may appear if the person who made the request trusts in that false answer. In order to minimize the problems that these kinds of patterns can cause, software engineers must receive a rigorous training by considering their culture.

3   Influence of Personal Aspects and Skills in GSD

Personal aspects play an important role in GSD, due to the fact that people make decisions by mixing feelings and logic in a different degree depending on their values, knowledge and personality [30]. As an example, extrovert people tend to pay attention on the external environment, while introverts are more focused on the internal environment when taking decisions [31].

Some studies have found that virtual team performance was directly related to leadership and interpersonal dimensions, which are influenced by personality and psychology factors [32]. Moreover, factors such as personality or charisma of an individual can also affect the overall team performance [33].

These factors are closely influenced by the participants culture, as well as their age, gender, experience and region, and the team size [33]. Moreover these attitudes directly affect colleagues' satisfaction, effectiveness and performance, all the more when the practitioner is in a position that requires leadership abilities. Extroverted behaviors, for example, tend to result in higher frequency of communication through electronic messages and an increase in the team performance [34]. In [35] it was found that high levels of positive personal traits, such as helpfulness and agreeableness increased team performance satisfaction.

GSD involves high requirements for communication and collaboration between its practitioners in a common language. Fluency is also a problem which produces misinterpretations, hesitancy or delay [22]. Native speakers have a natural tendency to assume facts that can affect negatively in project. These attitudes can lead to the loss of pertinent information and eventually damaging the team relationships being necessary to train the skills that allow to minimize these problems and also to deal with them when they occur.

Instant messaging, mail, phone, and video conferencing systems are the main media for both formal and informal communication in GSD [36], so it is necessary to have additional skills in their use in order to build trust and social relationships with co-workers by considering the characteristics of each communication mean. The aim of this proposal consists on providing training in instant messaging and mail communication considering some of the aforementioned personal factors.

4   VENTURE

The aim of this research work is to define a tool for providing training in same of the skills required in GSD, considering cultural and personal factors that can influence the development process. VENTURE (*Virtual ENvironment for Training cUlture and language problems in global softwaRe dEvelopment*) is intended to cover some of the following aspects in the training of the skills required in GSD:

The chat simulator would make it possible to create simulations with which to achieve the following:

1. Creating awareness of the different kinds of cultures and the problems that may appear during textual interactions.
   - Showing the typical language mistakes of the people from a particular culture.
   - Showing the different gestures, customs and behaviors of people from other cultures that could be misunderstood.
   - Showing ways in which to ask questions in an appropriate manner.
   - Using direct/indirect communicative style.
   - Using formal and informal communication skills.
2. Promoting skills for the development of relationships based on cultural diversity
   - Identifying issues that may cause conflict.
   - Showing tips to assist in reacting towards certain actions or to answer specific questions.

      - Teaching strategies by which to eliminate bias and discrimination. For instance avoiding the usage of sexist words.
      - Showing ways in which to establish a dynamic conversation.
3. Training the proper use of a second language
      - Ability to effectively communicate with multidisciplinary members using the same terminology.
      - Minimizing language mistakes and teaching structures to allow people to communicate in an effective manner.
4. Developing teamwork skills
      - Leadership and decisions making skills.
      - Time management skills.
      - Showing how to develop mutual trust and confidence.
      - Knowledge of negotiation skills.
      - Management of ambiguity and uncertainty.
      - Conflict resolution skills and critical reasoning skills.

VENTURE provides a platform in which users will acquire practice in these aspects by means of simulation. Users will confront common situations in which they could appreciate the problems of interacting in the distance with people with different personalities, experiences, skills and culture. For achieving this it uses Virtual Agents (VAs) playing a specific role in the Software Engineering process, as a mean to simulate any kind GSD scenario. These VAs are characterized by a specific culture and personality, and will textually interact with the student. Moreover, during the interactions, a Virtual Colleague (VC) will guide the user to address the simulation, giving advice and correcting the inappropriate interactions.

This section shows the main components of VENTURE (see Fig. 1), which follows a client-server architecture. An e-learning application is the core of the server side and is made up of the following components:

Resource repository (1): in which both the theoretical lessons and the simulators and artifacts are made available to the students.
Task area (2): which serves to control and schedule the practical activities. The students can also upload deliverables in this area.
Forum and wiki module (3, 4): through which students and instructors can keep in touch.
Evaluation area (5): in which students can do exams, fill in questionnaires, and review the evaluation and the instructor's comments for these activities.

Pedagogical Module

The *Pedagogical Module* (6) stores all the theoretical contents in the field of teaching GSD training and is structured with reference to the following knowledge areas: software requirements, software design, software construction, software testing, software quality, software maintenance, configuration management, software engineering management and software engineering process.

The difference between this module and the *Resource Repository* is that the latter contains the general contents that are available to all the students. The *Pedagogical module* also contains the different strategies needed to train specific skills according to the needs of each student.

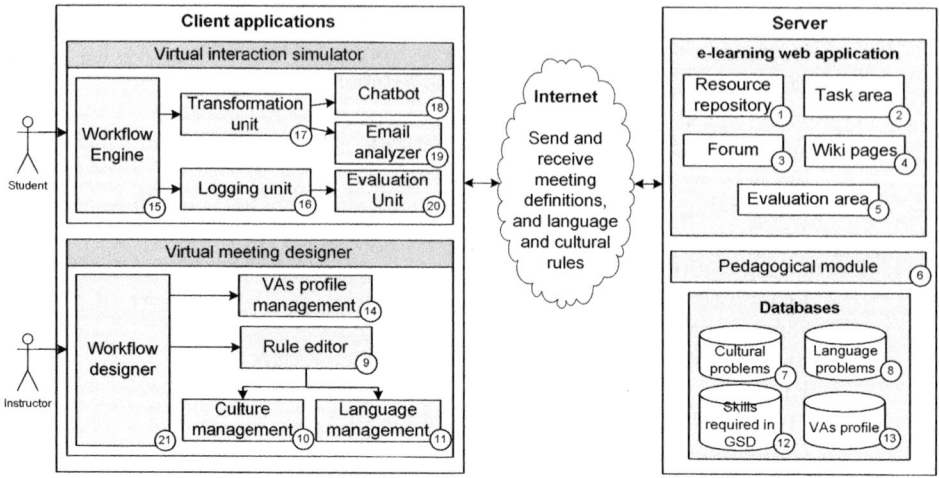

Fig. 1. VENTURE Architecture

Cultural Problems

The *cultural problems* database (7) contains the cultural rules that can be used in the simulations and which train cultural problems that might affect communication in GSD scenarios. They consist of VTRML (VenTuRe Markup Language) structures; a language specifically defined for VENTURE, containing the rules for each phase of the simulation as well as the necessary metadata required for the execution engine for the simulation.

Language Problems

The *language problems* database (8) contains the linguistic problems that may appear when participants interact textually using a non-native language. As in the previous case, the structures that serve to train these problems are defined in VTRML, and can be used in any simulator through their inclusion its definition by means of a wizard. The linguistic rules are classified by the kind of problem that they deal with and include any relevant information that may be useful for correcting the students' actions.

The information contained in both the *cultural database* and the *linguistic database* is managed by the *Rules Editor* interface (9), which is made available to the instructors through its *cultural management* module (10) and *language management* module (11).

Skills Required in GSD

The *skills required in GSD* are stored in the database (12) which contains best practices in the form of VTRML structures, as in the case of the cultural and language problems. This knowledge is classified into the following skills that they are intended to train.

VAs Profile Database

The *VA profile (13)* contains the information regarding the virtual characters involved in the training scenarios, and defines their appearance and gestures. This is used to teach users how they should understand and react to different customs during a conversation. The *VA profile management* module (14) permits these profiles to be maintained so that new characters can be included or existing ones can be modified.

Workflow Engine

The *Workflow Engine* (15) is responsible for executing the scenarios by interpreting the definition of the workflows, and orchestrating the corresponding phases. This engine interprets the VTRML definition of the workflows by extracting the conversational knowledge, together with the linguistic and cultural rules defined. This process is carried out by the *transformation unit* (17).

The conversational knowledge embedded in the workflow is defined in AIML language [37], which is interpreted by the *chatbot system* (18), in the case of synchronous interactions, and by the *Email analyzer* (19), in the case of dealing with asynchronous interactions.

The *login unit* (16) makes it possible to save the log of the conversation so that the instructor can evaluate it later.

Evaluation Unit

The *Evaluation unit* (20) gathers information about the course of the simulations in order to provide an evaluation that would serve to determine what skills a student must improve.

Workflow Designer

The *Workflow Designer* (21) allows the virtual meetings to be defined and customized in a graphical manner. The virtual meetings are thus designed as sequential workflows made up of a set of phases containing the specifics details of the conversation for each phase. Based on these graphical definitions, the definition of the meetings is automatically translated into VTRML format.

5   Simulating an Interaction

In this section a training scenario based on a real experience by members of a company is presented. In this training scenario, a Spanish user called Alberto, plays the role of developer and has to interact with another developer from Germany called Georg. Georg has developed a webservice, and Alberto has (supposedly) developed and application that have to consume that webservice. However, Alberto has problems to consume the service because it does not follow the WSDL standard. The task for the Alberto in this scenario consists on explaining Georg what the problem is and what changes would be necessary in the webservice for solving the problem.

The training is intended to train the following specific skills: questions formularization, negotiation skills, trust creation and linguistic problems in the context of the conversation. Before starting the simulation, the situation is explained to Alberto, so he has an idea of how he is going to interact in order to convince Georg, although the VC will guide him at any moment.

By attending to the cultural dimensions of House [26], for Germany and Spain, the differences in the cultural dimensions are depicted in Table 1 (on the 1-to-7 scale, where 1 is the lowest value of fulfillment for a dimension).

Table 1. Cultural dimensions for Germany and Spain. Summarized from [26]

House Dimensions/County	Germany	Spain	Difference
Assertiveness	4.66	4.39	0.27
Institutional Collectivism	3.97	3.87	0.1
In-Group Collectivism	4.16	5.53	**-1.37**
Future Orientation	4.41	3.52	0.89
Gender Egalitarianism	3.25	3.06	0.19
Human Orientation	3.30	3.29	0.01
Performance Orientation	4.42	4.00	0.42
Power Distance	5.48	5.53	-0.05
Uncertainty Avoidance	5.35	3.95	**1.4**

Considering that the cultural dimensions that differ more between these two cultures are in-group collectivism and uncertainty avoidance, Alberto must interact in a proper manner to cover the problems that these differences can entail:

- **In-group Collectivism** is the degree to which a community encourages and rewards the collective distribution of resources and collective action, including factors such as loyalty and cohesiveness of the individuals [26]. Members of individualistic cultures tend to be direct in their communication, expressing their inner opinions, whereas collectivist cultures tend to be more indirect. In this simulation Alberto will try to interact in an indirect manner, and the scenario will be focused this. Fig. 2 show an example of a fragment of a conversation in which Alberto interacts in a too direct way and the VC corrects him.

In this case, the VC detects a direct intervention based on the detection of the patterns: "I need", "you must", "you have to", etc. In case of detecting one of these patterns in the context of this part of the conversation, the VC will intervene to provide feedback. This rule is modeled in VENTURE as it follows, where the severity value is used for evaluation purposes, indicating the penalty that will receive the user if this rule is triggered:

```
<Skills type="direct-indirect style" severity="1">
    <pattern>"I need *"</pattern> <!—Formulate a request in a
    direct style"-->
    <pattern>"You must *"</pattern>
    <pattern>"You have to *"</pattern>
    <template>You should try to be more indirect</template>
</Skills>
```

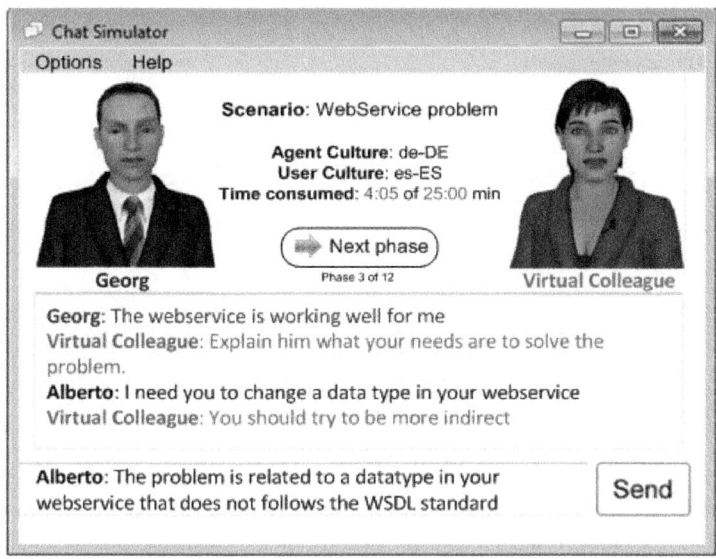

Fig. 2. Fragment of a conversation in the chat interface

- **Uncertainty Avoidance** is the degree to which the individuals feel 'comfortable' in new situations. Individuals tend to avoid uncertainty by relying on social norms, customs, and bureaucratic practices [26]. Individuals with high levels of uncertainty avoidance, tend to seek more feedback than those that are more tolerant to uncertainty, either by asking questions or observing. As Germans are less tolerant to ambiguity, Georg could feel anxiety and stress if Alberto is not clear with his proposal for a solution. Short-term feedback is a proactive method that Alberto should apply to avoid these feelings. Alberto should also try to minimize the uncertainty trying to give as much information as possible, avoiding, for example, misunderstandings or improper use of language. In the following fragment of a conversation, Alberto commits a mistake that could cause a misunderstanding:

   Alberto: Could you realize some changes in the webservice?
   Virtual Colleague: "Realize" is a false-friend in Spanish. Do you mean to "carry out"?
   Alberto: Could you carry out some changes in the webservice?
   Virtual Colleague: You should try to be more polite using "please"
   Alberto: Please, could you carry out some changes in the webservice?

In this case, a language rule has been triggered in order to correct a false-friend mistake. Moreover, in the same conversation, the VC has also detected that the formulation of a question has been too direct without using the word "please". These rules are modeled as it follows in VENTURE:

```
<LanguageProblem type="false friend" severity="2">
    <pattern>realize</pattern>   <!--Incorrect   use   of   the   word
    "realize"-->
    <template>"Realize" is a false-friend in Spanish. Do you mean to
    "carry out"?</template>
</LanguageProblem>

<Skills type="politeness" severity="3">
    <pattern>"!please + ?"</pattern> <!—Formulate a question without
    "please"-->
    <template>You    should    try    to    be    more    polite    using
    "please"</template>
</Skills>
```

The VA (Georg) can also commit mistakes during his interaction, so that Alberto must receive a certain training of what he can confront in this sense. In the following example, the VC warns him about that mistake:

Georg: I have not become any request on my webservice.
Virtual Colleague: Note that he has incorrectly used the word "become", when he wanted to say "received".

In this case "become" is a false-friend, related to the german word "bekommen", which means "to get or receive". So Alberto must know how to manage the uncertainty that generates this kind of answer. The training scenario can be designed to detect the word "become" in this specific context of the conversation and teach the problem to the user. Moreover, the text introduced by the user is automatically checked by a spelling dictionary which will provide him feedback in case of committing grammatical errors.

6   Conclusions and Future Work

In this work we present a training environment for providing rigorous training in the skills required in GSD activities. A feasibility evaluation of VENTURE, was carried out by four experienced members of multinational companies, that provided insights for improving some aspects of the environment. After presenting them the environment, they were interviewed about their perception with regard to the use of the environment in their companies, its usefulness, and its usability from the students' and instructors' perspectives.

They all agreed that it could be useful in their companies and that are interested in using it, although they remarked that the time available for training in their companies is quite limited. Two responders stated that one of the main difficulties that companies usually encounter when organizing training courses is related to the difficulty in finding experts and the time needed to develop these courses. For these reasons they believed that the use of a simulator was a good idea, because these problems might be avoided. The flexibility that would make it possible to improve the training scenarios was also well valued.

The future work will be mainly focused on the evaluation of the environment. Our preliminary planning includes testing our approach on various experimental settings in which students, engineers and conference participants will be invited to participate in order to provide feedback about the perceived usability, motivation and adequacy of the scenarios. We are therefore preparing surveys and structured interviews with the following goals:

Validation goal 1: effectiveness and efficiency of VENTURE. The effectiveness and efficiency can be determined by analyzing the data gathered during the simulations, and the correction of deliverables after the simulation.

Validation goal 2: evaluation of the degree of adaptability of VENTURE to different cultures, languages and training goals.

Finally, we are also planning to carry out experiments with students at universities in Spain, Ireland, Mexico and Germany so that we could compare their performance with other students of the same characteristics that have not used this simulation tool. Therefore, several scenarios must be designed to train students of these different cultures considering specific goals in their training. For this purpose, we will also count with the experience of professionals that will guide us to provide realistic training scenarios based on real cases.

Acknowledgments. This work has been funded by the PEGASO/MAGO project (Ministerio de Ciencia e Innovación MICINN and Fondos FEDER, TIN2009-13718-C02-01). It is also supported by ENGLOBAS (PII2I09-0147-8235), funded by the Consejería de Educación y Ciencia (Junta de Comunidades de Castilla-La Mancha), and co-funded by Fondos FEDER and ORIGIN (IDI-2010043 (1-5)) funded by CDTI and FEDER, as well as GlOBALIA (PEII11-0291-5274), Consejería de Educación y Ciencia, Junta de Comunidades de Castilla-La Mancha.

References

1. Monasor, M.J., Piattini, M., Vizcaíno, A.: Challenges and Improvements in Distributed Software Development: A Systematic Review. Advances in Software Engineering 2009, 1–16 (2009)
2. Acuna, S.T., Juristo, N., Moreno, A.M., Mon, A.: A Software Process Model Handbook for Incorporating People's Capabilities. Springer-Verlag New York, Inc. (2005)
3. Guzmán, J.G., Ramos, J.S., Seco, A.A., Esteban, A.S.: How to get mature global virtual teams: a framework to improve team process management in distributed software teams. Software Quality Control 18(4), 409–435 (2010)
4. Monasor, M.J., Vizcaíno, A., Piattini, M., Caballero, I.: Preparing students and engineers for Global Software Development: A Systematic Review. In: International Conference on Global Software Development (ICGSE 2010), August 23-26, pp. 177–186. IEEE Computer Society, Princeton (2010)
5. Acuna, S.T., Juristo, N., Moreno, A.M.: Emphasizing Human Capabilities in Software Development. IEEE Softw. 23(2), 94–101 (2006)

6. Abufardeh, S., Magel, K.: The impact of global software cultural and linguistic aspects on Global Software Development process (GSD): Issues and challenges. In: 4th International conference On New Trends in Information Science and Service Science (NISS), Gyeongju, South Korea, pp. 133–138 (2010)

7. Bordyuk, L.: Linguistic and culture-specific factors for professional success. In: Proceedings of the 7th International Conference The Experience of Designing and Application of CAD Systems in Microelectronics, CADSM 2003, February 18-22, pp. 530–532 (2003)

8. Deitersy, C., Herrmannz, C., Hildebrandtz, R., Knauss, E., Kuhrmannx, M., Rauschy, A., et al.: GloSE-Lab: Teaching Global Software Engineering. In: International Conference on Global Software Engineering (ICGSE), Helsinki, Findland, pp. 156–160 (2011)

9. Clear, T.: Replicating an 'Onshore' Capstone Computing Project in a 'Farshore' Setting – an Experience Report. In: International Conference on Global Software Engineering (ICGSE), Helsinki, Findland, pp. 161–165 (2011)

10. Braun, A., Dutoit, A.H., Harrer, A.G., Brüge, B.: iBistro: A Learning Environment for Knowledge Construction in Distributed Software Engineering Courses. In: Proceedings of the Ninth Asia-Pacific Software Engineering Conference, p. 197. IEEE Computer Society, Gold Coast (2002)

11. Swigger, K., Aplaslan, F.N., Lopez, V., Brazile, R., Dafoulas, G., Serce, F.C.: Structural factors that affect global software development learning team performance. In: Proceedings of the Special Interest Group on Management Information System's 47th Annual Conference on Computer Personnel Research, pp. 187–196. ACM, Limerick (2009)

12. Mandl-Striegnitz, P.: How to successfully use software project simulation for educating software project managers. In: Proceedings of the Frontiers in Education Conference, 2001 on 31st Annual, vol. 11, pp. T2D-19–T2D-24. IEEE Computer Society (2001)

13. van Solingen, R., Dullemond, K., van Gameren, B.: Evaluating the Effectiveness of Board Game Usage to Teach GSE Dynamics. In: International Conference on Global Software Engineering (ICGSE), Helsinki, Findland, pp. 166–175 (2011)

14. Drappa, A., Ludewig, J.: Simulation in software engineering training. In: Proceedings of the 22nd International Conference on Software Engineering, pp. 199–208. ACM, Limerick (2000)

15. Iwai, K., Akiyoshi, M., Samejima, M., Morihisa, H.: A Situation-Dependent Scenario Generation Framework for Project Management Skill-up Simulator. In: 6th International Conference on Software and Data Technologies, Seville, Spain, pp. 408–412 (2011)

16. Yilmaz, M., O'Connor, R.V.: An Approach for Improving the Social Aspects of the Software Development Process by Using a Game Theoretic Perspective. In: 6th International Conference on Software and Data Technologies, Seville, Spain, pp. 35–40 (2011)

17. Pelachaud, C.: Studies on gesture expressivity for a virtual agent. Speech Commun. 51(7), 630–639 (2009)

18. Bevacqua, E., Pelachaud, C.: Expressive audio-visual speech: Research Articles. Comput Animat Virtual Worlds 15(3-4), 297–304 (2004)

19. Kavakli, M., Rudra, T., Li, M.: An Embodied Conversational Agent for Counselling Aborigines. In: 6th International Conference on Software and Data Technologies, Seville, Spain, pp. 371–376 (2011)

20. Corder, D., U-Mackay, A.: Integrating Second Life to enhance global intercultural collaboration projects. ACM Inroads 1(3), 43–50 (2010)

21. Clear, T., Daniels, M.: 2D & 3D Introductory Processes in Virtual Groups. In: 33rd ASEE/IEEE Frontiers in Education Conference, November 5-8, pp. S1F1–S1F6. IEEE, Boulder (2003)
22. Parvathanathan, K., Chakrabarti, A., Patil, P.P., Sen, S., Sharma, N., Johng, Y.: Global Development and Delivery in Practice: Experiences of the IBM Rational India Lab. IBM Press (2007)
23. Casey, V.: Imparting the importance of culture to global software development. ACM Inroads 1(3), 51–57 (2011)
24. Hall, W.: Managing Cultures: Making Strategic Relationships Work, 1st edn. John Wiley & Sons (1996)
25. Hofstede, G., Hofstede, G.J.: Cultures and organizations: software of the mind, 2nd edn., New York, USA (2005)
26. House, R.J., Hanges, P.J., Javidan, M., Dorfman, P., Gupta, V.: Culture, Leadership, and Organizations: The GLOBE Study of 62 Societies. Sage Publications, Thousand Oaks (2004)
27. Trompenaars, A., Hampden-Turner, C.: Riding the waves of culture: understanding cultural diversity in global business. McGraw Hill (1998)
28. Hall, E.T.: Beyond Culture. Anchor Press (1976)
29. MacGregor, E., Hsieh, Y., Kruchten, P.: Cultural patterns in software process mishaps: incidents in global projects. In: Proceedings of the 2005 Workshop on Human and Social Factors of Software Engineering, pp. 1–5. ACM, St. Louis (2005)
30. Cunha, A.D.D., Greathead, D.: Does personality matter?: an analysis of code-review ability. Commun. ACM 50(5), 109–112 (2007)
31. Capretz, L.F.: Personality types in software engineering. Int. J. Hum.-Comput. Stud. 58(2), 207–214 (2003)
32. Tsai, M.-T., Huang, Y.-C.: Exploratory learning and new product performance: The moderating role of cognitive skills and environmental uncertainty. The Journal of High Technology Management Research 19(2), 83–93 (2008)
33. Strang, K.D.: Leadership substitutes and personality impact on time and quality in virtual new product development projects. Project Management Journal 42(1), 73–90 (2010)
34. Yoo, Y., Alavi, M.: Emergent leadership in virtual teams: what do emergent leaders do? Information and Organization 14(1), 27–58 (2004)
35. Kayworth, T.R., Leidner, D.E.: Leadership Effectiveness in Global Virtual Teams. J. Manage. Inf. Syst. 18(3), 7–40 (2002)
36. Dittrich, Y., Giuffrida, R.: Exploring the Role of Instant Messaging in a Global Software Development Project. International Conference on Global Software Engineering (ICGSE), Helsinki, Findland, pp. 103–112 (2011)
37. Wallace, R.S.: The Anatomy of A.L.I.C.E. In: Netherlands, S. (ed.) Parsing the Turing Test, pp. 181–210 (2008)

Improving IT Service Desk and Service Management Processes in Finnish Tax Administration: A Case Study on Service Engineering

Marko Jäntti

University of Eastern Finland, School of Computing
P.O. Box 1627, 70211, Kuopio, Finland
marko.jantti@uef.fi

Abstract. Due to success of IT service management frameworks, the service desk function and the incident management process are improvement targets of high priority for many IT companies at the moment. The main goal of the incident management process is to restore normal service operation as quickly as possible. The research problem of this study is: How service engineering processes and service desk can be improved by using ITIL-based best practices? The main contribution of this paper is to 1) describe the phases of a study that focused on improving service desk and incident management process from IT service management perspective and 2) provide lessons learnt from the study. The case study was carried out with a single case: Finnish Tax Administration.

Keywords: IT service management, incident management, ITIL, process.

1   Introduction

A service desk is a very important function for IT service companies. It handles incidents (hardware and software failures), service requests, complaints, feedback and requests for change reported by customers and users. Therefore, the service desk is a crucial part of the IT service provider's customer interface. Many IT service provider organizations are using IT Infrastructure Library (ITIL) to increase the quality of IT service support and to improve the service engineering processes. ITIL is the most widely used IT service management framework. ITIL best practices are used by thousands of IT organizations worldwide [1].

IT service management can be defined as "implementation and management of quality IT services that meet the needs of the business" [2]. IT companies may provide various types of IT services, such as application services, server services, data center services, desk top services, help desk services, data network services, and hardware lifecycle services. IT service management is performed by IT service providers through an appropriate mix of people, process and information technology.

O. Dieste, A. Jedlitschka, and N. Juristo (Eds.): PROFES 2012, LNCS 7343, pp. 218–232, 2012.

The ITIL framework consists of best practices and guidelines that can be used to improve IT service desk function and related processes. First, the goal is to establish a service desk that acts as a single point of contact by recording and classifying every support request from customers and users. These support requests are stored into a IT service management system. Second, the goal is to keep the customers and users informed. This means that they should receive incident confirmation receipts, enough information on the progress of incident resolutions and on services that are available for customers. Third, the goal is to establish clear escalation procedures that enable service desk workers to escalate and assign cases to other teams, such as second level support, field support teams or third-party service providers.

1.1   Related Work

Currently, there are many frameworks and standards that can be used to improve IT service management processes:

- IT Infrastructure Library version 2 [3], version 3 [1], edition 2011 [4]
- Control Objectives for IT and related Technology (COBIT) framework [5]
- Capability Maturity Model Integration (CMMI) for Services [6]
- IT Service Capability Maturity Model [7]
- ISO/IEC 20000-1:2005 Part 1: Specification for service management [8]
- ISO/IEC 20000-1:2005 Part 2: Code of practice for service management [9].
- ISO/IEC FDIS 20000-1:2010 Part 1: Service management system requirements [10]
- ISO/IEC TR 20000-3:2009 Part 3: Guidance for the scoping and applicability of ISO/IEC 20000-1 [11].

In this paper, we focus on the improvement of service desk function and the incident management process. Academic studies that deal with customer support can be classified into traditional customer support studies that use a term 'help desk' and service management studies that use a term 'service desk'. According to ITIL service support, the service desk extends the services that a traditional help desk provides [12]. Help desk studies have focused, for example, on examining the role of help desk in the strategic management of information systems [13], knowledge management-centric help desk [14], evolution of a knowledge management system in the help desk [15] and building IT help desk in the university environment [16].

The number of academic IT service management studies is rapidly increasing. Previous studies on IT service management have dealt with benefits of implementation of service-oriented IT management [17], creating taxonomy for ITIL processes [18], creating a maturity model for implementing ITIL v3 [19], and success factors in implementing IT service management [20,21]. Meziani and Saleh [22] have presented results of process maturity self-assessment in a government agency. Zhang et al. [23] have explored ITIL process integration architecture in the context of organization environment. Moreover, Iden and Eikebrokk [24]

have conducted a study on conceptualization and measurements of ITIL implementation project. There are also studies that are directly related to service
management processes, such as improvement of incident management processes
based on ITIL practices [25], creating a mature problem management process
[26], service testing [27], service level management [28] and change and configuration management [29]. Surprizingly few of ITSM studies have provided details
how ITIL-based process implementation has been done in government agencies
or presented feedback on ITSM trainings.

1.2   Our Contribution

This paper is related to IT service management research of the research project
Keys to IT Service Management and Effective Transition of Services (KISMET).
The main contribution of this paper is to

- describe the phases of a study that focused on improving service desk and
  incident management process from IT service management perspective and
- provide lessons learnt from the study regarding processes, tools and ITSM
  trainings.

Our research results might be useful for employees who are working for IT service desk improvement (service desk managers, incident managers and customer
service managers) or overall service quality improvement (CSI managers).

The rest of the paper is organized as follows. In Section 2, the research problem
and methods are described. In Section 3, we describe the process improvement
phases. In Section 4, we provide the analysis of findings in the form of lessons
learnt. The conclusions are given in Section 5.

2   Research Methods

In this study, the research problem is: How service engineering processes and
service desk can be improved by using ITIL-based best practices? We used a
case study research method to answer the research problem. The study was
carried out with a single case organization, Finnish Tax Administration that is
a member of the university's research project.

The case study approach was selected for the research method because it
suits well for studying service engineering processes that are linked to a complex
organizational context; a jungle of IT teams, software products, services and
suppliers. A case study is "a research strategy which focuses on understanding
the dynamics present with single settings" [30]. It can also be defined as "an
empirical inquiry that investigates a contemporary phenomenon within its real-
life context" [31]. Research settings consists of three main elements: research
problem, research methods and research data. Figure 1 describes the research
settings of this case study.

The research problem was further divided into following research questions
that provided a roadmap for the case study:

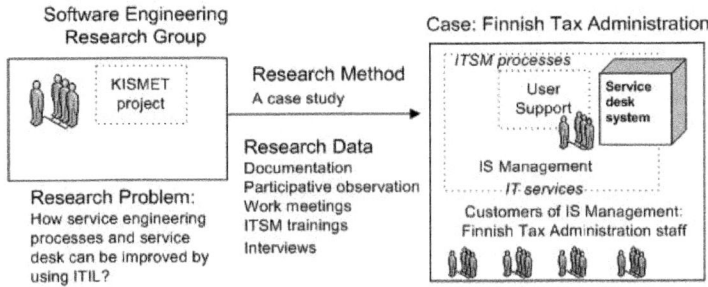

Fig. 1. The research settings of the case study

- What is the current status of the service desk tool and the incident management process?
- What types of challenges are related to service desk operations (Service desk and incident management)?
- How support requests should be classified and ITSM concepts integrated to the service desk?
- Which interfaces do service desk and incident management have?
- How IT service management trainings for service desk people should be conducted?
- What does Continual Service Improvement mean for service desk?

2.1   The Case Organization and Data Collection Methods

Our case organization is the Information System Management unit of Finnish Tax Administration that provides IT services (e.g. desktop services, service desk) to the tax administration staff. Regarding the case selection, Tax Administration was a representative case of a government agency with service desk tool development and ITIL-based process improvement. The organization had 5336 fulltime employees in 2010. The service desk improvement project had started in the organization in the end of 2010.

The user support services unit is responsible for the support services (use of the information technology and support services related to the management of production environment). User support services staff manages the support requests and service requests. User support services unit cooperates with other groups of the Information System Management, such as application support, infrastructure support and e-service support. Customers and users can use two main service channels (phone, service desk system) while submitting support requests to the service desk. User instruction documents are maintained in the intranet. Service desk is open for customers and users during the office hours (8.00-16.15). The following sources of evidence were used in data collection:

- Documentation (process descriptions, user support metrics, service desk system user manual, service descriptions, service area catalogue, event

management process description, error handling process description, change plan template)
- Archives and records (service categories, incident records, service request records, problem records, change records)
- Participative observation (weekly meetings, informal coffee table discussions, email discussions)
- ITSM trainings for user support staff (70 persons, September 2011)
- Physical artifacts (access to the organization's intranet and service desk system).

2.2 Data Analysis

Eisenhardt [30] reports that there are two main approaches that can be used to analyze the case study data: a case comparison analysis and a within-case analysis. The within case analysis focuses on examining cases carefully as stand-alone entities before making any generalizations. The purpose of the within-case analysis is to carry out a detailed level investigation in a case, for exa-ple, by creating a case study write-up that describes the behavior of the case. The cross-case analysis aims to search cross-case patterns and is suitable for multiple case studies.

In this study, a within-case analysis technique was used. Process improvement events were organized into chronological order according to the phases of KISMET model. Researcher triangulation (three researchers) was used both in data collection and in data analysis. Case study findings were validated in weekly meeting with the case organization's representatives. A summary report on the process improvement work was created and submitted to the case organization.

3 Improving Service Desk and Service Management Processes

The service desk process improvement with Finnish Tax Administration was based on KISMET (Keys to IT Service Management Excellence Technique) model. The model consists of the following seven phases: 1) Create a process improvement infrastructure, 2) Perform a process assessment, 3) Plan process improvement actions 4) Improve/Implement the process based on ITSM practices, 5) Deploy and introduce the process, 6) Evaluate process improvement and 7) Continuous process/service improvement.

3.1 Create a Process Improvement Infrastructure

Create a process improvement infrastructure phase includes the following steps: motivate the business decision makers to ITSM, define business goals for ITSM process improvement, select an improvement target and identify stakeholders that participate in the process improvement.

The goals for the improvement were discussed in the meeting of March 2011 between the research team and a service manager of the case organization. The goals were discussed again in August 2011. The first goal was to improve the service desk tool to match the IT service management requirements. To achieve this goal, the plan of KISMET research team was to carry out reviews for service categories, data fields, incident and problem records. The aim was to find out whether employees use the properties of IT service management tool effectively. The second goal was to improve and optimize the service support processes (incident and problem management). Especially, the interface between incident management, problem management and change management needed clarification. The third goal was to explore continual service improvement activities and organize a CSI workshop.

NDAs were signed, as usually, in industrial cases by research team members and access to the case organization's facilities was granted to two researchers. Researchers received a PC that enabled access to the organization's intranet, email and office applications. Additionally, researchers had access to the IT service management tool.

Stakeholders that would participate in the process improvement from the case organization's side were partly familiar to the research team, mainly service managers representing various IT services of the organization. We were also told that we could participate an informal Friday morning coffee table meetings with user support service staff.

3.2   Identify the Current State of the Processes

The *Perform a process assessment* phase includes steps, such as perform a process assessment for a selected ITSM process, document the challenges and difficulties in the current state of the process, identify the key concepts regarding the process, study how tools support the process and benchmark the process with ITIL best practices and ISO 20 000 requirements. This phase was carried out by multiple researchers and using various types of data sources, such as participative observation, organization's internal documentation, intranet, service desk records, and discussions with service managers and user support team members both in process improvement meetings and in coffee table.

The following strengths were observed during the phase. First, the selected service desk tool seemed to support well the IT service management and ITIL-based process improvement. Second, the case organization had put a lot of efforts on automatization of service requests. There were many electronic service request forms in daily use. The forms were connected to the service management system. Third, we observed that service desk roles and responsibilities had been well described and implemented in practise. Fourth, incident management activities had been described in the incident management process description and they seemed to match IT service management concepts. Fifth, service desk as a single point of contact seemed to be a common and a clear goal in the organization. Finally, the tool improvement team seemed to have a good knowhow how to configure the service desk system. This observation was based on the discussions with a member of the tool team.

The following improvement targets were observed during the phase. The list is not exhaustive.

- Classification of support requests in the service desk requires clarification (both from customer's and service desk worker's viewpoint).
- Identification of repeating incidents from the service desk system.
- Employees have problems to understand differences between ITIL concepts.
- The interface between incident management and problem management.
- Improvement ideas regarding IT services and processes should be recorded systematically into the service desk system.

3.3 Plan Process Improvement Actions

The *Plan process improvement actions* phase includes the following steps: Analyze the identified challenges, plan improvement actions, and validate the challenges and improvement actions. This phase focused on defining the process improvement actions based on the identified challenges and bottlenecks. For each improvement target, we documented the solution and the business benefit why it is important to resolve challenge.

- **Challenge:** Classification of support requests requires clarification. **Solution:** Clarify the options in 'Reason for Contact Request' field of the incident record. Make the difference between service requests and incidents visible. Service area and the type of of support requests should be different fields. Remove the classification option from customers and simplify the submission of support requests. **Business benefit:** Handling of the support request shall be faster. Service area can be used also in the problem records and incident records. Submitting support requests becomes easier for customers and users. The number of phone calls from customers and users shall decrease as they use the service desk system to report support requests.
- **Challenge:** It is difficult to identify repeating incidents from the service desk system. **Solution:** Mark the repeating incidents (for example, create an additional 'check box' type data field to an incident record: Repeating incident = x). Use the 'Relate Cases' function to establish relationships between similar cases. Create a problem record based on a repeating incident. **Business benefit:** Identification and reporting of repeating incidents shall be easier. Finding the root cause and solution for repeating incidents shall decrease the support request volume.
- **Challenge:** Employees do not understand differences between some ITIL terms. **Solution:** Collect 10 examples of each term. The service desk should separate service requests from incidents. **Business benefit:** Service requests are routine requests and handling of them is easier and faster than handling of incidents. In the future, there might be different SLAs for incidents and service requests.

 – **Challenge:** Interface between incident and problem management should
   be defined. **Solution:** Create and use a problem record. Establish a simple
   problem management procedure. **Business benefit:** Recording systematic
   incidents as problem records provides a way to identify the root cause of
   incidents. Proactive problem management enables monitoring trends (which
   services or products have caused the most incidents)
 – **Challenge:** Improvement ideas regarding IT services and processes should
   be recorded systematically into the service desk system. **Solution:** Create a
   CSI model. Assign improvement suggestions to change management. **Business benefit:** Management of improvement suggestions shall become more
   systematic. This ensures that each suggestion receives attention and review.

3.4   Improve/Implement the Process Based on ITSM Practices

The *Improve/Implement the process based on ITSM practices* phase includes
for example, the following steps: Define and document a) the process goals, b)
benefits that a process provides customers and IT organization's business, c) key
concepts, d) roles and responsibilities, e) actions, f) metrics and g) relationships
to other ITSM processes; improve tools that are used in the process and establish
a process manager role if it does not exist yet.

The case organization already had a good description of the incident management process. Thus, improvement of the support processes was started from
classification. There was a dropdown menu field *Reason for the service desk contact* in the incident record. We divided the contact categories according to ITIL
concepts: incident (error and failure reports), service request (request for user
rights, request for advice, request for reporting, request for examining, request
for update, order, other service request), feedback, improvement suggestion and
formal complaint. A member of the service desk tool improvement team told
us that they removed ''problem' from the list of contact reasons because some
service desk workers started to log incidents as problems.

We continued the improvement of classification by proposing a new service
area classification that could be used in the classification of incidents, service
requests, problems and requests for change. The new, proposed service area was
presented to the case organization's representatives that reviewed service areas
and created a new version of service areas. In order to show differences between
ITIL concepts (incidents, service requests, problems, requests for change), we
collected ten examples of each concept. That was a really good exercise because
researchers learned a lot of provided services and found good material for IT
service management trainings.

While examining the interface between incident and problem management,
the research team started to develop a simple model for problem management.
For example, the following guidelines were created for opening and creating a
problem record: A problem record can be opened by using two different ways: a)
Select from the menu *Create problem* b) Create a problem based on an existing
incident record by clicking the link *Create problem* in the incident record. Thus,
incident basic information shall be transferred to the problem record. One should

not define a *customer* field as a mandatory field because a service desk specialist must be able to record the problem without a customer's incident report.

Regarding problem management, the representatative of the tool improvement team reported that they had to remove terms 'problem' and 'request for change' from the categories of the service desk case because service desk workers had logged incidents as problems. Additionally, the following questions were posed for the researchers that acted as ITIL consults: what is the difference between a support request and a problem in practice, how a problem should recorded in the system, how configuration items should be categorized and how a service desk worker can convert the incident to the RFC? The final improvement target was continual service improvement. The research team organized a CSI workshop where a CSI process model was presented to the case organization. We shall discuss the model more detailed in our further paper.

3.5 Deploy and Introduce Processes

This phase includes the following steps: Deploy an ITSM process with a pilot group, create work instructions how to perform the process in practice, motivate the workers to ITSM, increase the ITSM awareness in the organization through training, organize ITSM workshops to clarify ITSM process interfaces. In this phase, the representatives of case organization asked whether the research team could organize ITSM trainings for Tax Administration employees. Instead of one large training event, the research team organized seven small ITSM awareness events (1 hour, 6-10 user support service workers in each event) and Basics of IT service Support (3 hour each event).

3.6 Evaluate Process Improvement

This phase involces collecting feedback regarding an improved process, tools and training, conducting fine-tuning if necessary, and deployment the processes to other organizational units or services. Regarding ITSM trainings, the research team collected the following comments:

- English ITIL terms seemed to be weird many years, now they look clearer
- Service desk workers should see the big picture behind the things; whether a single ticket is related to a large group of incidents.
- Until these days, we have thought that these improvement frameworks are only for managers.
- How other organizations use ITIL?
- We should start thinking about the ITSM certification courses.
- ITIL framework looks very complicated, like a blueprint of a nuclear plant.
- All support groups do not use automatic alert function that submits an email message when a new ticket has arrived.
- It would be nice if user support staff could send information on repeating incidents to process managers.
- The large number of support groups is a problem.

- Is it possible to conduct parallel handling for the tasks of an incident?
- Who is responsible for change management in the IS management unit?

In the feedback form, we asked how useful employees considered the ITSM awareness training by using 1 to 5 scale (1 =completely useless, 5= very valuable for daily work). We received 28/70 responses. The average score was 3.46. We also received free form feedback from participants that indicated that training had included concrete examples, participants had liked the face-to-face training, employees were interested in getting more training, and the timing for training had been good. In the end of the evaluation phase, we organized an end meeting of the study where the case organization gave feedback for the whole process improvement. They mentioned that the study helped the organization especially identifying connections between processes and increase the employee's awareness of ITSM processes and concepts.

3.7   Continuous Process/Service Improvement

Continuous process improvement phase includes, for example, the following steps: Conduct process reviews frequently, identify and report process improvement ideas or process-related problems to a process manager or the Continuous Service Improvement process and plan and implement improvement actions.

The interface between CSI and service desk means in practice monitoring, measurement and reporting capabilities for service desk function and incident management process. Additionally, CSI organizes reviews for the service desk service, systems and processes and analyzes improvement suggestions. According to our findings, the service desk and incident management metrics included incident throughput time, speed of ticket creation, ticket volume, average ticket resolution time, tickets by service channel(phone, email), and customer satisfaction.

4   Analysis

In the analysis phase of this study, we summarized case study findings in the form of lesson learned. A source for each lesson is presented in parentheses (AR= Archives and records, D= Documentation, ID= Interviews and discussions, O= Observation, PA= physical artefacts, ST= Seminars and trainings organized by the research group).

Lesson 1: Reserve time for informal discussions between ITIL consults and employees (Phase 1: ID, O). Informal discussions with user support team members turned out to be very valuable data collection method during the study. The reseach team participated, for example, in weekly coffee table meetings. These discussions worked as ice-breaking sessions and resulted in important information about the current state of the tools and processes. Discussions revealed that some of the workers were afraid of learning ITIL best practices. This observation put us to make big changes in ITSM training material.

Lesson 2: The classification of service desk cases is one of the key challenges in service desk (Phase 2: AR, PA, ID). The classification activity of the incident management has been a bottleneck or a challenge for many IT service provider companies. We started the improvement of classification by exploring service areas and ensuring that a service desk can create service requests, incidents, problems and RFCs and relate these to service areas. We observed that a service request term had been used in a different meaning than in ITIL and there were many request types that were clearly subcategories of service requests. Therefore, we proposed that incidents and service requests would be visible in the *Reason for contact* field's categories, for example, Order - Service request.

Lesson 3: Define clear escalation rules for the service desk (Phase 2: O, ID, DO). We observed that one should clarify the rules of escalating cases to other support levels. The application support team is responsible for handling application-related support cases and providing advice on applications. They had reported that they receive incidents and service requests that would be possible to solve on the first level support (service desk). The hardware technology group had reported the same issue that the service desk assigns the cases too easily for them. One had suggested that a case should be assigned to the hardware technology group not until one has identified that the case is a problem (according to ITIL).

Lesson 4: Identification of repeating incidents creates a natural bridge between incident management and problem management (Phase 3 and 4: O, ID). The interface between incident management and problem management has been among the most discussed challenges in ITIL implementation projects. Incident management and problem management have completely different goals. The main objective of incident management is to resolve incidents (unplanned interruptions to IT services) reported by customers and users as soon as possible while problem management aims to find a root cause for incidents. Thus, the speed of problem solving is not the issue in problem management. After employees have understood the basic meaning of incidents and problems, it is easy to train them that repeating incidents (also called systematic incidents) are potential problems.

Lesson 5: Create a problem management culture to the service desk (Phase 4: ID, ST). Based on the discussions between user support service workers and the member of the tool improvement team, we observed that the employees are not familiar with the problem management process that aims to create proactive customer support. We decided to create a draft problem record for trainings in order to show that there is a place for problem records and a simple instructions how to create them.

Lesson 6: Do not forget event management while improving service desk (Phase 4: O, ID, D, AR). Events are automatic alerts caused by the IT infrastructure. Event Management provides mechanisms for early detection of incidents [32]. The event management process includes the filtering step where a support engineer decides whether to assign the event to an ITSM tool or to ignore it. We almost forgot to define the interface between incident management and event management. We received very good and tough questions from event management people.

Lesson 7: IT service management trainings should be tailored by using practical examples (Phase 5: ST, O). Before this study, we had always started trainings with the same old picture of ITIL framework. After some informal discussions with user support staff, we decided to hide the ITIL framework from our slides and started training by explaining what are the services and motivating why IT service management is a good thing both from an organization's and employee's career perspective. We felt that this was a good solution. Additionally, we added a lot of organization-related examples to the training material instead of classic ITIL training examples. Finally, we removed all the ITIL abbreviations and translated the English terms in Finnish.

Lesson 8: Conduct ITSM trainings in small groups (Phase 5 and 6: ST). The research team considered important that trainings are organized in small groups and a trainer has a face-to-face contact to audience in awareness level trainings. Thus, employees feel more comfortable to ask questions. However, this required a lot of travelling in our case but we received good feedback. The trainer also decided not to sit in the front of the class but in the same row withi audience to create a feeling that a trainer is a part of the group.

Lesson 9: Use CSFs, KPIs and metrics as a basis of a process measurement program (Phase 4 and 7: D, ID, ST). Regarding Continual Service Improvement, we observed that critical success factors, key performance indicators and metrics provide a good basis to establish process measurement program. The case organization had defined several service desk metrics and created reports based on metrics. However, these metrics needed to be linked to critical success factors and key performance indicators. Defining these three elements creates the bridge between business goals and operational measurements.

Lesson 10: Define the interface between Continual Service Improvement and service desk and incident management (Phase 4 and 7: ST, D, ID). The interface between Continual Service Improvement and service desk and incident management means in practice that a service desk collects improvement suggestions from customers, creates improvement suggestions regarding the service desk and the incident management process, tools and people. CSI is also responsible for reviewing service desk as a service.

Both the case organization and the research team were satisfied with the case study results. This paper enables the research team to share ITSM process improvement experiences with other companies.

5   Conclusions

The research problem in this study was: How service engineering processes and service desk can be improved by using ITIL-based best practices? The main contribution of this study was to describe the phases of a study that focused on improving service desk and incident management process from IT service management perspective and provide lessons learnt from the study regarding processes, tools and people. The unit of analysis in the case study was a government agency, an IS management unit of the Finnish Tax Administration.

We used a phased approach (KISMET technique) with seven phases for IT service process improvement. The improvement focused on 1) classification of customer support requests 2) clarifying the interfaces of the incident management process, especially with problem, change, and event management, 3)increasing the employee's awareness of ITSM concepts and processes and 4) exploring CSI actitivies and organizing a CSI workshop.

This study included the following limitations. First, we used a single case structure in our study. Thus, the generalization of the results might be weaker compared to multiple case studies and quantitative studies. In order to increase the quality of the case study, we used the principles of data collection presented by Yin [31]: 1) using multiple sources of evidence, 2) creating a case study database and 3) maintaining a chain of evidence. This study provided us important feedback on ITSM trainings, valuable observations on process interfaces. Second, we could have had discussions with the employees from other service areas, such as hardware technology groups of Tax Administration. Unfortunately, the lack of time was a limiting factor. Third, due to research project, we had easy access to the case organization. Every project member receives certain amount of time for process improvement. Thus, the case was not randomly selected.

To conclude, more case studies are needed to examine interfaces between IT service management processes. Further work could focus on creating and validating a Continuous Service Improvement model in IT service provider organizations.

Acknowledgment. This paper is based on research in Keys to IT Service Management and Effective Transition of Services (KISMET) project funded by the National Technology Agency TEKES (no. 70035/10), European Regional Development Fund (ERDF), and industrial partners.

References

1. Office of Government Commerce: ITIL Service Strategy. The Stationary Office, UK (2007)
2. Office of Government Commerce: ITIL Continual Service Improvement. The Stationary Office, UK (2007)
3. OGC: ITIL Service Support. The Stationary Office, UK (2002)
4. Cabinet Office: ITIL Service Strategy. The Stationary Office, UK (2011)
5. COBIT 4.1: Control Objectives for Information and related Technology: COBIT 4.1. IT Governance Institute (2007)
6. Software Engineering Institute: CMMI for Services: Initial Draft. Carnegie Mellon University (2006)

7. Niessinka, F., Clerca, V., Tijdinka, T., van Vliet, H.: The it service capability maturity model version 1.0. CIBIT Consultants&Vrije Universiteit (2005)
8. ISO/IEC 20000: IT Service Management, Part 1: Specification for service management. ISO/IEC JTC1/SC7 Secretariat (2005)
9. ISO/IEC 20000: IT Service Management, Part 2: Code of practice for service management. ISO/IEC JTC1/SC7 Secretariat (2005)
10. ISO/IEC: ISO/IEC FDIS 20000:1. ISO/IEC JTC 1 Secretariat: ANSI (2010)
11. ISO/IEC: ISO/IEC TR 20000-3 Information Technology - Service Management - Guidance on scope definition and applicability of ISO/IEC 20000-1. ISO/IEC JTC1/SC7 Secretariat (2010)
12. Office of Government Commerce: ITIL Service Delivery. The Stationary Office, UK (2002)
13. Marcella, R., Middleton, I.: The role of the help desk in the strategic management of information systems. OCLC Systems & Services 12(4), 4–19 (1996)
14. Gonzalez, L.M., Giachetti, R.E., Ramirez, G.: Knowledge management-centric help desk: specification and performance evaluation. Decis. Support Syst. 40(2), 389–405 (2005)
15. Halverson, C.A., Erickson, T., Ackerman, M.S.: Behind the help desk: evolution of a knowledge management system in a large organization. In: Proceedings of the 2004 ACM Conference on Computer Supported Cooperative Work, CSCW 2004, pp. 304–313. ACM, New York (2004)
16. Evans, K., Jones, W.T.: Building an it help desk: from zero to hero. In: SIGUCCS 2005: Proceedings of the 33rd Annual ACM SIGUCCS Conference on User Services, pp. 68–74. ACM, New York (2005)
17. Hochstein, A., Zarnekow, R., Brenner, W.: Itil as common practice reference model for it service management: Formal assessment and implications for practice. In: EEE 2005: Proceedings of the 2005 IEEE International Conference on e-Technology, e-Commerce and e-Service, pp. 704–710. IEEE Computer Society, Washington, DC (2005)
18. Brenner, M.: Classifying itil processes; a taxonomy under tool support aspects. In: The First IEEE/IFIP International Workshop on Business-Driven IT Management, BDIM 2006, pp. 19–28 (2006)
19. de Sousa Pereira, R., da Silva, M.: A maturity model for implementing itil v3. In: 2010 6th World Congress on Services (SERVICES-1), pp. 399–406 (2010)
20. Tan, W.G., Cater-Steel, A., Toleman, M.: Implementing it service management: A case study focussing on critical success factors. Journal of Computer Information Systems 50(2) (2009)
21. Pollard, C., Cater-Steel, A.: Justifications, strategies, and critical success factors in successful itil implementations in u.s. and australian companies: An exploratory study. Information Systems Management 26(2), 164–175 (2009)
22. Meziani, R., Saleh, I.: e-government: Itil-based service management case study. In: Proceedings of the 12th International Conference on Information Integration and Web-based Applications & Services, IIWAS 2010, pp. 509–516. ACM, New York (2010)
23. Zhang, S., Ding, Z., Zong, Y.: Itil process integration in the context of organization environment. In: 2009 WRI World Congress on Computer Science and Information Engineering, vol. 7, pp. 682–686 (2009)
24. Iden, J., Eikebrokk, T.R.: Understanding the itil implementation project: Conceptualization and measurements. In: Proceedings of 2011 22nd International Workshop on Database and Expert Systems Applications. IEEE, Washington, DC (2011)

25. Jäntti, M.: Lessons Learnt from the Improvement of Customer Support Processes: A Case Study on Incident Management. In: Bomarius, F., Oivo, M., Jaring, P., Abrahamsson, P. (eds.) PROFES 2009. LNBIP, vol. 32, pp. 317–331. Springer, Heidelberg (2009)
26. Kajko-Mattsson, M.: Problem management maturity within corrective maintenance. Journal of Software Maintenance 14(3), 197–227 (2002)
27. Jantti, M., Kujala, T.: Exploring a testing during maintenance process from it service provider's perspective. In: 2011 5th International Conference on New Trends in Information Science and Service Science (NISS), vol. 2, pp. 318–323 (2011)
28. Kajko-Mattsson, M., Ahnlund, C., Lundberg, E.: Cm3: Service level agreement. In: ICSM 2004: Proceedings of the 20th IEEE International Conference on Software Maintenance, pp. 432–436. IEEE Computer Society, Washington, DC (2004)
29. Ward, C., Aggarwal, V., Buco, M., Olsson, E., Weinberger, S.: Integrated change and configuration management. IBM Syst. J. 46, 459–478 (2006)
30. Eisenhardt, K.: Building theories from case study research. Academy of Management Review 14, 532–550 (1989)
31. Yin, R.: Case Study Research: Design and Methods. Sage Publishing, Beverly Hills (1994)
32. Office of Government Commerce: ITIL Service Operation. The Stationary Office, UK (2007)

Experiences from Establishing Knowledge Management in a Joint Research Project

Sebastian Meyer[1], Anna Averbakh[1], Torsten Ronneberger[2], and Kurt Schneider[1]

[1] Software Engineering Group, Leibniz Universität Hannover
Welfengarten 1, 30167 Hannover, Germany
{sebastian.meyer,anna.averbakh,
kurt.schneider}@inf.uni-hannover.de
[2] Audi AG
85045 Ingolstadt
torsten.ronneberger@audi.de

Abstract. Joint research projects are create new knowledge and lessons learned from experience. A research project with several partners is a challenging environment for systematic reuse of knowledge and experience. Knowledge management is often considered overhead, with several tasks added to the workload of the project. This overhead can become overwhelming, since partners from academia and industry have different backgrounds, and may associate different goals and priorities with the project. Industry partners tend to follow strict security guidelines that hamper experience exchange. An extension of project duration is not possible in many publicly funded joint projects. In this paper, we describe our experiences from the initial phase of a major German joint research project with partners from academia and industry. We describe the applied techniques and the lessons learned during the first year the project. We derive conclusions and provide suggestions how to introduce knowledge and experience management in similar projects.

Keywords: experience report, case study, joint research project, knowledge management, experience lifecycle.

1 Introduction

Over the last years, research and development (R&D) has become more and more important in Germany. Funding for R&D rose from 20.2 billion EUR in 1982 to 62.2 billon EUR in 2007. Building up researching experience is an important factor in global competition.

Research initiatives usually consist of several smaller research projects. Because of innovative content and the different participants with different knowledge backgrounds, these are very complex projects [1]. This complexity poses a great challenge to project management. As knowledge is one of the most valuable results and assets of a research project, knowledge and experience management is needed to support knowledge generation, transfer and application throughout all organizational and procedural solutions.

O. Dieste, A. Jedlitschka, and N. Juristo (Eds.): PROFES 2012, LNCS 7343, pp. 233–247, 2012.

An ideal process for collecting and storing knowledge or experiences and making them accessible again is denominated by the experience lifecycle [2] as shown in Figure 1. In this model experiences are collected, structured and stored. After this they are made accessible and can be activated to help in the future. This, of course, leads to new experience, starting a new iteration of the lifecycle.

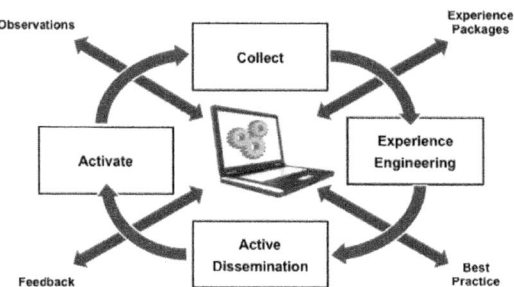

Fig. 1. Experience Lifecycle as described in [2]

In this paper, we show an instantiation of the experience lifecycle in a joint research project. We evaluate the experiences made during the first year of the project and derive lessons learned to take into account for a better instantiation.

The paper is structured as follows: Chapter 2 gives an overview of the general characteristics of a joint research project and the challenges for knowledge management. Chapter 3 relates our findings to existing literature. In chapter 4, we present the *e performance* project as a case study for a joint research project and show our instantiation of the experience lifecycle. After this, we give an evaluation of the usefulness and the appropriateness of the chosen result in chapter 5. The evaluation is based on experience made during the first year of the project. Chapter 6 summarizes the lessons learned during the project and presents recommendations for establishing knowledge management in similar joint research projects. We discuss our findings in chapter 7 and give an outlook to further work in this area.

2   Joint Research Projects

2.1   Project Management Characteristics

A joint research project is one frequently used option to close the gap between academia and industry. In the majority of cases, scientists and developers with various specializations and from different organizations are working together towards a defined research goal. They are distributed across different sites. Project members often have different R&D methodologies. They may even stem from different domains as well as disciplines. To effectively work as a project team, knowledge differences must be minimized to assure effective work during the project. Additional time is needed to minimize knowledge differences. That is often neglected or forgotten when partners agree on a project schedule. Project management must, therefore, adapt schedules during the whole project, opening opportunities for team building and installation of infrastructure. It is typically also distributed among different organizations.

Another essential characteristic of a joint research project are the different goals of each project partner. While the overall goal of the project is commonly agreed upon in the project description, each partner can strive after one or more sub-goals, aligned to their overall business. Although project management is in charge of overseeing the agreed goals, partners can distribute their manpower in order to achieve their own high priority sub-goals. Sometimes, reaching a sub-goal conflicts with working towards overall project goals.

2.2   Challenges in Knowledge and Experience Management

Having knowledge in a specific domain is an important competitive advantage. On the one hand, working together successfully in a joint research project depends on knowledge exchange between all contributors. On the other hand, sharing of knowledge with possible competitors or contractors is a fine-grained, often difficult process with many constraints and restrictions. Thus, a fundamental task of knowledge management in joint research projects is to motivate all knowledge carriers to share their knowledge in the context of the project and create the awareness for knowledge as a common resource in the project. Of course, this needs to be supported by the project partner organizations. They need to create a friendly knowledge-sharing environment, even among competitors and contractors working in the same project. There is an obvious tension.

Sharing organizational knowledge among all team members is a popular starting point for creating such an environment. Organizational knowledge can be project plans, competencies and roles of the project members, and contact information. This knowledge should already be in place when the project starts. It is not a competitive advantage, and it can send a signal that sharing knowledge freely is a basic concept of the project.

A much more difficult process is to level the different knowledge backgrounds. To establish a common ground of understanding, it is often necessary for different project members to share their competitive knowledge. As stated above, this is a critical case, since knowledge equals business value for most of the organizations.

At last, it is the function of knowledge management to encourage externalization of tacit knowledge so that the created knowledge will not be lost after the end of the project. Since knowledge management is not the main task for the project members, it is often seen as overhead work for which little time is dedicated.

3   Related Work

Knowledge Management in General. Original research on knowledge management is numerous. Polanyi [3] and Nonaka [4] coined the terms tacit and explicit knowledge. Tacit knowledge, like insights or intuitions, dwells in human mind and is hard to convey to others. Explicit knowledge can be expressed and shared in documents. The key to successful knowledge management is finding a way to transform tacit into explicit knowledge. Academia and industry have tried to implement tacit and explicit knowledge transfer. A well-known concept is the Experience Broker introduced by Ericsson [5]. An Experience Broker acts as communicator over projects providing support to other project members. Wenger [6] introduced communities of practice as a social approach to knowledge management and organizational learning. A fundamental work on knowledge and experience management is the Experience Factory by Basili [7]. An experience factory is a separate "logical and/or physical organization that supports project developments by analyzing all kinds of experience, acting as a repository for such experience, and supplying that experience to various projects on demand" [7]. These experiences are stored. The knowledge management initiative in the presented case study has been set up according to the Experience Factory concept.

Knowledge Management in Cooperative Projects. Nonaka et al. define a fundamental model (SECI) of a knowledge life cycle in an inter-organizational context, including a combination step, i.e. engineering explicit knowledge into more structured knowledge [8]. This model is a basis to our contribution. Jolly [9] and Soekijad [10] discuss decision and knowledge sharing problems in joint ventures but without giving a pragmatic solution. Trust between (R&D) cooperation partners as an important factor for knowledge sharing has been reported by Inkpen and Curall [11] as well as by Caloghirou et.al. [12]. Concerns of being dependent on the knowledge of joint venture partners are also discussed [13], though giving no implications for project management. Examining research joint ventures, Revilla proposed a taxonomy for knowledge management processes in such a setting [14]. It differentiates types of shared knowledge generated by the research joint venture. It is a conceptual framework and does not consider project management challenges in relation to knowledge management. Bhandar [15] describes how opportunity, motivation and ability can address conflicts like different business interests in collaborative projects and improve knowledge contribution and assimilation. He does not mention technical knowledge management challenges in joint ventures. Kastelli [16] mentions negative influence of rivalry and opportunism on organizational knowledge creation in cooperative R&D projects not giving solutions.

Experience Reports. In the past decade, a lot of experience reports on experience and knowledge management initiatives were published [17], [18], [19], [20], [21], [22], [23] in the field of software engineering. They describe company-wide and successful implementations, providing recommendations on how to success in this initiative. Akhavan [24] reports of an unsuccessful knowledge management initiative, mentioning problems like lack of cooperation and knowledge culture, absence of time and an unsuitable infrastructure. This was a company-wide initiative having different reasons for failing and conclusions. It does not give recommendations how to solve these shortcomings. Bass et al. [25] present experiences from a cooperative project on creating a knowledge base. This contribution concentrates on people- and communication-related aspects of distributed software development and does not consider hindrances to the knowledge life cycle.

To distinguish from related work, our experience report presents challenges in conducting a knowledge management initiative in a cooperative research project with industrial and academic partners. We present lessons learned on technical, social and content-related knowledge management problems. From these lessons learned we derive concrete and practical recommendations for similar project settings.

4   Case Study

The following chapter describes our instantiation of the abovementioned Experience Lifecycle on a concrete project. We describe the *e performance* project in the first section of this chapter. Based on the project, we will show how we planned to instantiate the Experience Lifecycle in the first instance.

4.1   Project Description

The *e performance* project is a joint research project that consists of industrial and academic partners with duration of three years. The goals of the project are to research innovative concepts to electrify the power train and to get the implication it has to a complete vehicle. According to this, AUDI AG (Audi), Audi Electronics Venture GmbH (AEV), Rheinisch-Westfälische Technische Hochschule Aachen (RWTH) and Bosch Engineering GmbH (BEG) cooperate to achieve these goals and to establish know-how in the field of electro mobility. These distributed partners have different competencies and specific experience in the development of conventional vehicles and in the area of electro mobility. These various characteristics have been brought together and have been applied to the goals of the project and to get an integrated concept for an electric car.

The *e performance* project is structured so that the characteristic components of an electric car can be analyzed in the work packages (WPs) separately. The WPs themselves are organizational units. They operate in parallel to each other. Agility inside work packages is encouraged to create the innovative concept ideas. In this context, agility denotes the operation of the teams without general process guidelines. This independency gives the WPs room for creativity. Different WPs can work together at the various concepts of vehicle components more easily in a distributed environment. In spite of the agile approach, the developed concepts must pass through predefined basic phases: conception, development/calculation, construction, production, integration/testing. Afterwards, the tested electric car concepts is assembled to a complete vehicle demonstrator to present an integrated solution based on individual solutions.

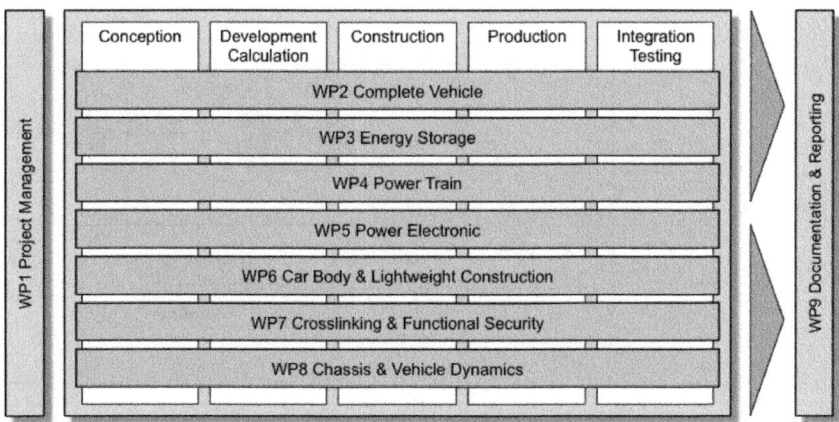

Fig. 2. Structure of the e performance project

The project structure is divided into 9 WPs as shown in Figure 2. WP 1 project management and WP 9 documentation and reporting are cross cutting units. The substantial work about the development phases will be made by WP 2-7. The knowledge management is assigned to WP 9. WP 2 complete vehicle has special role. This package coordinates the overall parallel activities of the other WPs and consolidates the integration concepts of the complete vehicle.

4.2   Instantiation of Lifecycle Phases

Figure 3 shows our knowledge management architecture for instantiating the Experience Lifecycle. A Wiki system was established as a central knowledge base. We used an integrated System based on Jira, Confluence and a WebDAV based document storage to implement our instantiation. This system is hosted at a project partners site and already in productive use. We will reference to it as the *productive system* throughout this paper.

For the first iteration, we started at the *collect* step. Since the main objective of the project members is doing research, they cannot afford to devote a lot of additional time to knowledge management. To create just minimal additional workload, we first looked at those documents that are supposed to be created during the project, regardless of knowledge management. These documents were evaluated whether they are suitable for knowledge management. We found the following two document types:

- **The project member list**

  The project member list contains all project participants. It lists each person with his respective contact information and his assignment to the organizational parts of the project. We used this document as a starting point for our FlowMaps [26] and for automatic notifications that are described in detail later on.

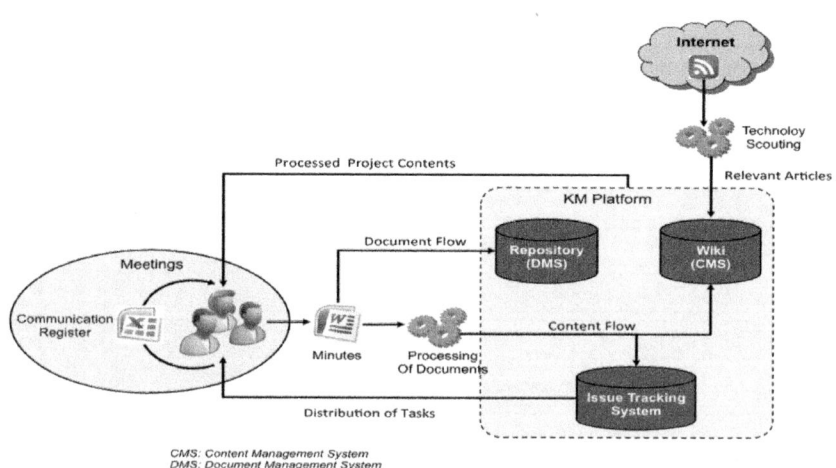

Fig. 3. Instantiation of the Experience Lifecycle

- **Meeting protocols**

  To create a protocol for each project meeting is mandatory. A meeting protocol lists all participants, discussed topics and assigned tasks during the meeting.

We used these two document types in the *collect* step of the experience lifecycle. Since documents of these types have to be created independently from knowledge management, it supports our goal to create just a minimal additional workload for the project members. We created protocol templates to facilitate their automatic processing.

The collected data about project organization, spatial distribution of project members, their contact information and assigned tasks were used for the second step of the experience lifecycle, the *experience engineering*. Here, the collected data has to be prepared and structured, generating new or newly arranged data.

Our infrastructure was designed to create a ticket in an issue tracking system for each assigned task. To add additional information (e.g. contact information) to a ticket that is not part of the protocol, the project member list is used. Additionally to the ticket creation, we create Wiki pages for the information that are contained in the protocol. These pages are grouped by topic and information types (tasks, information, etc.). People that are recognized based on the project member list, are linked to their respective Wiki sites. This is also true for already existing topic-specific sites.

Creating a linked structure from the extracted information is one of the main benefits gaining from using a Wiki. Since the link creation happens automatically, it generates additional value to already existing documents, while creating minimal additional overhead for the people.

During the *active dissemination* step the prepared data is actively distributed to all interested project members. In our instantiation, this phase starts when the Wiki pages and tickets have been created. Both systems – Wiki and issue tracking – inform appropriate members about the creation of new or updated content, to help the dissemination of the generated data. Additional material like presentation slides or CAD data is uploaded by the users to a shared project repository that is subject to access control. While access control may be hindering knowledge distribution, it is necessary in a joint research project to give each project partner sufficient control over their own data. They must be able to decide what they consider sensitive information. Access to relevant documents for the whole project is usually granted to all project members.

The last step in a complete lifecycle is the *activate* step. Since all collected and reorganized data is made available in the used systems (Wiki, issue tracking system, repository), each project member can access the needed data directly. The structuring of the data (linking, categorization) allows filtering and sorting the amount of data adequate for user needs, allowing a quick access to the needed information as well as directed search.

5   Evaluation

After the described instantiation of the Experience Lifecycle, we evaluated user acceptance of the knowledge management initiative. We turned the attention to the Wiki as central information storage, since we noticed that the Wiki's content did not grow as expected. We conducted a survey of 21 persons from all main project partners, most of them leaders of a working package.

Regarding the Wiki, we asked the following questions:

- **Question 1**: Do you use the Wiki?
- **Question 2**: If yes, how often do you use the Wiki?

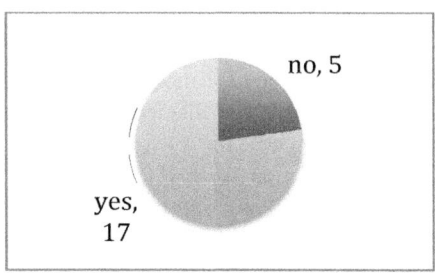

Fig. 4. Do you use the Wiki?

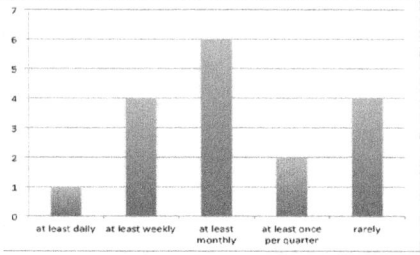

Fig. 5. How often do you use the Wiki?

The survey revealed that 17 out of 21 (approx. 81 %) users have at least used the Wiki once, as shown in Figure 4. From these 17 people, only five (approx. 29 %, i.e. approx. 24 % of all asked people) used it at least weekly (Figure 5). Of course, five people using the Wiki regularly is a ratio far too low in a research project.

To better understand why people were not using the Wiki, we asked them for their reasons. We then used Open Coding [27] to classify the answers. In the end, we derived three main categories of reasons from analyzing 65 answers: *Technical issues, social issues* and *issues directly related to knowledge management*. We will discuss each category and its sub-categories in the following sections.

5.1   Technical Issues

This category contains all issues caused by technical infrastructure. One of our main goals, when planning the instantiation, was to establish knowledge management without adding large overhead, i.e. minimizing the additional workload for the project members. To achieve this goal, the tools were supposed to support users to document their knowledge and use already documented knowledge. This category consists of two sub-categories:

- **System too slow**

  Project participants rated the system as generally too slow. This was especially the case for the shared document repository, when working with numerous and large files (e.g. CAD data).

  The logon to the system was also rated too cumbersome. This is true for the logon performance mechanism and for the time needed to initialize the additional security mechanisms like one-time password tokens.

Conclusion: Users that have to work with a system they consider too slow, will lose their interest in the system. They will start to avoid the system for smaller tasks and only use it, when it is absolutely necessary.

- **No access to system**

  Another technical problem is access restriction to the system. Lacking an (activated) account, users complained about not being able to access the system. Since we implemented the infrastructure on a project partners' productive system, clearance for accounts have to be done through their clearance process.

  Using a productive system makes the process of account clearance for other organizations a security relevant process. It has to be guaranteed that other internal projects cannot be accessed. Even if there are organizational reasons for a slow response to account applications, users only notice the missing access. To bypass the time without a working account, they use other applications.

  Conclusion: If organizational overhead for creating and clearing new accounts is too big, users have to wait too long. They start using another system during this time and lose interest in the original system. By the time their account is cleared, they will be accustomed to the alternative. This may leads to an inconsistent knowledge base, a tedious process to transfer the data, or the avoidance of the original system.

5.2   Social Issues

Social issues are triggered directly or indirectly by project members. These issues often hinder people from completing their tasks of knowledge sharing. In our case, we experienced the following four sub-categories of social issues:

- **System is external**

  Establishing the knowledge management environment, we decided to use a project partners' productive environment to host the infrastructure. From other partner organizations' perspectives the system is external. External systems are considered less trustworthy compared to own systems.

  An additional problem is the uncertainty of what happens to the data after the project is finished and who will have access to which data in what format. Since we used a proprietary system, it was not possible for external users to create a full system backup on their own.

  Conclusion: If one project partner hosts the system, at the beginning it is necessary to clearly commit to others what happens to the data at the end of the project. There should also be a possibility for external users to get a full backup of all data at any time.

- **System is too complex**

  Some users found that a system containing many sub-systems (like a Wiki, issue tracking, etc.) is too complex, especially as these several sub-systems were not integrated. This leads to ambiguity and confusion where to put which type of data and where to search for them.

Conclusion: If several non-integrated systems are used, there has to be a clear guideline about the use of each system for a certain type of data.

- **Not enough time**

  Users having not enough time are a common issue. Since knowledge management is not their main task, they are often not able to spent additional time for it.

  Conclusion: Tools and methods for knowledge management have to be designed to avoid any additional overhead, especially those operated by users whose main task is not knowledge management.

- **Does not fit into workflow**

  Even if the technical infrastructure is in place and all other issues (see above) are fixed, one limitation for productive usage stays: the inadequate workflow. In our case, all project members used e-mails to communicate with each other and to get informed about new content. Contrary to this, the Wiki implements a polling pattern, requiring from the users to ask proactively for new content. This interrupts the users' workflow, restraining instead of supporting them.

  An automatic e-mail notification about new content was not helpful. Many users were notified about content that was not relevant to them. The outcome was information overflow letting the users to ignore e-mails from this source.

  Conclusion: When installing new systems to support knowledge management, e-mails as a main component of a personal workflow should not be underestimated. E-mail should not be misused to send irrelevant or trivial information to the users.

5.3   Issues Directly Related to Knowledge Management

This category of issues is directly related to knowledge management. Contrary to social and technical issues, reasons for KM-related issues can usually be influenced. We found two KM related issues in our project:

- **No useful content** and **no need to use**

  These two issues depend on each other. As long as there is no enforcement to use a certain system, just a few people will use it voluntarily. As only a few people use a system and just a few of them add new information to the system, there will be no useful content for most users. As a consequence, they will still not use it. Another consequence from the lack of participation is old news remaining on the homepage and not being updated.

  Conclusion: A new system needs significant contribution from knowledge management to make it interesting for other users. Otherwise they won't use it.

5.4   Lessons Learned

In this section, we present lessons learned from our instantiation of the Experience Lifecycle and feedback we received from participants. For the next iteration of our instantiation architecture, these lessons have to be taken into account:

- **Fixed productive system**

Using a productive system, hosted at the site of a project partner was not an ideal decision. Needed adaptions of the system like a special view for agendas could not be implemented, since changing the base system could only be done after passing internal security tests. These tests usually last longer than a month. This is far too long for users to wait.

High security barriers around a productive system are another obstacle. They effectively prevent automation of tasks, which renders the implementation of additional tools impossible. Those tools could support low-effort knowledge work.

Conclusion: The use of productive systems for systems with unfinished or fast changing requirements is not adequate.

- **Volatile content**

Since the described project is a joint research project, the documented knowledge can be very short-lived. It may be outdated at a fast pace or should be enriched with new findings. This leads to problems, when trying to synchronize two different sources like documents and the Wiki.

This problem may be diminished by an automatic synchronization mechanism. However, depending on the complexity of the synchronization and the temporal distance between synchronizations, there may be a difference between actual data in the reference documents and the data in the knowledge base. Having a knowledge base that is filled with outdated or wrong data will lead the user to lose trust in it.

Conclusion: If reference documents for the data in the knowledge base change regularly, all changes must be adopted to the knowledge base immediately.

- **Unfamiliar Workflows**

Even though we carefully inspected the workflows and habits of the project members and optimized our tools to work with MS Office, we underestimated the importance of e-mail for the users. The change from the e-mail application into another, usually uncommon application, led to disruption of the workflow and has been therefore done reluctantly.

Additionally to this, many users experienced knowledge management as an additional task, since it has nothing to do with their regular workflow items. This is true for their main project task (i.e. researching) as well as for using additional tools for knowledge management. Even if the tools look and feel similar to the commonly used tools, they are still subtly different and may yield unexpected results.

Conclusion: Inspecting workflows, it must be considered that commonly used tools cannot easily be replaced by similar tools that may be subtly different. E-mail must be considered as the most important utility.

6   Recommendations for a Better Start

Based on the abovementioned lessons learned, we adjusted our instantiation of the Experience Lifecycle to antagonize the discovered issues. This chapter describes the adjustments and gives recommendations for similar projects.

- **A tool to collect data**

  The choice to use meeting protocols as a data source for the knowledge base was good, but not sufficient. We wanted project members to describe additional experiences and problems made during their daily work.

  We found that problems will only be documented at the time they occur. They will not be documented afterwards. To support documentation, we created an iPad application which is connected to our issue tracking system. As an advantage of this solution, project members can carry the tablet with them and document problems and experiences as they go, optionally adding additional media like photo. Since the application runs locally on the Apple iPad, this can also be done in cases of no Wi-Fi. Lack of Wi-Fi is common in secure manufacturing areas.

  Recommendation: If the documentation of problems is desired, project members need a tool to enter the problems directly as they happen. This tool must be able to completely capture the documentation, making it possible (but not necessary) to rework the documentation.

- **Using a version control system as project repository**

  After getting feedback about the shared project repository in use, we decided to introduce the Apache Subversion version control system instead. Apart from the automatic versioning of Subversion (which was not implemented in the old repository), another benefit is the possibility to get a complete copy of the contained documents at any time. The first feedback we received points to a much higher acceptance of the Apache Subversion than of the old system.

  Compared to a Wiki, the ability to create linking structures between the documents is lost. As compensation, we plan to implement a novel web platform, which will show categorized links to the documents. This should also eliminate the problem of outdated content, since the content is always contained in the reference documents and must not be transformed.

  Recommendation: If the content of a knowledge base is transformed from volatile reference documents, it is better practice to directly link to the documents and structure the links instead.

- **Better workflow integration**

  After getting feedback about the integration of our methods into the everyday workflow of project members, we stopped working with similar tools and concentrated on supporting the tool already in place.

Recommendation: When introducing new tools into existing workflows, it has to be precisely checked if already existing tools can substitute the new tools. In this case not using the ideal tool is often better. The familiarization process is then much shorter leading to higher productivity and more satisfied project members.

7   Discussion and Outlook

In this paper we described our experience made in the first year of establishing knowledge management in a joint research project. In the beginning we instantiated the Experience Lifecycle. The issues related to this instantiation were then inspected through interviews with the project members.

We described experiences and lessons learned during this year in detail. We hope to give similar project settings a better starting point to plan an instantiation of the Experience Lifecycle. These are our recommendations in short:

- Do not use a productive system as a knowledge base.
- Synchronize changes in referenced documents immediately to the knowledge base.
  – If this is not possible, just link to the original documents.
- Take already established workflows into account and try to support existing tools instead of introducing similar ones.
- Provide the possibility to document problems immediately when they occur.

From this analysis, we received a better awareness about the necessary adaption of our Lifecycle instantiation.

To prove the usefulness of our adaptation to the needs of the users, we will have a look at the usage pattern for this new approach. We expect the users to work more often with the new infrastructure, since it better supports their native workflow. Preliminary results from surveys concerning the changes indicate a much better acceptance rate.

Another area of research is structuring the data in the version control systems. For this, we plan to use the linking categorization to the documents and extract an ontology from them. This will help us to automatically categorize new documents as they are uploaded to the system. It also allows us to integrate a semantic driven search functionality for documents. Another use of the categorization is to generate comprehensive documentation from already existing documents.

References

1. Arranz, N., Fdez de Arroyabe, J.C.: Complex joint R&D projects: From empirical evidence to managerial implications. Complexity 15, 61–70 (2009)
2. Schneider, K.: Experience and Knowledge Management in Software Engineering. Springer (2009)
3. Polanyi, M., Sen, A.: The tacit dimension. Peter Smith Gloucester, MA (1983)

4. Nonaka, I., Takeuchi, H.: The Knowledge-Creating Company: How Japanese Companies Create the Dynamics of Innovation. Oxford University Press (1995)
5. Johannson, C., Hall, P., Coquard, M.: Talk to Paula and Peter - They are Experienced. In: International Conference on Software Engineering and Knowledge Engineering (SEKE 1999), Workshop on Learning Software Organizations (1999)
6. Wenger, E.: Communities of Practice - Learning, Meaning, and Identity. Cambridge University Press (1998)
7. Basili, V.R., Caldiera, G., Rombach, H.D.: Experience factory. Encyclopedia of software engineering, 469–476 (1994)
8. Nonaka, I., Toyama, R., Konno, N.: SECI, Ba and Leadership: a Unified Model of Dynamic Knowledge Creation. Long Range Planning 33, 5–34 (2000)
9. Jolly, D.: Sharing knowledge and decision power in Sino-foreign joint ventures. Asia Pacific Business Review 9, 81–100 (2002)
10. Soekijad, M.: The competitive factor in knowledge sharing networks. Presented at the (2002)
11. Inkpen, A.C., Currall, S.C.: The coevolution of trust, control, and learning in joint ventures. Organization Science, 586–599 (2004)
12. Caloghirou, Y., Vonortas, N.S., Ioannides, S.: European collaboration in research and development: business strategy and public policy. Edward Elgar Publishing (2004)
13. Walker, D.H.T., Johannes, D.S.: Preparing for organisational learning by HK infrastructure project joint ventures organisations. The Learning Organization 10, 106–117 (2003)
14. Revilla, E., Sarkis, J., Acosta, J.: Towards a knowledge management and learning taxonomy for research joint ventures. Technovation 25, 1307–1316 (2005)
15. Bhandar, M.: A Framework for Knowledge Integration and Social Capital in Collaborative Projects. Electronic Journal of Knowledge Management 8, 267–280
16. Kastelli, I.: Organisational Knowledge Creation in the Context of R & D cooperation. The role of absorptive capacity. Knowledge Creation Diffusion Utilization (2006)
17. Thomas, H., Davenport David, W., De Long, M.C.B.: Successful Knowledge Management Projects. Sloan Management Review (1998)
18. Jørgensen, M., Sjøberg, D.I.K., Conradi, R.: Reuse of software development experience at Telenor Telecom Software. In: European Software Process Improvement Conference (EuroSPI 1998), Gothenburg, Sweden, pp. 10.19–10.31 (1998)
19. Dingsoyr, T., Conradi, R.: A survey of case studies of the use of knowledge management in software engineering. International Journal of Software Engineering and Knowledge Engineering 12, 391–414 (2002)
20. Brössler, P.: Knowledge Management at a Software House: An Experience Report. In: Ruhe, G., Bomarius, F. (eds.) SEKE 1999. LNCS, vol. 1756, pp. 163–170. Springer, Heidelberg (2000)
21. Feldmann, R.L., Pizka, M.: An On-Line Software Engineering Repository for Germany's SME – An Experience Report. In: Henninger, S., Maurer, F. (eds.) LSO 2003. LNCS, vol. 2640, pp. 34–43. Springer, Heidelberg (2003)
22. Houdek, F., Bunse, C.: Transferring and Evolving Experience: A Practical Approach and its Application on Software Inspections. In: Ruhe, G., Bomarius, F. (eds.) SEKE 1999. LNCS, vol. 1756, pp. 210–226. Springer, Heidelberg (2000)
23. Schneider, K., Schwinn, T.: Maturing experience base concepts at DaimlerChrysler. Software Process: Improvement and Practice 6, 85–96 (2001)
24. Akhavan, P., Jafari, M., Fathian, M.: Exploring failure-factors of implementing knowledge management systems in organizations. Journal of Knowledge Management Practice 6, 1–9 (2005)

25. Bass, M., Herbsleb, J.D., Lescher, C.: Collaboration in global software projects at siemens: An experience report. In: Second IEEE International Conference on Global Software Engineering, ICGSE 2007, pp. 33–39. IEEE (2007)
26. Stapel, K., Knauss, E., Schneider, K., Zazworka, N.: FLOW Mapping: Planning and Managing Communication in Distributed Teams. In: 2011 6th IEEE International Conference on Global Software Engineering (ICGSE), pp. 190–199. IEEE (2011)
27. Corbin, J., Strauss, A.: Open Coding. In: Corbin, J., Strauss, A. (eds.) Basics of Qualitative Research: Techniques and Procedures for Developing Grounded Theory, pp. 101–121. Sage Publications, Thousand Oaks (1998)

The Impact of Lack in Domain or Technology Experience on the Accuracy of Expert Effort Estimates in Software Projects

Susanne Halstead, Rosario Ortiz, Mario Córdova, and Miguel Seguí

School of Business Administration, University of Puerto Rico, Mayagüez

Abstract. The study examines the impact of lack of experience in the domain problem or lack of experience with the technologies used in a software development project on the accuracy of single expert estimation of task effort, as measured by estimated versus actual effort. Expert judgment in the estimation of task effort is the most frequently used estimation technique for software projects. Estimators rely on their experience, business domain knowledge, and technical expertise. Occasionally, organizations lack experts on staff that have relevant prior experience on some business or technology related aspects of the project. This research investigates the impact of such incomplete expertise on the reliability of estimates.

Keywords: Software Projects, Software Development, Expert Estimation, Project Risk, Effort Estimation.

1 Introduction

Software development projects are known to have considerable risks associated to them [5]. Scheduling unreliability is among the most serious risks in software projects [15], [25]. The notion that software projects fail frequently and severely is ubiquitous in the practitioners' community. The findings of the Standish Group's CHAOS report [11] are widely cited in academic work and in practitioners' conferences. Several authors have since criticized the methodology and findings of the 1991 report and its subsequent issues [10], [19], [8]. Jørgensen and Molokken conclude that the actual failure rate of software projects and the severity of such failures are far lower than depicted in the Standish figures, yet still a significant problem. In all this research, the definition of failure or troubled projects is mainly marked by severe schedule and/or budget overruns. Several authors have criticized this narrow definition of project success. The assessment of project success cannot be solely based on whether the project met its schedule, cost budget and conforms to specifications, but should consider all stakeholders' expectations and long term product success [2], [4], [7], [29]. De Wit [7] points out that there should be a clear distinction between the success of the project management effort and project success. Nonetheless, organizations have a strong interest in making the software development process more predictable and in being able to plan development times and costs. The project

O. Dieste, A. Jedlitschka, and N. Juristo (Eds.): PROFES 2012, LNCS 7343, pp. 248–259, 2012.
© Springer-Verlag Berlin Heidelberg 2012

management framework relies greatly on the accuracy of task effort estimates. Project management tools such as the identification of critical activities, the baseline schedules, milestones, resource schedules, and cost baselines depend on the accuracy of task effort and the derived task duration estimates [13]. Expert judgment is the most frequently used technique for time estimations of software projects [24]. In order for expert judgment to be an efficient tool, however, the experts have to combine a specific set of skills and experience. They need to have (1) domain knowledge, (2) software engineering knowledge and knowledge of the particular software engineering process of the organization, (3) knowledge of the technology mix to be used, as well as (4) expertise in estimation. Many organizations are lacking in the latter aspect, as they do not formally strive to develop estimation skills in their personnel [18]. In practice, it is not unusual that the personnel entrusted with an estimate might also lack in domain knowledge or experience with the proposed technology mix for particular projects. This research is meant to assess the impact of such incomplete experience on the part of the estimator.

Project managers are aware of the importance of estimates. They might not be aware of the magnitude of the estimation risk created by relying on expert judgment of personnel that is unfamiliar with the domain problem or the technology mix to be used in the project. Such knowledge would aid project managers in their interpretation of estimates, risk assessment for projects, and contingency planning.

2   Related Work

Literature relevant to this subject was identified via online library database search and by using the BEST (Better Estimation of Software development Tasks) database, which is a catalog of relevant literature on estimation for software projects maintained by researchers at Simula Laboratory (Simula Laboratories, n.d.). Among the publications about estimation methods, most work focuses on regression models or seeks to create or propose a mathematical model for estimation. Relatively few publications focus on expert estimation [20]. This is in stark contrast to the fact that expert estimation is the most frequently used estimation technique [16], [20]. A systematic literature review gathering evidence for comparison between the performance of expert estimation and parametric models [17] found that the average accuracy of expert estimation was at least equal or better than the average accuracy of models, especially if models were not calibrated to the particular organization. There is no strong evidence that would suggest using expert estimation is not a valid practice [14], [17]. It is necessary, though, to better understand expert estimates and create processes that support estimators and avoid the introduction of biases and other distorting factors. Situational and human biases are the subject of several investigations. Some significant findings are that anchoring [3], goal setting [1] or known customer expectations [21] skew estimates. Even though lack of domain knowledge and technology risks have been identified as significant risk factors in projects [5], [27], no literature specifically investigating the impact of these particular risk factors on expert estimation for software projects was found during the literature search. There are studies on reliability of estimation methods [12], [22], [23] and expert estimation in particular [13], [24]. Furthermore, there are efforts to quantify estimation reliability and estimation risk from historic data and project portfolio data, which includes estimates created by expert judgment [22]. Eveleens and Verhoef, [9], explain the importance of quantifying forecast quality and present a model that would allow organizations to quantitatively assess accuracy of estimates, the conversion of actuals with estimates over the life of the project and systematic biases of estimates. In summary, to better understand and practically apply expert estimation, we need knowledge on factors affecting estimation reliability and models to quantify their impact.

3   Methodology

The research was carried out by means of a survey among experienced software development professionals in Puerto Rico. All survey participants have relevant university studies in Computer Science, Software Engineering or Information Systems. These backgrounds reflect a basic job requirement for their current positions. The questionnaire does not distinguish between these fields of study as the sample size attainable is too small to make such further fragmentation meaningful. In addition, the work performed and relevant experience between survey participants is similar, regardless of their respective degrees. The survey was deliberately directed at technology professionals fulfilling the job functions of senior developer or analyst, not project managers. The underlying assumption is that senior developers or analysts are the ones that give expert estimates, not project managers. Asking the person that will finally carry out the work to do the estimates is considered best practice in project management practitioner's literature [15].

For the purposes of the study, it is assumed that the personnel asked to perform the estimates have experience in software engineering practices and in the organization's software development process. Therefore, only experienced personnel were included as survey participants. The survey considers two scenarios. Scenario 1 is a situation in which the person asked to give the effort estimate for tasks has experience with the particular domain problem; however, a new technology will be used in the implementation of the solution. Scenario 2 is the inverse situation, in which the person asked to provide the estimate is experienced with the technologies to be used in the implementation of the solution, but lacks experience with similar domain problems. This does not imply that there was no analysis of requirements prior to the estimation process or that the domain problem was not properly defined. It only implies that the estimator has not worked on a similar project before. Therefore, the business requirements are not as well understood as in the case of familiar problems. The estimator would, for example, be less likely to consider overlooked requirements or tasks. It is also assumed that the personnel asked to provide the estimates will be lacking in

Table 1. Questionnaire Distributed to Software Development Professionals

---

SURVEY ON ACCURACY OF ESTIMATES AND EXPERIENCE EFFECTS

General Information
Education   ◯ Some College   ◯ Bachelor's Degree
                       ◯ Some Master's ◯ Master's Degree
                       ◯PhD   ◯Other, Specify:
Work Experience ◯ < 1 yrs   ◯ 1-5 yrs
                    ◯ 6-10 yrs   ◯ > 10 yrs

I . When faced with a task where you understand the business requirements well and have experience solving similar problems, however, the technology mix (e.g.databases, programming languages, frameworks, interfaces) is NEW to you:

1. How frequently do you need more time to complete your tasks than was allocated in the estimates?
Please provide percentage estimate. Valid values are 0% through 100 % ....

2. If you use more time than was allocated to the task, by what proportion do you typically overrun the time budget?
Please provide percentage estimate. Percentage values greater than 100 are possible.
For example a value of 120% means that you needed all the time allocated for the task and an additional 120%.
So if 10 hours were estimated for a task, you actually required 22 hours [10+12] ....

3. How many similar projects would you have to work in order to significantly reduce this overrun and give more accurate estimates?
Please state number:

II . When faced with a task where you DO NOT understand the business requirements well and DO NOT have experience solving similar problems, however, the technology mix (e.g. databases, programming languages, frameworks, interfaces) is FAMILIAR to you:

1. How frequently do you need more time to complete your tasks than was allocated in the estimates?
Please provide percentage estimate. Valid values are 0% through 100 % ....

2. If you use more time than was allocated to the task, by what proportion do you typically overrun the time budget?
Please provide percentage estimate. Percentage values greater than 100 are possible. For example a value of 120%
means that you needed all the time allocated for the task and an additional 120%.
So if 10 hours were estimated for a task, you actually required 22 hours [10+12] ....

3. How many similar projects would you have to work in order to significantly reduce this overrun and give more accurate estimates?
Please state number:

---

only one of the dimensions of domain knowledge or technology mix to be used. A lack of domain knowledge and inexperience with the technology would clearly disqualify the person form giving any estimates.

The survey participants were recruited from the researchers extended professional network and at professional development events. Participants were approached in person and asked to fill out the questionnaire. The questionnaire was accompanied by a consent form to participate in the survey and an instruction sheet. The background and instructions for the survey were explained to each individual, following the information on the instruction sheet. The format of the questionnaire is shown in table 1. The questionnaire asks survey participants to assess the probability and severity of time (task duration) overruns when compared with the original estimates under the two scenarios. In software development, person-hours are the greatest cost driver and the most frequently used measure for effort required. Since effort estimates are considered on a task level, an overrun in effort will typically directly translate to an overrun in time required, which in turn might lead to a schedule overrun, depending on the float of the tasks considered. It is seldom possible to prevent duration overrun by adding more resources [6]. Furthermore, survey participants were asked to indicate how many similar projects they would have to work on in order to feel more confident in their estimates.

4   Results

The survey produced 47 data sets. The response rate was 100 percent, as one
of the researchers approached participants personally. Participants filled out the
questionnaires in private and deposited them in a collection box, thus maintaining the anonymity of the questionnaire. The survey results were tabulated, and
the descriptive statistics were calculated using Excel statistics functions.

Of the 47 participants, 13 have 1-5 years of relevant work experience, 12 have
6-10 years of relevant work experience, and 21 have more than 10 years of relevant
work experience.

When partitioning the population according to the highest level of formal
education in computer science, software engineering or information systems, 25
participants hold a Bachelor's degree, 11 participants have partially completed
a Master's degree, and 9 participants have completed a Master's degree.

4.1   Descriptive Statistics

Scenario 1 describes a situation where the person asked to give an estimate
has experience with similar domain problems, but lacks experience with the
technologies that will be used. Table 2 summarizes the descriptive statistics for
effort overrun and the overrun factor for this scenario.

The overrun factor expresses the amount of time required additionally to
the time estimated relative to that estimate. Thus, the time actually required to
complete the task would be Actual Duration = Estimated Duration + Estimated
Duration x Overrun Factor.

For the whole population, the average probability of underestimating required
task effort is 52 percent, with a variance of 10 percent. When a time overrun
is incurred, the average overrun factor is 58 percent. These results indicate
that estimations under Scenario 1 create considerable risk exposure, as the

Table 2. Descriptive Statistics for Overrun Probability and Overrun Factor under
Scenario 1

	Whole Sample	5 years	10 years	more 10 years	Bachelor	Some Master's	Master's
SampleSize	47	13	12	21	25	11	9
Range	0.95	0.95	0.75	0.95	0.95	0.9	0.8
Mean	0.52447	0.56923	0.62083	0.44286	0.502	0.53182	0.59444
Variance	0.09814	0.11356	0.06657	0.10707	0.09635	0.11314	0.09465
Std.Dev.	0.31327	0.33698	0.25802	0.32722	0.3104	0.33636	0.30766
Scenario 1: Overrun Factor							
Range	1.35	1.2	1.2	1.3	0.95	1.1	1
Mean	0.58404	0.61538	0.62083	0.52381	0.4624	0.55909	0.57778
Variance	0.19012	0.21724	0.16112	0.2044	0.09584	0.14691	0.18194
Std.Dev.	0.43603	0.46609	0.40139	0.45211	0.30959	0.38329	0.42655

Table header: **Scenario 1: Probability of Effort Overrun**

Table 3. Descriptive Statistics for Overrun Probability and Overrun Factor under Scenario 2

	Scenario 2: Probability of Effort Overrun						
	Whole Sample	5 years	10 years	more 10 years	Bachelor	Some Master's	Master's
SampleSize	47	13	12	21	25	11	9
Range	0.95	0.95	0.95	0.95	0.95	0.95	0.9
Mean	0.51723	0.53923	0.5625	0.47857	0.4624	0.54091	0.56667
Variance	0.10248	0.12567	0.09869	0.10289	0.09584	0.14091	0.08438
Std.Deviation	0.32013	0.35451	0.31415	0.32077	0.30959	0.37538	0.29047
	Scenario 2: Overrun Factor						
Range	2.95	1.5	1.45	2.9	1.95	2.9	0.7
Mean	0.7383	0.70385	0.69167	0.77381	0.728	0.83182	0.67222
Variance	0.34904	0.28978	0.21038	0.5064	0.34418	0.68964	0.06257
Std.Deviation	0.5908	0.53831	0.45867	0.71162	0.58667	0.83044	0.25014

probability of occurrence and the impact of occurrence are large. On average, survey participants indicate they need to work on 3 (2.6) similar projects in order to give more reliable estimates. The values ranged from 1 project to 8 projects.

Scenario 2 describes the situation where the estimator is familiar with the technologies to be used in the implementation of the solution, but has not worked on a similar domain problem before. Table 3 summarizes the descriptive statistics for the probability of incurring in time overrun and the overrun factor under this scenario. Under Scenario 2, the average overrun probability is 52 percent, with an average overrun factor of 73 percent. Estimates made under the situation described in Scenario 2 have a high risk exposure, as the probability and severity of effort overruns are also high. Under scenario 2, survey participants indicated that on average, they have to work in 3 (calculated average is 2.65) similar projects, in order to be able to give more reliable estimates. The answers ranged from 1 to 10 projects.

We ran goodness of fit tests for the Normal Distribution of the samples using the Easy Fit statistics tool. The samples could be fitted to the Normal Distribution at significance level alpha of 0.05 using the Kolmogorow-Smirnow, the Anderson-Darling and Chi Square Test, allowing us to use t-test and ANOVA tests for further analysis of the data.

4.2 Comparisons between Scenario 1 and Scenario 2

In order to determine whether the means of overrun probability and the means of the overrun factors are different between scenario 1 and scenario 2, we performed t-tests. Prior to performing the t-tests, f-tests were performed to determine whether the variances are equal between the samples. Table 4 summarizes the results.

Table 4. Comparison of Variances and Means between Scenarios for Overrun Probability and Overrun Factor

Comparing Variances of Schedule Overrun between Scenario 1 and Scenario 2		
F-Test Two-Sample for Variances	Variable 1	Variable 2
Mean	0.524468085	0.517234043
Variance	0.098138298	0.102481314
Observations	47	47
df	46	46
F	0.957621389	
P(F <=f) one-tail	**0.441942783**	
F Critical one-tail	0.612570986	
Does not reject hypothesis that the samples have equal variance for alpha 0.05.		

Comparing Means of Schedule Overrun between Scenario 1 and Scenario 2		
t-Test: Two-Sample Assuming Equal Variances	Variable 1	Variable 2
Mean	0.524468085	0.517234043
Variance	0.098138298	0.102481314
Observations	47	47
Pooled Variance	0.100309806	
Hypothesized Mean Difference	0	
df	92	
t Stat	0.11072439	
P(T<=t) one-tail	0.456038048	
t Critical one-tail	1.661585397	
P(T<=t) two-tail	**0.912076096**	
t Critical two-tail	1.986086272	
Does not reject hypothesis that the samples have the equal mean for alpha 0.05.		

Comparing Variance of Overrun Factor between Scenario 1 and Scenario 2		
F-Test Two-Sample for Variances	Variable 1	Variable 2
Mean	0.584042553	0.738297872
Variance	0.190120259	0.349044866
Observations	47	47
df	46	46
F	0.544687167	
P(F <=f) one-tail	**0.020987837**	
F Critical one-tail	0.612570986	
Rejects hypothesis that samples have equal variance for alpha 0.05.		

Comparing Means of Overrun Factor between Scenario 1 and Scenario 2		
t-Test: Two-Sample Assuming Unequal Variances	Variable 1	Variable 2
Mean	0.584042553	0.738297872
Variance	0.190120259	0.349044866
Observations	47	47
Hypothesized Mean Difference	0	
df	85	
t Stat	-1.440217823	
P(T<=t) one-tail	**0.076739498**	
t Critical one-tail	1.6629785	
P(T<=t) two-tail	0.153478996	
t Critical two-tail	1.988267868	
Does not reject hypothesis that the samples have the equal mean for alpha 0.05.		

For the comparison of the probability of schedule overrun, the p-value of the f-test is 0.44, leading us to reject the hypothesis that the probability distributions of the occurrences of schedule overrun in the two samples have different variance for the significance level of 0.05. We therefore used a t-test, assuming equal variances. We use a two sample t-Test. This is appropriate, since even though, the samples are provided by the same person, the survey participants were asked to assess two mutually exclusive scenarios. The two-tailed p-value of 0.91 indicates that the two samples have equal means. For the overrun factors, the p-value of the f-test is 0.02. Thus, it cannot be assumed that the two samples have equal variances. The t-test was performed assuming unequal variances. The two-tailed p-value is 0.15, the one tailed p-value is 0.08. In personal conversations with the study participants, many indicate that the overrun factor in the case of lack of domain experience is larger than in the case of lack of experience with the technology to be used. Thus, considering the one-tailed p-value, it could be assumed with 0.08 confidence, that the sample mean of scenario 2 is larger than the sample mean of scenario 1. This confidence is larger than the confidence of 0.05 we chose for our data analysis, thus we do not consider this as a statistically relevant result. Nonetheless, we recommend further studies to probe whether this can be observed at a statistically relevant level using a larger sample, since from the professionals' accounts, it seems that lack of experience with the domain problem causes larger and more volatile overruns than lack of experience with the specific technology. Table 5 summarizes the means and variances for scenarios 1 and 2.

Table 5. Comparison of Overrun Factors between Scenarios

	Scenario 1	Scenario 2
Mean	0.5840	0.7383
Variance	0.1901	0.3490

4.3   Influence of Years of Experience and Level of Education

In order to assess the influence of years of experience, within each scenario, we partitioned the data in three groups according to the years of experience reported. ANOVA tests were then performed in order to compare means between experience groups in each scenario. In all cases, the sample means were found to be equal.

We used the same approach to compare sample means between the responses partitioned by level of education for each scenario. The ANOVA tests comparing the sample means between the three groups of education level also found that the means are equal between the groups in both scenarios.

From these tests, it seems, that neither having more years of experience nor a higher level of formal education greatly reduces the probability and severity of incurring in time overruns under either scenario. Table 6 summarizes our findings.

Table 6. Summary of ANOVA Results

	Level of Education	Years of Work Experience
Probability of Schedule Overrun Scenario 1	Do not reject hypothesis.	Do not reject hypothesis.
Probability of Schedule Overrun Scenario 2	Do not reject hypothesis.	Do not reject hypothesis.
Severity of Schedule Overrun Scenario 1	Do not reject hypothesis.	Do not reject hypothesis.
Severity of Schedule Overrun Scenario 2	Do not reject hypothesis.	Do not reject hypothesis.

Hypothesis: The groups have equal means.

5   Recommendations

Based on these findings, the most obvious recommendation is to carefully evaluate the level of experience with the domain problem and technology of the estimators when using the technique of expert judgment. In cases where the estimators lack domain knowledge or experience with a specific technology, more than one person should provide estimates and the differences between the estimates should be investigated. In any case, it seems that it is more advantageous to have experience with the domain than with the technology.

Many project managers might underestimate the magnitude of uncertainty in the estimates introduced by lack of experience with the domain problem or the technology mix. Contingency buffers of 10 to 20 percent might not be sufficient, considering the large average overrun probabilities and overrun factors. As it may not be acceptable or desired to introduce larger buffers, using alternate estimation methods and combining results becomes more important. Considering the significant uncertainty under these scenarios, it might not be a fair practice to hold estimators responsible for faulty estimates, for instance in performance evaluations.

Neither more formal education nor more years of experience seem to have a significant impact on average overrun probability and overrun factors under either scenario. Previous studies also found that increase in work experience does not necessarily lead to better estimates, as experience relevant to particular estimation tasks tends to be rather narrow. Instead, estimators need to receive feedback and need to receive training on how to estimate [16]. During our research, we found in interviews with study participants that none of the companies where the survey participants work have a formal training program on software project effort estimates, nor do they provide any formal structures for estimation feedback or process improvements. The experts depend solely on their own learning experience. To improve estimates, we therefore stress the importance of formally training personnel in estimation techniques and providing them structured opportunities to compare their estimates to historic data during the estimation process and actual results in retrospect. Overall, organizations should take better advantage of historical project estimate data available to them to assess their quality of estimates over time, support estimators, calibrate their estimation models, and determine contingencies. The data collection for projects should consider these goals explicitly.

6   Future Research and Weaknesses of Methodology

Since the research was carried out by means of a questionnaire, the results obtained reflect the professionals' perception of estimation uncertainty and learning effects in the estimation process. Therefore, results depend on the participants' ability to recall past experience. This recall might be incomplete, inaccurate, or tainted by psychological effects, such as self-perception or reluctance to admit failures in their full magnitude. In a research by M. Roy et al., it was found that people underestimate the duration of future events, not only because they take a too optimistic outlook, but also because their memories are systematic underestimations of how long past events lasted [26]. This effect might be reflected in the survey participants' answers. The fact that none of the employers of the survey participants offer ex post feedback on estimation accuracy means the survey participants depend fully on their perception of magnitude of time overruns. They have had no opportunities to compare their perception with actual results. The numbers obtained from this research are hence more of an indicator of observed scale of the impact of lack of domain or technology, than usable data for model calibration or other contingency determination. To obtain results based on data collection rather than recall, this same research question could be investigated by means of carefully designed experiments or project portfolio data analysis similar to the methodology explained in [22] and [28], rather than by means of questionnaire.

The sample size obtained was small. It would be interesting to repeat this research with a larger sample, in order to see if the results change. The study was geographically limited to Puerto Rico. Future research could use a more geographically dispersed sample, in order to cancel out any possible cultural bias in the results.

References

1. Abdel-Hamid, T.K., Sengupta, K., Swett, C.: The impact of goals on software project management: An experimental investigation. MIS Quarterly, 531–555 (1999)

2. Agarwal, N., Rathod, U.: Defining 'success' for software projects: An exploratory revelation. International Journal of Project Management 24(4), 358–370 (2006)
3. Aranda, J., Easterbrook, S.: Anchoring and adjustment in software estimation. ACM SIGSOFT Software Engineering Notes 30(5), 346–355 (2005)
4. Atkinson, R.: Project management: cost, time and quality, two best guesses and a phenomenon, its time to accept other success criteria. International Journal of Project Management 17(6), 337–342 (1999)
5. Barki, H., Rivard, S., Talbot, J.: Toward an assessment of software development risk. Journal of Management Information Systems 10(2), 203–225 (1993)
6. Brooks, F.P.: The mythical man-month: essays on software engineering, vol. 7. Addison-Wesley, Reading (1995)
7. De Wit, A.: Measurement of project success. International Journal of Project Management 6(3), 164–170 (1988)
8. Eveleens, J., Verhoef, C.: The rise and fall of the chaos report figures. IEEE Software 27(1), 30–36 (2010)
9. Eveleens, J.L., Verhoef, C.: Quantifying it forecast quality. Science of Computer Programming 74(11-12), 934–988 (2009)
10. Glass, R.L.: The standish report: does it really describe a software crisis? Communications of the ACM 49(8), 15–16 (2006)
11. The Standish Group. Chaos report (1991)
12. Heemstra, F.J.: Software cost estimation. Information and Software Technology 34(10), 627–639 (1992)
13. Hill, J., Thomas, L.C., Allen, D.E.: Experts' estimates of task durations in software development projects. International Journal of Project Management 18(1), 13–21 (2000)
14. Hughes, R.T.: Expert judgement as an estimating method. Information and Software Technology 38(2), 67–75 (1996)
15. Jones, C.: Assessment and control of software risks (1994)
16. Jørgensen, M.: A review of studies on expert estimation of software development effort. Journal of Systems and Software 70(1-2), 37–60 (2004)
17. Jørgensen, M.: Forecasting of software development work effort: Evidence on expert judgement and formal models. International Journal of Forecasting 23(3), 449–462 (2007)
18. Jørgensen, M., Carelius, G.J.: An empirical study of software project bidding. IEEE Transactions on Software Engineering 30(12), 953–969 (2004)
19. Jørgensen, M., Molokken-Ostvold, K.: How large are software cost overruns? A review of the 1994 chaos report. Information and Software Technology 48(4), 297–301 (2006)
20. Jørgensen, M., Shepperd, M.: A systematic review of software development cost estimation studies. IEEE Transactions on Software Engineering 33(1), 33–53 (2007)
21. Jørgensen, M., Sjøberg, D.I.K.: The impact of customer expectation on software development effort estimates. International Journal of Project Management 22(4), 317–325 (2004)
22. Kulk, G.P., Peters, R.J., Verhoef, C.: Quantifying IT estimation risks. Science of Computer Programming 74(11-12), 900–933 (2009)
23. Lederer, A.L., Prasad, J.: Information systems software cost estimating: a current assessment. Journal of Information Technology 8(1), 22–33 (1993)
24. Molokken, K., Jørgensen, M.: A review of surveys on software effort estimation, p. 223. IEEE Computer Society (2003)

25. Ropponen, J., Lyytinen, K.: Components of software development risk: How to address them? A project manager survey. IEEE Transactions on Software Engineering 26(2), 98–112 (2000)
26. Roy, M.M., Christenfeld, N.J.S., McKenzie, C.R.M.: Underestimating the duration of future events: Memory incorrectly used or memory bias? Psychological Bulletin 131(5), 738 (2005)
27. Schmidt, R., Lyytinen, K., Keil, M., Cule, P.: Identifying software project risks: An international delphi study. Journal of Management Information Systems 17(4), 5–36 (2001)
28. Verhoef, C.: Quantitative IT portfolio management. Science of Computer Programming 45(1), 1–96 (2002)
29. Wateridge, J.: How can IS/IT projects be measured for success? International Journal of Project Management 16(1), 59–63 (1998)

A Metrics for Meeting Quality on a Software Requirement Acquisition Phase

Noriko Hanakawa[1] and Masaki Obana[2]

[1] Hannan University,
5-4-33, Amami Higashi, Matsubara-si, Osaka 580-8502, Japan
hanakawa@hannan-u.ac.jp
[2] Nara Institute Science and Technology
8916-5 Takayama-cho, Ikoma, Nara Japan
masaki-o@is.naist.jp

Abstract. Requirement analysis of software is an important phase on software development. In practice, stakeholders discuss software requirements with system engineers on meetings. Quality of meetings influences quality of software requirements. Low quality of meetings will lead low quality software. However, measurement of meeting quality is difficult, because meetings for software requirements mainly perform oral discussions among stakeholders and system engineers.

Therefore, we propose a new metrics of meeting quality for software requirements are discussed. A feature of the metrics is to measure only when and who speaks. Because the metrics does not depend on analysis of conversations' contents by natural language techniques, the metrics can be easily adapted to various software domains. As a result of adapting practical software development projects, we extracted doubtful discussions in meetings. After that, we confirmed that the metrics can predict doubtful specifications that may lead specification faults in future.

Keywords: Meeting, software requirement, System engineer, discussion logs, meeting quality.

1 Introduction

Requirement analysis of software is important on large-scale software development. In industrial practice, software requirements are often defined at meetings with system engineers and stakeholders. We call such meeting "Specification meeting", "requirement analysis meeting", or "discussion of software specification". In the meetings, system engineers extract demands and concepts of target software from stakeholders. And system engineers also discuss a new business work flows, the details of system specifications, and GUI with the stakeholders. System engineers need high communication abilities, proposal abilities of software specifications, analysis abilities of problems, and proceeding abilities of meetings. On the other hand, stakeholders are required high decision-making skills, competence to judge correctness of software specifications, and regulating abilities of various opinions in their organizations. Although the requirement analysis is one of most difficult activities in

O. Dieste, A. Jedlitschka, and N. Juristo (Eds.): PROFES 2012, LNCS 7343, pp. 260–274, 2012.

software development, results of requirement analysis on meetings greatly influence software quality [1][5].

Many methods have been proposed for improving activities of a requirement analysis phase. Sawye et al. claimed that deep understanding of software requirement is performed on an early phase using descriptions written in a natural language from stakeholders' interviews [2]. Domain models are constructed in order to eliminate inconsistency of descriptions in documents of system specifications [3], a method of refining stakeholders' requirement at meetings is proposed [4]. These studies focus on important problems of requirements analysis such as vagueness of requirements written in a natural language, inconsistency of requirements, and not-refining requirements. However, these studies are depended a target system's domains and accumulated experiential knowledge. If a system belongs to a new domain and new development technologies, the above methods are not useful because experiential data and knowledge are not yet accumulated.

Therefore, we propose a new metrics for meeting quality on a software requirement analysis phase. Our original basic idea is "high quality of meetings lead high quality software requirement". In industrial practice, system engineers discuss software requirements with stakeholders at meetings on an analysis phase. The meeting quality greatly influences quality of software requirements. A feature of the metrics is to measure only when and who speaks at meetings. Contexts of speaking at meetings are not a target of the metrics. Hence, the metrics can adapt a new project using a new system domain and new development technologies without accumulated experiential data and knowledge.

In this paper, we show measurement of meeting quality in two projects. In addition, we call all activities such as "specification analysis", and "requirement definition" as "requirement analysis". And a meeting of requirement analysis means a meeting where system engineers and stakeholders define software requirements and specifications with deep discussions. Section 2 shows related works. In section 3, the meeting metrics is proposed. Section 4 shows examples of measuring meeting qualities, at section 5, we discuss efficiency of the metrics. Section 6 shows summary and future works.

2   Related Works

There are many empirical researches for communication at meetings on software development projects. Seaman et al. clarified relationships between efficiency of inspection meetings and organizational arrangements [6]. Organizational relationships among developers influence meeting time and meeting processes. Damian et al. studied synchronous or asynchronous negotiations of software requirements in distributed development [7]. They claimed that efficient negotiations are to discuss details of requirements at regular meetings after asynchronous discussion of vague requirements by e-mails. The approach of these researches is based on records of practical meeting logs. The approach is similar to our research. Although these researches focus on only meeting times and efficiency of meetings, meeting qualities and predictions of specification faults are not mentioned. Our research also mentions predictions of specification faults caused by low quality of meetings.

On the other hand, software requirements and specifications are discussed in natural languages such as Japanese. Therefore, Sawye et al. proposed a new analysis method for acquiring deep understandings from shallow knowledge using corpus linguistics [2]. After frequent words are extracted from stakeholders' interviews at a software requirement analysis phase, main concepts of the software domain are constructed in order to help analysts' understandings. Doi et al. proposed USP (User-oriented System Planning method) for capturing software requirements. USP presents problem solution graphs based on corpus. The corpus is constructed by recording stakeholders' utterance at requirement analysis meetings in a natural language. The solution graphs are useful for function analysis, quality analysis, and concern analysis on both online and offline methods. Purposes of these researches are improvement of software requirement analysis activities using natural language techniques based on records of utterance at meetings. These approaches need high cost. Each utterance at meetings should be correctly recorded. The activities of recording such utterances require expertise knowledge in order to understand correctly speakers' intentions. Moreover, because oral words at meetings include more vagueness than words written on paper documents, correct capturing of speakers' intentions at meetings is more difficult than capturing writers' intentions on paper documents.

In addition, many analysis techniques for meeting states are proposed using video pictures and audio recording. Miyata et al. proposed a technique of auto editing long meeting videos into a digest [8]. They find speakers' thinking statements and thinking stop scenes using an electroencephalograph. And a new metrics for meeting concentrate named "MS-Level" is proposed [9]. Values of the MS-Level present important thinking statements such as "concentration" and "concern" at a meeting. By indexing video pictures using the MS values, researchers are useful for analyzing meeting statements and thinking statements of participants. On the other hand, an auto zooming TV meeting system is proposed. In the system, a speaker's picture of videos is automatically zoomed up when the speaker start talking [10]. These systems and researches are a kind of analysis methods using video pictures in order to clarifying meeting quality and discussions. However, these researches need large-scale equipment such as electroencephalographs, many video cameras, and TV meeting systems. The preparing and setting the equipment at meeting rooms will be costly. Our proposed metrics for meeting quality needs only records: "who spoke, and when it was spoken". Because our approach does not need large-scale equipment, various meetings on various organizations can easily adapt our metrics for measuring meeting quality.

3   The Proposed Meeting Metrics

3.1   Background

In our university, two large-scale educational systems have been developed from October of 2007. After competitive bidding of the two systems, we ordered the systems to a system development company. One of the systems is version 2 of HInT system (Hannan Internet communication Tool) [11]. The HInT is an integrated educational system with a campus portal site system and an e-learning management system in order to communicate between teachers and students. Two new functions: a calendar function, an attendance management function are added to the first version of the HInT. On the other hand, another of the systems is p-HInT (portable HInT) system [12][13]. The p-HInT is a lecture support system for large-scale lecture rooms where 200 or more audiences attend a lecture using NINTENDO DS® (DS) [14].

To analyze requirements of these systems, we held many meetings with system engineers and stakeholders. The number of meetings is 16, total time of the meetings is about 32 hours. However, major problems caused by two specification faults of the HInT system occurred after the second version of the HInT system was released. The first problem is to send an e-mail of daily schedule in a remainder function even if there is no schedule on the day. That is, a "today has no schedule" e-mail sends to all teachers and all students. One of important concepts of the HInT is to avoid unnecessary e-mails as much as possible. The "today has no schedule" e-mail is obviously against the concept. The other problem is to lack an important function of sum calculation of attendance data every semester. Because stakeholders and system engineers pay attentions to only visual operationality of the attendance function, the sum calculation of the attendance data was inadvertently missed. In reality, causes of the specification faults already had occurred at meetings of a requirement analysis phase. The discussions of the meetings already included vagueness and a gap of the specifications between the system engineers and the stakeholders.

We became aware of meeting quality through many practical meetings with system engineers and stakeholders. For example, there is a good case in which a specification is smoothly determined through well‐regulated discussions. In contrast, there is a bad case in which discussions become complicated. In the bad case, stakeholders have only vague feelings "what was determined at the meeting?". In such way, each meeting has an each quality. Therefore, we clarify differences between a good meeting and a no-good meeting. After that, we propose a meeting metrics that measures quality of discussions and possibility of specification faults.

3.2   A Concept of Meeting Metrics

Fig.1 shows a typical discussion pattern when system engineers and stakeholders determine software specifications at a meeting. The discussion pattern is extracted from experiences of practical meetings. The pattern is a basis of our proposed meeting metrics. At first, a system engineer proposes a specification of a new function. The system engineer explains the specification to stakeholders using explanation documents or demonstrations (P1 of Fig.1). After the system engineer's explanation, a stakeholder asks a question about the specification to the system engineer (P2 of Fig.1). On another occasion, the system engineer asks a question to stakeholders. Next, the system engineer answers the stakeholder's question, or the stakeholder answers the system engineer's question (P3 of Fig.1). After a pair of a question and an answer is repeated, the stakeholders make a decision about the specification (P4 of Fig.1). Finally, the system engineer summarizes the final specification that was discussed in the iterations of the questions and answers.

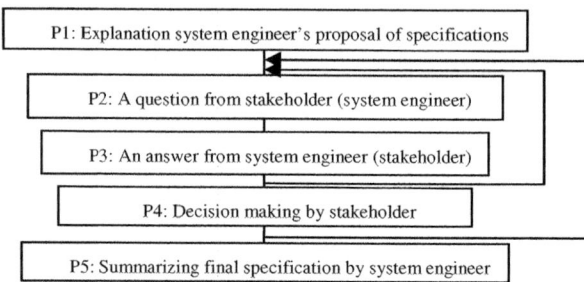

Fig. 1. A typical pattern of discussion with system engineers and stakeholders

However, if discussions between system engineers and stakeholders become complicated, the iterations of questions and answers will be thrown into disorder. The questions and answers are confused, or, stakeholders' decision making may be vague, or, system engineers may unilaterally talk without stakeholders' replies. Moreover, speaking time becomes long, the number of times of speaking increases. In such case, discussion often deviates from the typical discussion pattern of Fig.1.

Therefore, we make the new meeting metrics using the number of times of speaking and speaking time. The speaking of discussions is classified into system engineers' speaking and stakeholders' speaking. The number of times of speaking and speaking time can be easily collected without domain knowledge, and expertise knowledge. Our metrics is easily adapted to various projects because domain knowledge and expertise knowledge are not required.

3.3   Measuring the Value of the Metrics

Basic metrics of the proposed metrics are follows;

(1) Start time and end time of a speaking.
(2) Who speaks?
(3) Start time and end time of a theme.

Advanced metrics based on the basic metrics are follows;

— Metircs1: average of a system engineer's speaking time.
— Metrics2: average of a stakeholder's speaking time.
— Metrics3: the number of times of system engineers' speakings.
— Metrics4: the number of times of stakeholders' speakings.
— Metrics5: Ratio of system engineers' speaking time to all discussion time.
— Metircs6: Ratio of stakeholders' speaking time to all discussion time.
— Metrics7: Ratio of the number of times of system engineers' speakings to total number of time of speakings.
— Metrics8: Ratio of the number of times of stakeholders' speakings to total number of time of speakings.

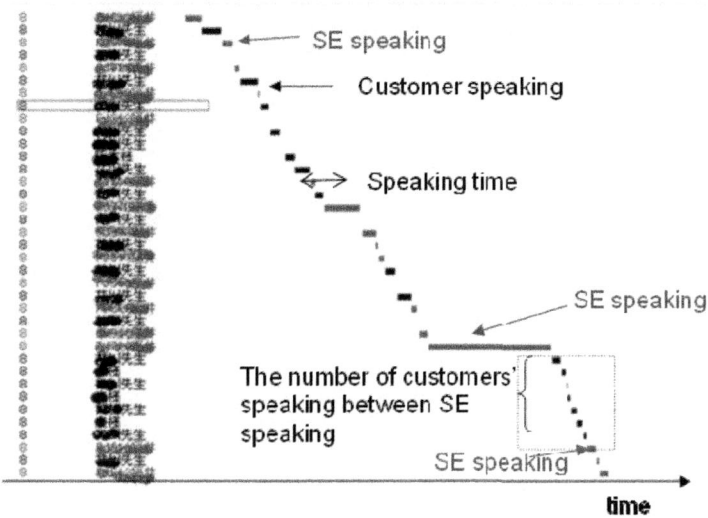

Fig. 2. A graph of system engineers and customers' speaking

— Metrics9: The maximum number of times of stakeholders' speakings between a system engineer speaking and a system engineer speaking (in Fig.1, a cycle between P2 and P3 is disordered. For example, stakeholders frequently speak without waiting of system engineers' answers).

The advanced metrics are measured on each theme. The theme means a discussion topic at a meeting. For example, in the third meeting of HInT system, there are 8 themes; (1) confirmation of pending issues, (2) confirmation of a list of new functions, (3) an operation flow of attendance management in a lecture, (4) an operation flow of making a time table of examination, (5) an operation flow of making a time table for extra classes, (6) an operation flow of changing lecture schedule, (7) an operation flow of making reports, (8) an operation flow of making messages to students. Usually, 5 to 8 themes are discussed at a meeting. The themes are easily collected from a resume of the meetings. By recording start time and end time of one theme's discussion, we can make relationships the system engineer's speaking and stakeholder's speaking with the same themes.

Fig.2 shows a visual graph of system engineers' speakings and stakeholders' speakings in the eighth theme of the third meeting of HInT system. The horizontal axis means time, the vertical axis means speakers. Red names of Fig.2 means system engineers, black names means stakeholders. By recording each speaking start time and end time, the graph of Fig.2 can be created. In the measurement of speakings, we recorded details of speaking such as "yes" and "I know". The length of the vertical bars of Fig.2 means speaking time of each speaker. In addition, the rectangle area with broken line in the lower part of Fig.2 shows the Metrics9 (the maximum number of times of stakeholders' speakings between a system engineer speaking and a system engineer speaking). In the rectangle area, a red bar means system engineer speaking, a

Fig. 3. An example video pictures of meetings

black bar means a stakeholder speaking. The number of black bars between two red bars is a value of the Metrics9. In the case of the rectangle area of Fig.2, the value of the Metrics9 is 7.

We measured values of the basic metrics while we referred video pictures (See Fig.3). The length of the meeting video is 32 hours. At the beginning, we tried automatic identification of speakers and speaking time using an automatic identification technique for speakers. However, correctness of the automatic identification was very low. Then we made a support tool for measuring values of the basic metrics (See Fig.4). The tool consists of a video running area and an identifying speaker area. In the tool, while the video running, a researcher clicks a "speaker" button at the identifying speaker area. For example, a researcher watched the movie at the video area. If a speaker changes to another speaker on the movie, the researcher clicks the new speaker's name button on the identification area. Although the change of the speaker is manual on the tool, the researcher is not required expertise knowledge and domain knowledge. In addition, the movies of the video area and the time stamp of the identification area are synchronized. Then, the work of identifying speakers can repeat like replaying videos.

3.4 Extracting Significant Metrics

From the basic metrics and the advanced metrics in the section 3.3, significant metrics are extracted. The steps of the extraction are follows;

- (Step1)All values of the basic metrics are measured. The all values of the advanced metrics are automatically calculated based on the values of the basic metrics.
- (Step2)By analyzing minutes of the meetings, we classify the themes to two categories; discussions including the specification faults, and discussions not including the specification faults. The specification faults are "sending a daily e-mail even if there is no schedule", and "lack of a function for calculating total sum of attendance data".
- (Step3)The significant differences of average values of each advanced metrics between the two categories are clarified by t-test. If the significant difference is large, the advanced metrics means a significant metrics for measuring meeting quality.

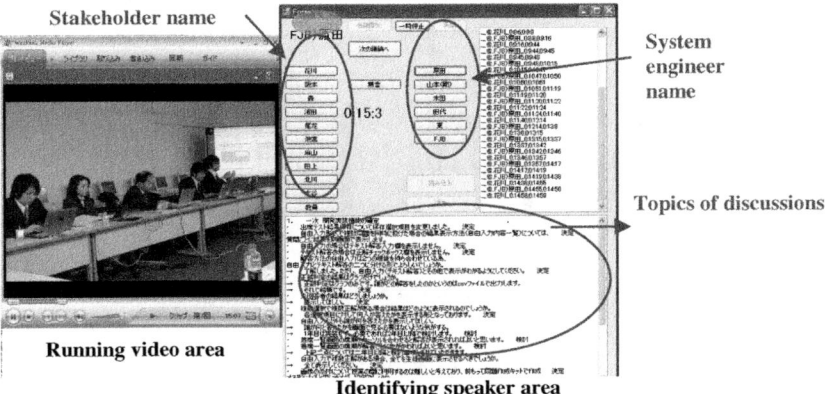

Fig. 4. A tool for measuring values of the basic metrics

In step 1, values of the basic metrics are measured by the tool of Fig.4. The values of the advanced metrics are automatically calculated. Fig.5 shows the values of the 9 advanced metrics in 8 themes of the third meeting of the HInT system. A value of Metris3 (the number of times of system engineers' speakings) and a value of Metrics4 (the number of times of stakeholders' speakings.) of the theme 3 are bigger than the values of the other advanced metrics. In step 2, we identified 8 discussions related with the specification fault; "e-mail sending", and 4 discussions related with the specification fault; "sum of attendance data". The way of the identification was to watch all video movies of the meetings, and manually identify the discussions of all minutes of the meetings. Then, the 8 discussions and the 4 discussions are categorized to a group related with the specification faults. The other discussions are categorized to a group with normal specifications. As a result, there are 12 themes related with the specification faults, there are 44 themes related with normal specifications.

In step 3, averages and distributions of the 9 advanced metrics are calculated. The averages of the advanced metrics between the two categories are shown in Fig.6. We confirmed that the average of Metrics1 of the group related with normal specifications was more than the average of Metrics1 of the group related with the specification faults. Moreover, the average of Metrics9 of the group related with the specification faults is more than the average of Metrics9 of the group related with normal specifications. The significant difference between the two categories is clear by t-test. With significant level 5%, there are significant differences between the two categories in Metrics1 and Metrics9. That is, if time of the system engineer speaking is short, and if stakeholders frequently speak between a system engineer speaking and a system engineer speaking, the possibility of the not-smooth discussion will be high. Quality of such discussions and meetings will be low. Then we can predict that the themes including such not-smooth discussions leads specification faults in requirement analysis.

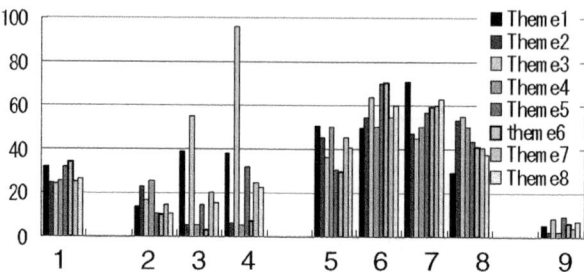

Fig. 5. Values of the 9 advanced metrics of 8 themes of the third meeting of HInT system

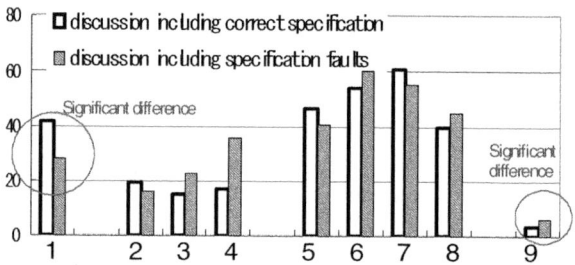

Fig. 6. Values of the advanced metrics categorized the two groups

In short, a high quality meeting is that system engineer spends much time to explain specifications (P1 of Fig.1), after that, a system engineer answers a stakeholder's question, or a stakeholder answers a system engineer's question (P2 and P3 of Fig.1). The "answers and questions" is near to "one answer and one question". In addition, the system engineer spends long time to summarize the discussions and the specifications (P5 of Fig.1). We predict that the specifications are correct because the specifications were discussed in high quality meeting. In contrast, a low quality meeting is that system engineer spends little time to explain specifications, moreover, stakeholders do not sufficiently understand a concept of specifications, and a system engineer's thought. Stakeholders ask many questions and claim their opinions without waiting system engineers' answers and explanations. Moreover, because stakeholders and system engineers repeat questions and opinions that are off the point of the discussion theme, it takes long time to discuss. Quality of meeting in such situations will be low. The situations of complicated discussions can be derived from values of the two advanced metrics; Metrics1 and Metrics9.

3.5   A Metrics for Meeting Quality

Based on the result of the section 3.4, the metrics for meeting quality has been proposed as follows;

$$Meeting = SE_{talk} \times 1 / CUS_{repeat} \tag{1}$$

Meeting: Value of the metrics for meeting quality.

SE_{talk} :   Metrics1(average of a system engineer's speaking time.).

CUS_{repeat}:   Metrics9 (the maximum number of times of stakeholders' speakings between a system engineer speaking and a system engineer speaking).

If a value of *"Meeting"* is low, quality of a meeting will be low, and possibility of including specification faults will be high.

4   Adapting the Meeting Metrics

4.1   Calculation of Values of *Meeting*

The proposed metrics is adapted to another project "p-HInT". In the p-HInT project, three system engineers were assigned. Stakeholders of the p-HInT were different from the stakeholders of the HInT. Although the project of the HInT is version up, the project of the p-HInT is completely a new system. The number of the meetings was 8, total number of the themes was 45. The all values of the themes are shown at Fig.9. Especially, Fig.7 shows values of *Meeting* of each theme of the first meeting and the third meeting. The values of theme 3 and theme 5 of the first meeting are low. Fig.8 shows values of two advanced metrics; Metrics1 and Metrics9. Bar charts mean values of Metrics1, a line chart means values of Metrics9. The values of Metrics1 of the theme 3 and theme 5 are about 5.5; it is smaller than the values in the other themes. Moreover, the value of Metrics9 of the theme 5 is 7; it is also bigger than the values in the other themes.

Then, we checked the video movies of the theme 3 and the theme 5 of the first meeting. In the theme 5, the discussions were off the point of the theme 5. The theme 5 was "How are late students marked on a student list?". However, stakeholders discussed "How do we visit other universities in order to investigate similar educational systems?". Of course, the stakeholders' discussions were not suitable of the theme 5. The discussions became obviously complicated. As a result, the specification of marking late students was vague. Quality of the meeting became low.

4.2   Evaluation of the Values of *Meeting* as Compared with Specification Faults

After the first release, the stakeholders claimed 48 specification problems from April to September of 2008. Range of the specification faults was wide from simple problems to significant problems. The categorized specification faults are shown at Table 1. The row named "Functions" means main 7 functions of p-HInT. The "Normal" row means that the specification faults occurred while users doing normal operations. The "no-normal, limit" row means that the specification faults occurred while users doing irregular operations. The "message" row means unclear messages for navigating users' operations. If the stakeholders and the system engineers more carefully had discussed the specifications in the meetings, we would be able to avoid almost all the specification faults.

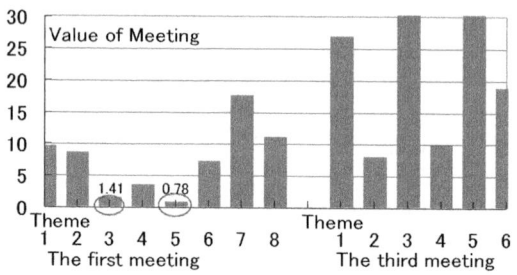

Fig. 7. Values of *Meeting* on each theme in the first meeting and the third meeting on p-HInT project

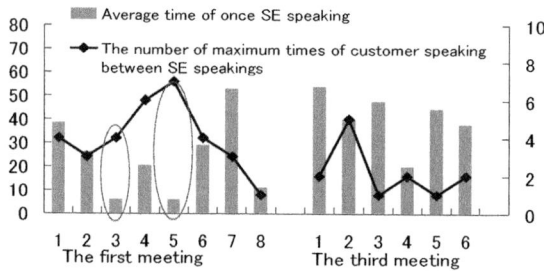

Fig. 8. Values of the two significant metrics on p-HInT project

Therefore we tried classifying the 48 specification faults into the 45 themes of the 8 meetings. The results of the classification are shown at Fig.9. The 36 specifications faults were able to be classified. The numerical values with white bold characters with a red filled rectangle of Fig.9 mean the number of the specification faults that should be discussed at the theme. For example, at the forth theme of the second meeting, three specification are classified. That is, the value "3" of the white bold character means a count number of specification faults that were discussed in the theme at the meeting. The 3 specification faults are derived from Table 1. In addition, the classification of the specification faults is in manual while we compared the faults with the discussions' contents using video records.

Table 1. Counts of the specification faults

Functions	Test	Log-in	Data format	Student list	Making test	Call the roll	Environment	Total
Normal	8	2	2	2	3	3	13	33
no-normal, limit	9	0	0	0	0	0	3	12
messages	3	0	0	0	0	0	0	3
Total	20	2	2	2	3	3	16	48

As shown in Fig 9, the values of *Meeting* of discussion including specification faults are lower than the values of *Meeting* of other discussions. If the stakeholders and system engineers more sufficiently discussed the specification, the specification

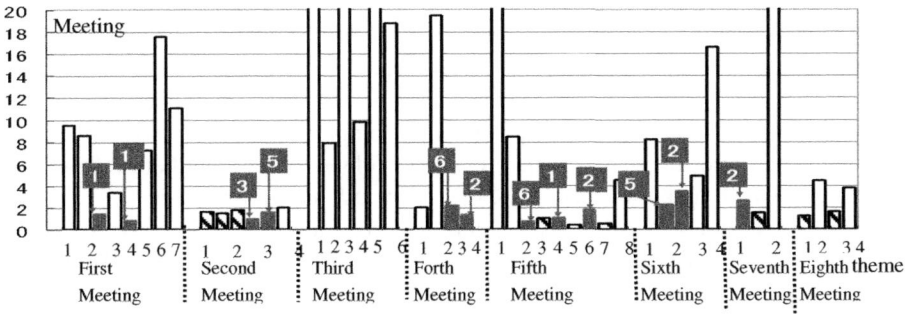

Fig. 9. Comparison the values of *Meeting* of p-HInT with the specification faults

fault might not occur. The value of *Meeting* of the third theme of the first meeting is 1.42. The value of *Meeting* is low. In addition, the value of *Meeting* of the third theme of the fifth meeting is 0.71. The third theme of the fifth meeting is "details flow of Test function". As shown in Table 1, many specification faults according to Test function occurred at not only no-normal operations but also normal operations. Therefore, we can predict that the discussion of the third theme of the fifth meeting was not sufficient.

One of purpose of *Meeting* metrics is prediction of specification fault occurrences at an early stage of development phase. Therefore, we evaluate whether the values of *Meeting* metrics of p-HInT indicate occurrence of the 36 specification faults. If a value of threshold of *Meeting* is 3.0, the number of doubtful themes is 22. For example, the sixth theme "detail flow of input key word" of the fifth meeting is lowest; 0.42. Therefore, we predict that the specification of the "detail flow of input key word" may be unclear. The recall of detecting the 36 specification faults is 91.7%, precision of detecting the specification faults is 50.0%. If the value of threshold of *Meeting* is 2.0, the number of doubtful themes is 17 (See striped pattern bars of Fig.9). The recall is 83.2%, precision is 59.0%. In short, the *Meeting* metrics can be predictable in short odds. At an early development stage such as requirement analysis phases, problematic specifications can be detected using the *Meeting* metrics. However, the value of precision of detecting the specification faults is low as compared with the value of the recall. The reasons of the low value of the precision are investigated at the following section "Discussion".

5   Discussion

5.1   Why the Value of Precision Is Low?

As mentioned above, when a value of threshold of *Meeting* is 2.0, although the value of recall of finding the specification faults is 83.2%, the value of precision is 59.0%. A reason of low value of the precision is discussed in this section.

At Fig.9, there are 9 themes that the specification faults were not occurred although the values of *Meeting* are low. These low values of the 9 themes do not indicate the specification faults. The 9 themes lead the value of the precision low. The 9 themes are categorized as Table2. At first, discussions of No.1 and No.7 of Table 2 are about "Meeting management". Because the discussions are not about software specification, of course, the discussions did not lead any specification faults. Similarly, No.9 discussion of Table 2 did not lead any specification faults because the discussion is about promotion activities of p-HInT. Therefore, we exclude these three themes from analysis of the above evaluation (section 4.2) by the recall and the precision.

Next, discussions of No.2, No.3, and No.8 of Table 2 are "Review". "Review" means re-checking development documents such as function lists, design documents among stakeholders and system engineers. Basically, a value of *Meeting* of a good review process is high. For example, the ninth theme of the fifth meeting, and the forth theme of the sixth meeting are review processes of reviewing design documents for user interface. Values of these themes are not so low; 4.5, and 4.9. The discussions of No.2 and No.3 are in similar review process about function lists. The function lists should be discussed previous meetings (the first meeting and the second meeting). However, because the discussions of the previous meeting were not sufficient, as a result, the discussions about the function list at review processes were not smooth. In addition, the discussion of No.8 at Table 2 is review of design documents for user interface of test function. That is, the previous discussions about the test function were not sufficient. In this way, because the values of *Meeting* of review processes are reflected by qualities of the previous discussions, naturally, the values of *Meeting* of review processes do not indicate the specification faults.

Here, we re-calculate a value of the precision of the section 4.2. The specification faults of No.1, No.2, No.3, No.7, No.8, and No.9 of Table2 are extracted the calculation of the precision. The value of the precision is improved to 73%.

Next, although No.4, No.5, and No.6 of Table 2 are just specification discussions, the discussions did not lead the specification faults. We check details of the discussions. The discussion of No.4 is a detail flow of the question function. The question function is similar to the test function. Moreover, the question function was not useful. No teachers used the question function in their lectures. Because of no user, the

Table 2. Details of themes that the specification faults were not classified

No.	Num. of meeting	Num. of theme	Contents of the discussion	Category
1	2	1	Confirmation of schedule, a way of sharing development data	Meeting management
2	2	2	Reviewing the previous discussion of the function list of this version	Review
3	2	3	Reviewing the missing description of the function list of this version	Review
4	5	4	A detail flow of question function	Specification
5	5	6	A detail flow of input keyword for DS	Specification
6	5	8	A detail flow of referring test results for DS	Specification
7	7	2	Schedule of making new functions for the next version	Meeting management
8	8	1	Reviewing the design documents for the user interface	Review
9	8	3	Demonstration of p-HInT system	Promotion

specification faults about the question function did not occur. To begin with, the question function may not be necessary. Of course, the necessary of the question function should be discussed more at the meetings of the requirement analysis phase. Therefore, the low value of *Meeting* of the No.4 of Table 2 may be appropriate.

Next, discussions of No.5 and No.6 are about specifications of students' operations on DS. To tell the truth, all of the specification faults were requests from only several teachers. Investigation from April to September of 2008, we collected requests and opinions of the first release p-HInT from only several teachers. Because teachers' requests and specification faults were too many, we were not able to collect students' requests and opinions. Therefore, there was no specification fault about operations on DS. After second release of October of 2008 students' requests and opinions were collected as same as teachers' requests. 4 specification faults about students' operations on DS occurred. One was a complicated operation of log-in process on DS. Another was about operations of a test function on DS. Of course, because the second version of the p-HInT was improved various functions' operations and performance, we can't simply compare the values of *Meeting* of the first version's meetings with the second version's specification faults. However, we think that several causes of the second version's specification faults had already been embedded at the first version's meetings. Using the values of *Meeting*, we can investigate essential causes of specification faults with tracing back to the past. Even if the tracing goes back previous versions, essential causes of specification faults will be detected by values of *Meeting*.

5.2   A Tool for Detecting Doubtful Specifications in Real Time

A most important point of *Meeting* metrics is measurement in real time. Doubtful specifications should be detected as early as possible. Therefore, we have developed a tool for detecting doubtful specifications. The tool consists of a tool for measuring basic metrics (See Fig.4) and calculations of *Meeting* metrics. A person operates the tool for measuring basic metrics of Fig.4 while he/she hears discussions in meetings. He/ she does only action of push buttons of the tool when a speaker changes. Just discussions of a theme finishes, the tool calculates a value of *Meeting* metrics. If the value of *Meeting* is lower than a threshold value, a warning of doubtful specifications informs in real time to stakeholders and system engineers. The tool is useful to improve specifications for avoiding specification faults after release.

6   Conclusion

We propose a new metrics for meeting quality at a software requirement analysis phase. The metrics needs only time of speaking, the number of times of speaking of system engineers and stakeholders. The metrics can distinguish smooth discussions with complicated discussions. As a result of application of p-HInT project, the values of the metrics were able to indicate occurrence of specification faults after release. Recall of detecting specification faults by values of the metrics is 83.2%, precision is 59.0%. The low value of the precision was caused by topics of meeting management, and reviewing documents. In addition, after second version release, we confirm that specification faults caused by the insufficient discussions of the first version.

In future, a tool for auto measuring when and who speaks at meetings will be developed. In addition, we will be clear relationships among various software development processes and methodologies, then, more details of relationships between values of the metrics and occurrence of specification faults will be clear.

Acknowledgement. This research was partially supported by KAKENHI, Grant-in-Aid for Scientific Research(C), 21500045, 2011.

References

1. Stellman, A., Jennifer, G.: Applied Software Management. O'Reilly Media, Cambridge (2005)
2. Sawye, P., Rayson, P., Cosh, K.: Shallow knowledge as an aid to deep understanding in early phase requirements engineering. IEEE Transactions on Software Engineering 31(11), 969–981 (2005)
3. Osada, A., Ozawa, D., Kaiya, H., Kaijiri, K.: The Role of Domain Knowledge Representation in Requirements Elicitation. In: Proc. IASTED International Conference on Software Engineering, pp. 84–92 (2007)
4. Doi, K., Horai, H., Watanabe, I., Katayama, Y., Sonobe, S.: User-oriented requirements capturing method in analyzing requirements capturing meeting requirements engineering. Transactions of Information Processing Society of Japan 44(1), 48–58 (2003)
5. Dyba, T., Dingsoyr, T.: Empirical Studies of agile software development: A systematic review. Information and Software Technology 50(9-10), 833–859 (2008)
6. Seaman, C., Basili, V.: Communication and Organization: An Empirical Study of Discussion in Inspection Meetings. IEEE Transaction on Software Engineering 24(6), 559–572 (1998)
7. Damian, D., Lanubile, F., Mallardo, T.: On the Need for Mixed Media in Distributed Requirements Negotiations. IEEE Transactions on Software Engineering 34(1), 116–132 (2008)
8. Miyata, A., Hayashi, T., Yamamoto, S., Hayashi, M., Shigeno, H., Okada, K.: Conference Movie Summarization Assistance Using Mental States and Speech Breakpoints. Transactions of Information Processing Society of Japan 47(3), 906–914 (2006)
9. Miyata, A., Hayashi, T., Yamamoto, S., Hayashi, M., Shigeno, H., Okada, K.: A Proposal of Indexing Conference Movies with Thinking States. In: Proce. Fifth International Conference on Creating, Connecting and Collaborating through Computing, pp. 54–61 (2007)
10. Tomino, T., Inoue, A., Ichimura, S., Matsushita, Y.: A Speaker Zooming Method for Room-to-room TV Conference. Transactions of Information Processing Society of Japan 47(7), 2091–2098 (2006)
11. Hanakawa, N., Akazawa, Y., Mori, A., Maeda, T., Inoue, S., Tsutsui, S.: A Web-based integrated education system for a seamless environment among teachers, students, and administrators. International Journal of System & Computer in Japan 37(5), 14–24 (2006)
12. http://www2.hannan-u.ac.jp/p-hint/index.html
13. Hanakawa, N., Obana, M.: Mobile game terminal based interactive education environment for large-scale lectures. In: Proc. the Eighth IASTED International Conference on Web-based Education, WBE 2010 (2010)
14. http://www.nintendo.co.jp/ds/index.html

Merging the Quality Assessment of Processes and Products in Automotive Domain

Morayo Adedjouma[1, 2], Hubert Dubois[2], François Terrier[2], and Tarek Kitouni[1]

[1] DELPHI France, 64 avenue de la plaine de France, 95572 ROISSY CEDEX, France
[2] CEA LIST, Nano-INNOV, Boîte 174, 91191 Gif-sur-Yvette Cedex, France
{Morayo.Adedjouma,Tarek.Kitouni}@delphi.com,
{Hubert.Dubois,Francois.Terrier}@cea.fr

Abstract. It is commonly accepted that the quality of a product depends on quality of a process. So, many industrial companies have put effort to improve their software processes, which are mainly based on CMMI or SPICE in automotive industry. However, these processes do not pay attention to safety-related dedicated issues. We propose in this paper an instrument that allows performing a SPICE assessment as well as a safety assessment regarding the ISO 26262 recommendations. The major benefit of our proposal is that it allows focusing on assessing software by both development process quality and product quality approaches.

Keywords: Quality assessment, certification, Automotive, HIS, ISO 26262.

1 Introduction

With the recent safety-related standard ISO 26262 [3], automotive industry is interested in strategies for mastering its processes. Indeed, in current situation, suppliers have to prove process capabilities to OEM (Original Equipment Manufacturers) through maturity models, and standards such CMMI (Capability Maturity Model Integration) [14], ISO/IEC 15504 also called SPICE (Software Process Improvement and Capability dEtermination) [15], HIS Automotive SPICE [5] in automotive domain, etc... These processes are described as being "process-based", in that they define a set of practices to be adhered during the development of software. They provide good strategies to assess organization's software development capability and, based on the resulted assessment, they allow identifying the process strengths, weaknesses and risks for preventing them. Unfortunately, because these last ones do not comprise safety aspects, they do not satisfy requirements for a consistent safety management. On the other side, ISO 26262 is the new software safety standard, derived from the IEC 61508 [16], specifically developed for automotive industry to handle this purpose. It is a certification system that focuses on end-product quality approach based on the construction of well-structured and reasoned safety arguments. Our work is an attempt to develop an assessment instrument for a specific automotive engineering organization that develops safety systems and that aims at supporting software certification by both end-product quality approach and

O. Dieste, A. Jedlitschka, and N. Juristo (Eds.): PROFES 2012, LNCS 7343, pp. 275–289, 2012.

development process approach. The instrument is built across a metamodel that is implemented in an Excel framework.

The paper is organized as follows: it starts with an overview of the two standards discussed in this article: HIS Automotive SPICE and ISO 26262. Section 3 presents the analysis that we realized about the overlapping between the two standards and about the identified gaps. Then, the considered methodology to unify them in a single process which corresponds to a full compliance of both standards is presented in section 4. In section 5, an assessment framework to measure process capability of a specific engineering organization that develops safety systems is proposed. Lastly, the paper presents some future works before concluding.

2   Motivation and Introduction to HIS and ISO 26262

For a long time now there have been demands for process-oriented developments according to Automotive SPICE [1], [2] in the automotive sector. Many companies have already set themselves up here, or accordingly aligned their improvement projects. In 2011, the new ISO 26262 safety standard has been released, with more stringent requirements on the development of a product. The current problematic for suppliers is to check if they have to completely adapt their current projects now; or to check what has already been achieved according to Automotive SPICE, what has effectively been used and integrated to meet the new ISO 26262 requirements as well.

2.1   Overview of HIS Automotive SPICE

The Automotive SPICE derived from the ISO/IEC 15504 standard [15], is an international standard used in major worldwide automotive firms, as a *"framework for the assessment of processes"*.   The automotive SPICE can be considered as representative software process assessment models since assessors assign ratings to indicators and metrics that measure the capability of software processes. It is a reference model for the maturity models which specifies requirements for Process Reference Models (PRM) [2] and Process Assessment Models (PAM) [1]. This reference model consists in some major components, namely: some lifecycle processes from different process categories for the process dimension, and six capability levels for the capability dimension.

Processes are the basic by which the software organization generates products. We rely in this paper on the HIS Automotive SPICE [5], a basic subset of processes (named HIS Scope), which has been defined above Automotive SPICE as a selection of a standardized assessment method mostly appropriated for determining suppliers software process capability and related to the sub models of the V-Model (Fig. 1).

Capabilities associated with their process attributes refer to the ability of the organization to produce these products predictably and consistently. It comprises a set of assessment indicators of process performance and process capability which are used as a basis for collecting the objective evidence that enables an assessor to assign ratings. The process attributes are based on the assessment model in ISO/IEC 15504-5 and provide the measurable characteristics of process capability (Fig. 2).

Engineering Process Group		Support Process Group	
ENG.2	System requirements analysis	SUP.1	Quality assurance
ENG.3	System architectural design	SUP.8	Configuration Management
ENG.4	Software requirements	SUP.9	Problem resolution management
	analysis	SUP.10	Change request management
ENG.5	Software design	**Management Process Group**	
ENG.6	Software construction		
ENG.7	Software integration	MAN.3	Project management
ENG.8	Software testing	**Acquisition Process Group**	
ENG.9	System integration	(optional)	
ENG.10	System testing	ACQ.4	Supplier Monitoring

Fig. 1. HIS Automotive SPICE Scope [5]

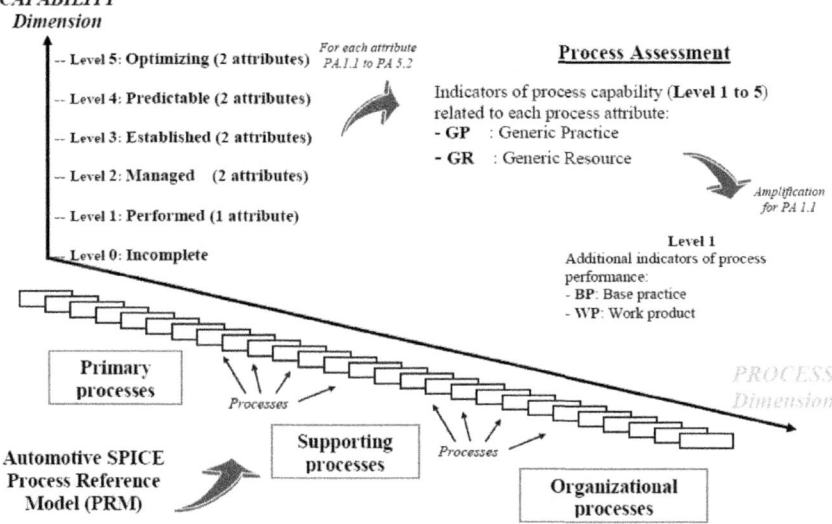

Fig. 2. Relationship between *Process Reference Model* and the assessment *indicators* [1]

2.2   Overview of ISO 26262

Safety is one of the key issues of future automobile development, as for other domains [19]. The new automotive standard ISO 26262 is the adaptation of IEC 61508 [16] to comply with needs specific to the application sector of safety-related electrical and/or electronic (E/E) systems within road vehicles. The standard, through an application model and framework, focuses on the assessment of functional safety by proposing an automotive safety lifecycle based upon a V-model, and tailoring the necessary activities during these lifecycle phases (Fig. 3).

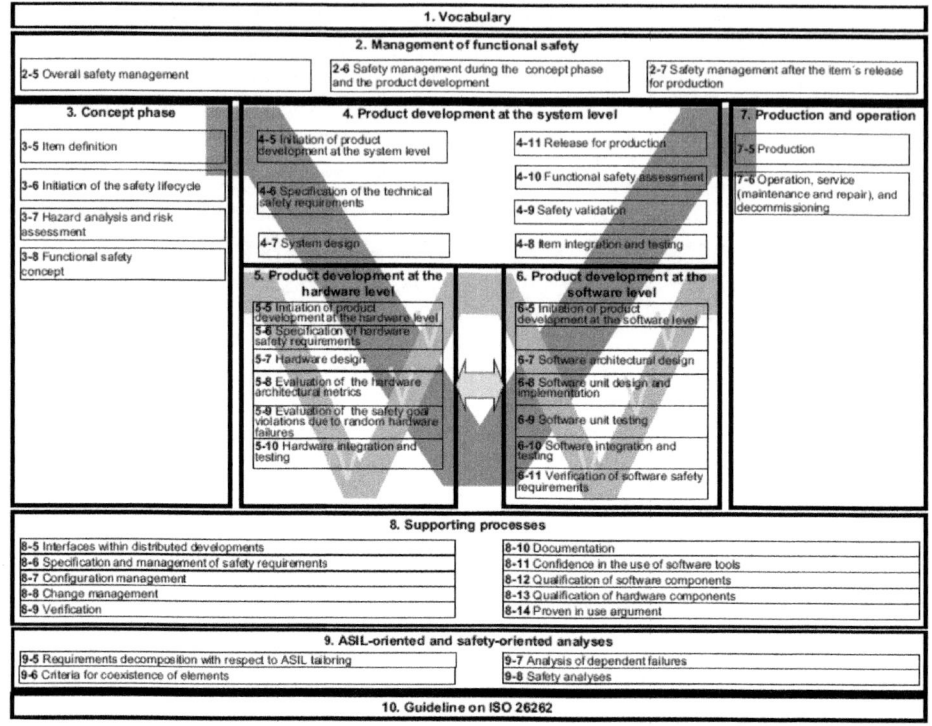

1. Vocabulary

2. Management of functional safety		
2-5 Overall safety management	2-6 Safety management during the concept phase and the product development	2-7 Safety management after the item's release for production

3. Concept phase	4. Product development at the system level		7. Production and operation
3-5 Item definition	4-5 Initiation of product development at the system level	4-11 Release for production	7-5 Production
3-6 Initiation of the safety lifecycle	4-6 Specification of the technical safety requirements	4-10 Functional safety assessment	7-6 Operation, service (maintenance and repair), and decommissioning
3-7 Hazard analysis and risk assessment		4-9 Safety validation	
3-8 Functional safety concept	4-7 System design	4-8 Item integration and testing	

5. Product development at the hardware level	6. Product development at the software level
5-5 Initiation of product development at the hardware level	6-5 Initiation of product development at the software level
5-6 Specification of hardware safety requirements	
5-7 Hardware design	6-7 Software architectural design
5-8 Evaluation of the hardware architectural metrics	6-8 Software unit design and implementation
5-9 Evaluation of the safety goal violations due to random hardware failures	6-9 Software unit testing
5-10 Hardware integration and testing	6-10 Software integration and testing
	6-11 Verification of software safety requirements

8. Supporting processes	
8-5 Interfaces within distributed developments	8-10 Documentation
8-6 Specification and management of safety requirements	8-11 Confidence in the use of software tools
8-7 Configuration management	8-12 Qualification of software components
8-8 Change management	8-13 Qualification of hardware components
8-9 Verification	8-14 Proven in use argument

9. ASIL-oriented and safety-oriented analyses	
9-5 Requirements decomposition with respect to ASIL tailoring	9-7 Analysis of dependent failures
9-6 Criteria for coexistence of elements	9-8 Safety analyses

10. Guideline on ISO 26262

Fig. 3. ISO 2626 overview on V-model [1]

It includes guidance to avoid unreasonable residual risk by providing an automotive-specific risk-based approach to determine Automotive Safety Integrity Levels (ASIL) [3] of system's elements; together with appropriate requirements, processes, techniques, methods and expected work products for validation and confirmation measures to ensure a sufficient and acceptable level of safety being achieved. The final goals is to provide evidence that all reasonable system safety objectives are satisfied, to justify the acceptability of safety based upon product-specific and finally to target evidences to illustrate the competence for managing systems.

2.3   Relationships between HIS and ISO 26262

Much researches are looking for a mapping between HIS and ISO 26262 [8], [9], [11]. General evidence is that there is a high coverage of the HIS scope by the ISO 26262 standard, but a low coverage of the safety standard by the HIS scope instead. This is in particular because, in addition of the requirements defined at process level as is the case in the HIS scope, the ISO 26262 standard also includes specific requirements to be considered at product level. According to our study, we reached the same result as in [18], [7]. Indeed, we note that for the HIS scope, all processes are fully supported by ISO 26262, failing processes SUP 8 and SUP 9 (respectively configuration and problem resolution management) that are only partially considered. Conversely, the process of ISO 26262 is only partially covered by the HIS SPICE or not at all for others activities. This is particularly true for the safety management, hazard analysis and risk assessment, safety concept definition, safety validation, production and operation, safety qualification, safety analyses processes. We present a quick overview of our results in Fig. 4.

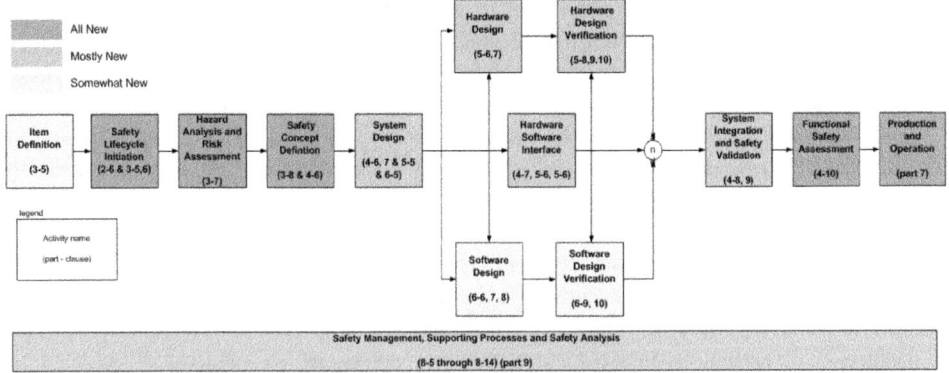

Fig. 4. HIS support in ISO 26262

In the following sections, we present our approach to allow through a unique framework, the assessment of both standards, despite this finding.

3   Certification Representation Model

In [3], an interesting note holds that *"an organization's process definitions must address multiple standards at the same time. If a SPICE assessment is performed, then this SPICE assessment and a functional safety audit can be simultaneously performed. There is sufficient commonality in content that can help to avoid duplication of work or process between both standards and to allow synchronization of the planning"*. For having these coordinated processes, we want to provide specific process cross references to ISO 26262 requirements and HIS. The enhanced obtained model is an integrated model which focuses on certification and assessment of software based on both product quality and process development approaches in a wider scope of requirements.

3.1   Algorithm of Metamodel Extension

Among the researches that are oriented towards the comparison between HIS and ISO 26262, some of them have opted to extend the HIS standard to ensure compliance [7], [8]. Specifically, these approaches update HIS (and more widely) processes according to some ISO 26262 processes that are already partially covered. In addition, they add, at the appropriate level, processes purely dedicated to safety as the identification of hazards, the safety case creation, the classification of safety requirements and so on.

We decide to follow another position that we believe more appropriate in a certification context. Our motivation relies on the following question: how to ensure good compliance to a standard that has been modified if the modification or the extension has not been approved by the certification body having published the original standard? Thus, in our compliance study, we rather have chosen to not modify any of the two standards, but to allow nevertheless a combined assessment method which corresponds to a full compliance for the two automotive standards.

The methodology used for that purpose is inspired by the model and metamodel composition paradigms (also called model combination or weaving) from model-driven engineering community [13], [23]. It is a structured approach that relies on the ontologies. Thus, the respective semantics of each standard are considered as the isomorph graph which needs to be matched to provide a single one that embodies all the different concepts [4]. In [6], the authors propose a generic framework based on an algorithm that follows two steps: (1) the matching step that identifies the models elements (nodes or edges) that describe the same concepts in different models and that have to be composed; (2) the merging step where the matched model elements are merged to create new models elements that represent an integrated view of the concepts.

This algorithm is improved by the application of some others main principles proposed in [12]: (1) the generalization of similarity of nodes; (2) the transitivity of similarity for edges and nodes and (3) the pattern matching.

3.2   Extended Metamodel for HIS Scope and ISO26262 Processes

We apply the full resulting algorithm in order to identify the extended metamodel corresponding to the ontology of both HIS (for which we listed 16 concepts) (Fig. 5) and ISO 26262 standards (for which we listed 21 concepts) (Fig. 6). Let us define the "*similarity*" as the different degree of equivalence greater than a certain threshold between two concepts according to their semantics. When a concept of a standard does not have a similar one in the second standard, the concept is reported in the common metamodel following the transitivity and inheritance rules.

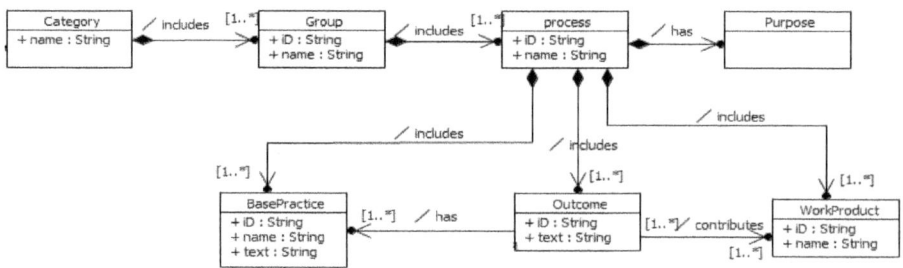

Fig. 5. Extract of the SPICE domain model

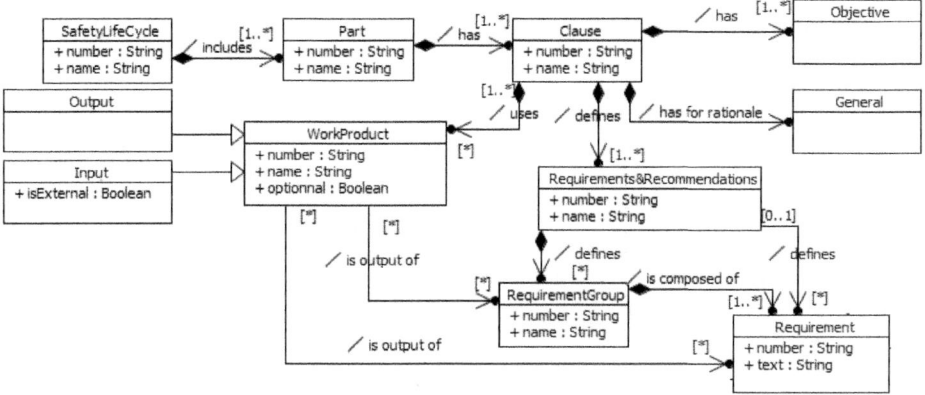

Fig. 6. Extract of ISO 2626 domain model

We start by determining the similarity of *Category, Group, Process* and *Purpose* concepts in SPICE that can be considered similar respectively with *Safety Lifecycle, Part, Clause* and *Objective* concepts in ISO 26262, based on our understanding of their semantic definitions. We apply the pattern matching principle: as they form a connected graph in ISO 26262, the edges connecting them are similar with the edges connecting the concepts in SPICE.

With regard to their semantics, we establish that *Outcome* and *Requirement* concepts are similar. Because *RequirementGroup* concept has an inheritance hierarchy with *Requirement* concept, we apply the generalization of similarity of nodes and stated then *Outcome* concept is also similar of *RequirementGroup*. In the same meaning, a similarity degree is founded between *Outcome* and *Requirements& Recommendations*. Outcome is then similar to several nodes.

Outcome concept is connected with *Workproduct* and *Process* concepts through edges. By transitivity of similarity of edges, we analyze that *Clause* concept is similar to *Process* concept whereas *Workproduct* is similar concept in both standard.
Output, Input, BasePractice and *General* concepts have not matching concepts: they are copied in the common metamodel as such (see Table 1).

Table 1. Example of some matching concepts

HIS concept	ISO 26262 concept	Final Concept
Category	Safety Lifecycle	Category
Workproduct	Workproduct	Workproduct
Outcome	Requirement	Requirement
BasePractice	N/A	BasePractice
N/A	ASIL	ASIL

The resulting metamodel that we obtained allows us to describe the two standards in a single way with one language (Fig. 7). It also allows having an assessment framework able to measure both process capability and product quality about the safety systems development that will discussed in the following sections.

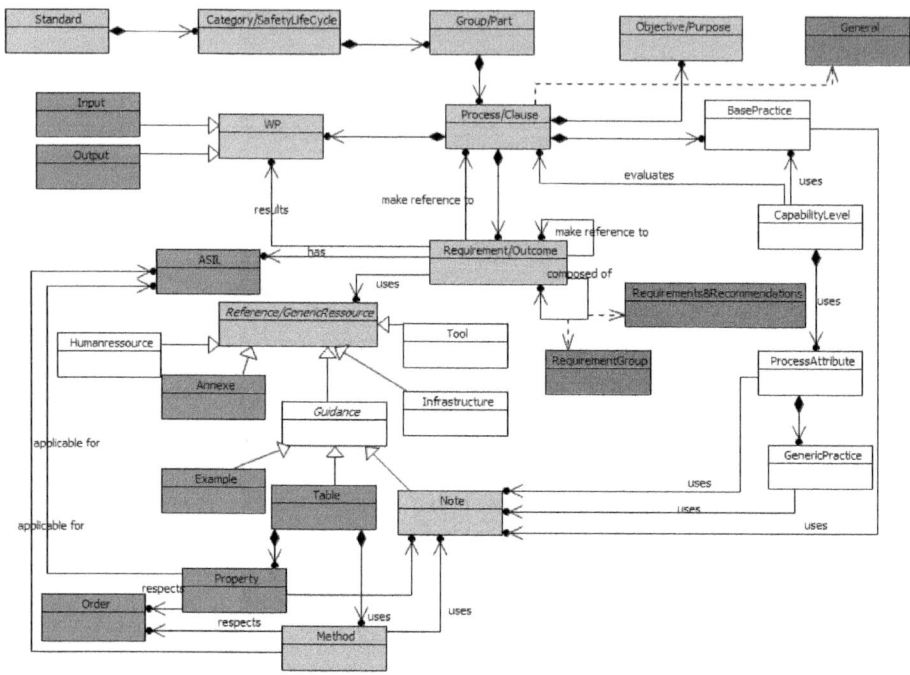

Fig. 7.   Overview of the common metamodel for HIS and ISO 26262. The concepts only present in ISO 26262 are in red. Respectively, the concepts only present in HIS are in White. Blue ones are those common.

4   Integrated Assessment Model

To implement our metamodel, we decide to use an Excel framework. As in [11], we choose this tool because, first of all, it is widely used in automotive industry as it is quite simple to manipulate; furthermore, it served as an experimental tool for interpreting the suitability of our metamodel before we translate it in a more formal way.

4.1   Boundaries of the Context Evaluation

Before starting an audit [3], it is necessary to precise its boundaries. Indeed, the users have an opportunity to select their interesting quality factors to be applied in the certification exercise depending on the organizations requirements:

- What is the system (subsystem) under evaluation?
- Given that each HIS process may be audited individually, and that in this case, they can achieve different maturity level, it is necessary to identify the specific processes that will be subject to evaluation. The term "maturity" relates to the degree of formality and optimization of processes, from ad hoc practices, to formally defined steps, to managed result metrics and to active optimization of the processes [21].

- Concerning ISO 26262, given that the number of requirements to cover increases following the higher severity to achieve (around 1300 requirements for *ASIL A* and more than 1450 requirements for *ASIL D* for instance), it is necessary to define the ASIL as referred to its system (or subsystem). Moreover, if we do not want to cover the entire standard, the processes (i.e. parts) integrated as part of the assessment have to be precised. For instance, if it is the ASIL A that is referred to the system, all requirements that are specifically valid for the others severities (*B, C, or D*) are hidden by an algorithm defined in the framework. It is the same for methods and tools tables recommended by the standard that can also be filtered. For generalization, all the HIS requirements have their ASIL put to "*All*", i.e. they are to be considered for all ASIL levels.

- The certification includes three pillars: product, process and people [20]. Software engineering is a creative, intelligent kind of work, which highly depends on well skilled people. Assigning well-equipped and educated people to a software project is a critical success factor reported from industry. Therefore, we also need to take into consideration the human resources dimension. We have identified a role responsible for each workproduct. If desired, the framework can also be filtered by competency.

These different settings can be parameterized in our framework. After having fixed the quality factors, we can exactly know how many requirements must be met in total for the two standards coverage, and also the needed number to be covered for each standard.

4.2   Description and Usage Rules of the Framework

We may consider two different cases for the audit. The first one is to identify which requirements of the safety standard ISO 26262 already have a good support if we suppose an HIS compliance process ready. The second one is to identify which requirements of the safety standard ISO 26262 will not be fulfilled assuming the same prerequisite.

We start with an analysis of the overlapping and the gaps existing between the standards HIS and ISO 26262 [22]; this analysis allows us to identify how HIS requirements are covered in the safety standard. Regarding that, for each requirement, some parameters have been added. This results in the addition of new columns in the framework used for implementation, that's mean an extension of the metamodel's core. Let's consider the example of a requirement *ReqA* of the standard A (Fig. 8):

- The column *ISO 26262 compliance* (respectively *HIS compliance*) indicates the level of coverage of *ReqA* in the standard B. Three values are possible: "*OK*" (*ReqA* is completely covered); "*Partially*" (*ReqA* is partially covered), "*NOK*" (*ReqA* is not covered at all).
- The column *Clauses references* indicates the clause(s) reference(s) of the requirement(s) corresponding in the standard B.
- The column *Workproducts References* indicates the associated workproducts reference(s) of the requirement(s) corresponding in the standard B.
- The column *Rating* to assign a rating value to the requirement.
- *Recommendation level* is an attribute attached to *Table* and *Property* concepts (see Fig. 7) following the ASIL value. It takes the value "highly recommended", "recommended" and "no recommendation".

Deliverable	Change report		Selected ASIL = D							
Responsible	System Engineer		Capability Level					D		

Clauses	Requirements	ASIL	Recommendation level	Notes	Examples	Rating	HIS Compliance	Clauses SPICE	Workproducts Refereces
8.6.4.5.3	The documentation of the change shall contain the following information:	All				N	OK		
a	the list of changed work products at an appropriate level including configurations and versions, in accordance with Clause 7 (Configuration management).	All				N	OK	SUP 10 - BP 11 SUP 10 - BP 12 SUP 9 - BP 8	13-21 Change control record [Outcome 8] 13-16 Change request [Outcome 2, 3, 5, 6, 7] 21-00 Work product [Outcome 7] 13-07 Problem record [Outcome 3, 5] 15-12 Problem status report [Outcome 6]
b	the details of the carried out change, and	All				N	OK	SUP 10 - BP 10 SUP 9 - BP 8	13-16 Change request [Outcome 2, 3, 5, 6, 7] 21-00 Work product [Outcome 7] 13-07 Problem record [Outcome 3, 5] 15-12 Problem status report [Outcome 6]
c	the planned date for the deployment of the change	All		In the case of a rejected change request, the change request and the rationale for the rejection are also documented		N	OK	SUP 10 - BP 10 SUP 9 - BP 6	13-16 Change request [Outcome 2, 3, 5, 6, 7] 21-00 Work product [Outcome 7]

Fig. 8. Extract of a requirement specification with HIS references columns

Note that we rely on the availability of deliverables to assess the maturity level since, in principle, a process is validated only when all its output workproducts are available. Our resulting metamodel allows us to get the information about the (required or optional) output and input workproducts of each process (see Fig. 7).

Identically, a deliverable is available only if all requirements to which it refers are satisfied. We believe that focusing the assessment on requirement level ensure a more detailed assessment, in contrast to SPICE which focuses on base practice, an concept that regroups a set of outcomes of a process.

We have defined an Excel spreadsheet for each workproduct with all requirements relating to it. Then, we have as many Excel spreadsheets as available workproducts. We use the SPICE rating scale [1], [10] generically to assess the satisfaction status of a requirement in the framework, that means the values *"N", "P", "L" and "F* (Table 2) *" and we add the value "N/A" (Not Applicable)* for follow-up questions.

Table 2. SPICE rating scale

N	Not achieved	0% - 15%	There is little or no evidence of achievement of the defined attribute in the assessed process.
P	Partially achieved	16% - 50%	There is some evidence of an approach to, and some achievement of, the defined attribute in the assessed process. Some aspects of achievement of the attribute may be unpredictable.
L	Largely achieved	51% - 85%	There is evidence of a systematic approach to, and significant achievement of, the defined attribute in the assessed process. Some weakness related to this attribute may exist in the assessed process.
F	Fully achieved	86% - 100%	There is evidence of a complete and systematic approach to, and full achievement of, the defined attribute in the assessed process. No significant weaknesses related to this attribute exist in the assessed process.

In HIS, as well as in the ISO 26262, a requirement may participate in multiple workproducts. Our method avoids redundant work because once a requirement is validated, it will also be validated wherever else it is specified: we propagate the information. In addition, each validated requirement automatically validates all relevant requirements whose references are in column "*Reference*". Several cases are possible to assign the rating in this case (Table 3). Let us consider an example: the requirement *ReqA* which has already its rating value and its reference requirement *ReqB*:

- if the requirement *ReqB* is completely covered by the requirement *ReqA* (equivalent to *"OK"* value), then the rating assigned to the requirement *ReqA* is automatically carried to the requirement *ReqB*.
- if the requirement *ReqB* is partially covered by the requirement *ReqA* (equivalent to *"Partially"* value), then the rating assigned to the requirement *ReqB* is directly below that of the requirement *ReqA,* when it is possible.

The table below summarized the different rating values applied to *ReqB* according to the *ReqA* rating in case of partial coverage.

Table 3. *ReqB* rating values applied following the *ReqA* rating value in case of partial coverage of a requirement *ReqB* by a requirement *ReqA*

ReqA rating	ReqB rating
F	L
L	P
P	N
N	N
N/A	N/A

If the requirement *ReqA* has no corresponding reference in the standard B (*"NOK"* value), then, obviously, nothing is postponed. The staining tab quickly lets us check that a workproduct is available. The coloration follows the same ones associated to SPICE rating scale, i.e. green when all clauses are fully achieved (*F*), yellow when they are largely achieved (*L*), orange when they are partially achieved (*P*), and red when they are not at all achieved (*N*); which by transitivity allows to know the maturity level for each process.

5   Case Study and Future Works

5.1   Case Study Discussion

We applied it on a trivial industrial case study. The process can be indifferently started with the HIS requirements or the ISO 26262 requirements, as the work done on one affects the other. Nevertheless, as presented in section 2, it is better to start with the ISO 26262 requirements because it has a broader spectrum. Some studies have concluded that covering the ISO 26262 standard (regardless of *ASIL* level) corresponds to cover the capability level 2 of the HIS Automotive SPICE standard at least [18]. The opposite is not true.

We considered a subset of the ISO26262 (only activities associated with the specification of functional and technical requirements) and the results are more or less consistent with those expected. After performing the audit of all the requirements of a given standard, it is possible to verify, through a summary sheet, the maturity level for each process being evaluated, derived from rating of workproducts (Fig. 9).

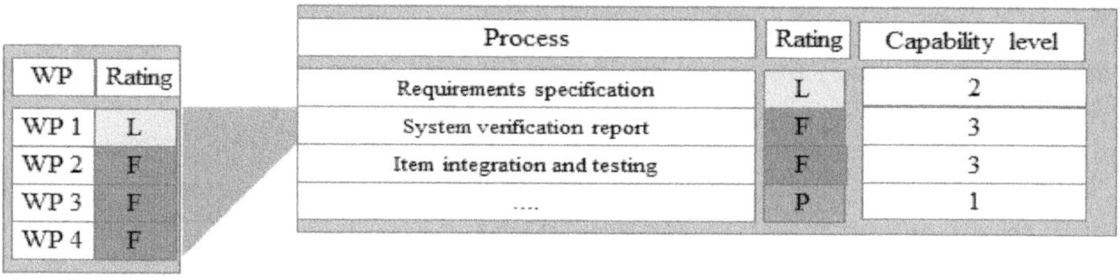

Fig. 9. Method for deriving maturity level of ISO 26262 processes

Furthermore, having a partial evaluation of the other standard greatly helps since to perform a complete assessment, it is only necessary to review, for each deliverable of this standard, the requirements that have not been automatically validated. This would be those whose the reference column contains the *NOK* on the staining tab in red. For SPICE audit, we obviously have to switch to the terminology given in the standard (that means *Base Practice, Process Attribute, Generic Practice*, etc.) (Fig. 10) that we can find again regarding the matching concepts (see Table 1).

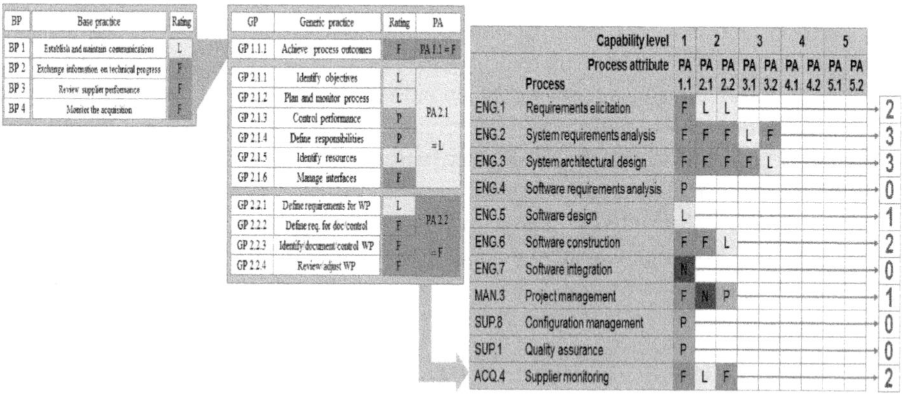

Fig. 10. Maturity level Calculus of SPICE processes. The number in blue (from *0* to *3*) represents the final maturity level achieved by the process derived from rating on their process attributes.

The saving of time and effort is undeniable as we avoid some redundancy in the requirements verification. Nevertheless, it would be used carefully in general, only in the scope of an audit-line evaluation to one project. Indeed, assessing processes in an organizational unit to a certain capability level means much more than requirements conformity: for instance, level 3 in SPICE means having the processes institutionalized in the organization and just a requirements' conformity is not enough sufficient for judging this fact.

It was also a first solution to evaluate the feasibility, costs and additional efforts that would require the full deployment of the ISO26262 standard on a large scale projects within the organization.

5.2   Future Works

The tool selected for the implementation of our framework is Excel. Nevertheless, given the amount of data and the numerous algorithms implemented, we meet difficulties to maintain or to add other features. It would be wise to find a more appropriated format to ensure an efficient and effective assessment like in [11]. A comparison of our common metamodel with SPEM metamodel [17] suggests us that it would be possible to translate it in this process language; even if some extensions will have to be developed to cover all our concepts.

We also remain that this work is based on a partial view of the HIS and therefore needs to be completed to allow a future application in an engineering organization. In addition, the matching between the ISO 26262 requirements and HIS which is the foundation of some features for the assessment requires a great review of certification experts, although this does not undermine the proposed methodology.

6   Conclusion

Certification is commonly a hard expectation in safety-critical industries like rail, aerospace, automotive, etc. The probably most well-known process certificate in automotive domain is the certification based on SPICE, which defines the necessary activities of a general quality management process. However, its application that warrants a better process is not an assurance of getting a higher product quality. At best, it offers an increased confidence of this quality. Hence, the recent definition of the ISO 26262 standard that focuses on the certification of a product and its (safety-) related artifacts which were created during its development. Although disjoined, all these types of certifications affect software quality.

This work was then conducted with the objective to propose a solution in an acceptable certification perspective that focuses both on end-product quality approach and process development approach in automotive domain, where a HIS assessment and a functional safety audit simultaneously performed is becoming a great need. In particular, we propose an extended metamodel that describe the two standards in a common way without altering their respective contents and it had implemented in an Excel framework for experimentation objectives. Considering the assessment purpose, we apply the SPICE assessment method [1] also to the ISO 26262 requirements as today no method has yet been formally established in this regard for the safety standard. Moreover, the framework avoids redundant work because it is used to validate all at once the requirements that an expert would have found similar in the two standards: thus, it greatly reduces the effort required to be compliant with the new standard.

The proposed solution can be seen as an initial response for the actual automotive needs and future works are still under development to integrate these results in a more generic process-based language (like SPEM) that will ensure a wide usage of our results.

References

1. Automotive SIG: Automotive SPICE, Process Assessment Model (PAM). Version 2.5 (2010), http://www.automotivespice.com (status: released May 10, 2010)
2. Automotive SIG: Automotive SPICE, Process Reference Model (PRM). Version 4.5 (2010), http://www.automotivespice.com (status: released May 10, 2010)
3. International Organization for Standardization: ISO International standard ISO 26262 (all parts) Road vehicles – Functional safety (2011) (Status: First Edition November 15, 2011)
4. Kolovos, D.S., Di Ruscio, D., Pierantonio, A., Paige, R.F.: Different models for model matching: An analysis of approaches to support model differencing. In: International 2009 ICSE Workshop on Comparison and Versioning of Software Models, pp. 1–6. IEEE Computer Society (2009)
5. HIS automotive SPICE, http://www.automotive-his.de/
6. France, R., Fleurey, F., Reddy, R., Baudry, B., Ghosh, S.: Providing Support for Model Composition in Metamodels. In: 11th IEEE International Enterprise Distributed Object Computing Conference, p. 253. IEEE Computer Society, Annapolis (2007)
7. Petry, E.: How to Upgrade SPICE-Compliant Processes for Functional Safety. Tutorial, SPICE Conference 2010, Pisa (2010)
8. Lami, G., Fabbrini, F., Fusani, M.: ISO/IEC 15504-10: Motivations for Another Safety Standard. In: Flammini, F., Bologna, S., Vittorini, V. (eds.) SAFECOMP 2011. LNCS, vol. 6894, pp. 284–295. Springer, Heidelberg (2011)
9. Lami, G.: ISO/IEC 15504-10 Safety Extension, Yet Another Safety Standard? Report, Eight Automotive SPIN Italia Workshop (2011)
10. Hoermann, K., Mueller, M., Dittmann, L., Zimmer, J.: Automotive SPICE in Practice: Surviving Interpretation and Assessment, Rocky Nook (2008)
11. Messnarz, R., Ross, H.-L., Habel, S., König, F., Koundoussi, A., Unterrreitmayer, J., Ekert, D.: Integrated Automotive SPICE and safety assessments. Software Process: Improvement and Practice 14(5), 279–288 (2009)
12. Chiprianov, V., Kermarrec, Y., Rouvrais, S.: Practical meta-model extension for modeling language profiles: an enterprise architecture modeling language extension for telecommunications service creation. In: 7th Days of Model Driven Engineering, Lille, pp. 85–91 (2011)
13. Barbero, M., Jouault, F., Gray, J., Bézivin, J.: A Practical Approach to Model Extension. In: Akehurst, D.H., Vogel, R., Paige, R.F. (eds.) ECMDA-FA 2007. LNCS, vol. 4530, pp. 32–42. Springer, Heidelberg (2007)
14. CMMI, http://www.sei.cmu.edu/cmmi

15. International Organization for Standardization: ISO/IEC International standard 15504 (all parts), Information technology – Process assessment (status: release 2004)
16. International Electrotechnical Commission: IEC 61508 (all parts), Functional safety of electrical/electronic/programmable electronic safety-related systems (status: release 2010)
17. Object Management Group: OMG Software & Systems Process Engineering MetaModel (SPEM). Version 2.0 (2008), OMG document number: formal/ 2008-04-01
18. Petry, E.: Automotive SPICE® & ISO/CD 26262, Their Mutual Relationship. Report, Fifth Automotive SPIN Italia Workshop (2009)
19. Machrouh, J., Blanquart, J. P., Baufreton, P., Boulanger, J. L., Delseny, H. Gassino, J., Ladier, G., Ledinot, E., Leeman, M., Astruc, J. M., Quéré, P., Ricque, B. : Cross domain comparison of System Assurance. In: ERTS^2 2012 Congress, Toulouse (2012)
20. Voas, J.: The Software Quality Certification Triangle. CrossTalk, The Journal of Defense Software Engineering (1998)
21. Humphrey, W.S.: The IBM Large-Systems Software Development Process: Objectives and Direction. IBM Systems Journal 24(2), 76–78 (1985)
22. Adedjouma, M., Dubois, H., Maaziz, K., Terrier, F.: A Model-Driven Requirement Engineering Process Compliant with Automotive Domain Standards. In: 3rd Workshop on Model-Driven Tool & Process Integration, Paris (2010)
23. Noyrit, F., Gérard, S., Terrier, F., Selic, B.: Consistent Modeling Using Multiple UML Profiles. In: Petriu, D.C., Rouquette, N., Haugen, Ø. (eds.) MODELS 2010. LNCS, vol. 6394, pp. 392–406. Springer, Heidelberg (2010)

Improving Unfamiliar Code with Unit Tests: An Empirical Investigation on Tool-Supported and Human-Based Testing

Dietmar Winkler[1], Martina Schmidt[1], Rudolf Ramler[2], and Stefan Biffl[1]

[1] Vienna University of Technology, Institute of Software Technology, Christian Doppler
Laboratory "Software Engineering Integration for Flexible Automation Systems" (CDL-Flex)
Favoritenstrasse 9-11/188, A-1040 Vienna, Austria
{Dietmar.Winkler,Martina.Schmidt,Stefan.Biffl}@qse.tuwien.ac.at
[2] Software Competence Center Hagenberg
Softwarepark 21, A-4232 Hagenberg, Austria
rudolf.ramler@scch.at

Abstract. Software testing is a well-established approach in modern software engineering practice to improve software products by systematically introducing unit tests on different levels during software development projects. Nevertheless existing software solutions often suffer from a lack of unit tests which have not been implemented during development because of time restrictions and/or resource limitations. A lack of unit tests can hinder effective and efficient maintenance processes. Introducing unit tests after deployment is a promising approach for (a) enabling systematic and automation-supported tests after deployment and (b) increasing product quality significantly. An important question is whether unit tests should be introduced manually by humans or automatically generated by tools. This paper focuses on an empirical investigation of tool-supported and human-based unit testing in a controlled experiment with focus on defect detection effectiveness, false positives, and test coverage of two different testing approaches applied to unfamiliar source code. Main results were that (a) individual testing approaches (human-based and tool-supported testing) showed advantages for different defect classes, (b) tools delivered a higher number of false positives, and (c) higher test coverage.

Keywords: Software Product Improvement, Software Testing, Random Test Case Generation, Manual and Tool-Supported Tests, Controlled Experiment.

1   Introduction

Software testing is a well-established quality assurance approach to identify defects in source code documents during software and systems development. Software processes, e.g., traditional and agile process models, aim at introducing (unit) tests as mandatory activities in software engineering projects. Traditional – rather sequential – development processes (e.g., Waterfall and V-Model process approaches) typically consider software testing with a focus on integration, system, and acceptance tests late

O. Dieste, A. Jedlitschka, and N. Juristo (Eds.): PROFES 2012, LNCS 7343, pp. 290–304, 2012.

in the project [15]. Nevertheless, V-Model process models can support the early definition of test cases in the analysis and design phases and the execution of test cases depending on the availability of the code. More recent approaches apply concepts from agile software development, e.g., Test-Driven Development (TDD) [13], where tests are designed, implemented, and executed prior (or at least in parallel) to the implementation of the source code on unit test level. Agile software development processes like eXtreme programming [4] and Scrum [21] apply unit tests as an integral part of the software construction phase.

Observations in industry projects show that not all projects achieve full code coverage [12][16] and, in some cases, investments in systematic testing have to be traded off against functionality and time to market [14]. Yet existing software solutions with a lack of software tests might hinder software maintenance, enhancements, and evolution. Similar arguments apply to legacy systems including a lack of documentation and unit tests [9]. In addition, sufficient unit tests on various levels and documentation support engineers in better understanding existing code. Thus, it might be reasonable to introduce unit tests after deployment to enable (a) better understanding of the software product and code, (b) increased product quality by executing unit tests more frequent, and (c) automated testing for continuous integration and test strategies [13]. An important question is whether unit tests should be introduced manually by experts (requiring additional effort) or whether these unit tests could be generated with tools, e.g., using Randoop[1] for JUnit[2] tests in Java.

In this paper we report on a controlled experiment investigating effects of different testing strategies, i.e., tool-supported and human-based testing, for introducing unit tests based on unfamiliar source code with respect to effectiveness (i.e., share of identified real defects), false positives (i.e., wrongly reported defects), and test coverage (i.e., method coverage). The remainder of this paper is structured as follows: Section 2 describes related work. Section 3 summarizes research issues and hypotheses. We present the study design and arrangements in Section 4, results in Section 5, and the discussion of the finding in Section 6. Finally, Section 7 concludes and identifies future work.

2   Related Work

This section summarizes related work on software testing in the software product life-cycle (2.1), software testing strategies (2.2), and test case generation (2.3).

2.1   Testing in the Software-Life-Cycle

Software Testing is an integral part of software development processes as a part of traditional engineering processes (e.g., Waterfall-Model, Spiral Model, and Rational Unified Process) and agile software development approaches, e.g., eXtreme Programming (XP) [4] and Scrum [21]. Traditional software processes (e.g., based on

---

[1] Randoop: http://code.google.com/p/randoop/
[2] JUnit: http://www.junit.org/

well-defined sequences of engineering steps) typically consider testing on various levels: (a) Unit tests on code implementation level; (b) Integration tests with emphasis on interfaces and the software architecture; and (c) System tests with focus on the overall system's behavior from user perspective. Agile software engineering processes apply testing techniques embedded within code construction activities, e.g., Test-Driven Development [11][13] on unit level and/or on higher levels. Independent of the applied software process, the scope of testing can focus on individual units (classes), subsystems (interfaces and components), or the entire system [13]:

- *Unit Testing* refers to the smallest executable part of a system, e.g., components, classes, or methods in Java. In agile software engineering practice, unit tests are typically embedded within a test-driven (test-first) development approach.
- *Integration Testing* focuses on the interaction between software components [10] to test communication and data exchange between individual software components on architecture level (e.g., focus on subsystems).
- *System Testing* focuses on testing the overall systems behavior from user perspective, including verification and validation of functional and non-functional requirements (e.g., performance) of the system [13]. In the software life-cycle system testing is applicable late in the development project where most of the subsystems and components are available.

During software maintenance, enhancement, and evolution, these tests can help engineers (a) in better understanding the software product and (b) testing new and/or modified software artifacts (i.e., units, components and subsystems, and systems) more efficient. Additional challenges arise if tests are missing, i.e., how can engineers introduce test for unfamiliar source code effectively and efficiently.

2.2   Software Testing Strategies

Following software engineering best-practices two basic testing strategies are applicable: (a) test-first development and (b) test-last development.

Test-First (Test-Driven) development (TDD) [11][13] refers to agile software development best practices, i.e., defining test cases prior (or in parallel) to software construction, following a set of defined steps: (a) selection of the most valuable requirement (prioritization of backlog items [21]) and definition of a set of test cases to test the selected requirement; (b) test case execution with failed test results because no implementation is available; (c) fast source code implementation to pass the test case successfully; (d) refactoring of the source code to meet source code requirements (e.g., coding guidelines and source code optimization) and test case execution; (e) after passing all defined tests, selection of the next pile of requirements (step a). Figure 1 (left hand-side) presents a basic workflow of the test-first approach. Frequent test runs can be executed within a continuous integration and test strategy (including regression tests after source code changes) [7] and will lead to observable software projects. In addition some studies [8][13] reported that TDD also promotes productivity of programmers. However, the application of TDD might also be limited to testing vulnerable source code if development time is scarce. Thus, there might be a lack of test cases even if TDD is applied.

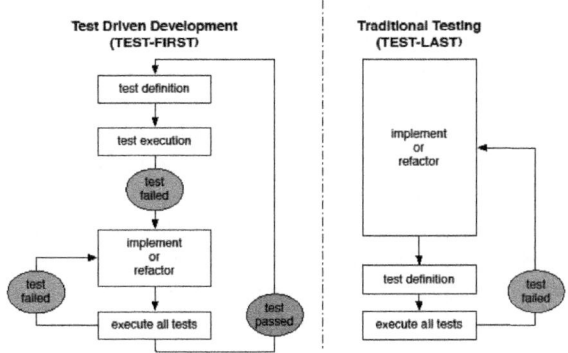

Fig. 1. Test-First and Test-Last Approach

Traditional software processes (e.g., the Waterfall Process Approach) typically follow the test-last approach, i.e., writing/executing test cases after the software construction phase has been completed. Figure 1 (right hand side) presents this traditional testing approach. Based on the specification and the source code test cases are constructed/generated and executed. Modifications and refactoring activities are necessary in case of defects and/or deviations. If development (and testing) time is scarce, the test activities are in danger to be skipped at the end of the projects.

A lack of tests might raise quality issues (e.g., undetected defects and deviations or limitations of test case coverage) and might lead to source code, which is hard to understand and to maintain by engineers during software maintenance, enhancement, and evolution. A key question is how test cases can be included after deployment to overcome these issues: (a) human-based test case definition or (b) tool-supported test case generation based on already delivered source code.

2.3   Human-Based and Tool-Supported Test Case Generation

Nowadays, changing product requirements, enhancements, and evolution of software products will require testing after deployment and during maintenance processes. New and missing test cases need to be written so that existing systems can be maintained properly. The question is how test cases should be introduced.

Human-Based Test Case Construction. Obviously, introducing test cases manually by experts and/or testers might be a promising but challenging option. Writing test cases manually will require (a) a deep understanding of the requirements and the source code and (b) additional effort. Typically test cases are based on the specification, pre-conditions, input parameters and expected output values [15]. Test execution, e.g., supported by a test framework, includes comparing the expected outcome with the current result and leads to decisions whether test cases have been passed successfully or fails.

Tool-Supported Random Test Case Generation. A second promising approach is the automated generation of test cases based on specifications, models or the source code [5]. Furthermore, random testing refers to choosing input values at random from the input domain, selecting test points independently, executing the system under test with these inputs and comparing the results to the program specification (test oracle) [1]. No test points are considered "similar" and input sampling is usually done over the entire input domain. The application of random testing depends only on knowledge of the input domain and the ability to map pseudorandom values into that domain [1]. Tools for generating unit tests for Java code include academic tools such as JCrasher [6], Eclat [20], Jartege [17], and Randoop [18], and commercial tools, for instance, JTest[3] and Agitator[4]. Instead of automatically inferring properties like its predecessor Eclat, Randoop [18] uses a set of universally applicable object contracts [18][19]. Automatic tools are really fast: they produce test cases for a big number of classes in a very short time and they scale much better than manual implementations [2]. Nevertheless, it remains open whether there are benefits of applying an automation-supported test case generation tool and a human-based testing approach in a test-last strategy with respect to test performance.

3   Research Questions and Hypotheses

The major goal is to investigate the effects of human-based testing and tool-supported test case generation in terms of effectiveness (share of defects found), false positives (share of wrongly reported defects), and method coverage. To investigate the effects of test case generation and the effects on product quality we conducted a controlled experiment including two groups: (a) tool-supported test case generation and (b) human-based test case construction, where participants were asked to write test cases in a short time interval of about 60 minutes. Section 4 and [24] present the study description and arrangements in more detail.

3.1   Variables

According to Wohlin *et al.* [23] we defined a set of variables: *Independent variables* include the testing strategy applied and number of seeded defects within a given experiment setup. Dependent variables are study duration, number of test cases, defect detection effectiveness (Eff), false positives (FP), and method coverage (MC).

3.2   Hypothesis

To investigate the effects of human-based test case definition and tool-supported test case generation we derived the following null hypotheses:

H0.1: Defect Detection Effectiveness. Human participants developed test cases and tool-generated test cases enable similar defect detection effectiveness (i.e., share of found seeded defects).

H0.2. False Positives. The share of false positives is similar for human-based test case development and tool-supported test case generation.

---

[3] JTest: http://www.parasoft.com
[4] Agitator: http://www.agitar.com

H0.3. Method Coverage. Human participants and Randoop covers a similar number of methods, i.e., achieve a similar method coverage level.

The alternative hypotheses for this research are:

H1.1. Defect Detection Effectiveness. We assume that Randoop will find more defects than the participants, since the tool generates tests for the entire software package while the participants are only able to test a portion of the package within the given time interval of about 60 minutes. The alternative hypothesis is that tool-supported testing with Randoop is more effective than human-based testing regarding defect detection. *Eff(Randoop) > Eff(Participants).*

H1.2. False Positives. We assume that tool-supported testing with Randoop will report more false positives than human-based testing, because the tool can only rely on its predefined contracts. Randoop is not able to comprehend and test against the contract described in the documentation for a particular class. Human developers are able to understand documentation of the requirements hence they are able to avoid false positives. *FP(Randoop) > FP(Participants).*

H1.3. Method Coverage. We assume that tool-supported testing will achieve higher overall method coverage, because more test cases can be generated in contrast to human-based test case construction. *MC(Randoop) > MC(Participants).*

4   Study Description

This section summarizes the study process (4.1), material (4.2), Randoop configuration (4.3), subjects (4.4), and identifies a set of threats to validity (4.5).

4.1   Study Process

The study includes three main phases in a sequential order, (a) study preparation, (b) study execution, and (c) analysis and evaluation: The *study preparation phase* includes the preparation of the study material, i.e., selecting the source code components, preparation of questionnaires, and the configuration of Randoop. Furthermore, the human participants received a short tutorial including a brief overview on the study setting and the study process. The *study execution phase* for human participants includes (a) individual test case construction activities and (b) completing an experience and feedback questionnaire at the end of the study. The challenge for the participants was to write as many JUnit test cases (based on the black-box approach [15]) as possible within the given time interval of about 60 minutes in order to identify defects in the software package. Source code, test cases, and questionnaires had to be delivered electronically via a course administration system. The *execution phase* of the tool-supported test case generation approach focuses on executing Randoop (based on the tool configuration) including capturing test cases and defects.

Figure 2 presents the study execution process for human-based test case construction (Session 1) and tool-supported test case generation (Session 2).

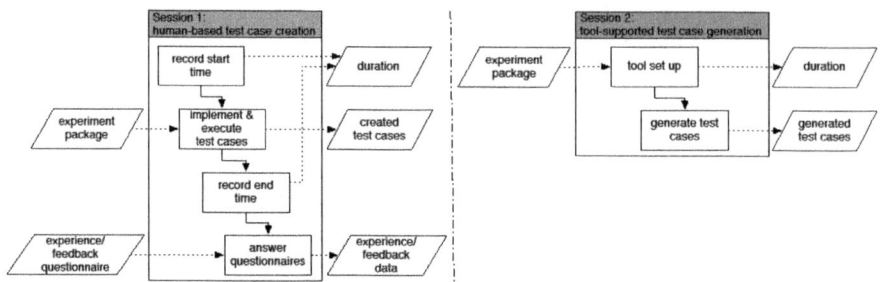

Fig. 2. Study Process for Human-Based (Session 1) and Tool-Supported Testing (Session 2)

During the *study analysis and evaluation phase* the experiment team (guided by the authors) scanned the reported/generated test cases, executed them and recorded the outcome of the test runs for every participant (results were lists of candidate defects and executable test cases). Reported defects were matched to the seeded defects (i.e., matched defects) by the experiment team. Note that identified matched defects were counted once, skipping multiple reported defects. Additionally wrong configured test cases (i.e., test cases which could not be executed) were excluded from the evaluation. We applied a set of tests regarding consistency and correctness of submitted data. After study completion the participants got a de-briefing session and a presentation on the results of the study. For statistical evaluation we used descriptive statistics and conducted the Mann-Whitney Test at a significance level of 95% (1-sided) for hypotheses testing.

4.2   Study Material

The material used during the study includes a software package (i.e., compiled class files) with their API documentation, as well as two questionnaires to be completed by the participants after submitting their tests and defect reports.

The software package is based on a previously published study [24] and includes Java Collection Classes provided for courses on algorithms and data structures in software engineering education [22]. The software package includes approximate 2800 lines of code in a total number of 34 interfaces and classes, and 164 methods.

Table 1. Allocation of Seeded Defects

	Defect Classes				
	Algorithm	Assignment	Checking	Data	Total
Number of defects	6	15	10	4	35
Share of defects [%]	17%	43%	29%	11%	100%

The experiment package was provided as an Eclipse project comprising the compiled collection classes with 35 seeded defects as jar archive and the corresponding Javadoc API documentation. Table 1 presents the share of seeded defects in the software package. See Wolfmaier *et al.* [24] for a more detailed description on the experimental material and the seeded defects. Expert seeded defects focus on:

- *Algorithm.* Problem in a method that describes a service offered by an object, e.g., a method is not implemented or memory is not allocated for a given task.
- *Assignment.* Values are assigned incorrectly or not assigned at all. Multiple assignment faults in a method may be of type *algorithm*, e.g., wrong arithmetic operator used.
- *Checking.* Failure to validate values before they are used, leading to the wrong control flow path in a program to be taken, e.g., missing or incorrect predicate(s) in conditional statements.
- *Data.* Incorrect use or implementation of a data structure, e.g., incorrectly determining the index for the last element in a data structure.

Note that we only provided class files and the Javadoc API documentation to force black-box testing and prevent participants from deducing the seeded defects by directly inspecting the source code. Additional material includes questionnaires to capture software engineering and testing background (experience questionnaire) and feedback on the study and the individual study results (feedback questionnaire).

4.3   Randoop Configuration

We used the Randoop Eclipse plugin to automatically generate tests for the compiled classes of the experiment package. Output was a test suite with 500 regression tests per JUnit test-fixture and defect revealing tests, each segregated into their own test fixture. We applied a default configuration with an upper execution time limit of 2 minutes (i.e., 120 seconds).

4.4   Study Subjects

Subjects were 48 master students at TU Vienna with software engineering and software testing background. To capture individual experience we applied an experience questions including six questions on a nominal scale from 1 (no experience) to 5 (professional experience). The mean experience levels of individual participants were calculated and assigned to three experience levels: (a) less experience (11 participants, 23%), medium experience (17 participants (35%) and high experience (20 participants, 42%). In addition, 35 (74%) participants out of 48 participants worked at least part-time in software engineering projects in industry context. The study was integrated as an optional exercise in the practical part of a software testing course on master level. Study participants got additional extra points for the course. In addition the study was executed as a competition, i.e., the participants with the highest number of identified defects received a small gift.

4.5   Threats to Validity

Every empirical study has to deal with several threats to validity. This subsection includes a set of major threats to this study and the countermeasures we applied:

Conclusion validity. The study included 48 participants and one tool with one test run. We applied the Mann-Whitney-Test at a significance level of 95% (1-sided) for hypothesis testing. To address *internal validity,* experts (i.e., the authors and externals) reviewed the material and the experiment package for correctness. Note that the source-code and class-files were already used in previous studies [24]. We avoided *communication* between the participants of the experiment. To capture the skills of the participants we applied an *experience questionnaire.* The *study duration* was limited to about 60 minutes for the participants and 2 minutes for the tool application. *Construct validity* focuses on the relation between theory and observations. The study is based on related work and previous experiments [24] and addresses effectiveness, false positives, and method coverage, common variables in empirical studies. *External threats to validity* focus on the participants, i.e., master students in software engineering. We used a classroom setting to monitor and control study variables. Although most of the participants (74%) work at least part-time in industrial environment, we see the participants as semi-professionals in the field of software testing. Finally, study objects have already been used as standard libraries in industry and are widely distributed and well known in practice.

5   Experiment Results

This section summarizes the results of the empirical study with respect to effort and performance measures, i.e., effectiveness, false positives, and method coverage.

5.1   Study Effort

The study effort summarizes the overall effort by participants and tool execution. Note that the effort of both testing strategies, presented in Table 2, does not include the individual preparation duration for participants training (i.e., approximately a 15 min briefing session) and the tool configuration effort (i.e., 2 hours effort). Randoop generates tests within a pre-defined time interval of 2min (defined during Randoop configuration). The upper test case construction time limit for participants was set to about 60min. The mean value of 48 participants was 59min (SD: 2min). Nevertheless, the maximum duration was 68min. A more detailed investigation showed that this maximum duration was caused by one participant who needed more time for completing and submitting the results and the questionnaire.

Table 2. Study Effort

Test Strategy	Study Effort [min]				
	No.	Min.	Max.	Mean	SD
Randoop	1	2 min	2 min	2 min	0 min
Participants	48	52 min	68 min	59 min	2 min

5.2   Reported/Generated Test Cases

The main tasks include test case generation (Randoop) and test case construction (participants) based on given artifacts in order to find defects. Table 3 presents the number of delivered test cases by Randoop and by the participants.

Table 3. Reported/Generated Test Cases

Test Strategy	Delivered Test Cases				
	No.	Min.	Max.	Mean	SD
Randoop	1	5 368	5 368	5 368	0
Participants	48	1	92	27.1	21.23

While the number of generated test cases for one test run carried out by Randoop (5 368 test cases) seems to be no surprise, the participants delivered 27.1 test cases on average (SD: 21.23) and up to 92 test cases in a 60 minutes working period.

5.3   Effectiveness

The quality of a software product is not limited to the number of test cases of a defect detection strategy but on the number of identified defects and the effectiveness of the strategy. Defect detection effectiveness is defined as the number of defects found in relation to the overall number of seeded defects (35 defects have been introduced by the experiment team). Randoop had the ability to test the entire experiment package automatically (2 minutes were defined for this test run). Because of the upper time limit of about 60 minutes for participants, testers had to prioritize components of the software under test to focus on the most important components of the package (from tester perspective). No guidelines were given for prioritization.

Table 4 shows the defect detection effectiveness of the testing strategies. Randoop reached a defect detection effectiveness of 25.7%, similar to the maximum effectiveness of most efficient testers. We observed an average effectiveness of 10.6% (SD: 10.66%) for participants and no significant differences ($p = 0.082(-)$).

Table 4. Reported Defects and Effectiveness

	Identified Defects (Matched Defects)		Effectiveness [%]	
	Randoop	Participants	Randoop	Participants
Minimum	9	0	25.7%	0%
Maximum	9	**9**	25.7%	**25.7%**
Mean	**9**	3.7	**25.7%**	10.6%
SD	0	2.68	0.0%	7.66

A more detailed investigation of the findings identified whether there are advantages of the tool/participants with respect to different defect classes (see Table 1 for details on the seeded defect classes). Figure 3 shows the box plots and Table 5 presents the descriptive statistics of this evaluation step. The results showed significant advantages of Randoop for algorithm (p = 0.041(s)) and checking defects (p=0.041(s)) and no significant advantages for assignment (p=0.735(-)) and data (p=0.898(-)) defects. We applied the Mann-Whitney test at a significance level of 95%, 1-sided, for hypothesis testing.

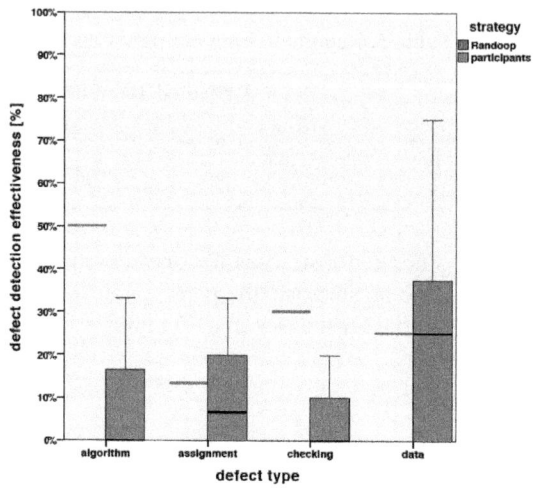

Fig. 3. Defect Detection Effectiveness per Defect Class

Table 5. Defect Detected per Defect Class

Defect Class	No of Defects					Effectiveness					P-Value
	Tool	Human Participants				Tool	Human Participants				
	No.	Min	Max	Mean	SD	Eff	Min	Max	Mean	SD	
Algorithm	3	0	2	0.7	0.78	50.0	0.0	33.3	11.1	13.02	0.041(s)
Assignment	2	0	5	1.6	1.63	13.3	0.0	33.3	11.0	10.87	0.735(-)
Checking	3	0	2	0.4	0.61	30.0	0.0	20.0	4.2	6.13	0.041(s)
Data	1	0	3	1.0	0.98	25.0	0.0	75.0	24.5	24.46	0.898(-)
Total	9	0	9	3.7	2.68	25.7	0.0	25.7	10.6	7.66	0.082(-)

A more detailed investigation of defects found by Randoop and by the participants showed advantages for the tool and the participants with focus on individual defects:

- *Advantages for Tool-Supported Test Case Generation with Randoop.* Four defects were detected by Randoop and not by any of the participants: 1 checking defect and 3 algorithm defects (cyclic data). Common to these defects is that a higher number of test cases or a sequence of cyclic operations is required to identify the defect correctly – a clear advantage of a tool-supported test.
- *Advantages for Human-Based Testing.* Even when the 2 minutes time limit for generating tests was extended to three hours, Randoop did not find any further defects. In total, 19 various defects were detected by the participants, which

Randoop was not able to find. For finding these defects, it was an advantage to understand the context of tests/requirements and to have the ability of abstraction and reflection of humans. For instance, the participants were able to identify documentation aspects associated with classes and to derive test cases appropriately.

5.4   False Positives

False positives (FP) refer to wrongly reported defects, i.e., candidate defect which does not match to seeded defects. Note that we checked all reported candidate defects for correctness and added newly found defects in the list of seeded defects. Nevertheless, no new defect was found. It is notable that false positives require similar effort as real defects to be found and even more effort to be identified as wrongly reported. Since this is extremely time consuming and wastes resources, the amount of false positives should be minimized.

Analyzing the test results provided by Randoop, we noticed 17 reported defects, including 9 real defects and 8 false positives. Thus, the share of FP was 47.1%. Table 6 presents the descriptive statistics of human participants.

Table 6. Reported Defects and False Positives for Human Participants

	No. Reported Defects	No. Matched Defects	No. False Positives	False Positives [%]
Minimum	0	0	0	0 %
Maximum	17	9	11	100 %
Mean	5.6	3.7	1.9	30.4 %
SD	4.11	2.68	2.50	31.36 %

In contrast to Randoop, human participants reported 30.4% (SD: 31.36%) false positives, a better rate than the tool-supported test case generation result. Nevertheless, by applying the Mann-Whitney Test at a significance level of 95%, we did not observe any significant differences between human-based and tool-supported testing (p-value: 0.653(-)). Participants who did not identify false positives (0%) either did not report many tests or they had enough experience to avoid false positives entirely. On the other hand side, participants who did not find real defects, i.e., FP rate of 100%, did not write many proper tests (2-18 tests). Additional investigations are required to identify the reasons for these findings; experience could be one reason.

Summarizing these results the human-based test generation approach delivers a fewer number of false positives on average; a main reason might be additional knowledge (i.e., context, requirements and design specification) which could be applied during test case generation and might reduce false positives.

5.5   Method Coverage

Identifying defects in source code artifacts and software products is the common goal of software testing. If some methods are not covered by tests, defects could not be found in the related methods. Thus, method coverage is a first measure to see whether all possible defective methods have been covered, either by the tool-supported approach or by human-based testing. Note that the overall study (software) package includes an overall number of 164 methods to be tested. Table 7 summarizes the results of the study with respect to method coverage for Randoop and the human participants.

Table 7. Method Coverage Overview

Test Strategy		Number of Covered Methods				Method Coverage [%]				P-Value
	No.	Min.	Max.	Mean	SD	Min	Max	Mean	SD	
Randoop	1	115	115	115	0.0	70	70	70	0.0	0.041(s)
Participants	48	8	101	48.1	22.89	5	62	29.3	13.96	

The human participants gained a method coverage value of 29.3% on average (SD: 13.96), while Randoop achieves quite higher method coverage, i.e., 70%. Applying the Mann-Whitney-Test we observed significant advantages for Randoop (p=0.041(s)). It is notable that the maximum method coverage achieved of the participants is 60% that is only 10% less than Randoop. We assumed that Randoop would achieve extremely high method coverage. Since only public methods of implementations could be tested, Randoop was not able to achieve method coverage higher than 70%. Thus, a mix of tool-supported and human-based testing approaches seems to be reasonable to merge benefits from both testing strategies.

6   Discussion

The main goal of this paper was to investigate the effects of human-based testing and tool-supported unit test case generation in a test-last testing strategy with respect to defect detection effectiveness, false positives, and method coverage. Based on the material and previously published studies [24], we compared Randoop, a tool for generating unit tests randomly, and human participants who have to write unit test in Java within a short time interval of about 60 minutes.

Defect Detection Effectiveness (Eff). Randoop gained a defect detection effectiveness of 25.7% while human participants achieved 10.6% (SD: 7.66%) on average. The results did not show significant differences, i.e., p=0.082(-). Thus, H0.1 that participant-developed test cases and tool-generated test cases enable similar defect detection effectiveness cannot be rejected. In addition H1.1, i.e., Eff(Randoop) > Eff(Participants), must be rejected.

An interesting finding was that most effective testers and the tool-supported test case generation approach achieved similar effectiveness. A more detailed view on defect classes highlighted significant benefits for Randoop for *algorithm* (p = 0.041(s)) and *checking defects* (p=0.041(s)) and no significant differences for *assignment* (p=0.735(-)) and *data* (p=0.898(-)) defects. In addition we noticed 4 defects that could only be found by Randoop and 19 other defects that could only be found by humans. The reasons are most likely that (a) Randoop enables defect detection for defects which require more iterations and a higher number of data and (b) human participants apply context, specification, and abstraction to derive more focused test cases. More detailed investigations are necessary to verify these results.

False Positives (FP). We assumed a higher share of false positives for generated test cases, i.e., Randoop, because human developers are able to understand documentation of the requirements hence they are able to avoid false positives. The results showed that human participants reported on average 30.4% false positives (SD: 31.36%) while Randoop reported 47.1% false positives. Applying the Mann-Whitney Test we did not identify any significant differences (p=0.653(-)). Thus H0.2 that the share of false positives is similar for human-based test case development and tool-supported test case generation cannot be rejected. In addition H1.2 must be rejected.

Method Coverage (MC) is a simple but common testing measure in software engineering practice. If methods are not covered by tests, defects could not be found. Thus, the third research question focused on investigating the method coverage of Randoop and human participants. Because of the automation supported approach, we could have expected higher method coverage of Randoop. The results showed that Randoop gained a MC of 70% while human participants achieved a MC of 29.3% on average (SD: 13.96). Applying the Mann-Whitney test, we observed significant advantages for Randoop, i.e., p=0.041(s). Thus we have to reject H0.3 that human participants cover a similar number of methods. In addition the results supported H1.3 that MC(Randoop) > MC (Participants).

7   Conclusion and Future Work

In many cases, software projects show a lack of documentation and unit tests, which hinders effective and efficient maintenance, enhancement, and evolution after deployment. Thus, it might be reasonable to implement test cases after deployment, i.e., in a test last strategy. The main question is whether these test cases should be implemented manually by human experts orsupported by tools for test case generation. This paper reported on an empirical study in the area of software testing to investigate the effects of human-based testing and tool-supported test case generation (i.e., Randoop) in a test last scenario. The findings of the study did not reveal one testing strategy (i.e., human-based and tool-supported) superior over the other. However, it showed that a mixture of the two testing strategies might be reasonable because both strategies focus on different defect classes, i.e., algorithm, checking, assignments, and data in this study.

Future work will include a more detailed investigation of the individual test cases with respect to test case quality and an initial investigation of the impact of tester qualification with respect to written test cases and defect detection capability. Additionally, alternative configurations of Randoop might be promising to strengthen the benefits of the tool-supported test case generation approach. Finally, a replication of the study (a) in a larger environment as well as (b) in an industry setting is required to verify the results and get a deeper understanding of the study objects with respect to testing strategies.

Acknowledgements. This work has been supported by the Christian Doppler Forschungsgesellschaft and the BMWFJ, Austria. We want to thank Erik Gostischa-Franta and the participants of the study in the course "Software Testing" at the TU Vienna.

References

1. Andrews, J.H., Haldar, S., Lei, Y., Hang Li, F.C.: Tool support for randomized unit testing. In: Proceedings of the 1st Int. Wsh on Random testing, RT 2006, pp. 36–45 (2006)
2. Bacchelli, A., Ciancarini, P., Rossi, D.: On the Effectiveness of Manual and Automatic Unit Test Generation. In: Proc. of the 3rd Int. Conf. on SE Advances, pp. 252–257 (2008)
3. Baker, P., Dai, Z.R., Grabowski, J., Haugen, Ø., Schieferdecker, I., Williams, C.: Model-Driven Testing: Using the UML Testing Profile. Springer (2007)
4. Beck, K., Andres, C.: Extreme Programming Explained: Embrace Change, 2nd edn. Addison-Wesley (2004)
5. Ciupa, I., Meyer, B., Oriol, M., Pretschner, A.: Finding Faults: Manual Testing vs. Random+ Testing vs. User Reports. In: Proc. of the 19th Int. Symposium on Software Reliability Engineering, pp. 157–166 (2008)
6. Csallner, D., Smaragdakis, Y.: JCrasher: An Automatic Robustness Tester for Java. Software Pract. Exper. 34, 1025–1050 (2004)
7. Duvall, M.P., Matyas, S., Glover, A.: Continuous Integration: Improving Software Quality and Reducing Risk. Addison-Wesley (2007)
8. Erdogmus, H., Morisio, M., Torchiano, M.: On the Effectiveness of the Test-First Approach to Programming. IEEE Trans. Softw. Eng. 31, 226–237 (2005)
9. Feathers, M.: Working Effectively with Legacy Code. Prentice-Hall, Upper Saddle River (2004)
10. IEEE Computer Society: Software Engineering Body of Knowledge (SWEBOK) (2004)
11. Koskela, L.: Test Driven: Practical TDD and Acceptance TDD for Java Developers. Manning Publications (2007)
12. Larndorfer, S., Ramler, R., Federspiel, C., Lehner, K.: Testing High-Reliability Software for Continuous Casting Steel Plants - Experiences and Lessons Learned from Siemens VAI. In: Proc. of the 33rd EUROMICRO SEAA Conference (2007)
13. Madeyski, L.: Test-Driven Development: An Empirical Evaluation of Agile Practices. Springer (2010)
14. Martin, D., Rooksby, J., Rouncefield, M., Sommerville, I.: 'Good' Organizational Reasons for 'Bad' Software Testing: An Ethnographic Study of Testing in a Small Software Company. In: Proc. of the 29th ICSE (2007)
15. Myers, G.J., Sandler, C., Badgett, T., Thomas, T.: The Art of Software Testing, 2nd edn. John Wiley & Sons (2004)
16. Nagappan, N., Maximilien, E.M., Bhat, T., Williams, L.: Realizing quality improvement through test driven development: results and experiences of four industrial teams. Empirical Software Engineering 13(3), 289–302 (2008)
17. Oriat, C.: Jartege: A Tool for Random Generation of Unit Tests for Java Classes. In: Reussner, R., Mayer, J., Stafford, J.A., Overhage, S., Becker, S., Schroeder, P.J. (eds.) QoSA-SOQUA 2005. LNCS, vol. 3712, pp. 242–256. Springer, Heidelberg (2005)
18. Pacheco, C., Ernst, M.D.: Randoop: Feedback-Directed Random Testing for Java. In: Proc. of the 22nd ACM SIGPLAN Conf. on OOPSLA, pp. 815–816 (2007)
19. Pacheco, C., Lahiri, S.K., Ernst, M.D., Ball, T.: Feedback-Directed Random Test Generation. In: Proc. of the 29th Int. Conf. on Software Engineering, ICSE, pp. 75–84 (2007)
20. Pacheco, C., Awasthi, P.: Eclat: Automatic Generation and Classification of Test Inputs. In: Gao, X.-X. (ed.) ECOOP 2005. LNCS, vol. 3586, pp. 504–527. Springer, Heidelberg (2005)
21. Schwaber, K.: Agile Project Management with Scrum. Prentice Hall (2004)
22. Weiss M.A.: Data Structures and Problem Solving Using Java. Addison-Wesley (1997)
23. Wohlin, C., Runeson, P., Höst, M., Ohlsson, M.C., Regnell, B., Wesslén, A.: Experimentation in software engineering: an introduction. Kluwer Academic Publishers (2000)
24. Wolfmaier, K., Ramler, R., Dobler, H.: Issues in Testing Collection Class Libraries. In: Proc. of the 1st Workshop on Testing Object-Oriented Systems, ETOOS, pp. 4:1–4:8 (2010)

Self-Organizing Systems and the Like

An Innovative Vital Perspective in Mutual Inspiration with Application Areas

Horst F. Wedde

School of Computer Science, TU Dortmund, Germany

Problem Statement

This contribution is a short introduction into the Special Session "Software Engineering Problems and Solutions in Self-Organizing Systems".

Computer Technology, as it has developed over the past 60 years, has undergone a tremendous development ending up in invading, or being indispensable for, most areas of scientific, technical, social, economic, political, and even cultural life. There is no other example in History comparable to the speed and the paradigmatic change that have come about under the influence of this technological novelty which is *both a scientific and engineering effort*. (No divergence like between Physics and Mechanical or Electrical Engineering has yet occurred.)

As part of its consolidation process within the new scientific/ engineering discipline, the efforts have led into different methodological directions creating areas like

- Theoretical Computer Science (including like Complexity and Automata Theory)
- Software Engineering (comprising such classical sub-areas as Operating systems, Data Bases etc.)
- Computer Architecture and other hardware-related themes.

Researchers and developers in each of these fields were, over a long of time, seriously involved in creating and studying their specific problem approaches. While it was necessary for an appropriate understanding of the problems to reach a high technical clarity and depth their efforts resulted at the same time in a separation between theoretical and practical areas, between software and hardware research, as easy examples. Gradually the major amount of scientific and engineering discussion took mostly place between the specialists in each sub-area. Not only were there strong tendencies towards pure insider discussions or *l'art-pour-l'art* work on the conceptual level: The solutions presented turned out to be of ever less practical value.

As an example, let us consider the extensive research and development efforts which, for more than 25 years, had been devoted to problems in real-time, safety-critical, and embedded systems. Security issues were considered crucial in mission-critical systems. While all such constraints had been derived as design problems for software control systems in real-world applications *they had been treated as separate*

O. Dieste, A. Jedlitschka, and N. Juristo (Eds.): PROFES 2012, LNCS 7343, pp. 305–308, 2012.

aspects since these partial problems proved difficult enough in themselves. This resulted gradually in nearly different scientific disciplines in their own right (with the *real-time community, the safety community ...* behind), yet turned out to be increasingly inadequate for the design of large control systems, in particular for applications with (partially) autonomous entities and decision-making: As a well-known example, optimal real-time performance in such applications may then be adverse to optimal overall throughput, and vice versa, while both requirements may well be equally important.

Novel R&D Perspectives in Software

This eventually came to the awareness of commercial sponsors and public funding agencies (at first in the US, subsequently in Europe, in particular through EU-programs), creating new R&D initiatives and programs over the years. So, in 2008 a special initiative of the US NSF agency succeeded in collecting the relevant experts from academia and industry for a 2-day workshop in Troy, Michigan, with the task to overcome the crisis. The concept of *Cyber-Physical Systems* was put forward for general discussion, and we coined a definition which gradually became generally agreed upon: For the design and analysis of such systems, it is *requested that the structures and relationships of the software and physical/real-world layers be as similar as possible, ideally even isomorphic or congruent.* (In an easy example, if the physical system exhibits a certain amount of autonomy for the actors, say in a large traffic system, then the control system should exhibit an explicit concept of distributed control.) In the meantime this concept has provided a steadily growing momentum for quite a number of successful key research projects.

Particular attention in our special session is given to a quickly emerging new class of cyber-physical systems, so-called *Self-Organizing Systems*, coming from a joint initiative of researchers from the Artificial Intelligence and Distributed System communities. In self-organizing systems, *highly autonomous* software processes or *agents* adapt through their own decisions to changing environmental conditions and/ or to modifications from other software processes, and in coordination with such processes. (In the singular case of a central control scheme supervising the agents, such systems are termed *self-adaptive. Self-organizing Maps (SOM)* are a particular example.)

Traditional approaches for modeling and analyzing systems (e.g. optimization or other classical theoretical methods) normally fall short concerning efficient solutions in practice. They often do not really scale: With the system size growing the computation time may well explode (e.g. for problems that can be reduced to TSM), and once requirements such as real-time conditions are concerned the solutions exhibit a practically very cumbersome, if not inadequate, timing behavior.

In several novel application areas like Smart Power Grids, Renewable Energy and power management, routing in today's and future Internet applications, Transportation Planning or Traffic Control systems in Logistics, novel technological developments have posed a class of novel challenges that have been interpreted, with growing success, as self-organizing phenomena. As a characteristic novelty for their modeling, implementation, and analysis the R&D tasks have to be treated as *transdisciplinary* problems which require a (so far unusually) close collaboration between researchers and developers in the different disciplines involved. In this way self-organizing systems have become a leading edge of current research and development in modern Technology.

Solutions have been pursued, and even implemented, which borrow principles from Natural Computing or from Swarm Intelligence. Also, they replace conventional approaches issuing exact solutions which are practically irrelevant, through iterative methods which are faster to obtain and at he same time of top quality (like Self-Organizing Maps (SOM)). Open problems such as on-line organization, consistency, and availability of mobile and dynamic geographic data (in Outer Space, in widespread maritime operations etc.) have been identified as particular candidates for self-organizing research.

For me, the most exciting experience in Cyber-Physical and Self-Organizing Systems research has been the mutual inspiration coming from getting involved in the challenges in the different application areas while a the same time experiencing, through the necessary cooperation with researchers and developers in the different application areas, how the discussions across the borders lead to substantial and novel ideas in one's own area of expertise: Reality and its R&D treatment get visibly closer!

The Papers Comprising the Special Section

The special session on Self-Organizing Systems consists of 3 papers. Each of them gives an example of ongoing and promising work in a specific field of interest.

The first paper (authored by S. Senge and H.F. Wedde) deals with a novel Swarm Intelligence concept as it applies the principles of honey bee behavior to handling road traffic in metropolitan areas, with the twofold objective of minimizing both the average driving times and traffic congestions (BeeJamA project). The convincing results are demonstrated through extensive simulation experiments in a realistic large environment where the best existing routing algorithms that are commercially available are compared to the new algorithm. For the latter one no global information would be collected however, similar to path finding of forager bees, the available information, although *nearly* accurate only, is made available on a very short notice. As in this way corrections come in extremely timely the effect is better than with global information that may well be late.

In the second paper the authors (K.-E. Großpietsch and T. Silayeva) lay the ground for an innovative approach for allowing robots in dangerous environments to perform coordinated operations based on autonomous decisions in situations where unpredictable events (e.g. the unexpected phasing out of a robot) and incomplete information still require timely and appropriate reactions. An example might be the potential disaster handling in a nuclear reactor (Fukushima). Robots could even exploit short-term learning about the next (suboptimal) actions following rules in an appropriately adapted Adaptive Resonance Theory (ART) model (from the area of Neural Networks). The model, while not yet experimentally evaluated, is quite ingenious and elegant, and certainly opens new avenues in Artificial Intelligence.

The third paper (by Sv.-Ch. Müller, U. Häger et al.) presents a thorough discussion of the potential which self-organizing systems have for the treatment of stability problems in large electric power grids. Due to the liberalization of the European power market on the one hand, also as a result of the quickly growing amount of power from renewable sources (wind, solar,...) with its high production fluctuation, unpredictable grid instability may have a disastrous effect (black-outs) for a power grid state. The authors make a well-supported strong plea for a distributed self-organized approach (based on autonomous agents) which they term *functional*, pointing to huge advantages in reactive flexibility as well as in timing accuracy, over a control concept based on global or centralized information which is called *comprehensive*. They make their point very clear by addressing and discussing it in the context of an ongoing large power grid project.

The papers have been solicited through a separate Call for Papers, and they have undergone a rigid peer-to-peer evaluation. As a result it is hoped that this selection may provide stimulating insight into novel research which has been triggered by, and borrowed from, challenging problems in various application areas. I would like to give the reviewers my sincere thanks for their very professional job which has led to substantial improvements of the originally submitted versions of the contributions.

Special Section Reviewers

Karl-Erwin Großpietsch, St. Augustin
Ulf Häger, TU Dortmund
Robert Keller, TU Dortmund
Oliver Kramer, U of Oldenburg
Sven-Christian Müller, TU Dortmund
Sebstian Senge, TU Dortmund
Tanya Silayeva, Moscow

Modified ART Network Architectures
for the Control of Autonomous Systems

Karl-Erwin Grosspietsch[1] and Tanya A. Silayeva[2]

[1] EUROMICRO, P.O. Box 2043, Sankt Augustin, Germany
karl-erwin.grosspietsch@online.de
[2] Moscow Aviation Institute, Volokolamsk Highway 4, Moscow, Russia
ta.silaeva@mail.ru

Abstract. In this paper, the potential of adaptive resonance theory (ART) networks for the dependable control of autonomous systems is considered. First a short survey about existing ART network approaches is given. A combination of such networks with counterpropagation networks is described which provides fast access to control procedures corresponding to the different classes of situations to be treated. Moreover, it is discussed how the observed success or failing of such a procedure can be utilized to influence the learning of the ART network.

Keywords: autonomous systems, neural networks, self-organizing maps, adaptive resonance theory (ART) networks, combination of long term memory and short term memory, combined dependability / performance issues, health functions.

1   Introduction

Autonomous systems as e.g. robots are starting to have a growing impact within the spectrum of technical systems. The control of their operation is non-trivial because usually a complex interaction is necessary to produce their coordinated actions; moreover, threre might be unknown situations (e.g. unknown territory, unknown combinations of sensor unput signals etc) where the autonomous systems on their own have to find a solution what to do. Usually the design and implementation of control software for such systems is complex as it has to face numerous possible problem constellations so that it is practically impossible to consider all of them in a comprehensive a priori model. Instead, solutions are needed which enable some kind of learning from examples, i.e. to derive some generalizable behaviour pattern from them. Here, as well-known means neural networks have gained growing importance.

Additionally, as it is holding for most IT systems, such a derivation of the control software is realized under observing constraints as costs and resulting perfomance. Dependability issues usually have to be brought into compliance with these two major requirements. In real-time computing, this need is explicitly shining up in the requirement that the system is not only correctly working, but guarantees to fulfil tasks within given upper time bounds: I.e. functioning alone is not enough, sufficiently quick functioning is necessary.

O. Dieste, A. Jedlitschka, and N. Juristo (Eds.): PROFES 2012, LNCS 7343, pp. 309–319, 2012.

In many applications the relation between performance orientation and dependability orientation should not be fixed, as dependability-critical and -uncritical situations may quickly follow each other. Consider e.g. a robot moving in unknown territory. The cautious control approach always to move very slowly, always to perfectly check for all possible dangers might imply too much loss of velocity to reach the goal location in the required time. So, what we would need is a flexible strategy which also considers performance issues while not neglecting some background cautiousness.

Here, a special class of neural networks, the adaptive resonance theory (ART) networks [1] could be an intesting choice as they are intrinsically based on the idea of the cooperation of some short term memory catching sight of actual, local input patterns, with a long term memory storing some larger history of background experience. We also propose a modification of the architecture with regard to its application for the control of autonomous systems. Here the main idea is to additionally influence the updating of the network´s experience during system operation according to the observed success or failing of activated control procedures. To measure such success we consider the health functions of autonomous systems, monitored concurrently to system operation [2].

The paper is organized as follows: Section 2 introduces the basic properties of ART networks, and in section 3 some variants of this architecture are described. Then section 4 shows how by a combination of the ART network approach with the so-called counterpropagation networks [3], the step from classifying a problem situation to accessing control patterns for the management of this situation can easily be implemented within the neural network frame. Section 5 finally describes a heuristic approach for updating the long term memory, controlled by the changes of the health function of autonomous systems.

2   Basic Structure of ART Networks

With regard to learning, neural networks can be divided into two main classes:

- supervised learning where the neural network in a training phase gets input patterns together with the desired output patterns, and is to learn from these associations how to sufficiently exactly produce from similar, but not identical inputs adequate output patterns;
- unsupervised learning where the neural network without help from outside tries to cluster similar patterns to certain classes ("self-organizing maps" [4]).

Standard neural networks for supervised learning as e.g. backpropagation networks try to systematically minimize the error in the output by changes of the weight factors of the neurons until the error reaches 0 or a sufficiently small value. After the end of the training period these values are frozen so that no change of the learned experience is possible any more. Then, in the recognition phase the network is to classify unknown input patterns as similar to certain learned inputs and, thus, to sufficiently exactly derive from them the required output patterns.

A classical example of self-organizing maps is the Kohonen Network, where each implemented pattern class is represented by just one neuron. Here again learning is confined to an initial phase during which the pattern classes are formed; at the end of this phase the number of pattern classes is fixed.

In many applications, however, as e.g. for the movement of autonomous robots in unknown territory, it would be desirable to adapt again the experience of the network to the changing environment. But simply extending the training to the operational phase of the system causes the tradeoff that this treatment would destroy part of the experience learned during the initial learning phase.

Here, ART networks have been proposed as a remedy [1]. In the basic ART architecture, the entire recognition process mainly proceeds as follows (see also Fig. 1): The input pattern inp is implemented as a vector of Boolean numbers. It activates the neurons i (i=1,...,m) of the so-called comparison layer F1. The output of the layer neuron i is a function $s_i= f(inp_i)$; often simply the identical reproduction of the input vector inp is assumed: $s_i=inp_i$ (i=1,...m).

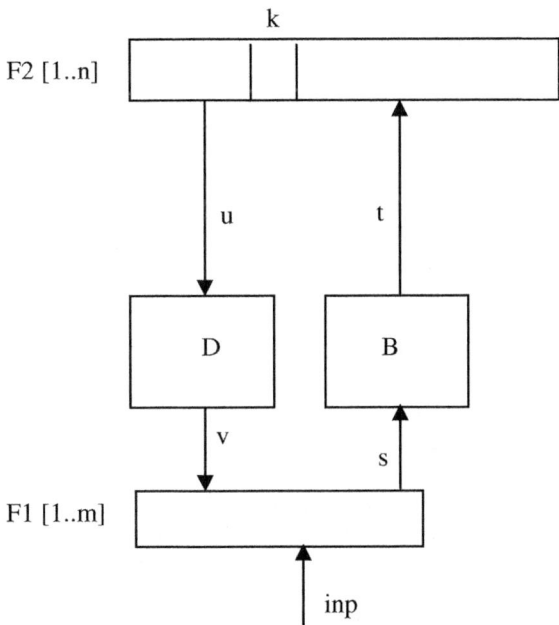

Fig. 1. Basic architecture of ART networks (according to [1], [4])
F1 comparison layer, F2 recognition layer, k winning neuron of layer F2
B bottom-up matrix, D top-down matrix
inp input vector; s, t, u,v generated vectors (see text)

The vector s is multiplied by the so-called bottom-up matrix B the elements of which are real numbers. This produces a real number vector t comprising as components the weighted sums

$$t_j = \sum_{i=1}^{m} B_{ij} * s_i = B_j * s \quad (j=1,..,n; \; B_j \text{ being the row vector } j \text{ of matrix } B)$$

The maximum of these sums is determined:

$$t_k = \max(\{t_1,..,t_n\})$$

Neuron k of the recognition layer F2 is then set to 1; all other neurons of this layer are set to 0 (neuron k is the „winner neuron"). I.e. the neuron k of F2 represents the class of patterns to which the input pattern inp is, in this first selection, estimated to belong.

Subsequently, this decision is checked by a control computation. To do so, the vector u of the Boolean values of the recognition layer neurons is multiplied by a second matrix, the so-called top-down matrix D, producing a Boolean vector v:

$$v_i = \sum_{j=1}^{n} D_{ij} * u_j = D_{ik} * u_k = D_{ik} \text{ for } i=1,..,m$$

By AND ing the components of vector v and of the input vector inp of layer F1, a check vector c is formed:

$$c = AND(v_{i1}, inp_{i1}),.., AND(v_m, inp_m)$$

Finally, the similarity of c and input vector inp is compared. This similarity is measured by counting the numbers n_c and n_{inp}, respectively, of 1s in both vectors, and forming their quotient $q = n_c/n_{inp}$. If q is larger than a previously selected value of a so-called tolerance parameter p, the input inp is assumed to be sufficiently close, „in resonance", to the column vector D_k of matrix D corresponding to the winner class k. If this is not the case, the classification is decided to be not fitting. Then the entire recognition process is repeated, with the previous winner neuron k being excluded from the selection process. This causes a new maximum $t_l = \max(\{t_1,..,t_{k-1}, t_{k+1},..,t_n\})$ so that now another neuron l is the winner neuron and is then checked for its resonance with the input vector inp.

The search loop is repeated until a resonant solution is found. If all the actual n class representations of the neural network do not fit to the input vector, an additional neuron n+1 is created in layer F2, and is set to 1. Correspondingly, the number of pattern classes distinguishable by the ART network increases by one. So, the network is able to respond to the appearance of unidentified patterns by the creation of new classes.

After the search process has been completed, the elements of the matrices B and D are updated. Updating of bottom-up matrix B is done by changing the row vector B_k which had produced the maximum sum; this row vector is torn towards the input vector inp. All other rows of matrix elements remain unchanged. Updating of the top-down matrix D is done by tearing the column vector D_k towards vector s. For the mathematics of the update formulas, and also the influence of some additional so-called gain factors see [1], [5] which provide a comprehensive discussion of these details.

As the main advantage of ART networks their „plasticity" is claimed, i.e. the ability to integrate new knowledge into the network without destroying old one. Moreover, this is done in a balanced way where still the attempted changes are checked aginst the memorized knowledge stored in the top-down matrix. So, the network to a certain degree emulates the cooperation between short term storage and long term storage known from biological systems: Actual on-the-fly experience or situation estimation might flow into the current system input, and then can be integrated into memory under the surveillance of the long-term knowledge stored in the top-down matrix D.

3   Modifications of the Basic ART Architecture

In the years 1988-93 the group of Grossberg and Carpenter developed a number of extensions of the basic architecture ART-1 described in the previous section. A second class of ART networks, ART-2 [6], enables the use of real number input patterns. In addition to the layers F1 and F2, ART-2 networks additionally contain a preprocessing layer F0. This layer first carries out a Euclidean normalization, representing the influence of shunting effects. The output of F1 is non-linear by means of using a threshold function :

$$\text{if (inp>Th) THEN s=inp ELSE s=0 ,}$$

Th is the value of the threshold. The change of weights on the long term memory here also depends on feedback control signals and is described by differential equations; this makes the convergenceof the network quite complex.

A further extension was reached by the ART-3 class [7] which enables to model in more detail also biological mechanisms. Especially details of the transmitter dynamics at chemical synapses are described: Consider two biological neurons i and j, connected by a chemical synapse. Bridging the synaptic gap for an electric signal is realized by a chemical process. An activation potential in neuron i at its side of the gap, at the so-called presynaptic membrane, generates presynaptic neurotransmitters the concentration of which shall be denoted by u_{ij}, and the maximum concentration by z_{ij}. These presynaptic neurontransmitters cause the release of movable neurotransmitters having a concentration v_{ij} (part of which, however, is lost again on the way through the gap, by means of recombination processes). This process system can be described by two differential equations for the time derivatives $u_{ij}{}'(t)$ and $v_{ij}{}'(t)$:

$$u_{ij}{}'(t) = (z_{ij} - u_{ij}(t))-u_{ij}(t)*[\text{release rate}]$$

and

$$v_{ij}{}'(t) = v_{ij}(t)+ u_{ij}(t)*[\text{release rate}]-v_{ij}(t)*[\text{recombination rate}]$$

Neglecting the influence of inhibiting and amplifying feedback loops, the resulting electric signal strength x_j arriving at cell j can be approximated by $x_{ij}=v_{ij}$.

However, Zell states [5] that outside the group of Grossberg and Carpenter not many applications of this extended model were realized, as the model from the viewpoint of neurobiology was still too simplified, but with regard to technical realization too complex.

In a later development, the ART-1 approach has also been combined with fuzzy logic. In [8] it is shown that mainly by replacing the AND operator by the fuzzy AND operator FAND(x,y)=min(x,y), ART-1 can be transformed so that it is able to process real number inputs. It has been proven that the learning algorithm is stable, as during learning the adjustable weights can only shrink. It is stated that in comparison to back propagation algorithms, the Fuzzy ART algorithm yields an improvement of the learning speed by a factor of more than 1000.

As one example of the algorithmic changes let us consider the preparation of ART-1´s check operation c= AND(v,inp) which in Fuzzy ART is replaced by

$$c^*=FAND(v,inp)=min(v_1,inp_1),..,min(v_m,inp_m)$$

The column vector D_k of matrix D is updated according to

$$D_k(t+1)=a^*FAND(inp,D_k(t))+(1-a)^*D_k(t)$$

where a is the so-called learn parameter. Fast learning is represented by a=1; in this case the second term vanishes.

Some additional variants of the described basic theory were created at the begin of the nineties [8]. But larger ART applications were rare, probably due to the complex mathematic details, and the potentially resulting computing time problems on sequential computers.

In connection with the flourishing of research in the nineties for hardware architectures to support neural networks, Serrano-Gotarredona, Linares-Barranco and Andreou 1998 published a book on the design of microcircuits for the emulation of ART networks [9]. But it seems that this effort, as it happened also to nearly all the other hardware designs for the support of neural networks, did not find resonance in industry.

In the recent decade, apparently only very few publications on ART networks appeared. In 2007, Teles Vieira and Lee described an approach to combine ART networks with recurrent neural networks. Outside the neural network research community, so far the impact of ART networks seems to be quite low. E.g. in the field of computing for safe and dependable systems, to our knowledge so far no attempt to apply adaptive resonance theory has been made.

But nowadays, more than twenty years after the introduction of adaptive resonance theory, the implementation conditions have considerably changed: Today´s standard technology offers the use of multicore/manycore architectures. So, e.g. the computations of matrix vector multiplications can be parallelized. Additionally it even would be possible to utilize parallel „lookahead" techniques so that the search loop to find the adequate winner neuron can at least partially be parallelized, either in a pipeling or a fully parallel computation aproach.

Thus, we think the time is ripe to re-consider ART networks and their principle of balanced learning based on a cooperation between short term and long term memory. In the following sections, we shall sketch an approach to utilize this framework to organize the control of autonomous systems. This will be discussed in two steps. First, in the subsequent section we shall describe how within the framework of neural networks the access to more detailed control procedures can be incorporated. Then in section 5 a heuristic approach   for controlling balanced learning in autonomous systems is sketched.

4   Access to Control Pattterns for Classes of Situations

In the literature presented in section 2 and 3, applications are confined to pure pattern recognition. This restriction does not seem really necessary: In many applications inputs (e.g. from certain sensors) encode an actual external situation which has to be classified, and then also to be managed. Here, the tradeoff of pure ART networks is that it is left open how as response to a input also a certain output is generated, for controlling the system or its environment in that specific situation. This output might either be a complex pattern of control bits, or, in most cases more practical, the address of a control procedure. In the following we shall address the second approach.

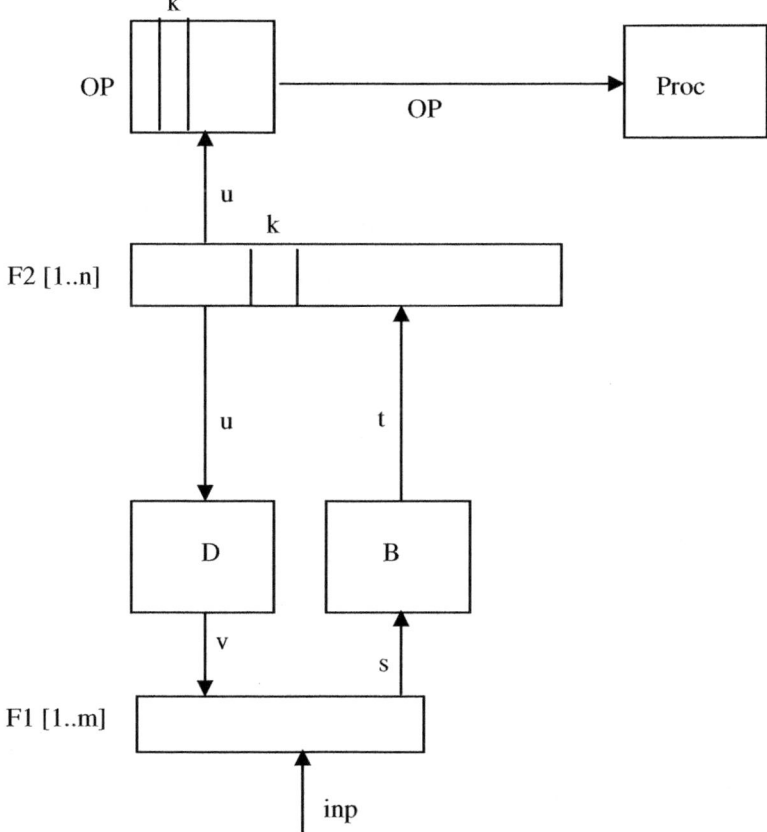

Fig. 2. Extension of the ART network by an associative memory
F1 comparison layer, F2 recognition layer, k winning neuron of layer F2
B bottom-up matrix, D top-down matrix
inp input vector; s, t, u,v generated vectors (see text)
Prock procedure triggered by column vector OPk to manage situations of class k

For the case that this mechanism is to be provided within the frame of neural networks, we propose to adopt a solution used e.g. in counter-propagation networks [3]. In that approach, after having completed the search for the winner neuron, the vector u is additionally fed into a matrix vector multiplication with an additional matrix, called here the output pattern matrix OP (see Fig. 2):

$$o_i = \sum_{j=1}^{n} OP_{ij} * u_j = Op_{ik} (i=1, ..., n^*) ,$$

here k is the index of the winning neuron in F2, and n^* the number of rows in matrix OP. That means the result vector o is just the column vector OP_k of matrix OP. So, depending on the contents of the input vector inp (not via a memory address !) the output pattern is accessed from the „memory" OP,   i.e. OP functions like an associative memory.

Computionally this can be achieved even simpler: if we want to access the control pattern for a problem class j, we have just to read out the column vector OP_j of matrix OP. So, the organization of this control scheme is easily scalable: For a larger size of the stored control patterns, we have just to add additional rows to the matrix OP.

5   Updating the Experience of the ART Network

When applying advanced resonance theory for the selection of control procedures, the update of the long term memory should not only be influenced by the choice of of a situation class, but also by the success of the corresponding control procedure. So, in contrast to the ART-1 description of section 2, the updating of the matrices B and D is carried out only after finishing of the triggered the control procedure. Here we propose a pragmatic modification of ART network architecture, according to the principles of Organic Computing   [9], [10] to achieve self-organization, self-optimization, and self-healing in ways similar to those of biological entities. Let us depict that again by the example of an autonomous robot.

To do so, as base we have to utilize a metric measuring the aspect of success or failing of the robot when solving required movement tasks. We build up this metric from a small   number of essential, critical parameters of the autonomous robot, as e.g.

- the inclination angle of the main robot body,
- battery power consumption,
- temperature of servo motors,
- number (or weighted sum) of components diagnosed to be partially or completely faulty.

It should be noted that these entities not only describe cases or parts of the system which are already defective, but mainly critical issues which relatively easily might turn into component or system failure. The parameter values are mapped into a scalar function, the so-called general health function GHF.

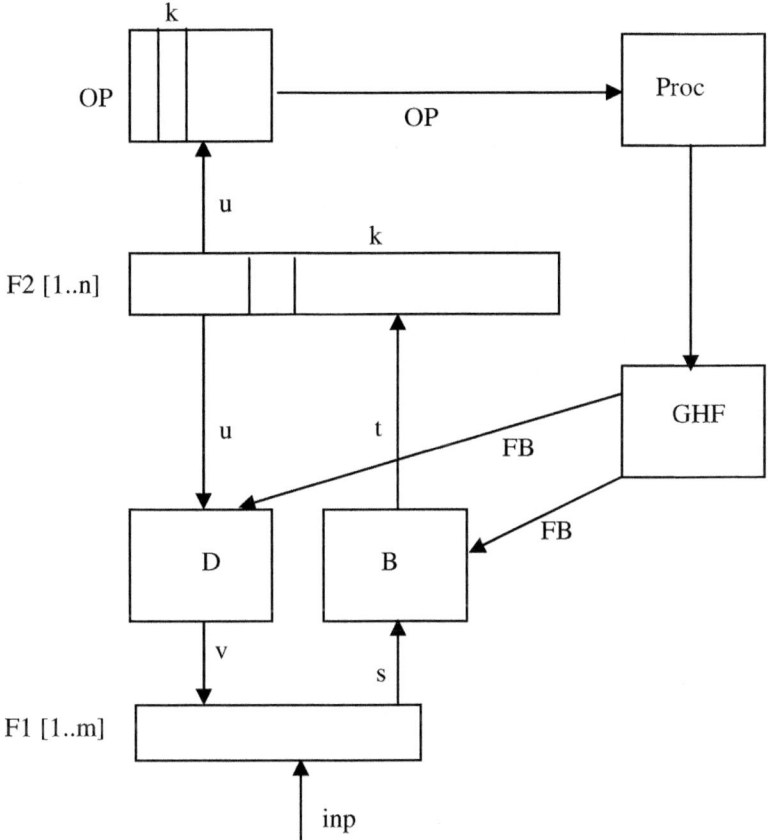

Fig. 3. Additional feedback of the general health function
F1 comparison layer, F2 recognition layer, k winning neuron of layer F2
B bottom-up matrix,D top-down matrix
inp input vector; s, t, u,v generated vectors (see text)
Prock procedure triggered by column vector OPk to manage situations of class k
GHF general health function
FB additional feedback control of GHF on the update of the matrices B and D

   For each execution of a control procedure, the effect of the resulting movement is checked whether it has increased or decreased the GHF, or has left it unchanged.
   The use of the actual GHF value measured after the completion of a control procedure is as follows: Here, the similarity measure for the check of the input inp against column vector D_k of matrix D introduced in section 2 appears to be too simple: When comparing e.g. two pixel patterns for similarity, the number of pixels identical in both pictures might be a reasonable measure. But in case of an autonomous system, for the input pattern inp that is to select the control procedure, it can be assumed that its bits usually do not have identical influence with regard to the survival of the system. So let us, without loss of generality, discuss that by the example case that the bits of the pattern inp belong to two main classes:

- class A: bits influencing life-critical properties of the autonomous system, i.e. with regard to its safety and security
- class B: bits influencing other, less critical system properties.

Without loss of generality, just for simpler discussion let us further assume that the class A bits of vector inp constitute its m_A leftmost bits, and the remaining $m_B = m - m_B$ bits belong to class B; these two parts of inp shall be called inp_A and inp_B. Correspondingly, also each of the row vectors B_j (j= 1,...n) of matrix B are partitioned into two parts of m_A and m_B bits, respectively; called B_{jA} and B_{jB}. In the same way the column vectors D_j of D (j=1,...,n) are partitioned into two parts (called D_{jA} and D_{jB}) which comprise m_A and m_B bits, respectively.

Let us now consider the excution of a control procedure $Proc_k$ for a previously selected situation class k. Our approach for defining update is based on three principles:

a) An update is allowed if the procedure $Proc_k$ has a sufficiently large success. This is expressed by the condition that the difference between the new and the old GHF value is larger than a given threshold value Th. The condition avoids that just fluctuation influences or noise lead to changes in the matrices.

b) If the condition is fulfilled, the parts B_{kB} and D_{kB} (which are related to non-essential system properties) are changed according to

$$\text{IF } ((GHF_{new} - GHF_{old}) > Th) \text{ THEN } B_{kB,new} = B_{k\,B,old} + C*(B_{kB,old} - s)$$
$$\text{ELSE } B_{kB,new} = B_{kB,old}$$

$$\text{IF } ((GHF_{new} - GHF_{old}) > Th) \text{ THEN } D_{kB,new} = D_{kB,old} + C*(D_{kB,old} - inp)$$
$$\text{ELSE } D_{kB,new} = D_{k\,B,old}$$

Here C is a learning parameter.

c) A change of part B_{kA} of B_k and part D_{kA} of D_k, however, is not allowed, i.e. they constitute an „iron kernel". This assures that even in case of permanent successes of a control procedure, its guardian function stored in the matrices B and D is not by and by weakened by updates.

Thus, with relatively moderate changes the use of the ghf function for the control of long term memory can be realized. We have demonstrated the use of adaptive resonance theory for autonomous systems by the example of robot systems. We would like to stress that the described strategy can be applied in the same way to the input and decision spaces of other autonomous systems, e.g. software agents.

6   Conclusion

In this paper, the potential of adaptive resonance theory (ART) networks for dependability issues in autonomous systems has been discussed. As introduction, the basic properties of ART architectures were outlined. A combination of such networks with counterpropagation networks was described which provides a fast access to control procedures corresponding to the different classes of situations to be treated. Moreover, it was discussed how the observed success or failing can be utilized to influence the learning of the ART network.

References

1. Carpenter, G.A., Grossberg, S.: The Art of Adaptive Pattern Recognition by a Self-Organizing Neural Network. Computer, 77–88 (March 1988)
2. Maas, R., Maehle, E.: Fault Tolerant and Adaptive Path Planning of Mobile Robots Based on Health Signals. In: Karl, W., Soudris, D. (eds.) ARCS 2011 Workshop Proceedings, pp. 58–63. VDE Verlag GmbH, Berlin (2011)
3. Hecht-Nielsen, R.: Applications of Counterpropagation Networks. Neural Networks 1, 131–139 (1988)
4. Kohonen, T.: Self-Organization and Associative Memory. Springer, Berlin (1984)
5. Zell, A.: Simulation neuronaler Netzwerke. R. Oldenbourg Verlag, München (1997)
6. Carpenter, G.A., Grossberg, S., Rosen, D.B.: ART-2A: An Adaptive Resonance Algorithm for Rapid Learning and Recognition. Neural Networks 4, 493–504 (1991)
7. Carpenter, G.A., Grossberg, S.: Hierarchical Search Using Chemical Transmitters in Self-Organizing Pattern Recognition. Neural Networks 3, 385–396 (1990)
8. Carpenter, G.A., Grossberg, S., Rosen, D.B.: Fuzzy ART: Fast Stable Learning and Categorization of Analog Patterns by an Adaptive Resonance System. Neural Networks 4, 759–771 (1991)
9. Serrano-Gotarredona, T., Linares-Barranco, B., Andreou, A.: Adaptive Resonance Microchips. Springer, Berlin (1998)
10. Teles Vieira, F.H., Lee, L.L.: A Neural Architecture Based on the Adaptive Resonant Theory and Recurrent Neural Networks. International Journal of Computer Science and Applications 4(3), 45–56
11. Grosspietsch, K.-E., Silayeva, T.A.: Organic Computing – A New Paradigm for Achieving Self-Organized Dependable Behaviour of Complex IT Systems. In: Hoyer, C., Chroust, G. (eds.) Proc. IDMIT 2006, Ceske Budejovice 2006, pp. 127–131. Trauner-Verlag, Linz (2006)
12. Brockmann, W., Maehle, E., Grosspietsch, K.-E., Rosemann, N., Jakimovski, B.: ORCA – an Organic Robot Control Architecture. In: Müller-Schloer, C., et al. (eds.) Organic Computing – A Paradigm Shift for Complex Systems, pp. 385–396. Springer, Basel (2011)

Application of Self-Organizing Systems in Power Systems Control

Sven C. Müller[1], Ulf Häger[1], Christian Rehtanz[1], and Horst F. Wedde[2]

[1] Institute of Energy Systems, Energy Efficiency and Energy Economics,
TU Dortmund University of Technology, Dortmund, Germany
{svenchristian.mueller,ulf.haeger,
christian.rehtanz}@tu-dortmund.de
[2] Chair of Operating Systems and Computer Architecture,
TU Dortmund University of Technology, Dortmund, Germany
horst.wedde@udo.edu

Abstract. The European electrical transmission network is operated increasingly close to its operational limits due to market integration and increased feed-in by renewable energies. For this reason, innovative solutions for a reliable, secure and efficient network operation are requested. The application of self-organizing systems promises significant potential in real-time control. This paper outlines the challenges of power system operation, gives a brief overview of relevant system characteristics and discusses the applicability of self-organizing systems for different fields of power system control. As a result of current research, the application of an agent-based decentralized power flow control system is presented and discussed in comparison to current practice based on central decision making.

Keywords: Self-organizing systems, power system control, smart grids, multi-agent systems, power flow control, FACTS.

1 Introduction and Scope

Large-scale power systems like the European electrical transmission system constitute safety-critical physical systems of a high degree of complexity. The electrical transmission network allows for the synchronous operation on alternating current (AC) of almost all parts of continental Europe and forms an interconnected system supplying millions of loads by several hundred conventional power plants as well as more than a million distributed generation units based on renewable energy sources. Due to the liberalization of the European electricity market and feed-in from renewable energies the transmission network has to adapt to a higher base loading and increasing volatility of power flows. It is becoming more and more important to develop innovative solutions to operate the system reliably and securely close to its operational limits in real-time.

The network operation is managed by Transmission System Operators (TSOs) which have to ensure reliability, security and efficiency [1]. Typically there is one

O. Dieste, A. Jedlitschka, and N. Juristo (Eds.): PROFES 2012, LNCS 7343, pp. 320–334, 2012.
© Springer-Verlag Berlin Heidelberg 2012

national TSO being state-owned or regulated by a national regulatory authority. Much of operation related decision making is undertaken centrally by the TSOs or is out of its controllability in the current regulatory framework. Intelligent distributed control plays a minor role in practice so far, although autonomous control systems have been developed in the last decade [2]. Recently the research on decentralized approaches based on multi-agent systems has been intensified and new flexible solutions have been proposed [3-5]. This paper gives an overview about decision making in power systems operation as of today, investigates the applicability of self-organizing systems, and outlines an exemplary application from current research in decentralized power flow control.

2   Self-Organizing Systems in Power Systems Operation

In this section, an overview of challenges as well as important physical characteristics of power systems is given followed by a discussion of decision making in system operation and the applicability of self-organizing systems in real-time control.

2.1   Challenges of Power Systems Operation

Reliability and security of power supply are closely linked to maintaining three kinds of system stability [6]:

- Frequency stability: supply and demand of active power need to be balanced, otherwise frequency exceeds acceptable limits and loads or generators need to be shedded.
- Rotor angle stability: all synchronous generators in power plants need to maintain synchronism of their rotors, otherwise the generators are disconnected from the system which leads to a sudden loss of feed-in and thus frequency instability.
- Voltage stability: local demand of reactive power needs to be met, otherwise voltage can drop irreversibly. Supply of reactive power is typically provided by neighboring synchronous generators or special reactive power compensation equipment.

If one of these conditions is violated system-wide black-outs can occur. A major challenge is to fulfill these conditions at any time even though the system changes dynamically. In particular, contingencies have to be taken into account, e.g., the outage of a major transmission line. For this reason, TSOs operate the system in accordance with the N-1 criterion that requires an operational state in which any single piece of equipment can fail without yielding in an inacceptable post-contingency state (N representing the total number of pieces of equipment in operation). In this context, it has to be taken notice of protection devices that protect equipment from overload by disconnecting it from the system. Therefore, a failure that leads to an overload of equipment can cause cascading disconnection of further equipment and thus loss of stability. The prevention of such a cascade is one aim of the N-1 criterion and overloads can only be accepted for a certain time period ranging from milliseconds to some minutes depending on the type of equipment and severity of overload.

Since rotor angle stability is so far of minor importance in the meshed European transmission network, the focus will be set on contributions to frequency stability, voltage stability and prevention of overloads by power flow control in the following parts.

2.2   Modeling of Power Systems

In the following an approach to power system analysis typical in electrical engineering is presented to give a basic overview of important physical linkages and elements relevant for application of self-organizing systems.

Power systems can be modeled as a network of branches and nodes. Nodes represent sinks or sources of active power P and reactive power Q (for sustaining electromagnetic fields) as a net value of generator feed-in and load consumption at each node. Branches represent the network topology consisting of transmission lines and additional equipment such as transformers or controllable devices designed to influence the parameters of the topology. Each branch element connected between node i and j can be represented by three complex admittances $\overline{Y}_{i,0}$, $\overline{Y}_{j,0}$ and $\overline{Y}_{i,j}$ derived from its equivalent circuit diagram (shown in Figure 1 with voltages $\overline{V}$ and currents $\overline{I}$).

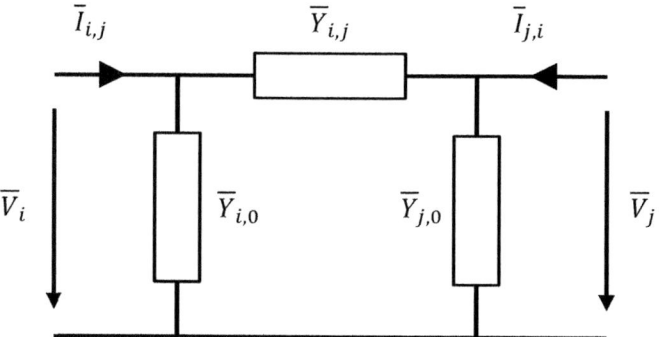

Fig. 1. Equivalent circuit diagram for branch elements (single-phase)

The branch elements need to be protected from overload which is typically regarded as a maximum of the current $\overline{I}_{el}$ flowing through the element. Given P and Q at each node n as well as the network topology, the resulting complex voltage $\overline{V}$ at the nodes as well as the complex currents $\overline{I}$ can be derived from equations (1-2) [7].

$$P_n + jQ_n = \overline{V}_n \Sigma_m \overline{y}_{nm}^* \overline{V}_m^* \tag{1}$$

$$\overline{I}_{el-i,j} = (\overline{V}_i - \overline{V}_j)\overline{Y}_{el-i,j} + \overline{V}_i\overline{Y}_{el-i,0} \tag{2}$$

Here, $\overline{y}_{nm}$ is the element from the n-th row and the m-th column of the node admittance matrix which comprises the admittances of all branch elements and their topological interconnection. For details on the formation rules of this matrix see [6-7].

In addition, the following physical linkages should be taken into account:

- The voltage magnitude V is closely linked to the local availability of reactive power Q. Reactive power can also be transported between nodes but its flow causes a higher loading of the corresponding transmission lines as well as active power losses. Also the flow of power through any kind of conducting equipment requires reactive power.
- The voltage angle φ between two nodes is closely linked to the active power flow P between the nodes.
- Deviations from the nominal frequency f_n (in Europe 50 Hz) evolve when supply of active power differs from the active power consumption by loads.

2.3   Decision Making and Control Actions in Real-Time Operation

Considerations of applying self-organization to power systems operation require knowledge about the decision making and potential actions in the system. In the following typical means of influence in power systems operation are summarized.

For generators the values of its active power feed-in P_{gen} as well as the reactive power supply Q_{gen} can be controlled. The base active power feed-in $P_{gen,base}$ is set by the power plant operator and follows a schedule derived from supply obligations mainly generated at the electricity market. It is constant for a certain supply period (e.g., 15 min). If the market clearing results in transmission system overloads the TSO can enforce a (mostly costly) change of generation schedules referred to as redispatch. In addition, the active power can temporarily differ from $P_{gen,base}$ by a value $P_{gen,r}$ for ancillary system services to ensure frequency stability by balancing system-wide supply and demand at any point of time (known as primary, secondary and tertiary reserve, see [8]). The value of $P_{gen,r}$ depends on control parameters defining how a generating unit contributes to mediating frequency deviations - e.g., due to noise and forecasting errors of load and renewable energy feed-in - and can be controlled on demand of the corresponding TSO (the contribution of a generator can, e.g., result from special control reserve markets). Additionally, the set point of the node voltage V_{gen} or – due to the strong coupling of voltage magnitude and reactive power – almost equivalently reactive power Q_{gen} can be set on demand of the TSO in order to achieve a desired voltage profile throughout the system and to optimize reactive power flows.

Loads are typically considered as demands of active power P_{load} and reactive power Q_{load} which cannot be controlled during normal operation and which can only be shedded in an emergency case. However, recent developments (e.g., in the fields of demand side management and smart grids) could change these conventional assumptions and could offer a superposing value of $P_{load,r}$ and $Q_{load,r}$ controllable in a certain range to a base load of $P_{load,base}$ and $Q_{load,base}$ [9]. Active and reactive power consumption are tightly linked and control of either value results in an approximately proportional change of the corresponding value. As the electricity service demanded by consumers usually regards active power, the typical control parameter is $P_{load,r}$.

Transmission lines themselves are uncontrollable and the only action available is to disconnect them from the system (e.g., in case of overload or failure). Nevertheless, the admittances being part of equations (1-2) can be influenced by the use of special equipment such as controllable transformers, compensations, HVDC (High-Voltage Direct Current) and FACTS (Flexible AC Transmission Systems) devices being under control of the TSO. These can be classified as series controlled, shunt controlled and combined shunt and series controlled devices. Series controlled devices are installed in series with a transmission line and their admittance influences voltage magnitude and angle resulting in control over voltage drop over the line and power flows. Its control value $ctrl_{series}$ changes the admittance $\bar{Y}_{i,j}$. Shunt controlled devices are installed line to ground, thus giving control over $\bar{Y}_{j,0}$ and $\bar{Y}_{i,0}$. Their control values $ctrl_{shunt}$ mainly influences reactive power and reactive power flows. Combined controlled devices influence all aforesaid element admittances by their control value $ctrl_{combined}$ and thereby combine the effects of shunt and series devices. For details on types and modeling of controllable devices see [10], Figure 2 gives an overview over relevant devices in practice and under development.

Additionally, every element of the topology as well as every generator and load can be disconnected from the system by triggering a breaker. This can be described as changing a binary control value $break_{el}$ from *on* to *off*. As mentioned, a typical case is the protection against overloads or load shedding in order to ensure frequency or voltage stability. Disconnection is either undertaken automatically or it can be initiated by the TSO. For loads and generators, a disconnection means a sudden change in P and Q at a node. Disconnection of topological network elements results in a sudden change of the admittances in equations (1-2). A similar effect has the change of interconnection of lines with couplers at certain nodes in the system (with a control value $couple_{bus}$).

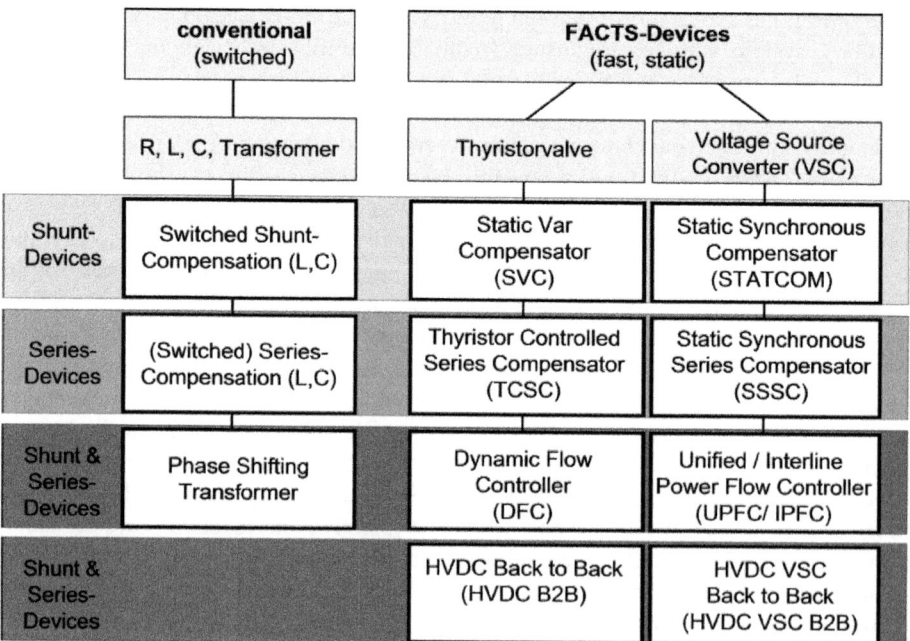

Fig. 2. Overview of controllable network devices (Source: [10])

Furthermore, from equations (1-2) it can be obtained that - at least to some extent - all state variables are interdependent and thus have impact on all examined fields of interest. However, the influence of different control values varies significantly and can be neglected depending on the application. Table 1 summarizes dynamically changing values in the system and shows qualitatively their influence on frequency stability, voltage stability and overload prevention. The table can serve to determine the decisive control values for new applications of power system control, nevertheless, a detailed system analysis including all control values should be undertaken to determine their influence in the specific scenario and whether or not they can be neglected.

Table 1. Dynamic values in power systems, entity in charge, and influence on stability and overloads (qualitative range: +++/++/+/0)

Dynamic value	Control sphere	Influence on frequency stability	Influence on voltage stability	Influence on overload prevention	Comment
$P_{gen,base}$	Market (TSO)	+++	0	+++	Possibly redispatch by TSO
$P_{gen,r}$	TSO	+++	0	+	Ancillary service purchased by TSO
Q_{gen}	TSO	0	+++	+	
$P_{load,base}$	Market	+++	Indirectly (by $Q_{load,base}$)	+++	Consumer behavior, possibly price-dependent
$Q_{load,base}$	-	0	+++	+	Follows mainly $P_{load,base}$
$P_{load,r}$	- (Future: TSO)	+++	Indirectly (by $Q_{load,r}$)	+	(Future: Ancillary service purchased by TSO)
$Q_{load,r}$	-	0	+++	+	Follows mainly $P_{load,r}$
$ctrl_{series}$	TSO	0	+	++	
$ctrl_{shunt}$	TSO	0	+++	+	
$ctrl_{combined}$	TSO	0	+++	++	
$break_{el}$	TSO	0	+++	+++	
$couple_{bus}$	TSO	0	+	+	

As another aspect for designing innovative and applicable control systems, the critical time for reactions, the control ranges and times for response of controllable devices, and the extent of coordination needed have to be taken into account. Table 2 gives a brief overview regarding these concerns.

Table 2. Coordination extent, critical times for reaction, and response times of devices for frequency stability, voltage stability and overload prevention

	Coordination	Critical time for reaction	Response time of devices
Frequency stability	System-wide	some 100 ms (major disturbance, keep frequency in boundaries) to some min (adjust frequency)	some 100 ms (local controller with limited range for ancillary services, load shedding) to some min (base feed-in)
Voltage stability	Local	some s (major disturbance) to several min	some ms (fast FACTS, HVDC) to some s or min (conventional controllable network devices, reactive power supply by generators)
Overload prevention	Region	100 ms (short circuit) to some min (moderate overload)	some ms (fast FACTS, HVDC, breaker) to some s or min (conventional controllable network devices)

2.4   Applicability of Self-Organizing Systems

Based on the characteristics of power systems control presented above, the applicability of self-organizing systems in this matter is discussed. In the following, self-organizing systems are understood as software processes being adaptive to changes in environment, capable of coordination and own decisions making without the need of a central hierarchic instance. A significant potential is seen in the capability of such decentralized systems to adapt in real-time compared to centralized decision making as of today that can take up to several minutes. This long time makes it necessary to operate the system in a possibly inefficient state because any contingencies need to be addressed upfront without accounting for the adaptiveness of the system. A first methodology for the economic assessment of such real-time control capabilities has been developed in [11] and indicates significant economic benefit. In addition, real-time adaptiveness can contribute decisively maintaining reliability and security of operation in an N-1 case.

Some insights for the targeted design of decentralized control systems that can be gained from Tables 1 and 2 are:

1. Not all relevant control values are in the sphere of influence of the same entity in the current regulatory framework, thus either the values not under control of the TSO are taken as external inputs in control systems or the framework needs to be changed.
2. Control values for frequency stability, voltage stability and power flow control are often interdependent, thus either all fields of interest are considered at the same time in a self-organizing system, or it must be assumed or verified that other fields are not critically influenced.
3. Time ranges of critical time for reaction as well as for the control capabilities of the devices vary widely. A detailed analysis must be undertaken specifying the

objective and constraints of application of the control system under consideration of the speed of the controllable devices as well as potentially occurring actions by other decision making processes in the meantime (e.g., a fast controlling FACTS device could react to a short circuit in time, whereas a conventional device could not serve for this purpose but is still sufficient to react in case of moderate overloading).

Taking these insights in mind, it can be distinguished between two general concepts for self-organizing systems:

- *Comprehensive Self-Organizational Approach*: all control values are controllable and emerge from self-organization.
- *Functional Self-Organizational Approach*: a specific problem is addressed by a self-organizing system complementing partially centralized or locally controlled systems.

The comprehensive self-organizational approach involves all system elements and needs to address both kinds of stability as well as overload prevention. This approach is of highest complexity but enables to gain the full benefit of self-organizing systems. However, this approach requires a change of the framework of European power systems as the existing market structure would have to be renewed. Such a bottom-up approach based on multi-agent-systems has been published in [12] and is still under development. As of today, this approach only makes use of control actions regarding active and reactive power supply and demand, but the system architecture generally offers the flexibility required to extend it in order to include topological actions as well.

The functional self-organizing approach has the advantage to be more easily applicable to an existing framework. Depending on the challenges to meet and the actions available, it can be identified how available controllable equipment could contribute. It must be assured that control actions do not cause violation of other operational requirements, thus (ii.) and (iii.) discussed above need to be specifically addressed. In the following, the applicability of functional approaches to the fields of interest in this paper is discussed.

Self-Organizing Systems for Frequency Stability

In order to ensure frequency stability in case of major disruptions (e.g., outage of a power plant), a fast and extensive response in the time range of some 100 ms by $P_{gen,r}$ and $P_{load,r}$ needs to be achieved in a coordinated process of power generation units and loads throughout the system. To apply self-organizing systems to this problem is challenging as a huge amount of communication over a wide-spanned area is needed. However, in a functional approach, this first reaction could be undertaken by local control systems (as of today by proportional and integral controllers) responding immediately to frequency deviations in order to avoid exceeding acceptable boundaries (e.g., 49 Hz) and the latter process of adjusting frequency to f_n as well as the transition to an improved configuration of $P_{gen,r}$ and $P_{load,r}$ could be organized decentralized (e.g., by application of self-organization in tertiary control).

Self-Organizing Systems for Voltage Stability
Voltage stability is of a rather local character and of a less critical time range, thus communication and coordination processes could be more easily executed in time than in the application for frequency stability. In addition, the most decisive control values with the exception of Q_{load} can be controlled by the TSO. Therefore, voltage stability constitutes a promising field for the application of self-organizing systems.

Self-Organizing Systems for Overload Prevention
Power flows are only partially in control of the TSO as they primarily derive from active power supply and demand configuration ($P_{gen,base}$, $P_{load,base}$). Nonetheless, controllable devices (particularly $ctrl_{combined}$, $ctrl_{series}$) offer influence in a limited range. As in the case of frequency stability, some applications (e.g., reaction to a short-circuit on the line) require a short response time of 100 ms. In the case power flow control, this time could be met more easily, as coordination is only needed regionally, nevertheless, achieving the response in time including communication and decision making is still challenging. Therefore, a functional approach for improved reconfiguration of control values as a complement to short-term local control or protection could be of high potential. An example for this application is presented in the next section.

3   Self-Organization in Coordinated Power Flow Control

In the following, a decentralized power flow control system as an example for applications of functional self-organizing approaches from recent research is presented [13-15]. First, the need of coordination of controllable devices in power flow control and the current practice of centralized coordination are outlined. Then, the agent-based decentralized approach is explained and investigated in detail.

3.1   Need for Coordination in Power Flow Control

In meshed transmission networks in a current framework with externally defined generation and load configuration, power flows can mainly be influenced by series or combined controlled devices such as Phase Shifting Transformers (PSTs) as well as certain FACTS and HVDC devices (see section 2.3). These devices are referred to as Power Flow Controllers (PFCs) in the following. Each PFC has a significant influence only in a certain neighborhood. Dimension and shape of this neighborhood depend on the type of device and the surrounding network. This influence can be determined by a sensitivity analysis using power flow analysis methods [6]. Figure 3 shows an example of a grid with several PFCs.

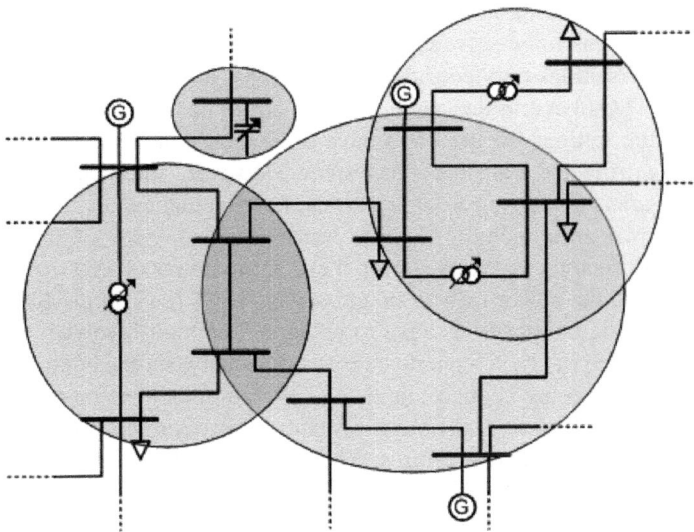

Fig. 3. Transmission network with generators (G), loads (Δ), and controllable network devices (marked with →)

The simplest way to implement a control system for PFCs is the use of a local control for each device. Local control means that one or several PFCs only address the control of the transmission lines within a certain region (which could be the control area of a TSO) while the neighborhood of influence of these PFCs could cover additional uncontrolled transmission lines from a control area of another TSO. Input values of local control are measurements of transmission line power flows. Further interaction with other controlling devices is not foreseen for local control. If several PFCs with mutual influence are integrated into the transmission system, the combination of several local controls might not always provide the optimal operation of the overall transmission system. A coordinated control system can provide several operational benefits which cannot be achieved by local control:

- Uncoordinated operation of PFCs may cause overcompensation of transmission lines within their neighborhood of mutual influence.
- When PFCs located in several control areas have mutual influence, counterproductive control actions may happen.
- In case of changing network topology (e.g., caused by a major line outage) local control of PFCs will not be able to adapt to the new network topology.

In general, the installation of multiple PFCs with mutual influence requires sophisticated coordination mechanisms in order to increase the overall transmission capacity and to avoid conflicts that may lead to unexpected behavior.

3.2   Current Practice: Central Coordination

Each day after finalization of the market bidding procedures each TSO analyses the day-ahead system security for its own transmission network. This analysis includes an

N-1 security analysis with an estimation of the PST settings in order to determine if there are congestions to be solved, e.g., by topology or redispatch measures. The estimation of PST settings only considers local control of the devices. During real-time operation the TSOs have to deal with forecast errors of the day-ahead security planning. Hence, the settings for the PSTs have to be determined based on real measurements coming from the transmission system. However, since currently there is no general wide-area monitoring system (WAMS) implemented in Europe, each TSO monitors its own grid, including a few transmission devices of the neighbouring TSOs. This information is the basis for the determination of PST settings. If PSTs have influence on the power flow of neighbouring TSOs (e.g., in the Benelux region), then changes of the tap positions have to be agreed with all involved TSOs. This coordination is carried out by telephone conversations between the control centres. Usually the time for agreeing about a tap change operation can last up to 15 min. A first step towards more efficient real-time coordination between the TSOs is made by the establishment of joint security centres. The participating TSOs submit their current system measurements as snapshots to the security centre, which then merges the individual data to a complete dataset which is basis for security analysis. As an example, the Coordination of Electricity System Operators (CORESO) provides such a quasi real-time analysis of the overall transmission system of the participating TSOs since July 2009. By performing a permanent monitoring of the transmission grid, updated through periodical snapshot, a security analysis is provided every 15 min.

However, all real-time control features which are planned for installation are until today based on a centralized data collection, which cannot provide coordination of PFC with a higher frequency than every 15 min. For responding to contingencies during unforeseen emergency situations this frequency is too small to protect the system against cascading events. Optimization tools are not applied for the coordination of PFC set-points, among others because they are yet too time consuming. Instead the coordination is performed by telephone conversations and based on expert knowledge supported by security calculations.

3.3   New Approach: Agent-Based Decentralized Coordination

This sub-section presents a new approach (still under development) for a coordinated control system. In contrast to existing coordination methods, this multi-agent based coordinated control system does not have any hierarchical structures. All communication and decisions are taken directly on the device level. This structure allows fulfilling the following requirements:

- To reduce the amount of data to be exchanged between neighboring control areas.
- System topology changes are detected automatically to be able to adapt the control immediately after the occurrence of contingencies
- The control system is robust in case of system disturbances. In particular during cascaded events (N-2 situations or higher) the coordinated control stabilizes the system with corrective control actions.

Description

The control variables are the set-points of PFC devices. The controlled variables are the power flows on transmission lines. Disturbances to be compensated by the coordinated control are caused by changes in load and generation or by tripping of transmission system devices (e.g., caused by a fault).

For the implementation of a multi-agent based coordinated control system with respect to the conditions described above an adequate communication network is needed. For this purpose each serial device of the power system (transmission line, transformer and PFC) is represented by a software agent. There are two kinds of agents, controlling (active) agents and non-controlling (passive) agents. Each PFC is equipped with a controlling agent. Each non-controllable electrical device within the area of influence of PFCs is equipped with a non-controlling agent (e.g., equipped with a Phasor Measurement Unit (PMU)).

The non-controlling agents permanently submit messages about local state information to their neighboring agents. These agents update the messages with local data and forward them to the next neighboring agents. In this way the messages are submitted along the power system topology until a stop criterion is reached. Controlling agents installed at each PFC receive these messages to gather information about the current system topology, the sensitivity for control actions on network devices and the demand for such actions. An example for this procedure is explained below, based on the network situation presented in Figure 4.

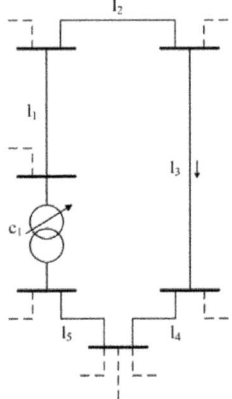

Fig. 4. Exemplary network situation

The agent of transmission line l_3 submits one message to every agent of its neighboring devices. These messages contain information about the impedance of transmission line l_3 and the identifier of the sending end-node from which the message was submitted. All agents of the devices physically connected to the sending end-node receive the message and add the impedance of their own transmission line. The accumulated impedance of one message expresses the transmission path impedance. Subsequently the messages are updated and forwarded along the topology. Finally the controlling agent of PFC c_1 receives one message from line l_3 at each end-node of the PFC. The first message was submitted along the transmission lines l_3, l_2 and l_1, while the second message was transmitted along the transmission lines l_3, l_4 and l_5. By analyzing these two messages the controlling agent concludes that the transmission line l_3 is located on a transmission path connecting the two end-nodes of the PFC and determines the total impedance of this transmission path by summing up the accumulated impedances stored in the two messages.

Each controlling agent evaluates this information by use of certain functions in order to determine the appropriate control actions. In this evaluation control requests of all transmission lines in the sphere of influence of a PFC are compared concerning severity of the request and the expected influence of the PFC for controlling the power flow on this device. Simulation results have shown that the multi-agent control reacts correctly and efficiently on detected overloading of transmission system devices in due time before cascading faults occur. The fact that the agents can exert efficient coordinated control without knowledge about the global system topology shows the immense potential for scalability and fault-tolerance of this distributed coordination of PFCs. Figure 5 visualizes the procedures of the control system.

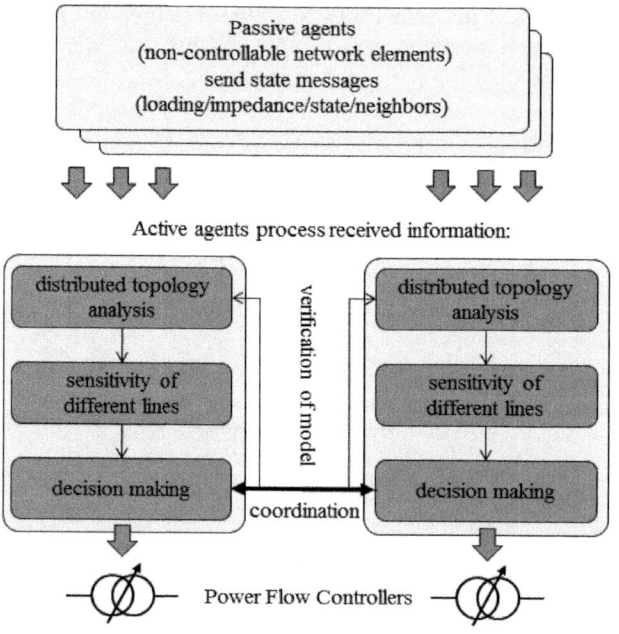

Fig. 5. Schema of a multi-agent-system for decentralized power flow control

Discussion

This coordination method allows for the coordination of series connected FACTS devices and PSTs. Up to now the implementation includes devices with discrete control steps which have a linear characteristic. The implementation of further types of PFCs including HVDC links is possible.

This coordination method adapts the control of PFCs when contingencies occur. This means that the set point of PFC devices can be modified timely in post-disturbance situations. Such corrective actions allow the TSO to operate the system without satisfying the strict N-1 security criterion. Since system topology changes are detected fully automatically without any necessity of communication with the control center, this approach is also robust in contingency situations of any grade.

This coordination method does not require any global data of the transmission system. The agents only submit information which is necessary for the coordination. The multi-agent system is supposed to be installed across the borders of system operators. However, the agents of neighboring system operators will only receive data from the neighboring networks which is required for the coordination (only from the area where the PFC has influence).

Field of Application and Requirements for the Implementation
The field of application of the multi-agent approach is real-time coordination. The method can be applied to perform an adequately fast automatic response to system events. This also includes severe system disturbances.

To achieve the benefits of this coordination method concerning fast reaction in contingency situations, fast PFC devices (of the FACTS family) have to be applied.

Since this approach is fully distributed significant modifications to the control centers are not required. However, the N-1 security constraints have to be adapted in the day ahead planning process and for the operation in the control centers. This softening of the N-1 criterion is required in order to achieve an increase of transmission capacity as response to the increased flexibility gained by using FACTS devices.

The majority of the modifications have to be made on the substations level. Agents have to be installed for each transmission line and for each PFC within the area to be coordinated. Each non-controlling agent must be connected to measurement devices which observe the loading and the status of the corresponding transmission line. Each controlling agent must be connected to a PFC controller to transmit the control signals. Between neighboring agents there must be appropriate communication channels.

4   Outlook

The application of self-organizing systems in power systems control promises significant potential to contribute to a reliable, secure and efficient network operation by enabling real-time adaptivity in contrast to current practices of centralized decision making. The capabilities of self-organizing systems particularly meet the challenges of ensuring voltage stability and preventing overloads. Therefore, research and development in these functional approaches should be continued with a close consideration of time constraints and interdependencies with other critical measures of system operation. Furthermore, the extension of recent comprehensive bottom-up approaches by inclusion of topological actions would be eligible. For power flow controllers, a decentralized coordination system based on agents has been developed. Benefits include increase of operational security by increased real-time adaptiveness in N-2 cases as well as improvement of operational efficiency by enabling corrective real-time measures, thereby possibly allowing for relaxation of strict N-1 security planning.

Acknowledgment. This work has been funded by the German Research Foundation (DFG) as part of research unit FOR1511 "Protection and Control Systems for Reliable and Secure Operation of Electrical Transmission Systems".

References

1. European Parliament, Council: Directive 96/92/EC (1997)
2. Rehtanz, C.: Autonomous Systems and Intelligent Agents in Power System Control and Operation. Springer, Heidelberg (2003)
3. Wedde, H.F., Lehnhoff, S., Rehtanz, C., Krause, O.: Intelligent Agents under Collaborative Control in Emerging Power Systems. International Journal of Engineering, Science and Technology 2(3), 45–59 (2010)
4. Häger, U., Lehnhoff, S., Rehtanz, C., Wedde, H.F.: Multi-Agent System for Coordinated Control of FACTS Devices. In: Proceedings of the 15th IEEE International Conference on Intelligent System Applications to Power Systems. IEEE Press, Curitiba (2009)
5. Voropai, N.I., Kolosok, I.N., Massel, L.V., Fartyshev, D.A., Paltsev, A.S., Panasetsky, D.A.: A Multi-Agent Approach to Electric Power Systems. In: Alkhateeb, F., Al Maghayreh, E., Abu Doush, I. (eds.) Multi-Agent Systems - Modeling, Interactions, Simulations and Case Studies. InTech (2011)
6. Kundur, P.: Power System Stability and Control. McGraw-Hill, Inc., New York (1993)
7. Handschin, E.: Elektrische Energieübertragungssysteme. Dr. Alfred Hüthig-Verlag, Heidelberg (1987)
8. Rebours, Y.G., Kirschen, D.S., Trotignon, M., Rossignol, S.: A Survey of Frequency and Voltage Control Ancillary Services—Part I: Technical Features. IEEE Transactions on Power Systems 22(1), 350–357 (2007)
9. Heffner, G., Goldmann, C., Kirby, B., Klintner-Meyer, M.: Loads Providing Ancillary Services: Review of International Experience. Lawrence Berkeley National Laboratory (2008)
10. Zhang, X.-P., Rehtanz, C., Pal, B.: Flexible AC Transmission Systems: Modelling and Control. Springer, Heidelberg (2006)
11. Rehtanz, C.: Dynamic Power Flow Controllers for transmission corridors. In: 2007 iREP Symposium on Bulk Power System Dynamics and Control - VII. Revitalizing Operational Reliability (2007)
12. Wedde, H.F., Lehnhoff, S., Handschin, E., Krause, O.: Real-Time Multi-Agent Support for Decentralized Management of Electric Power. In: Proceedings of the 18th Euromicro Conference on Real-Time Systems. IEEE Press, Dresden (2006)
13. Lehnhoff, S., Häger, U., Krause, O., Wedde, H.F., Rehtanz, C.: Towards Autonomous Distributed Coordination of Fast Power Flow Controllers in Transmission Networks. In: Proceedings of the 4th International Conference on Liberalization and Modernization of Power Systems: Coordinated Monitoring and Control towards Smart Grids. IEEE Press, Irkutsk (2009)
14. Häger, U., Lehnhoff, S., Rehtanz, C., Wedde, H.F.: Applicability of Coordinated Power Flow Control based on Multi-Agent Systems. In: Proceedings of the 8th IEEE International Conference on Bulk Power System Dynamics and Control. IEEE Press, Rio de Janeiro (2010)
15. Häger, U., Rehtanz, C., Lehnhoff, S.: Analysis of the Robustness of a Distributed Coordination System for Power Flow Controllers. In: Proceedings of the 17th International Power Systems Computation Conference. IEEE Press, Stockholm (2011)

Minimizing Vehicular Travel Times Using the Multi-Agent System BeeJamA

Sebastian Senge and Horst F. Wedde

TU Dortmund, Department for Computer Science

Abstract. We present and evaluate our self-adaptive and distributed vehicle route guidance approach, termed BeeJamA, which provides drivers safely with routing directions well before each intersection. Our approach is based on a multi-agent system which is inspired by the honey bee behavior and relies on a decentralized vehicle-to-infrastructure architecture. On the basis of microscopic traffic simulations under varying penetration rates it shows that BeeJamA has the tendency to outperform dynamic shortest path algorithms with respect to (global) travel times.

Keywords: vehicle route guidance, distributed system, swarm intelligence.

1 Introduction

Through the past few years the economical and ecological damage from increasing vehicular traffic resulting in more and more traffic congestions has been widely recognized and discussed [1]. Especially in metropolitan areas building new high capacity roads to reduce travel times may be to costly or even not possible for reasons of space. Cooperative vehicle route guidance can lead to a more efficient usage of the road network. However, commercially available state-of-the-art navigation approaches route vehicles solely based on static information or in the best case (like TMC) based on dynamic traffic utilizations but with rather high update intervals of several minutes. Nevertheless, such approaches rely on centralized processing of the involved data, a major shortcoming naturally limiting the covered area or the minimal update interval. In contrast, we argue that a distributed, self-adaptive vehicle route guidance does not suffer from these drawbacks.

In this paper our distributed routing protocol BeeJamA [2,3] is described and evaluated on the example of a Shanghai road network. BeeJamA (for Bee Jam Avoidance) is a multi-agent system (MAS) based on the BeeHive routing algorithm [4] for computer networks and makes use of principles derived from honey bee swarm intelligence behavior.

The most recent work that is close in spirit to our approach is based on ant swarm intelligence [5,6]. So far it appears that the aspect of scalability has not been dealt with so far.

The remainder of this paper is structured as follows. In the next section, we propose a vehicle-to-infrastructure architecture necessary for our MAS (Sec. 4). Our simulation studies are presented in Sec. 5 and discussed in Sec. 6.

O. Dieste, A. Jedlitschka, and N. Juristo (Eds.): PROFES 2012, LNCS 7343, pp. 335–349, 2012.
© Springer-Verlag Berlin Heidelberg 2012

2   Proposed Vehicle-to-Infrastructure Architecture

In this section, we propose a vehicle-to-infrastructure (V2I) [7] based architecture for the necessary bi-directional V2I communication in our BeeJamA system. The cornerstone of the architecture is a decentralized network of so-called *navigators*. A navigator has a spatially limited area of responsibility, its *navigation area*, where it handles the communication with each vehicle and returns routing instructions on request. An example of this concept is depicted in Fig. 1a. There, the map is splitted in four areas $A_1, \ldots, A_n$ and each area A_i is associated in a one-to-one relation to navigator N_i. After the driver specified a destination, a (GPS-enabled) personal navigation assistant (*PNA*), e.g. a smart cell phone, continuously submits the vehicle's position to its responsible navigator. Otherwise, state-of-the-art approaches like Floating Car Data (FCD) or anonymous cell phone position tracing may serve as a source of road utilization. We assume that at least approximations of these local utilizations are known to the associated navigator. The callout shows a junction and four vehicles (rectangles) as a part of area A_2 in greater detail. N_2 is the responsible navigator for all vehicle communication in A_2. Then, the interaction protocol between a vehicle and its navigator is simple: a routing instruction request for the next intersection (hop) is sent from the PNA to the navigator each time a vehicle enters a new road. The navigator calculates an instruction (see Sec. 4.4) based on up-to-date traffic information and returns it to the vehicle's PNA.

The navigators themselves communicate by flooding bee agents as described in Sec. 4.3. Navigators may be deployed as distributed road-side hardware (like GSM base stations) or (with lower total cost) as processes in a cloud environment (as indicated in Fig. 1a).

Ultimately, a hop-to-hop routing emerges, where each vehicle receives an individual next-hop instruction, in the best case, before each intersection in due time. This is a serious real-time problem as the individual deadlines depend on the speed of the vehicles moving within the area of their responsible navigator.

3   Generic Routing Framework

In order to conduct simulations easily, we developed a middleware, termed *Generic Routing Framework* (GRF), to hide the complexity of traffic simulation from the routing algorithms and to offer a common interface to routing algorithms for the simulation tools. In such a way we could easily switch to another simulator, or use a different set of routing algorithms. Figure 2 highlights the most important parts the GRF consists of. The GRF supports initializing from different data and configuration sources and formats, manages relevant graph and token (vehicles in this case) structures, simple automated analysis features and provides visualization for graph and token states. The routing algorithms access these features through a well defined set of interfaces and the simulators, called mobility world (mob world), are connected through exchangeable adapters. To add another simulator, only a new adapter has to be implemented,

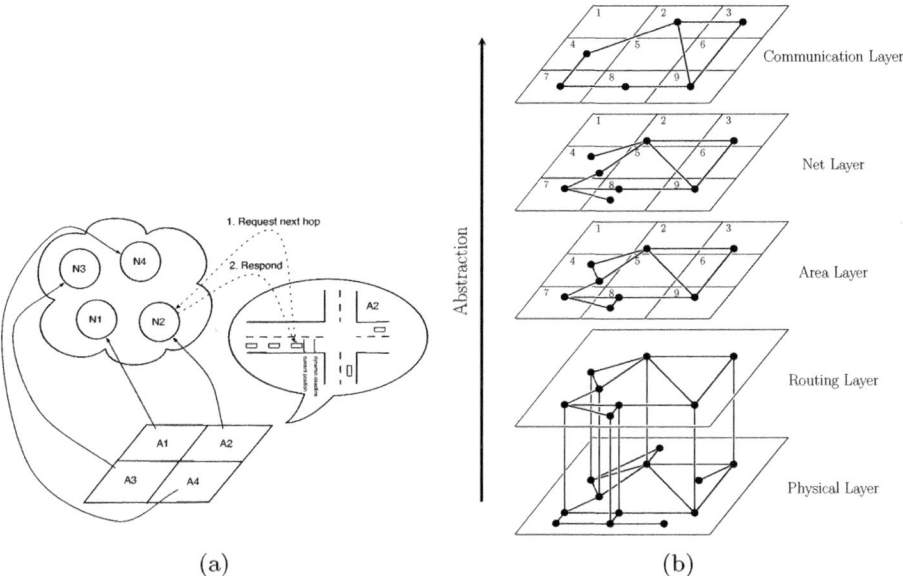

(a)   (b)

Fig. 1. Vehicle-2-Infrastructure architecture and Layered Routing Model

everything else, especially including the routing algorithms, remains unchanged. Basically, the only requirement for a simulator to be added as an GRF mob world, is that it uses a microscopic traffic, i.e. vehicle oriented, simulation model. At the moment, adapters exist for MATSim and SUMO. The GRF maintains two graphs, each on a separate layer, to satisfy the specific needs of both sides of the middleware, the mob world and the routing algorithms:

1. The *physical layer* corresponds to the actual road network (e.g. exported from OpenStreetMap); nodes correspond to intersections or are simply used to model the shape of a road. Traffic simulators operate on this graph to calculate the travel times of the individual vehicles and to visualize the road network, which is why a fine grained model of the underlying road network is best.

2. However, networks with more nodes and edges increase the runtime (or number of exchanged messages for distributed algorithms) and memory consumption of routing algorithms. Therefore, on the *routing layer*, irrelevant nodes, which do not represent an intersection, are pruned since no turning is possible and thus no routing at these nodes is necessary. Routing algorithms may only access this graph, not the original physical layer graph. Formally, the routing layer graph is given by $G = (V, E, w)$, where V is the set of vertices, E the set of edges and $w : E \times \mathbb{N} \to \mathbb{R}^n, n \in \mathbb{N}$ a time variant weight function mapping an edge $e \in E$ and a discrete time step $t \in \mathbb{N}$ to an n-dimensional weight vector. In this paper, however, we use a simple scalar weight value that expresses averaged vehicle travel times on this edge as returned by the road traffic simulation tools. The graph is assumed to be strongly connected.

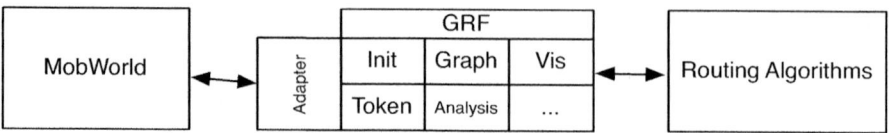

Fig. 2. Structure of the Generic Routing Framework

4   The BeeJamA Routing Protocol

The BeeJamA algorithm protocol is designed for routing vehicles with the intention of avoiding traffic congestions. It is based on the BeeHive[4] packet switching algorithm which, in turn, has been partially derived from the honey bee foraging behavior. The basic idea in BeeJamA, as well as in BeeHive, is that infrastructural components inform their vicinity how to reach them best by means of agents, the *bees*. In BeeHive these infrastructural components are the network routers, in the road traffic context the navigators take over this task. From a logical point of view each node in the road network can send and receive bees, physically are these bees handled by the associated navigator. To inform nodes in the vicinity, each node emits bees regularly and resends received bees, thus a flooding emerges. This is an adaption of the flexible scout and forager swarm intelligence behavior. A comprehensive presentation of the underlying natural behavior and the mapping to the routing context can be in [4].

BeeJamA regards the total delay $\eth$ vehicle experiences as a combination of two components: the *free flow delay* $\mathfrak{f}$ and the *traffic congestion delay* $\mathfrak{c}$, hence $\eth = \mathfrak{f} + \mathfrak{c}$. The first represents the minimal (and constant) travel time when driving with the maximum speed allowed. The latter is an indicator of the load on the path and thus is used by the algorithm to proactively decrease the number of vehicles forwarded over an already overcrowded path. In this paper, however, we use a simple path quality function weighting $\mathfrak{f}$ and $\mathfrak{c}$ equally, namely the inverted total delay $q = \eth^{-1}$.

Basically, the BeeJamA protocol works as follows. Emitted bees traverse the routing graph in the opposite direction of travel and report on delays a vehicle experiences on the path from the current node i to their launching node d. Let S be set the (direct) successors of node i and $s \in S$ the last node an incoming bee visited before reaching i. The current node i then stores the reported delays as a tuple $(\mathfrak{f}, \mathfrak{c})_{d,s}$ in a local routing table. Tab. 1 shows a generic table T of node i. As bees arrive at i the initially empty table grows. The column index is associated to the bee's launching node, the row index to the bee's path predecessor. Let S_r be the set of successors over which node i received a bee from launching node d, $S_r = \{s_j | (\mathfrak{f}, \mathfrak{c})_{d,s_j} \in T(i)\} \subseteq S, 1 \le j \le |S|$. Then, vehicles at node i with destination d are forwarded to a successor $s \in S_r$ biased by the quality q_s calculated from the tuple $(\mathfrak{f}, \mathfrak{c})_{d,s}$. In other words, vehicles will be forwarded to a specific next hop if a bee before discovered a path from the vehicle's destination over this node.

Table 1. Structure of a routing table

$T(i)$	d_1	$\cdots$	d_n
s_1	$(\mathfrak{f},\mathfrak{c})_{1,1}$	$\cdots$	$(\mathfrak{f},\mathfrak{c})_{n,1}$
$\vdots$	$\vdots$	$\vdots$	$\vdots$
s_m	$(\mathfrak{f},\mathfrak{c})_{1,m}$	$\cdots$	$(\mathfrak{f},\mathfrak{c})_{n,m}$

4.1   Area Layer

The BeeJamA protocol divides the road network into smaller independent parts called *navigation areas* (done on the area layer) and connects them to allow inter-area trips (done on the net layer). So each navigator will be released from maintaining global information and thus maintains only small routing tables with local (and therefore simple to keep up-to-date) information.

Areas on the *area layer* are completely self-contained in the sense that for intra-area routing no remote information is necessary. Each area belongs to a navigator which is responsible for sending and receiving bee agents, updating routing table updates and for satisfying routing requests within the area. Bees on the area layer never leave their source area, so that the information dissemination is limited to a local area only.

Technically, the area layer's set of vertices and edges are equal to their counterparts in the routing graph, $G_A = (V_A, E_A) = (V, E)$. Areas are defined using an node partition of the routing graph, currently we use a simple grid algorithm. Informally, an area consists of the nodes in a grid box and the edges having their source in the same box. Thus, given an grid-induced node partition $V_{A,1}, \ldots, V_{A,n}$, an area is a subgraph $A_i = (V_{A,i}, E_{A,i})$ with $E_{A,i} = \bigcup_{v_k \in V_{A,i}, v_l \in V} (v_k, v_l)$.

The set of border nodes $B(A)$ of an area A is given by the area's nodes with edge destination in a different area, i.e. $B(A) = \{b \in V_A | \exists i \in V \setminus V_A : (b, i) \in E\}$ and the set of inner nodes by $I(A) = V_A \setminus B(A)$.

For each node $v \in V_{A,i}$ its navigator maintains a IFZ_{area} (intra foraging zone) table, where incoming bees can store their intra-area delays. The table is then utilized for intra-area next hop routing (see Sec. 4.4).

4.2   Net Layer

Typically vehicles may drive across several areas to reach their individual destinations. To satisfy those routing requests, for each area on the area layer a *net area* on the *net layer*, is created. These net areas are mapped onto fixed *foraging regions*, modeling the vicinity of a destination node. For far distance routing in the rough direction of a destination (see Sec. 4.4 for details), each foraging region is represented by a *representative node*. In this paper, we use one foraging region per area. Informally, a net area consists of all fully connected border nodes of the corresponding area on the area layer plus all inter-area edges with their source in the net area. Let $A_1, \ldots, A_n$ be the areas on the area layer, then the net area N_i is given by the fully connected graph $N_i = (B(A_i), E_i)$ with $E_N = \bigcup_{i=1}^{n} \{(v_1, v_2) \in E | v_1 \in B(A_i) \wedge v_2 \in B(A_i)\}$.

In addition, each net area maintains a specific *foraging zone* FZ_{net}^r that consists of all neighboring areas within a certain hop range r. It models the direct vicinity of a source node for which accurate routing information is available.

The net area's navigator (the same as for the associated area on the area layer) maintains two tables: for each node $v \in B(A_i)$ the next hop tables IFZ_{net} (inter foraging zone) and IFR_{net} (intra foraging region). The IFZ_{net} table (in analogy to the IFZ_{area} table) stores costs from each neighbor to each node in the same foraging zone on the net layer. In addition, the IFR_{net} table stores costs from each neighbor to each representative node and is used to forward vehicles if the destination is far away (see Sec. 4.4 for more details).

Finally, the *communication layer* represents a communication network necessary for the MAS. Each node corresponds to a navigator and an edge corresponds to a communication link (e.g., via public internet or private networks) used to exchange agents between navigators. Such an edge is present if and only if two areas are connected by at least one edge (on the net layer). Vice versa, navigators not sharing edges do not communicate directly.

4.3   Bee Agents

Our multi agent system makes use of three different types of bee agents, all responsible for collecting and disseminating travel delays in the opposite direction of travel. They only differ in the distance that they are allowed to travel starting from their launching node. On the area layer, area bee agents are used to keep IFZ_{area} tables up-to-date. On the net layer, we use two types of agents, inspired by the honey bee behavior: the majority of the foragers exploit food sources in the direct vicinity of the hive, while a minority visit food sources which are further away. We adapted this concept into *Short Distance Bee Agents* (updating IFZ_{net} tables) and *Long Distance Bee Agents* (updating IFR_{net} tables). For a comprehensive overview of the natural background of our approach see [4].

All three agent types have in common that they traverse directed edges in opposite direction of travel, thus agents are sent to predecessors of the current node. An agent launched from node d to predecessor p, thus traversing an edge $(p, d) \in E$ in the routing graph in opposite direction, requests the free flow delay $\mathfrak{f}$ and the current traffic congestion delay $\mathfrak{c}$ across the edge (p, d) from the local navigator, proceeds and updates the routing tables in subsequent nodes. Before proceeding, the agent updates its carried delay information to its launching node d by means of the traversed path's $(d, \ldots, s, i)$ normalized quality with respect to the already known paths via $s' \in S_r$

$$\hat{q}_s = \frac{q_s}{\sum\limits_{s' \in S_r} q_{s'}}, \tag{1}$$

Algorithm 1. Launch and Transmit Bees

```
 1: procedure LAUNCH(type, srcNodes, waitLength)
 2:     gen← 1
 3:     while true do                              ▷ Start new generation of bees
 4:         for each node n ∈ srcNodes do
 5:             bee ← create new bee
 6:             bee.gen ← gen
 7:             bee.type ← type
 8:             if type = AREA or (type = NET and n is representative node) then
 9:                 bee.limit ← 1
10:             else
11:                 bee.limit ← SL
12:             transmit(bee, n)
13:         gen ← gen+1
14:         sleep waitLength
15: procedure TRASNMIT(bee, d)
16:     if bee.type = AREA or (bee.type = NET and A(d) = A(i) then
17:         enqueue bee in local receive queue for node d
18:     else
19:         transmit bee to remote node d via communication network
```

---

where the necessary total delays $\eth'_s$ can be looked up in the table. Then, the scalar product $(\mathfrak{f}, \mathfrak{c}) \cdot \hat{q}_s$ can be interpreted as the weighted delays for the path.

In this way, the delays reported by an incoming agent are composed of the (weighted) delays carried from the last node plus the delay of the last edge. A node i that receives an agent via successor s learns about the delays to the launching node d of the agent and can probabilistically forward vehicles with destination d based on this information. Unfortunately, probabilistic routing without any further measurements may lead to loops, i.e. a vehicle passes an already visited node. It is important to distinguish between two kind of loops. The first kind occurs if the situation in the network changes in such a way that a detour including an already node seems appropriate and is expressly desired. However, probabilistic routing may even lead to loops in situations without changes in the network utilization. As a counter measurement to this second kind of loops the BeeJamA version presented in this paper only forwards vehicles to successors with lesser *distances* in the sense of total delays. Then loops of the second kind cannot occur because the distance in a loop would increase.

Navigators call the *launch* procedure (Alg. 1, see Tab. 2 for used symbols) once for the area (type = AREA, srcNodes ≡ nodes in the area) and once for the net layer (type = NET, srcNodes ≡ border nodes of the area), the *receive* procedure (Alg. 2), however, is called once for each received bee agent. In the *launch* procedure, every second each node sends a bee agent to each predecessor in the routing graph. Predecessors in the same area are managed by the same navigator, so agents for these nodes are added to an internal queue, other nodes are sent across the communication layer (see *transmit* procedure in Alg. 1). Non-representative nodes on the net layer launch short distance bee agents (with a

Table 2. Used symbols, procedures and functions

Symbol	Meaning
bee	A bee agent
bee.src, bee.last	The agent's source and last visited node
bee.gen	The generation the bee was launched
bee.f	The agent's accumulated free flow delay
bee.c	The agent's accumulated traffic congestion delay
bee.dist	The agent's accumulated distance value
bee.limit	The agent's hop limit
bee.areas	The agent's number of visited areas
bee.type	The agent's type (AREA or NET)
i,d	Current and destination node
SL	Short bee distance limit
$dist$	Best known distance (total delay) to the destination
table[d][l]	Table entry with the delays (ffd, tcd) from i to d via l
table[d][l].dist	The agent's distance value that updated this table entry last
$A(i)$	Nodes of i's area
$B(i)$	Border nodes of $A(i)$, $B(i) \subseteq A(i)$
FZ(d)	Foraging zone of node d
bestSucc, bestDist	Maps for storing the best successor and distance
S_r	Successors of node i lying on a known path to d
$\hat{q}_s$	Normalized quality at node i for a path via s to d
$\mathfrak{f}(s,d), \mathfrak{c}(s,d)$	Free flow / traffic congestion delay from i to d via s
$IFZ_{area/net}(i)$	The IFZ area or net table for node i
$IFZ_{area/net}(i,s)$	The minimal IFZ area or net table entry with destination d for node i w.r.t. the total delays
$IFZ_{area/net}(i,s,d)$	The IFZ area or net table entry with destination d via s for node i
waitLength	Time between two generations, in this paper: 1 second

hop range of two in this paper) to inform their foraging zone about delay changes and representative nodes launch long distance bees (unlimited hop range in this paper, since only one net layer is present).

Alg. 2 shows the *receive* procedure. In line 3 of the listing, bees that arrive too late are killed. Then, if the first bee of a new generation arrives, the best distance value and the successor of the last generation are saved (line 6-7). If the distance value the bee is less than currently known value, a bee is allowed to update the table entry to its source node via the last node on the agent's

Algorithm 2. Receive and Resend Bees

```
1:  procedure RECEIVE(bee)
2:      if bee.gen < latestGen[bee.src] then
3:          return                                              ▷ Kill bee, too old
4:      if bee.gen > latestGen[bee.src]  then
5:          ŝ ← arg max_{s∈S_r}{table[bee.src][s].dist}
6:          bestSucc[bee.src]← ŝ
7:          bestDist[bee.src]← table[bee.src][ŝ].dist
8:          clear all successors marked with node bee.src
9:          dist = ∞
10:         latestGen[bee.src] ← bee.gen
11:     if bee.dist < dist then
12:         bee.f = bee.f + f(i, bee.last)                      ▷ Update delays
13:         bee.c = bee.c + c(i, bee.last)
14:         if bee.type = AREA then
15:             table ← IFZ_{area}(i)
16:         else if bee.type = NET then
17:             if bee.areas ≤ SL then
18:                 table ← IFZ_{net}(i)
19:             else
20:                 table ← IFR_{net}(i)
21:         table[bee.src][bee.last] ← (bee.f,bee.c)            ▷ Update table
22:         table[bee.src][bee.last].dist ← bee.dist
23:     bee.dist ← bee.dist + f(i, bee.last) + c(i, bee.last)   ▷ Update distance
24:     if bee.dist < dist then
25:         dist ← bee.dist
26:         remove all table entries table[bee.src][·].dist ≥ dist
27:     if bee.last = bestSucc[bee.src] or bee.dist < bestDist[bee.src] then
28:         resend ← true
29:         if bee.areas ≤ SL and A(bee.last) ∩ A(i)=∅ then
30:             bee.areas ← bee.areas + 1                       ▷ Update traversed areas
31:     if bee.areas ≤ bee.limit and resend = true then
32:         succs ← S(i) \ {bee.last,bee.src} ∪ {successors marked with node bee.src}
33:         for s ∈ succs do                                    ▷ Resend bee
34:             bee' ← clone bee
35:             bee'.last ← i
36:             bee'.f ← ∑_{s∈S_r}(f_s · q̂_s)
37:             bee'.c ← ∑_{s∈S_r}(c_s · q̂_s)
38:             bee'.dist ← dist
39:             transmit(bee', s)
40:             mark successor s with node bee'.src
```

path (line 11-22). If called on the area layer, the functions $f()$ and $c()$ (in line 12,13) return the corresponding edges weights in the routing graph, on the net layer, however, the delays are looked up in the routing tables. In line 23, the *bee.dist* variable is updated and it is checked once again if the bee's distance is better. If so, the best known distance value at node i is updated and worse

---

Algorithm 3. Next Hop Selection

1: **procedure** NEXTHOP(i,d)
2:     $T \leftarrow \emptyset$
3:     **if** $d \in Area(i)$ **then**   ▷ Routing case 1
4:         $\forall s \in S_r$: calculate $\hat{q}_s$ from $IFZ_{area}(i), T \leftarrow T \cup \{(s, \hat{q}_s)\}$
5:     **else if** $B(i) \subseteq FZ(d)$ **then**   ▷ Routing case 2
6:         $\forall s \in S_r$: calculate $\hat{q}_s$ from $IFZ_{area}(i)$ and $IFZ_{net}(i), T \leftarrow T \cup \{(s, \hat{q}_s)\}$
7:     **else**   ▷ Routing case 3
8:         $\forall s \in S_r$: calculate $\hat{q}_s$ from $IFZ_{area}(i), IFR_{net}(i), T \leftarrow T \cup \{(s, \hat{q}_s)\}$
9:     select a tuple $(s^*, \hat{q}_{s^*})$ from $T = \{(s_1, \hat{q}_1), \ldots, (s_m, \hat{q}_m)\}$ as per goodness
10:    **return** s^*

---

table entries are deleted accordingly. This ensures that vehicles are forwarded only to successors with lesser distances. Basically, a bee is allowed to travel further if the agent arrived over the successor with the best distance value of the last generation (first condition in line 27). This is an approximation of the idea that only the best path information should be disseminated in the network. The only way, however, to decide precisely which bee carries the best distance value, one must wait until all agents of a generation have arrived. Unfortunately, this waiting time accumulates along a agent's path through the network, since any node cannot resend a bee with source d until all bee flooded by d in the current generation have arrived. To avoid such an stop-and-wait protocol, we assume that the quality of a path does not drastically change between subsequent generations and identify the bee on the best path as the bee on the best path of the last generation. The notable exception is if the agent's distance value is already better than the best distance value of the last generation (see second condition in line 27). Afterwards, if necessary, the number of an agent's traversed areas is updated. Finally, the bee is flooded to eligible predecessors.

As a result of this flooding based approach, each node receives up-to-date delay information about the nodes in its own foraging zone and to representative nodes of destinations farther away at short time intervals. The size of routing tables stay small because short distance bee agents on the net layer never leave the local vicinity of their launching nodes. Just in case the IFR_{net} tables get too big nevertheless due to long distance bee agents (which are allowed to travel through the whole network in this paper) additional net layers may be added to cover larger networks. On each additional net layer the size of the foraging regions is increased and the hop limit of lower layers' bee agents is decreased. Finally, only on the highest net layer long distance bee agents must have unlimited hop limits to disseminate delays to the (then much lesser number of) representative nodes. Of course, each reduction leads to an intrinsically loss of precise and up-to-date traffic information, however, this has not to adversely affect routing precision in general, since traffic information from destinations far away may not have great relevance until the vehicle approaches its actual destination in which case BeeJamA provides accurate information.

4.4 Vehicle Forwarding

The MAS disseminates delays in the opposite direction of travel starting from node d. This information is then used to forward vehicles in the direction of d as explained in the this section. There are three possible cases for routing a vehicle from current node i within area $A(i)$ to a destination node d within a destination area $A(d)$ (see Alg. 3):

1. The destination node lies within the current area, $d \in A(i)$
2. The destination node's area lies within the foraging zone of the current area, $B(i) \subseteq FZ(d)$
3. Else (i.e., case 1 and 2 are not true).

The cases above reflect a sequence of scenarios in which the destination node d lies further and further away from the current area.

With BeeJamA, no complete paths are calculated in advance at all, only next hops. To do so, perspective successors, i.e. $s \in S_r$, get weighted, i.e. a normalized quality $\hat{q}_s$ is calculated. Finally, s is chosen as next hop with probability $\hat{q}_s$ (see Alg. 3). In the following, we describe how BeeJamA calculates successor's overall quality in the three aforementioned routing cases.

In routing case 1, the idea is that the destination is near enough, so that leaving the current area is not necessary. Thus, all possible paths from the current node to the destination considered lie entirely in the current area. Therefore, the vehicle's next hop is chosen according to the entries in the IFZ_{area} table of the current node i, i.e. for each successor $s \in S_r$, the quality $\hat{q}_s$ (as in Eq. 4.3) is calculated and the next the hop chosen probabilistically biased by the qualities. In case 2, the navigator tries to forward the vehicle so that it will leave the current area using border nodes promising good travel times to the destination. Possible paths via successor $s \in S_r$ comprise two components:

- a path from i via s to a border node b_1 of the current area (consult $IFZ_{area}(i)$).
- a path with minimal total delay $\mathfrak{f} + \mathfrak{c}$ from b_1 over an arbitrary border node b_2 of the destination area on the net layer (consult $IFZ_{net}(b_1)$) to d (consult $IFZ_{area}(b_2)$).

Please note that only the border node b_1 in the current area is a *degree of freedom*, because the choice of the local border node determines a remote border node b_2 over that d is reachable with minimal delay. Thus, for each successor s considered, $|B(i)|$ path combinations are possible (assuming areas are strongly connected). First, for each possible path from i via $s \in S_r$ to d the accumulated delays $(\mathfrak{f}_s^j, \mathfrak{c}_s^j), 1 \le j \le |B(i)|$ are calculated:

$$(\mathfrak{f}_s^j, \mathfrak{c}_s^j) = IFZ_{area}(i, s, b_1^j) + IFZ_{net}(b_1^j, b_2^j) + IFZ_{area}(b_2^j, d), \qquad (2)$$

where $b_j^2 \in B(d)$ is the remote border node that lies on the minimal path to d.

Table 3. Number of nodes and edges

	Nodes	Edges
Physical Graph	3813	7570
Routing Graph	2112	5539
Net Graph	1519	1503
Com Graph	164	409

In total, there are $|S_r \cdot B(i)|$ delay tuples, namely one for each possible path of each successor $s \in S_r$. To normalize the total delay $\mathfrak{d}_s^j = \mathfrak{f}_s^j + \mathfrak{c}_s^j$, a quality $\hat{q}_s^j$ with respect to all paths is calculated:

$$\hat{q}_s^j = \frac{q_s^j}{\sum\limits_{m=1}^{|S_r|} \sum\limits_{k=1}^{|B(i)|} q_m^k} \tag{3}$$

The overall quality q_s for s is then defined as $\hat{q}_s = \sum_{j=1}^{|B(i)|} \hat{q}_s^j$.

In case 3 a similar procedure as in case 2 is applied. Possible paths also consists of two components, however, the representative node of the destination foraging region $FR(d)$ is used as a destination substitute:

- a path from i via s to a border node b of the current area (consult $IFZ_{area}(i)$).
- a path with minimal total delay $\mathfrak{f} + \mathfrak{c}$ from b to the representative node r of $FR(d)$ (consult $IFR_{net}(i)$).

Vehicles starting far away from their destinations are first routed according to routing case 3 and as they approach according to case 2 and finally case 1.

5   Simulation Studies

We compared BeeJamA's (BJA) performance against a dynamic shortest path algorithm, i.e. an online A* implementation with access to up-to-date traffic information from time to time (Dynamic Shortest Path, DynSP), similar to commercially available systems like TMC. Please note that such algorithms rely on global information and therefore suffer from scalability issues that limits in reality the covered area and/or update interval. Unrealistically, our DynSP implementation, however, gets weight updates on every edge in the network.

For the simulations which were performed on MATSim [9] we extracted a part of Shanghai (see Fig. 3a) from Open Street Map covering 23km×28km, featuring 2112 intersections and 5539 connecting road sections (see table 3). Fig. 3b depicts the resulting routing graph, Fig. 3c shows the grid used by BeeJamA as area structure. In this example, the length of a square grid box is $1500m$, resulting in 161 areas. In reality areas can get as large as a single navigator can manage it

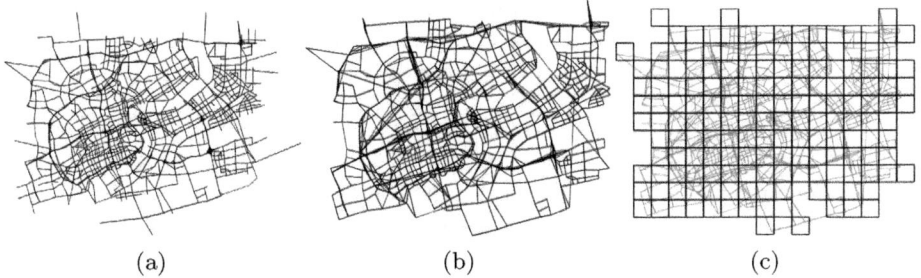

Fig. 3. Physical layer, routing layer and area layer graph

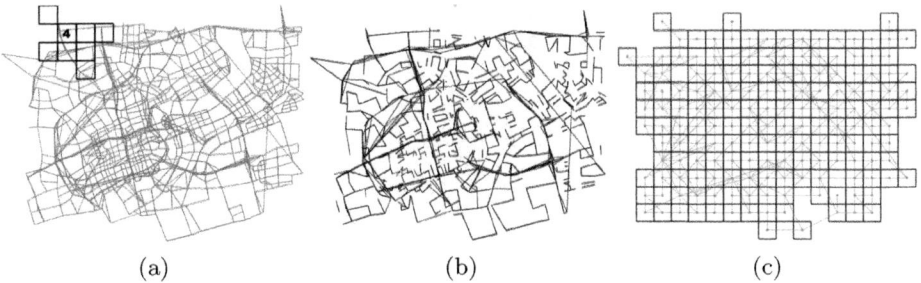

Fig. 4. Foraging zone of area 4, net layer and communication layer graph

computationally, here the rather small size highlights the protocol's scalability. Fig. 4a highlights the foraging zone of area 1. Finally, Fig. 4b shows the net layer (omitting intra-area edges) and Fig. 4c the communication layer.

We prepared two simulation setups. In the first we compare BeeJamA with DynSP with an update interval of 5min, i.e. the A* algorithm has every 5min access to updated edge weights. In the first five hours of simulation 60000 vehicles/hour are launched and the simulation then continues until all vehicles have arrived. The launching times, start and destinations are randomly chosen (evenly distributed), saved and reused in later simulations. We ran the simulations with penetration rates of 30% and 100%, where the remaining 70% in the first case equipped with a DynSP router with an 30min update interval. The travel times of all vehicles is accounted. The second setup consists of an scenario with 125.000 vehicles running an static shortest path algorithm as background traffic for creating partially jammed roads and an amount of 100.000 vehicles routed by an varying mix of BeeJamA and DynSP with an 30min update interval. In this scenario only the travel times of the dynamically routed vehicles are evaluated.

Tab. 4 and Fig. 5a presents the results for the first setup. The free flow time (FFT) distribution is a lower bound virtually impossible to achieve in reality since it assumes no interfering traffic at all. In queue-based simulations (like MATSim performs), however, the BeeJamA protocol is quite close to this lower bound. Under realistic circumstances this seems not likely to happen but at least

Table 4. Travel times (in minutes)

	1st Quartile	Median	Mean	3rd Quartile	Max
Free Flow Time	7.70	11.73	12.25	16.23	42.15
BeeJamA (100% pen. rate)	8.95	13.85	14.67	19.48	71.60
DynSP (5min update / 100% pen. rate)	11.65	21.00	26.43	35.93	196.80
BeeJamA (30% pen. rate)	20.98	58.58	94.96	148.80	564.10
DynSP (5min update / 30% pen. rate)	28.15	98.68	150.60	259.20	687.00

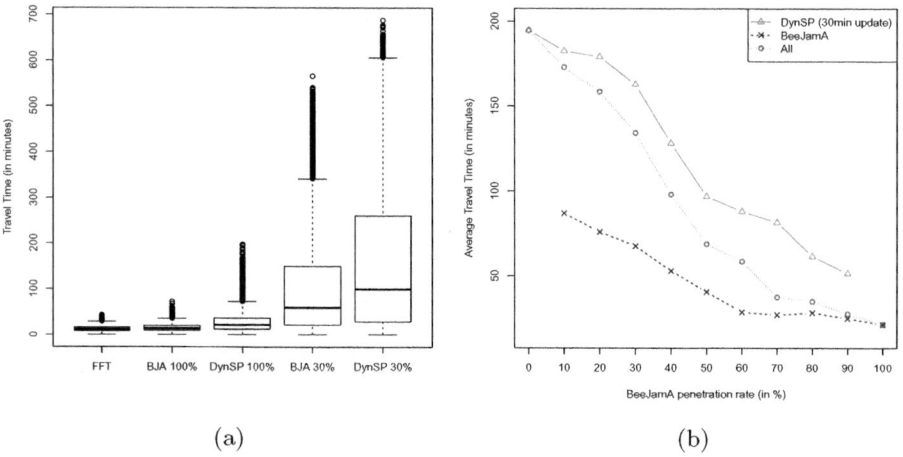

(a)   (b)

Fig. 5. Simulation results

there is a recognizable tendency in comparison to the DynSP results, e.g. the mean difference of the 100% simulations is about 12min. The results differ even more for the 30% simulations but it is obvious that maximum travel time of 687min in contrast to a maximum free flow travel time of about 42min is a simulation artifact due to necessary abstraction of the underlying traffic simulation model. Fig. 5b depicts the results of the second simulation setup. Once again there is clear tendency that 1) BeeJamA routed vehicles reach their destination faster (in average) and that 2) the travel times of accounted vehicles decrease as the penetration rate of BeeJamA increase.

6   Conclusion and Future Work

The distributed, self-adaptive BeeJamA routing protocol for minimizing travel times by avoiding traffic congestions has been presented. Simulation results indicate that the protocol is able to outperform dynamic shortest path approaches.

The main advantage of a distributed protocol is the (more or less) arbitrary high frequency of delay updates in large regions that centralized algorithms relying on global information cannot achieve easily. So, without any restriction to high-capacity roads - which is needed for any practical realization of a dynamic shortest path algorithm - BeeJamA is very flexible and sensitive to unexpectedly changing traffic patterns.

In order to get realistic insights beyond the necessary abstractions that traffic simulators depend on for the purpose of high efficiency, we have meanwhile started to run experiments such as reported here by operating the routing protocols through the generic routing framework on other simulators like SUMO [10]. Furthermore, due to the underlying BeeHive algorithm it is possible to extend BeeJamA to much larger traffic areas, and this can be done in a completely incremental fashion. This will all be subject to forthcoming publications.

Acknowledgements. This work was supported by the Deutsche Forschungs-gemeinschaft (DFG) under grants WE2816/10-1 and WE2816/8-1.

References

1. Rothengatter, W.: External costs of transport (2004),
   http://www.uic.org/html/environnement/cd_external/pages/
   introduction.html (last access at: February 03, 2012)
2. Wedde, H.F., Senge, S., et al.: Bee Inspired Online Vehicle Routing in Large Traffic Systems. In: Proc. of the Second Int. Conf. on Adaptive and Self-Adaptive Systems and Applications, IARIA, Lisbon, Portugal (2010)
3. Wedde, H.F., Senge, S., et al.: Towards Hybrid Simulation of Self-Organizing, Online Distributed Vehicle Routing in Large Traffic Systems. In: Proc. of the 7th ICNC Conf., Shanghai, China (2011)
4. Farooq, M.: Bee-Inspired Protocol Engineering - From Nature to Networks. Springer, Berlin (2009)
5. Claes, R., Holvoet, T., Weyns, D.: A Decentralized Approach for Anticipatory Vehicle Routing Using Delegate Multiagent Systems. Trans. on ITS 12(2) (2011)
6. Tatomir, B., Rothkrantz, L.J.M.: H-ABC: A scalable dynamic routing algorithm. In: Recent Advances in Artificial Life. World Scientific Publishing, Singapore (2005)
7. Faezipour, M., Nourani, M., Saeed, A., Addepalli, S.: Progress and Challenges in Intelligent Vehicle Area Networks. Communications of the ACM 55(2) (2012)
8. Kerner, B.S., et al.: Traffic State Detection with Floating Car Data in Road Networks. IEEE Intelligent Transportation Systems (2005)
9. MATSim - Multi-Agent Transport Simulation Toolkit, official homepage, http://www.matsim.org, (last access at: February 03, 2012)
10. SUMO - Simulation of Urban Mobility, official homepage, http://sumo.sf.net (last access February 03, 2012)

A Study on Predictive Performance of Regression-Based Effort Estimation Models Using Base Functional Components

Sousuke Amasaki and Tomoyuki Yokogawa

Department of Systems Engineering, Okayama Prefectural University
Soja, Okayama Japan 719–1197
{amasaki,t-yokoga}@cse.oka-pu.ac.jp

Abstract. Some study claim that Base Functional Components (BFCs) contributes to effort at different levels and thus using BFCs instead of Function Points (FP) is better for effort estimation. This study examined the claim with sound filtration and extra-sample error, which were lacked in the past study. As a result, we confirmed that BFCs-based modelings used in the past study was statistically inferior to a FP-based model. We also demonstrated that a BFCs-based model could become comparable to the FP-based model with suitable transformations for BFCs. The result contributes to understand the importance of transformations for BFCs.

Keywords: effort estimation, function points, regression models.

1 Introduction

Model-based effort estimation models have been studied well[7]. Size measure is considered as the most influential predictor for estimation. One criticism is that measuring size with a single measure such as Function Points (FP) and SLOC involves uncertainty[9]. In [2,3], the authors demonstrated that using Base Functional Components (BFCs) instead of FP, which are smaller components constituting FP, improved fitting of a regression-based effort estimation model. However, they did not validate the improvements with statistical test and in terms of predictive performance.

In this paper, we thus examined whether BFCs-based models can improve predictive performance. This paper provides the following insights: 1) All BFCs had significant contributions to effort, and 2) BFCs-based models could become comparable to the FP-based model with suitable transformations for BFCs.

2 Experiment Settings

2.1 Dataset

This study used the ISBSG R11 database[5] as same as [2] but we adopted different filtration process. Normalized Work Effort was used as effort in [2].

O. Dieste, A. Jedlitschka, and N. Juristo (Eds.): PROFES 2012, LNCS 7343, pp. 350–354, 2012.

Table 1. Filtration on the ISBSG R11 Database (based on [2,10])

Step Attribute	Filter	Excluded	Remaining
0 —	—	—	5052
1 Counting Approach	= IFPUG	1253	3799
2 Data Quality Rating	= {A|B}	185	3614
3 Quality Rating for Unadj. FP	= {A|B}	735	2879
4 BFC Types	≠ Empty	1397*	1482*
5 FP Standard All	≥ IFPUG 4	974	508
6 Summary Work Effort	= Normalized Work Effort	132	376
7 Resource Level	= 1	104	272
8 Language Type	≠ Empty	8	264
9 Development Platform	≠ Empty	5	259
10 BFC Types	$\sum$ BFCs > 0	23	236

*they were inverted in [2].

However, it is criticized in [10] because Normalized Work Effort may include estimated effort by ISBSG. We thus mixed filtrations in [2] and [10].

Table 1 shows our filtration criteria. We focused on projects adopting IFPUG Function Point Analysis (FPA)[6] as same as [2]. IFPUG FPA defines 5 BFC types: External Input (EI), External Output (EO), External Inquiry (EQ), Internal Logical File (ILF), and External Interface File (EIF). With step 6 and 7, we selected projects recording actual development team effort. We adopted 3 categorical attributes identified in [10] as candidate predictors: *Language Type*, *Development Type*, and *Development Platform*. We did not select subsets based on the same organization types as [2] because the subsets become too small.

The filtration reduced the number of projects from 5052 to 236. We then removed one apparent outlier. Eventually 235 projects were remained.

2.2 Effort Estimation Models Based on Linear Regression

While log-transformation is recommended for skewed effort and predictors[10], they were used as-is in [2]. We thus compared the four linear regression models:

$$\text{Effort} = \beta_0 + \beta_1\text{FP}, \tag{1}$$
$$\text{Effort} = \beta_0 + \beta_1\text{BFC}_1 \cdots + \beta_p\text{BFC}_p, \tag{2}$$
$$\log(\text{Effort}) = \beta_0 + \beta_1\log(\text{FP}), \tag{3}$$
$$\log(\text{Effort}) = \beta_0 + \beta_1\log(1+\text{BFC}_1) \cdots + \beta_p\log(1+\text{BFC}_p). \tag{4}$$

Here, categorical predictors are omitted for simplicity. We added 1 to BFCs so that log functions require a value more than 0.

As preparation, we examined significance of the three candidate categorical predictors with these models. As a result, we treated them as follows: 1) Merge Language types into 2 levels: 4GL and Other, 2) Merge Development platform types into 2 levels: Multi platform and Other, and 3) Drop Development types.

Table 2. The results of experiments

Model	adj.R^2	AIC	Dropped	MMRE	MMAE	PRED(25)	MABRE
(1)	0.37	3688	–	0.81	1806	0.29	13.96
(2)	0.38	3685	EI	0.82	1850	0.27	10.05
(3)	0.48	383	–	0.57	1658	0.34	3.19
(4)	0.47	390	–	0.61	1776	0.28	3.46

We also removed influential data points (outliers) based on Cook's distance[8] before our experiment. Eventually, 200 projects were remained in total.

2.3   Performance Measures

Performance measures for effort estimation models are based on the difference between estimate and actual effort [12,11]. We adopted the following definitions:

$$\text{MRE} = \frac{\|\text{Act} - \text{Est}\|}{\text{Act}}, \ \text{MAE} = \|\text{Act} - \text{Est}\|, \text{ and } \text{ABRE} = \frac{\|\text{Act} - \text{Est}\|}{\min(\text{Est}, \text{Act})}.$$

The performance measures we used are: MMRE, PRED(25), MMAE, and MABRE. MMRE and MMAE are arithmetic means of MREs and MAEs, respectively. PRED(25) is a percentage of estimates with MREs being smaller than 0.25. MABRE is an arithmetic mean of absolute value of ABREs. Some effort estimation models we evaluated may estimate an negative effort. We thus used absolute value so as to avoid spuriously good results.

2.4   Experiment Procedure

In this study, we first evaluated *in-sample error*[4] with adjusted R^2 and AIC as same as [2,3]. Predictors were selected by stepwise regression. Next, we evaluated *extra-sample error*[4] with cross-validation (CV) and the performance measures. Extra-sample error is based on predictive performance for future or unseen projects. We adopted 10×10-fold CV followed with t-test as evaluation procedure in order to avoid inflated Type I error[1].

3   Results

Table 2 shows results of the experiments. In contrast to [2,3], all BFCs were remained in almost all models and FP-based and BFCs-based modelings showed comparable performance regarding R^2, AIC. It was also found that using log-transformation was effective for improving performance measures. According to p values of statistical comparisons for performance measures, the improvement with log-transformation was significantly effective in most performance measures with significance level at $\alpha = 0.01$.

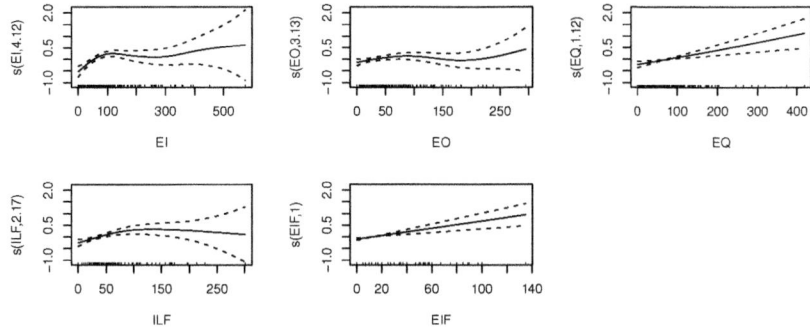

Fig. 1. Relationships between effort and BFCs by GAM

The performance measures indicates comparable performance of BFCs-based models to FP-based models. In fact, statistical tests revealed that BFCs-based models were significantly lesser or insignificantly different than the FP-based model with log-transformation. These results are contrasting to [2,3].

4 Discussion

Our experiment revealed that all BFCs had contributions to effort in the BFCs-based models. The experiment also revealed that the BFCs-based models were significantly inferior to the FP-based model with log-transformation.

While we confirmed log-transformation improves performance, it is still unclear what trasformations on each BFCs are effective. We thus examined effective transformations by using *Generalized Additive Models (GAM)*. GAM is used to identify and characterize nonlinear regression effects[4].

Figure 1 shows relationships between effort and BFCs. X-axis represents BFC values and Y-axis represents standardized values of an estimated function for corresponding BFC values. From this figure, we developed the following model:

$$\log\left(\text{Effort}\right) = \beta_0 + \beta_1 \log\left(1 + \text{EI}\right) + \beta_2 \text{EO} + \beta_3 \log\left(1 + \text{EQ}\right)$$
$$+\beta_4 \log\left(1 + \text{ILF}\right) + \beta_5 \text{EIF}. \tag{5}$$

Table 3 shows results of the same experiment on Model (5). All BFCs were also statistically significant in contrast to [2,3]. All figures became closer to those of the best FP-based model in Table 2. In fact, the results of statistical test show no significant difference between Model (5) and Model (4) while Model (5) became statistically better than Model (3). Thus, we concluded that selected transformations were more effective than log-transformation for all BFCs.

We also examined the numbers that Model (5) was better than Model (3) in 100 folds of 10×10 CV regarding performance measures. The numbers suggests that Model (5) was slightly better than Model (4) in all performance measures. This suggests that BFCs-based model might become superior when dataset is collected from a more specific domain or an organization as well as [2,3].

Table 3. The performance results for improved BFCs-based modeling

Model	adj.R^2	AIC	Dropped	MMRE	MMAE	PRED(25)	MABRE
(5)	0.50	377	–	0.56	1664	0.34	3.14

5 Conclusion

This study revealed that all BFCs had significant contribution on effort and a BFCs-based model could become comparable to the conventional FP-based model with suitable transformations for BFCs. We also demonstrated that the improved BFCs-based model may have superior performance though there was no statistical significance. Further study on a specific domain is needed.

References

1. Bouckaert, R.R.: Choosing between two learning algorithms based on calibrated tests. In: Proc. of ICML 2003, pp. 51–58 (2003)
2. Buglione, L., Gencel, C.: The significance of ifpug base functionality types in effort estimation: An empirical study. In: Proc. of ISMA5 2010 (2010)
3. Ferrucci, F., Gravino, C., Buglione, L.: Estimating web application development effort using cosmic: Impact of the base functional component types. In: Proc. of Smef 2010 (2010)
4. Hastie, T., Tibshirani, R., Friedman, J.: The Elements of Statistical learning: Data Mining, Inference, and Prediction. Springer (2009)
5. International Software Benchmarking Standards Group (ISBSG): ISBSG estimating, benchmarking and research suite release 11 (2004)
6. ISO: ISO/IEC 20926: Software Engineering – IFPUG 4.1 Unadjusted functional size measurement method – Counting practices manual. ISO (2003)
7. Jørgensen, M., Shepperd, M.: A systematic review of software development cost estimation studies. IEEE Trans. Softw. Eng. 33(1), 33–53 (2007)
8. Maxwell, K.D.: Applied Statistics for Software Managers. Prentice Hall, Inc. (2002)
9. McConell, S.: Software Estimation: Demystifying the Black Art. Microsoft Press (2006)
10. Mendes, E., Lokan, C.: Replicating studies on cross- vs single-company effort models using the isbsg database. Empirical Software Engineering 13(1), 3–37 (2008)
11. Miyazaki, Y., Takanou, A., Nozaki, H., Nakagawa, N., Okada, K.: Method to estimate parameter values in software prediction models. Information and Software Technology 33(3), 239–243 (1991)
12. Port, D., Korte, M.: Comparative studies of the model evaluation criterions MMRE and PRED in software cost estimation research. In: Proc. of ESEM 2008 (2008)

Managing Process Model Compliance in Multi-standard Scenarios Using a Tool-Supported Approach

Martin Kowalczyk and Silke Steinbach

Fraunhofer IESE Kaiserslautern, Germany
{martin.kowalczyk,silke.steinbach}@iese.fraunhofer.de

Abstract. The increasing number of standards and requirements makes compliance management in software organizations complex, time-consuming, and costly. This paper describes a tool-based approach for systematic compliance management and initial evaluation results for the suggested approach.

Keywords: Software Process Management, Process Model Maintenance, Compliance Management.

1   Introduction

Nowadays organizations must increasingly deal with multi-standard scenarios in which their software processes have to comply with a multitude of requirements from different international and national standards. These include general software development standards (e.g., ISO/IEC 12207 or ISO/IEC 15504) and standards dealing with more specific topics (e.g., IEC 61508 or ISO 26262 for functional safety). In mature safety- and security-critical domains, organizations typically have to comply with several such standards. Process guides, which document an organization's process models, must fulfill requirements that are demanded by external standards.

We focus on the creation and maintenance of compliance between process guides and standards in multi-standard scenarios. This is a major challenge and is becoming increasingly cost-intensive due to the growing number of standards [1]. This situation is aggravated by the fact that usually only experienced process engineers in an organization are assigned the task of compliance management, as they know the most about processes. This creates a bottle-neck with respect to resource availability and finally leads to situations in which compliance management is neglected. If compliance management is not performed systematically, compliance erosion is likely to happen. This means that over the course of time, the compliance of an organization's process model will decrease, which is often observed in industrial practice [2]. There are two main reasons that lead to compliance erosion:

- External standard(s) change, e.g., due to an update of the respective standard(s), but these changes are not reflected within the organization's process guide(s).
- The organization makes changes to its process model(s) or guide(s), but these changes are not in line with several requirements from all the standards the organization has to comply with.

O. Dieste, A. Jedlitschka, and N. Juristo (Eds.): PROFES 2012, LNCS 7343, pp. 355–360, 2012.
© Springer-Verlag Berlin Heidelberg 2012

This paper suggests a systematic, tool-based approach for compliance management in multi-standard scenarios that aims at improving the efficiency and effectiveness of compliance management. An additional goal is to reduce the involvement of experienced process experts by making it possible to assign routine compliance management tasks to less experienced process engineers.

In the following, Section 2 presents related work. Section 3 gives an overview of the approach. Section 4 presents the evaluation approach and initial results. Finally, Section 5 provides a summary and an outlook on future work.

2   Related Work

The challenge of working with multiple standards or process models has been reported by several authors (e.g., [1, 2]). The current approach for managing multi-standard scenarios is to reduce complexity by harmonizing related standards into consistent lists of requirements by comparing the respective standards and consolidating their requirements by removing redundancies. This approach is particularly beneficial when the targeted standards are quite similar. In such cases, large overlapping leads to a reduction of redundancies. In situations that are characterized by heterogeneous standards, a pure harmonization strategy will only have limited benefits. Typically, organizations need to consider standards from different domains, which consequently only have a limited number of redundancies. In these cases, the reduction of complexity that can be achieved through harmonization is limited.

The approach described in this paper is based on the work presented in [3] for tracing process model evolution and focuses on working with multiple standards. It can complement harmonization by using harmonized sets of requirements as one type of input for compliance management.

3   Compliance Management Approach

The overall compliance management approach consists of two phases, a specification phase and a maintenance phase. In the specification phase, compliance relations are defined and compliance is initially evaluated using the provided tool support (PET). This tool support focuses on scenarios that use word-based process descriptions, which are still very common in industrial practice. In the maintenance phase, compliance can be managed systematically for three maintenance scenarios by using this tool support (PET). The addressed scenarios encompass (S1) standard change, (S2) ad-hoc process guide change, and (S3) planned process guide change.

3.1   Specification Phase

In order to obtain trustable results, the specification phase must be performed or supervised by a process expert. During this phase, three activities can be distinguished:

1. **Define requirements set:** The process engineer defines the relevant set of standards that he would like to address. From these standards he needs to elicit the respective requirements and document them in requirements lists.
2. **Specify compliance relations:** The process engineer performs a section-wise analysis of the organization's process guide with respect to his defined sets of requirements and specifies compliance relations. Each relation specifies the related standard, requirement id, influence (positive, negative, neutral), and whether the relation is sufficient or supporting with respect to compliance. These requirements relations are documented in a table using the XML format, which can also be read by a standard word processing program. Our tool support provides a template for these tables that can be easily added to a word-based process guide.
3. **Perform initial analysis:** The requirements lists and the process guide document with the specified compliance relations are imported into the tool and an initial compliance analysis is performed. The tool evaluates all relationships and provides tabular and graphical compliance analysis results. In particular, the results of the initial analysis contain a list of candidates that need further manual compliance re-evaluation. The tool supports the process engineer during these re-evaluations.

The finalization of the initial analysis updates the overall set of compliance relations and closes the specification phase. Subsequently, the tool can be used for compliance management and tasks can be handed over to less experienced engineers.

3.2   Maintenance Phase

The maintenance phase addresses the three maintenance scenarios (S1) standard change, (S2) ad-hoc process guide change, and (S3) planned process guide change. For each of these scenarios, the following activities need to be performed:

1. **Identify changes:** In all three scenarios, changes occur that need to be identified. In (S1), the updated standard needs to be analyzed with respect to changes in requirements. In (S2) and (S3), the relevant sections of the process guide in which changes have been performed (S2) or will be performed (S3) need to be identified.
2. **Analyze change impact:** Tool support is used to identify the impact of the changes. Using the tool in (S1) provides those process guide sections that are impacted by requirements changes. Subsequently, the previously defined list of requirements can be updated to reflect changed, added, or removed requirements. Using the tool in (S2) and (S3) helps to identify the requirements that are in the scope of a process guide change. In (S2), the change has already been performed and the tool provides the possibility to identify the impact of such changes. In (S3), this impact analysis is performed upfront and can therefore be part of the rationale for process changes.
3. **Update compliance relations:** Compliance relations that are impacted by a change of a standard (S1) or a process guide (S2) need to be updated. Additionally, cases in which new relations need to be specified can be identified easily by using the analysis capabilities of the tool, as it provides a checklist of missing relations.

These three maintenance phase activities allow managing standard compliance systematically. If a new standard or process guide is to be included in the existing set, the overall process starts again with the specification phase.

4   Evaluation

4.1   Evaluation Approach

The purpose of the evaluation was to find out if the suggested tool-based approach provides the expected benefits with respect to efficiency, effectiveness, and suitability for novices. The object of the evaluation was the tool support (PET) for compliance management in scenarios that deal with changes (compare S1-S3).

The experimental design focused on three hypotheses:

H1 (efficiency): The identification of changes is more efficient when using PET than paper-based identification of changes. Efficiency is measured by how much time is needed to identify changes.

H2 (effectiveness): The identification of changes is more effective when using PET than paper-based identification. This means that if PET is used, more corresponding sections will be found. Effectiveness is measured by checking the completeness and correctness of the task results compared to a sample solution.

H3 (suitability for novices): PET is also suitable for novices, not only for experts who are very familiar with specific standards and norms, because it is easy to use and provides correct results. Suitability for novices is evaluated by means of the effects concerning efficiency and effectiveness. Additionally, the ease of use of PET was evaluated based on the Technology Acceptance Model (TAM) [4].

The design consisted of a comparing paper-based and tool-based task performance, followed by a questionnaire and a semi-structured interview. The current sample consisted of two experts (senior process engineers) and two novices (computer science students). We plan to replicate this evaluation.

4.2   Evaluation Procedure

The evaluation was conducted at our institute and the subjects worked on their assignments during the same time. At the beginning, all subjects were informed about the evaluation procedure and received the materials (one standard for functional safety and one document referring to that standard). After a reading period (approx. two hours), the subjects were given twelve tasks (six paper-based and six tool-based). The assigned tasks varied in the level of difficulty in order to differentiate the complexity of the changes (Task level A: Only one change in one section; Task level B: Several changes in one section; Task level C: Several changes in several sections) The subjects had to identify all relevant sections of the referring document possibly requiring correction in order to maintain conformance between both documents. First they had to perform the paper-based tasks, then the tool-based tasks.

4.3   Evaluation Results

H1 (efficiency): Comparison of the task durations for each task level shows a clear difference between the paper-based and the tool-based tasks (see Fig. 1). Particularly evident is the difference on task level C. On average, experts and novices needed 12.9 minutes to find all matching sections. Using PET helped to reduce task performance time for all tasks to less than 1.5 minutes.

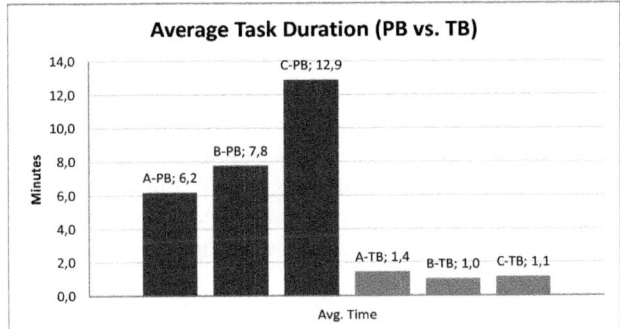

	A-PB	A-TB
Expert	4,7	1,0
Novice	7,7	1,8
	B-PB	B-TB
Expert	5,5	1,0
Novice	10,0	1,0
	C-PB	C-TB
Expert	6,8	1,0
Novice	19,0	1,3

Fig. 1. Comparison of task durations: Total averages (left) vs. expert-level averages (right)

H2 (effectiveness): Neither the experts nor the novices found all matches in the paper-based task fulfillment (see Fig. 2, left). The higher the task level, the lower the matching rate. The experts found only 50% of all correct matches on the A and B levels, while the novices found no correct matches on the C level. Using the PET tool helped to nearly achieve 100% completeness and correctness on the A and B levels (except for the novices achieving only 83.3% on the A level). Both, experts and novices achieved 75% correctness and completeness on the C level (see Fig. 2, right).

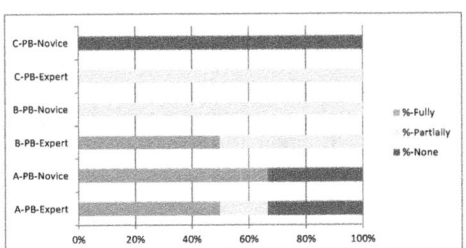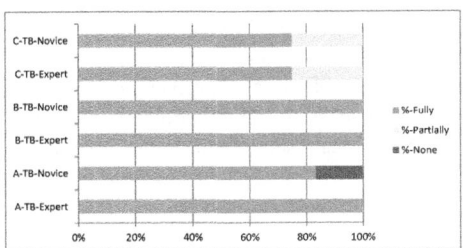

Fig. 2. Identified changes: Paper-based (left) vs. tool-based (right)

H3 (suitability for novices): As already shown, the results of the experts and the novices achieved higher correctness and completeness when using PET. Both experts and novices benefitted from time savings (see Fig. 1). The novices saved even more time as it took them longer to identify changes without tool support (see Fig. 1, right).

The analysis of the TAM questionnaire shows very good results in all four dimensions (ease of use: 4.25, perceived usefulness: 5, attitude towards using: 4.75, and intention to use: 3.75).

As part of the qualitative feedback, the experts and novices rated the overall performance of PET as "very good" (3x) and "good" (1x). In their opinion, PET supports the identification of changes very well. The actual change to maintain compliance still has to be done by an expert. Nevertheless, the experts expect a total efficiency gain of 20-30% on the complete maintenance activity. All subjects trusted the results because the upfront modeling of relations had been done by a domain expert.

5   Summary and Outlook

This paper presented a tool-supported approach for systematic management of process model compliance in multi-standard scenarios. This approach is part of ongoing research work and the results of an initial empirical evaluation have been presented. These preliminary results show that the tool supports experts and even novices in identifying changes in reference documents very efficiently and very effectively. Based on our results from the current development and evaluation, further research work and developments are planned.

Acknowledgment. This work was supported by the German Federal Ministry of Education and Research (BMBF) (grant number 01IS09049B).

References

1. Baldassarre, M.T., Caivano, D., Pino, F.J., Piattini, M., Visaggio, G.: Harmonization of ISO/IEC 9001:2000 and CMMI-DEV: from a theoretical comparison to a real case application. Software Quality Journal (July 2011)
2. Siviy, J., Kirwan, P., Marino, L., Morley, J.: The value of harmonization multiple improvement technologies: A process improvement professional's view. Software Engineering Institute Carnegie Mellon (2008)
3. Armbrust, O., Ocampo, A., Soto, M.: Tracing Process Model Evolution: A Semi-Formal Process Modeling Approach. In: Proc. ECMDA Traceability Workshop (November 2005)
4. Venkatesh, V., Davis, F.D.: A theoretical extension of the technology acceptance model: Four longitudinal field studies. Management Science 46(2) (2000)

Towards a Framework to Evaluate and Improve the Quality of Implementation of CMMI® Practices[*]

Isabel Lopes Margarido[1,**], João Pascoal Faria[1],
Raul Moreira Vidal[1], and Marco Vieira[2]

[1] Faculty of Engineering, University of Porto, Portugal
{isabel.margarido,jpf,rmvidal}@fe.up.pt
[2] Faculty of Sciences and Technology, University of Coimbra, Portugal
mvieira@dei.uc.pt

Abstract. CMMI practices can be poorly implemented leading to weak performance gain. SCAMPI verifies model compliance but not performance. Hence, a framework to evaluate the quality of implementation of each practice, based on compliance and performance results, will prevent poor implementation, locate and fix problems, and ultimately achieve better results. In this paper we propose such a framework, based on a combination of leading and lagging indicators measuring compliance, efficiency and efficacy.

Keywords: Capability Maturity Model Integration, Measurement, Performance Indicators, Quality of Implementation, Software Process Improvement.

1 Introduction

Capability Maturity Model Integration® (CMMI®) is a process improvement model of products and services, composed of 5 maturity levels (ML) achieved via implementation of the specific and generic goals of that ML and all the preceding ones. To satisfy a goal the generic and specific practices or acceptable alternatives to them need to be fulfilled [1]. Organisations that implement CMMI typically improve their performance in terms of predictability, productivity and product quality. Consequently, processes become more predictable and customer satisfaction increases [2]. However, not all organisations have the same performance results; this depends not only on the business context, projects and team but also on the methodologies used in implementation of the model. In a study presented in [3], organisations using the Team Software Process[SM] (TSP[SM]) achieved better product quality performance than the average of organisations appraised as CMM® (Capability Maturity Model®) level 5. There is more variance in performance results when using CMMI, as it is a generic model telling what to do but not how to do it. When using a prescriptive process like TSP, results are more predictable.

---

[*] Work partially funded by Fundação para a Ciência e a Tecnologia (FCT): Programa Operacional Potencial Humano (POPH) of QREN, and Fundo Social Europeu (FSE).
[**] Corresponding author.

O. Dieste, A. Jedlitschka, and N. Juristo (Eds.): PROFES 2012, LNCS 7343, pp. 361–365, 2012.
© Springer-Verlag Berlin Heidelberg 2012

CMMI Version 1.3 emphasises improvements in organisations performance [1], i.e., it clarifies that organisations need to focus processes on business goals and implement performance improvements to achieve goals that are continuously evolving. The Standard CMMI Appraisal Method for Process Improvement^{SM} (SCAMPI^{SM}) appraises compliance of organisation processes, activities and outcomes with CMMI, however evaluating performance lies outwith its scope.

CMMI compliance is not a guarantee of good performance *per se*, i.e., there is high variance in performance results within a maturity level [4, 5]. There are several causes for this problem, in particular: **1)** Practices are not used organisation wide [7]; **2)** Poor, or highly varied, implementation of practices leading to multiple solutions results in a lack of clear impact on performance or project improvement [5]; **3)** Baselines quickly erode after achieving a certain maturity level [7]; **4)** Measurement problems, such as metrics uncorrelated and meaningless to upper management, being useless [9]; measures that are unrelated to customer and business objectives [6]; process performance baselines that are not applicable to all projects [7]. In conclusion, as Peterson stated, the big issue is CMMI implementation [5]. To help prevent these problems we propose a framework that provides a catalogue of performance metrics, mapped with CMMI practices and potential organisation goals, used to monitor CMMI implementation across the organisation and through time, to evaluate quality of implementation of CMMI practices and measure effects of process improvements. The framework is inspired by TSP, which is focused on performance results and defines quantitative criteria for process and product quality [8].

2   Framework Proposal

We present the proposed framework in the upper left corner of Fig.1, including its components and how organisations can apply it in practice. The framework is composed of a **metamodel**, shaping a **repository** of performance indicators, to evaluate the quality of implementation of CMMI practices, possibly dependent on the methods used to implement those practices. The performance indicators will be tailorable, defined as mandatory or optional, and will be mapped with profiles according to maturity level and methods of the organisation. Additionally, the framework includes **procedures** for setup (tailoring), use in practice and supporting choice of indicators. The framework is developed in two stages: the first is presented in this paper, defining structure, concepts and metamodel; the second is building a repository, calibrated with historical data, which will be object of our future research work.

In general, we propose to characterise the **quality of implementation** of a CMMI practice by a combination of **efficiency** and **efficacy** of implementation, on one hand, and **compliance** of implementation on the other (i.e., alignment with CMMI recommendations or with what is prescribed by the concrete implementation method used), all measured by appropriate **performance indicators** (PI), possibly dependent on the practice and implementation method used. By considering these three quality characteristics, we are looking both at **how** the work is done and **what** its performance results are. For instance, assume we want to evaluate the quality of implementation of specific practice "SP2.2 Conduct Peer Reviews" of the Verification process area. Assume that

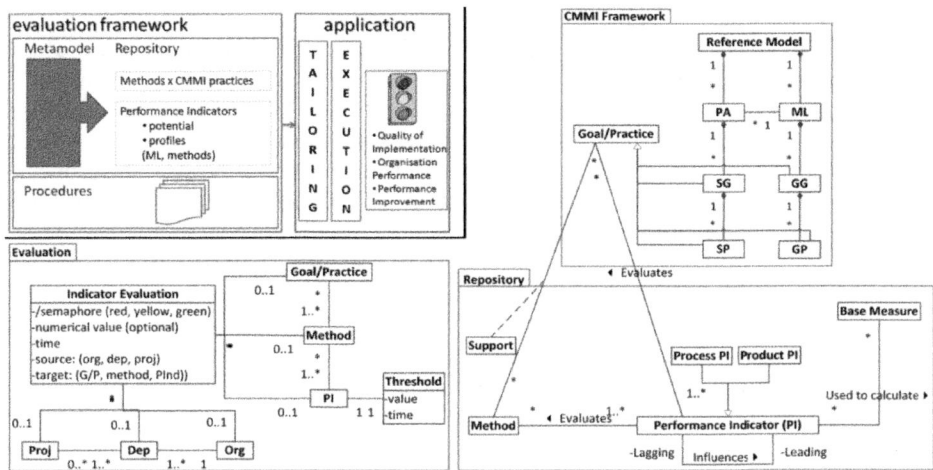

Fig. 1. Framework structure and metamodel: org-organisation, dep-department, proj-project [7]

reviewing follows two TSP guidelines: use checklists derived from historical data, and review at a moderate pace. Here, one can measure efficacy by *review yield* (percentage of defects detected), efficiency by *defect detection rate* (defects detected per hour), and compliance by *checklist usage* (a qualitative PI with values, *not used, had-hoc checklist*, and *checklist derived from historical data*) and *review rate* (size reviewed per hour), compared with some recommended values.

A rich set of PI usually combines **process** and **product** indicators, and **leading** and **lagging** indicators. In the given example, *review yield* is a **lagging performance indicator**, as the remaining defects can only be known *a posteriori*. Compliance indicators are often **leading indicators**; they influence and can be used to predict and control the values of lagging indicators. In the example, *review rate* is commonly considered a leading indicator of the *review yield* in TSP literature. The *density of defects* found in a review is a **product performance indicator**, whilst the *review rate* is clearly a **process performance indicator**. To evaluate the quality of implementation of methods and CMMI practices, organisation data is analysed through **indicators evaluation**. For that, PI are collected (normally in projects), at a given **time**, and their **numerical value** is compared with a **threshold**. Thresholds have different levels, used to determine the PI **semaphore** colour (red, yellow, green), established according with the organisation quantitative business goals and processes baselines, and define its normal behaviour regarding a PI.

There are three dimensions of aggregation of evaluation results: time, target and source. Aggregation in **time** is done by analysing organisation data in a selected period, given the methods and thresholds at that moment. The **target** of the evaluation can be a PI, a method or a CMMI practice. For each method it may be necessary to monitor one or more PI. A method is evaluated through a semaphore, whose colour is given by the analysis of the PI semaphores. For that reason **numerical value** is optional and **semaphore** is mandatory. Since we map methods with CMMI practices, the aggregation of the evaluation of each method used (mandatory, alternative or optional) gives the semaphore colour of the practices. The **source** of the evaluation can be: a **project**, evaluated by aggregating PI evaluation; a **department**, evaluated by aggregating its projects' evaluation; or the entire **organisation**, evaluated by aggregating its departments' evaluation. Aggregation at organisation level indicates the degree of institutionalisation of the practices necessary to achieve generic goals and high maturity, and consequently allow their evaluation. A project, department or organisation can also use target aggregation to evaluate a method or a CMMI goal/practice. The evaluation by aggregation of colours is done as follows: green – all green; yellow – at least one yellow and no reds; red – at least one red. We are aware that results aggregation can be more complex.

To find the adequate PI to populate the framework repository, we will undertake bibliographical research and analyse industry data. The value of a PI (e.g. *effort estimation error*) is influenced by two parcels: one is related to process (e.g. *estimate effort*) definition and execution, comprised of **controllable factors** (e.g. *size, historical data*); the other is comprised of **non-controllable factors**, related to project execution and other environment, complexity and context variables (e.g. *change requests, complexity*). Controllable factors (leading indicators) can be used to improve PI in advance. By experiment we will analyse organisations data to determine the percentage of each one of these parcels, to know the percentage of the PI value which may be influenced in advance. We will also analyse effects of individual controllable factors, determine recommended values for each one of them and consequently guarantee that implementation of CMMI practices leads to better performance. This step of the research is under development. For calibration we will use different organisations projects data and, when completed, the framework will be tested in an organisation.

3   Related Work

There are several frameworks to evaluate success factors in metrics programs [9] and in Software Process Improvements (SPI) [10]. The analysed success factors are related to the way SPI is done, and not to improving processes outputs. There are object-oriented models [11] and metamodels that can be used to develop measurement repositories [12, 13], which can also be aligned with CMMI [11, 14-16] and shape processes [15, 16]. Similar metamodels can be useful to unambiguously define PI. [13] describes a framework to measure processes based on their structure and relations. In our research, when measuring a practice we are focused not only on compliance but also on its efficacy and efficiency. In addition, there are tools to collect and align SCAMPI evidences. [17] proposed a method introducing quality metrics to evaluate SCAMPI, but does not evaluate how CMMI practices are implemented or organisation performance. [18] designed an evidence repository to assess projects activities by number of executions. Nonetheless, it is possible that an evidence is generated but empty, showing that the activity was not performed.

In the case of our framework, the primary evaluation criterion is not the way process improvement implementation is done, but the value, i.e. the outcome for the organisation, of the goal/practice itself. For that we need to understand what the advantage of using it is and whether the organisation benefits from it or not.

4   Conclusion

The proposed framework shall support organisations to: 1) implement CMMI by providing a pool of methods, aligned with practices, and performance indicators to monitor them; 2) choose methods for their adequacy and performance in context; 3) evaluate quality of implementation of CMMI practices early; 4) monitor process performance to act before problems occur; 5) anticipate impact of process changes on performance indicators; 6) understand, more accurately, causes of problems; 7) prioritise performance improvements. SEI will be able to assess performance improvements from one appraisal to the next. Aggregation is particularly relevant to evaluate Generic Goals and High Maturity Levels and performance indicators are useful to evaluate quality of implementation.

References

1. Chrissis, M.B., Konrad, M., Shrum, S.: CMMI for Development: Guidelines for Process Integration and Product Improvement. Addison-Wesley, Massachusetts (2011)
2. Goldenson, D.R., Gibson, D.L., Ferguson, R.W.: Why Make the Switch? Evidence about the Benefits of CMMI. In: SEPG 2004. CMU/SEI (2004)
3. Davis, N., Mullaney, J.: The Team Software Process^{SM} (TSP^{SM}) in Practice: A Summary of Recent Results. Technical Report, CMU/SEI, 105 (2003)
4. Radice, R.: Statistical Process Control in Level 4 and Level 5 Software Organizations Worldwide. In: Software Technology Conference. CMU/SEI (2000)
5. CMU/SEI: Accelerated Improvement Method (AIM). Technical Report, CMU/SEI (2010)
6. Leeson, P.: Why the CMMI® does not work. In: SEPG Europe. CMU/SEI, Prague (2009)
7. Lopes Margarido, I., Faria, J.P., Vieira, M., Moreira Vidal, R.: CMMI Practices: Evaluating the Quality of the Implementation. In: SEPG Europe. CMU/SEI, Dublin (2011)
8. Humphrey, W.S.: Introduction to the Team Software Process^{SM}. Addison Wesley (2010)
9. Jeffery, R., Berry, M.: A framework for evaluation and prediction of metrics program success. In: Software Metrics Symposium (1993)
10. Niazi, M., Wilson, D., Zowghi, D.: A maturity model for the implementation of software process improvement: an empirical study. J. Syst. Softw. 74(2), 155–172 (2005)
11. Palza, E., Fuhrman, C., Abran, A.: Establishing a generic and multidimensional measurement repository in CMMI context. In: SW Engineering Workshop (2003)
12. Goulão, M.: Component-Based Software Engineering: a Quantitative Approach. Ph.D. Thesis. Departamento de Informática, FCT/UNL (2008)
13. García, F., Ruiz, F., Cruz, J.A., Piattini, M.: Integrated Measurement for the Evaluation and Improvement of Software Processes. In: Oquendo, F., et al. (eds.) EWSPT 2003. LNCS, vol. 2786, pp. 94–111. Springer, Heidelberg (2003)
14. Colombo, A., et al.: The Use of a Meta-Model to Support Multi-Project Process Measurement. In: 15th Asia-Pacific Software Engineering Conference, APSEC (2008)
15. Hsueh, N.-L., et al.: Applying UML and software simulation for process definition, verification, and validation. Inf. Softw. Technol. 50(9-10), 897–911 (2008)
16. Mishra, S., Schlingloff, B.H.: Compliance of CMMI Process Area with Specification Based Development. In: SERA. SERA (2008)
17. Pricope, S., Lichter, H.: Towards a Systematic Metric Based Approach to Evaluate SCAMPI Appraisals. In: Bomarius, F., Oivo, M., Jaring, P., Abrahamsson, P. (eds.) PROFES 2009. LNBIP, vol. 32, pp. 261–274. Springer, Heidelberg (2009)
18. Sunetnanta, T., Nobprapai, N.-O., Gotel, O.: Quantitative CMMI Assessment for Offshoring through the Analysis of Project Management Repositories. In: Gotel, O., Joseph, M., Meyer, B. (eds.) SEAFOOD 2009. LNBIP, vol. 35, pp. 32–44. Springer, Heidelberg (2009)

INTEAMSE 2012
1ˢᵗ Workshop on Managing the Influence of People and Team Factors in SE

Silvia Teresita Acuña Castillo, Marta Gómez, and Kostadin Koroutchev

1 Description and Goals

Software engineering (SE) studies software development principles, processes, methods and tools. SE is based not on well-grounded scientific principles but on a compendium of disciplines that are refined and evolved through application into a body of knowledge. Nowadays, key software development issues are primarily concerned not with techniques but with sociological aspects and human nature. More importantly, people play a major role as sources of information, activity performers and product users.

Human aspects have been studied in different fields of SE. Analysed topics tend to overlap (e.g., quite a lot of research has addressed the expert/novice or introverted/extroverted dichotomy or teams in agile/heavy processes). However, results have not been disseminated outside their respective area.

Understanding what influence human and social issues have on the performance of a set of activities related to software development can improve the quality of the software process and product. It can also be beneficial for the team of professionals building the software, increasing their satisfaction with teamwork. Learning more about these issues can be helpful for selecting people to form work teams. This will improve the formation and maintenance of more effective teams.

This workshop specifically calls for the discussion of human and social aspects that have an impact on software development. Our position is that human factors are a single research field applicable across the board. The overall goal of the workshop is for people from one field to learn about methods and results from others, leading to productive feedback.

2 List of Topics

Submissions should examine the influence of the following factors on the development process (regarding development, management or support processes):

1. Personality factors (extroversion, conscientiousness, neuroticism...)
2. Soft skills (teamwork, cooperation, negotiation, team leadership competencies...)
3. Group processes (conflict, communication, cohesion, work climate...)
4. Cultural factors (beliefs, values, preferences...)
5. Social issues (rules, organisational stress level, reward structure…)
6. Technical issues (experience, training, organizational competencies...)

O. Dieste, A. Jedlitschka, and N. Juristo (Eds.): PROFES 2012, LNCS 7343, pp. 366–367, 2012.
© Springer-Verlag Berlin Heidelberg 2012

3   Targeted Outcome and Targeted Audience

The primary goal of this workshop is to set up a forum to debate the influence of human and social factors on software development. To date, human factors research has been compartmentalized into separate communities concerned with different development issues. We believe that this slows down progress in this field, as there is no cross-pollination. We believe that effects could be consistent irrespective of development issues. We propose to bring everyone together to exchange opinions and improve research. Our aims are modest: set up a standing forum, an information community.

Human and social issues can be studied from many viewpoints. Some communities focus on issues of cooperation, communication or stakeholder participation levels (e.g., traditional vs. agile processes). Although these issues are within the scope of INTEAMSE, we are primarily concerned with the inherent characteristics of the people, groups and cultures participating in software development, such as personality types, conflicts or values, to name but three examples. We target aspects that are unchanging across projects, team types, development processes or even organizations. In other words, we are interested in the inherent characteristics of the people that develop software in order to discover factors that influence and are able to improve their activity.

4   Workshop Format

We plan for a half-day or day-long workshop. The workshop will be discussion-oriented. It will start with a keynote, followed by paper presentations, and end with a roundtable. All accepted papers will be published in paper and electronic proceedings with an ISBN code.

5   Workshop Organizers

- Silvia T. Acuña Castillo. Escuela Politécnica Superior. Universidad Autónoma de Madrid. E-mail: silvia.acunna@uam.es
- Marta Gomez Pérez. Escuela Politécnica Superior. Universidad San Pablo CEU de Madrid. E-mail: mgomez.eps@ceu.es
- Kostadin Koroutchev. Escuela Politécnica Superior. Universidad Autónoma de Madrid. E-mail: k.koroutchev@uam.es

6   Program Committee

- Emilia Mendes. College of Information Technology, Zayed University, UAE.
- Richard Torkar. Blekinge Institute of Technology, Sweden.
- Dietmar Pfahl. Faculty of Engineering, Lund University, Sweden.
- Marcela Fabiana Genero, Universidad de Castilla-La Mancha, Spain.
- Norsaremah Salleh. Department of Computer Science, International Islamic University Malaysia.

VALOIR 2012
2nd Workshop on Managing the Client Value Creation Process in Agile Projects: Message from the Chairs

Jennifer Pérez[1], Luigi Buglione[2], and Maya Daneva[3]

[1] Technical University of Madrid-UPM, Spain
jenifer.perez@eui.upm.es
[2] ETS / Engineering.IT SpA, Italy
luigi.buglione@eng.it
[3] University of Twente, Netherlands
m.daneva@utwente.nl

Welcome to the 2nd Workshop on Managing the Client Value Creation Process in Agile Projects (VALOIR) at the PROFES 2012 conference!

The overall goal of VALOIR is to make the knowledge on value creation and management explicit, encouraging the discussion on the use of measurement and estimation approaches in managing value in agile project.

Agile methodologists tacitly assume that for SE professionals it is self-evident to figure out how exactly the application of the agile practices would create product and business value on an ongoing basis throughout a project, but little has been done to systematically aggregate the empirical evidence that can possibly confirm or disconfirm the claims of how the different (commercially viable) agile approaches create client's value (both product and business value) and how some agile-unique practices (as on-site site clients, story point counting, reprioritization) solve particular value-creation challenges.

In particular, we'd like to stimulate an explicit discussion on uncovering the mechanisms through which combinations of agile practices create client's value in agile projects in specific contexts. We consider both product and business value. We promote the position that for the agile organizations to make a lasting impact on the product and business value creation, the interplay between organizational context and use of agile practices needs to be understood in sufficient depth so that the organizations know the challenges specific to value creation through agile practices in certain contexts and the remedies that are likely to confront these challenges.

This second VALOIR edition includes 6 papers that are accepted for presentations. Papers cover a broad range of issues, including portfolio management using a combination of QFD and functional size measurement (FSM) methods, agile quality management, a tailored SCRUM for agile architectures, using systematic literature review techniques for finding sources for value creation, analyzing the advantage in using standards in agile projects, the value brought out from proper people and knowledge management to agile (and non-agile) projects, each one describing a helpful piece of an interesting puzzle, useful for stimulating a wide discussion during the workshop.

O. Dieste, A. Jedlitschka, and N. Juristo (Eds.): PROFES 2012, LNCS 7343, pp. 368–369, 2012.
© Springer-Verlag Berlin Heidelberg 2012

In addition, our second edition of VALOIR features the keynote of Alan W. Brown as an opening session of the workshop. Alan W. Brown is an IBM Distinguished Engineer at IBM Rational Software, where his main responsibilities are to define product direction and consult with product teams to help clients improve software development efficiency and value.

Also, the workshop has organized a round table as a closing event. Our round table was moderated by Prof. Dr. Juan Garbajosa from the Technical University of Madrid. Juan Garbajosa is actively involved in agile research projects and in the agile community. A major line of research among his main research topics are agile methodologies and software product value.

We would like to thank all researchers and practitioners who helped us make this workshop possible. In particular, we are indebted to all members of the Program Committee for their valuable comments and suggestions to authors. We also thank the workshop Program Chair at PROFES 2012 Burak Turhan, and the PROFES conference organizers. Last but not least, we acknowledge the continual support of Oscar Dieste whose prompt responses made a difference to the workshop planning and publicity.

VALOIR 2012 Program Committee

Pekka Abrahamsson, Free University of Bolzano, Italy
Silvia Abrahao, Universitat Politècnica de València, Spain
Jutta Eckstein, IT Communications, Germany
Thomas Fehlmann, Euro Project Office, Switzerland
Juan Garbajosa, Technical University of Madrid, Spain
Cigdem Gencel, Free University of Bolzano, Italy
Smita Ghaisas, Tata Consulting Services, India
Andrea Herrmann, Infoman AG, Germany
Eric Knauss, University of Victoria, Canada
Michele Marchesi, FlossLab/University of Cagliari, Italy
Sandro Morasca, University of Insubria, Italy
Outi Salo, Nokia, Finnland
Darja Smite, Blekinge Institute of Technology, Sweden
Miroslaw Staron, University of Gotteborg, Sweden

Tutorial: Business IT Alignment
Using the GQM⁺Strategies® Approach

Jens Heidrich and Martin Kowalczyk

Fraunhofer IESE, Fraunhofer Platz 1, 67663 Kaiserslautern, Germany
{jens.heidrich,martin.kowalczyk}@iese.fraunhofer.de

Keywords: Alignment of business strategies and goals, goal-oriented measurement, quantitative management of business goals, decision-making.

1 Introduction

Most of today's products and services are software-based. Organizations that develop software want to maintain and improve their competitiveness by controlling software-related risks. To do this, they need to align their business goals with software development strategies and translate them into quantitative project management. There is also an increasing need to justify cost and resources for software and system development and other IT services by demonstrating their impact on an organization's higher-level goals. For both, linking business goals and software-related efforts in an organization is necessary. However, this is a challenging task, and there is a lack of methods addressing this gap.

The popular Goal Question Metric (GQM) approach has served the software industry well for several decades in defining measurement programs. However, it does not provide *explicit* support for motivating and integrating measurement at various levels of the organization. On the other hand, approaches such as Balanced Scorecard address mainly business-level goal-setting activities, and do not support the alignment of objectives at different levels of the organization with an integrated methodology. To fill this gap, we propose GQM⁺Strategies®: an integrated approach that is based on GQM and adds the capability to create measurement programs that ensure alignment between goals and strategies at different levels, from the highest strategic levels of the business to the level of individual development projects. The approach is based on rationales for deciding about options when operationalizing goals and for evaluating the success of strategies with respect to goals.

2 GQM⁺Strategies® Modeling Concepts

Modelling strategic measurement systems that link and control organizational goals and strategies across multiple organizational levels requires concepts for adequately representing organizational goals and strategies as well as concepts that support the definition of corresponding measurement models. The GQM⁺Strategies® conceptual model (see Fig. 1) addresses both aspects.

O. Dieste, A. Jedlitschka, and N. Juristo (Eds.): PROFES 2012, LNCS 7343, pp. 370–373, 2012.
© Springer-Verlag Berlin Heidelberg 2012

Goal⁺Strategies elements (see left side of Fig. 1) provide the capability to define linked sequences of goals and associated strategies. Strategies describe a planned and goal-oriented course of actions for achieving the defined goals at the respective organizational level. The conceptual model allows multiple goal levels and permits deriving multiple strategies for each of these goal levels. A goal may be realized by a set of strategies, which may in turn lead to a set of goals. Additionally, Goal⁺Strategies elements provide the capability to capture the underlying rationales for the defined goals, strategies, and their linkages using context factors and assumptions.

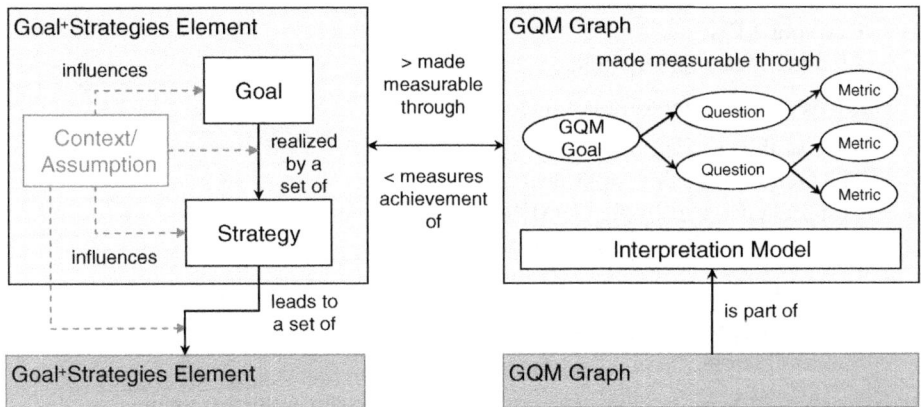

Fig. 1. GQM+Strategies® conceptual model

GQM⁺Strategies® provides support for defining measurement consistent with high-level organizational goals and for interpreting and rolling up the resulting measurement data at each level. For this purpose, the GQM approach is used, which constitutes the main element within the GQM graphs representing the measurement part of the conceptual GQM⁺Strategies® model (see right side of Fig. 1). A GQM graph consists of a GQM goal (that measures a Goal⁺Strategies element), corresponding questions, metrics, and additional interpretation models. At each goal level, such a GQM graph is modelled in order to measure the achievement of the defined goal in combination with the chosen strategy. Accordingly, the definition of a complete measurement plan includes the definition of GQM measurement goals, the derivation of questions and metrics, as well as the definition of an interpretation model that determines whether the measurement goal has been achieved.

3   Tutorial Contents and Organization

The tutorial will illustrate the GQM⁺Strategies® approach using practical examples from industry, present related approaches, and provide practical exercises on how to actually apply the method. The tutorial will focus on the following topics in detail:

- Introduction
  - What is measurement?
  - Related Standards (ISO/IEC 15939, 15504)
  - Process KPIs (IEEE 1045)
  - Product KPIs (ISO/IEC 9126, 14598, 25000)
- Basics of goal-oriented measurement
  - Typical problems in setting up KPI systems
  - The GQM approach
  - Determining measurement goals
  - Deriving KPIs
  - Creating measurement plans
- KPI-based monitoring of goals and strategies
  - State of the practice
  - The GQM$^+$Strategies® approach
  - Comprehensive example GQM$^+$Strategies® model
  - Related Work: BSC, SixSigma, and COBIT
- Conclusion
  - Costs and benefits of KPI systems
  - Success factors

Participants will learn how to apply the basic approach as part of practical exercises. This includes the following activities:

- Modeling and structuring of goals and corresponding strategies across different levels of an organization.
- Mapping goals and strategies to concrete metrics and indicators.
- Integrating measurement programs into the organization.
- Assessing the efficiency of strategies with respect to achieving goals.

The tutorial is planned for one day. The ideal number of participants is between 10 and 20; to ensure good discussions, we see 30 as a maximum practical figure.

The tutorial will have three theoretical sessions and one practical exercise session, where the participants will apply the presented approach on their specific business strategies and goals and exchange experiences with all participants.

4   Target Group

This tutorial addresses managers in the area of software development and IT, project managers, quality assurance managers, and controllers.

5   Presenters' CV

Jens Heidrich is Division Manager for Processes Management at the Fraunhofer Institute for Experimental Software Engineering (IESE) in Kaiserslautern, Germany.

He received his PhD in computer science (Dr. rer. nat.) from the University of Kaiserslautern in 2008. He is one of the co-developers of the strategic software measurement method GQM⁺Strategies®. He has been member of the program committee of numerous software engineering conferences and workshops (such as PROFES and Mensura/IWSM).

Martin Kowalczyk is researcher at the Department of Measurement, Prediction, and Empiricism at the Fraunhofer Institute for Experimental Software Engineering (IESE) in Kaiserslautern, Germany. He is member of the core development team of the GQM⁺Strategies® method.

References

1. Trendowicz, A., Heidrich, J., Shintani, K.: Aligning Software Projects with Business Objectives. In: Proceedings of IWSM/Mensura 2011, Nara, Japan, November 3-4 (2011)
2. Kaneko, T., Katahira, M., Miyamoto, Y., Kowalczyk, M.: Application of GQM+Strategies in Japanese Space Industry. In: Proceedings of IWSM/Mensura 2011, Nara, Japan, November 3-4 (2011)
3. Kowalczyk, M., Münch, J., Katahira, M., Kaneko, T., Miyamoto, Y., Koishi, Y.: Aligning Software-related Strategies in Multi-Organizational Settings. In: Proceedings of the International Conference on Software Process and Product Measurement (IWSM/MetriKon/Mensura 2010), Stuttgart, Germany, November 10-12 (2010)
4. Basili, V., Heidrich, J., Lindvall, M., Münch, J., Regardie, M., Rombach, D., Seaman, C., Trendowicz, A.: Linking Software Development and Business Strategy Through Measurement. IEEE Computer, 57–65 (April 2010)
5. Basili, V., Heidrich, J., Lindvall, M., Münch, J., Seaman, C., Regardie, M., Trendowicz, A.: Determining the impact of business strategies using principles from goal-oriented measurement. In: Business Services: Konzepte, Technologien, Anwendungen. 9. Internationale Tagung Wirtschaftsinformatik, Österreichische Computer Gesellschaft, Vienna, Austria (2009)
6. Basili, V., Heidrich, J., Lindvall, M., Münch, J., Regardie, M., Trendowicz, A.: GQM⁺Strategies® – Aligning Business Strategies with Software Measurement. In: Proceedings of the 1st International Symposium on Empirical Software Engineering and Measurement (ESEM 2007), Madrid, Spain, September 20-21 (2007)

Requirements Meet Interaction Design

Hermann Kaindl

Vienna University of Technology
Gußhausstr. 27-29, A-1040 Vienna, Austria
kaindl@ict.tuwien.ac.at

Abstract. Even if all the real needs are covered in the requirements and also implemented, errors may be induced by human-computer interaction through a bad interaction design and its resulting user interface. Such a system may even not be used at all. Alternatively, a great user interface of a system with features that are not required will not be very useful as well. So, the main topics of this tutorial are requirements and interaction design, as well as their joint modeling through discourse models and ontologies. Our discourse models are derived from results of human communication theories, cognitive science and sociology (even without employing speech or natural language). While these models were originally devised for capturing interaction design, it turned out that they can be also viewed as specifying classes of scenarios, i.e., use cases. In this sense, they can also be utilized for specifying requirements. Ontologies are used to define domain models and the domains of discourse for the interactions with software systems. User interfaces for these software systems can be generated semi-automatically from our discourse models, domain-of-discourse models and specifications of the requirements. This is especially useful when user interfaces for different devices are needed. So, requirements meet interaction design to make applications both more useful and usable.

Keywords: Requirements, interaction design, (semi-)automatic generation of user interfaces, automatic optimization for small devices, smartphones.

1   Tutorial Objectives

This tutorial has the primary objective to address a potential separation of requirements engineering and interaction design. In order to improve the development of useful and usable software systems, an approach to precisely specify use cases in terms of interaction design is presented. As a positive 'side-effect', supporting user interfaces can be generated semi-automatically, even optimized ones for smartphones.

2   Key Learning Outcomes

In this tutorial, participants learn about modeling discourses using a new approach inspired by human-human communication. They will know how such models can be utilized for specifying classes of scenarios, i.e., use cases. They will also see that such models can be the basis for semi-automatic generation of user interfaces.

O. Dieste, A. Jedlitschka, and N. Juristo (Eds.): PROFES 2012, LNCS 7343, pp. 374–376, 2012.
© Springer-Verlag Berlin Heidelberg 2012

3   Outline of Topics

- *Background*
  - Requirements
  - Scenarios / Use Cases
  - Interaction design
  - Widgets for user interfaces
  - Ontologies
  - Speech acts

- *Interaction design based on discourse modeling*
  - Communicative Acts
  - Adjacency Pair
  - Rhetorical Structure Theory (RST) relations
  - Procedural constructs
  - Conceptual Discourse Metamodel

- *Use case specification*
  - Use case report (RUP)
  - Use case diagram
  - Sketch of flow of events through scenarios
  - Specification based on discourse modeling

- *Exercise*
  - Try to understand the model sketch of a discourse
  - Try to model a discourse yourself

- *Sketch of automated user-interface generation*
  - Process of user-interface generation
  - Examples of generated user interfaces
  - Unified Communication Platform

4   CV of the Presenter

Hermann Kaindl is the director of the Institute of Computer Technology and a member of the senate at the Vienna University of Technology. He joined this institute in early 2003 as a full professor. Prior to moving to academia, he was a senior consultant with the division of program and systems engineering at Siemens AG Austria. There he has gained more than 24 years of industrial experience in software development and human-computer interaction. He has published 5 books and more than 130 refereed papers in journals, books and conference proceedings. He is a *Senior Member* of the IEEE and a *Distinguished Scientist* Member of the ACM, a member of the INCOSE and the AAAI, and he is on the executive board of the Austrian Society for Artificial Intelligence.

References

1. Bogdan, C., Falb, J., Kaindl, H., Kavaldjian, S., Popp, R., Horacek, H., Arnautovic, E., Szep, A.: Generating an Abstract User Interface from a Discourse Model Inspired by Human Communication. In: Proceedings of the 41st Annual Hawaii International Conference on System Sciences (HICSS-41). IEEE Computer Society Press, Big Island (2007)
2. Bogdan, C., Kaindl, H., Falb, J., Popp, R.: Modeling of interaction design by end users through discourse modeling. In: Proceedings of the 2008 ACM International Conference on Intelligent User Interfaces (IUI 2008). ACM Press, Maspalomas (2008)
3. Falb, J., Kaindl, H., Horacek, H., Bogdan, C., Popp, R., Arnautovic, E.: A discourse model for interaction design based on theories of human communication. In: CHI 2006 Extended Abstracts on Human Factors in Computing Systems, pp. 754–759. ACM Press, New York (2006)
4. Falb, J., Kavaldjian, S., Popp, R., Raneburger, D., Arnautovic, E., Kaindl, H.: Fully Automatic User Interface Generation from Discourse Models. In: Proceedings of the 2009 ACM International Conference on Intelligent User Interfaces (IUI 2009). ACM Press, Sanibel Island (2009) (Tool demo paper)
5. Falb, J., Popp, R., Röck, T., Jelinek, H., Arnautovic, E., Kaindl, H.: UI Prototyping for Multiple Devices Through Specifying Interaction Design. In: Baranauskas, C., Abascal, J., Barbosa, S.D.J. (eds.) INTERACT 2007. LNCS, vol. 4662, pp. 136–149. Springer, Heidelberg (2007)
6. Kaindl, H.: A Design Process Based on a Model Combining Scenarios with Goals and Functions. IEEE Transactions on Systems, Man, and Cybernetics (SMC) Part A 30, 537–551 (2000)
7. Kaindl, H.: Adoption of Requirements Engineering: Conditions for Success. In: Proceedings of the Fifth IEEE International Symposium on Requirements Engineering (RE 2001), pp. 156–163. IEEE, Toronto (2001); Invited State-of the-Practice Talk
8. Kaindl, H.: A Scenario-Based Approach for Requirements Engineering: Experience in a Telecommunication Software Development Project. Systems Engineering 8, 197–210 (2005)
9. Kaindl, H., Constantine, L., Pastor, O., Sutcliffe, A., Zowghi, D.: How to Combine Requirements Engineering and Interaction Design? In: Proceedings of the 16th IEEE International Requirements Engineering Conference (RE 2008), pp. 299–301 (2008)
10. Kaindl, H., Svetinovic, D.: On confusion between requirements and their representations. In: Requirements Engineering, vol. 15. Springer (2010)
11. Kavaldjian, S., Bogdan, C., Falb, J., Kaindl, H.: Transforming Discourse Models to Structural User Interface Models. In: Giese, H. (ed.) MODELS 2008. LNCS, vol. 5002, pp. 77–88. Springer, Heidelberg (2008)
12. Raneburger, D., Popp, R., Kaindl, H., Falb, J., Ertl, D.: Automated Generation of Device-Specific WIMP-UIs: Weaving of Structural and Behavioral Models. In: Proceedings of the 2011 SIGCHI Symposium on Engineering Interactive Computing Systems (EICS 2011), pp. 41–46 (2011)
13. Raneburger, D., Popp, R., Kavaldjian, S., Kaindl, H., Falb, J.: Optimized GUI Generation for Small Screens. In: Hussmann, H., Meixner, G., Zuehlke, D. (eds.) Model-Driven Development of Advanced User Interfaces. SCI, vol. 340, pp. 107–122. Springer, Heidelberg (2011) (selected from MDDAUI 2010 Workshop papers)

Author Index

GPSR Compliance

The European Union's (EU) General Product Safety Regulation (GPSR) is a set of rules that requires consumer products to be safe and our obligations to ensure this.

If you have any concerns about our products, you can contact us on ProductSafety@springernature.com

In case Publisher is established outside the EU, the EU authorized representative is:

Springer Nature Customer Service Center GmbH
Europaplatz 3
69115 Heidelberg, Germany

Batch number: 09490872

Printed by Printforce, the Netherlands